DEUTERONOMY
A Commentary in the Wesleyan Tradition

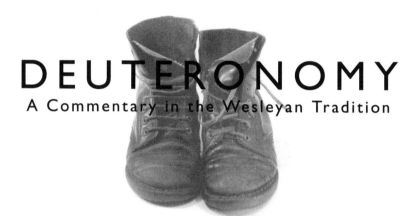

DEUTERONOMY

A Commentary in the Wesleyan Tradition

Stephen G. Green

BEACON HILL PRESS
OF KANSAS CITY

Copyright 2016
by Beacon Hill Press of Kansas City

ISBN 978-0-8341-3240-5

Printed in the United States of America

Cover Design: J.R. Caines
Interior Design: Sharon Page

Library of Congress Cataloging-in-Publication Data

Names: Green, Stephen G., 1952- author.
Title: Deuteronomy / Stephen G. Green.
Description: Kansas City, MO : Beacon Hill Press of Kansas City, 2016. |
  Series: New Beacon Bible commentary | Includes bibliographical references.
Identifiers: LCCN 2015045900 | ISBN 9780834132405 (pbk.)
Subjects: LCSH: Bible. Deuteronomy—Commentaries.
Classification: LCC BS1275.53 .G74 2016 | DDC 222/.1507—dc23 LC record available at http://lccn.loc.gov/2015045900

10 9 8 7 6 5 4 3 2 1

DEDICATION

To Elaine
The love of my life, an exemplar of someone who
follows the Lord wholeheartedly . . .
(Deut. 1:36)

COMMENTARY EDITORS

General Editors

Alex Varughese
Ph.D., Drew University
Professor of Biblical Literature
Mount Vernon Nazarene University
Mount Vernon, Ohio

Roger Hahn
Ph.D., Duke University
Dean of the Faculty
Professor of New Testament
Nazarene Theological Seminary
Kansas City, Missouri

George Lyons
Ph.D., Emory University
Professor of New Testament
Northwest Nazarene University
Nampa, Idaho

Section Editors

Robert Branson
Ph.D., Boston University
Professor of Biblical Literature
  Emeritus
Olivet Nazarene University
Bourbonnais, Illinois

Alex Varughese
Ph.D., Drew University
Professor of Biblical Literature
Mount Vernon Nazarene University
Mount Vernon, Ohio

Jim Edlin
Ph.D., Southern Baptist Theological
  Seminary
Professor of Biblical Literature and
  Languages
Chair, Division of Religion and
  Philosophy
MidAmerica Nazarene University
Olathe, Kansas

Kent Brower
Ph.D., The University of Manchester
Vice Principal
Senior Lecturer in Biblical Studies
Nazarene Theological College
Manchester, England

George Lyons
Ph.D., Emory University
Professor of New Testament
Northwest Nazarene University
Nampa, Idaho

CONTENTS

GENERAL EDITORS' PREFACE

The purpose of the New Beacon Bible Commentary is to make available to pastors and students in the twenty-first century a biblical commentary that reflects the best scholarship in the Wesleyan theological tradition. The commentary project aims to make this scholarship accessible to a wider audience to assist them in their understanding and proclamation of Scripture as God's Word.

Writers of the volumes in this series not only are scholars within the Wesleyan theological tradition and experts in their field but also have special interest in the books assigned to them. Their task is to communicate clearly the critical consensus and the full range of other credible voices who have commented on the Scriptures. Though scholarship and scholarly contribution to the understanding of the Scriptures are key concerns of this series, it is not intended as an academic dialogue within the scholarly community. Commentators of this series constantly aim to demonstrate in their work the significance of the Bible as the church's book and the contemporary relevance and application of the biblical message. The project's overall goal is to make available to the church and for her service the fruits of the labors of scholars who are committed to their Christian faith.

The *New International Version* (NIV) is the reference version of the Bible used in this series; however, the focus of exegetical study and comments is the biblical text in its original language. When the commentary uses the NIV, it is printed in bold. The text printed in bold italics is the translation of the author. Commentators also refer to other translations where the text may be difficult or ambiguous.

The structure and organization of the commentaries in this series seeks to facilitate the study of the biblical text in a systematic and methodical way. Study of each biblical book begins with an **Introduction** section that gives an overview of authorship, date, provenance, audience, occasion, purpose, sociological/cultural issues, textual history, literary features, hermeneutical issues, and theological themes necessary to understand the book. This section also includes a brief outline of the book and a list of general works and standard commentaries.

The commentary section for each biblical book follows the outline of the book presented in the introduction. In some volumes, readers will find section *overviews* of large portions of scripture with general comments on their overall literary structure and other literary features. A consistent feature of the commentary is the paragraph-by-paragraph study of biblical texts. This section has three parts: **Behind the Text**, **In the Text**, and **From the Text**.

The goal of the **Behind the Text** section is to provide the reader with all the relevant information necessary to understand the text. This includes specific historical situations reflected in the text, the literary context of the text, sociological and cultural issues, and literary features of the text.

In the Text explores what the text says, following its verse-by-verse structure. This section includes a discussion of grammatical details, word studies, and the connectedness of the text to other biblical books/passages or other parts of the book being studied (the canonical relationship). This section provides transliterations of key words in Hebrew and Greek and their literal meanings. The goal here is to explain what the author would have meant and/ or what the audience would have understood as the meaning of the text. This is the largest section of the commentary.

The **From the Text** section examines the text in relation to the following areas: theological significance, intertextuality, the history of interpretation, use of the Old Testament scriptures in the New Testament, interpretation in later church history, actualization, and application.

The commentary provides **sidebars** on topics of interest that are important but not necessarily part of an explanation of the biblical text. These topics are informational items and may cover archaeological, historical, literary, cultural, and theological matters that have relevance to the biblical text. Occasionally, longer detailed discussions of special topics are included as **excurses.**

We offer this series with our hope and prayer that readers will find it a valuable resource for their understanding of God's Word and an indispensable tool for their critical engagement with the biblical texts.

Roger Hahn, Centennial Initiative General Editor

Alex Varughese, General Editor (Old Testament)

George Lyons, General Editor (New Testament)

ACKNOWLEDGMENTS

Some of the earliest memories I have are of my father, who was also my pastor. These memories are of him reading the Scriptures and then adding his words to them. He preached consistently from the pulpit in our church and sometimes from the couch in our living room, but always with his own form of life. He preached what he and my mother practiced and they practiced what he preached. Their embodiment of the Scriptures allowed my three brothers and me to dare to believe its central message.

I remember as a young person three unique responses I would have to this language event. There were times when something new would come into view and my eyes would dance with glee as this strange new picture would invade what I had known of the text. There were also times when my eyes would glaze over. Perhaps it was because my picture of the world excluded any meaningful interpretation that these words may have for my life. And then there were times when a tear would form in my eye, and as I blinked away the tear the world appeared different. One could almost say in those moments I was not interpreting the words of the sacred texts but the words were interpreting my world and me. It seemed as if I inhabited a new world that solicited wonder, love, and praise.

The forming and reforming of the horizon of my life has taken place slowly across time with many influential people. Besides my own preacher-father and mother I owe much to the teachers in my life. My first Hebrew professor at Nazarene Theological Seminary, Charles Isbell, opened my eyes to the gift of the Hebrew language. My professors and mentor at Vanderbilt University I owe a gratitude that would take more than a lifetime to repay. To James Crenshaw and Mary Ann Tolbert I say thank you for giving me the tools to closely read the biblical text. To Douglas A. Knight I have a deep sense of gratitude for introducing me to an academic reading of the Pentateuch, to tradition criticism, and to my very first attempt to deliberately read the Bible through the lens of a philosopher: Paul Ricoeur's *The Symbolism of Evil* (1967). My deepest gratitude goes to my mentor at Vanderbilt University, Walter Harrelson. His dedication to both the academy and the community of faith are an influence that has incessantly shaped my ministry to this day.

The nomadic wanderings of my life escorted me through two wonderful pathways: the parish and the academy. Congregants, students, and colleagues have all expanded my horizon to the mysteries of Scripture and the world. My life is full of gratitude to those I have been privileged to pastor for over thirty years and teach for the rest of my ministerial career. They have opened my eyes to the wonder of grace and have served as a sacrament of that same grace; because of that my life will never be the same.

It became obvious to me, after a decade of ministerial service, that there was still an aspect of my ministry that was woefully lacking: a well-defined philosophical and theological framework. Looking for mentors became an obsession in my nomadic wanderings. By providence I began to read Nancey Murphy, which led me into a mentorship and friendship that would change my life and ministry forever. While doing postdoctoral work at Fuller Theological Seminary, she introduced me to her husband, James McClendon, and for the next three years they expanded my horizon to include an understanding of the philosophy of language, postmodern thought, virtue ethics, Wittgenstein, and the Radical Reformation. I would not be the theologian that I am today without the mentorship of Nancey; thank you.

I am indebted to Southern Nazarene University, my alma mater, which I have called my ministerial home for the past sixteen years. The support and encouragement of colleagues and students have been a means of grace across these days. I am very grateful for the university granting a sabbatical leave that allowed the space and time for a great portion of this project to be written. I am also sincerely grateful to Beacon Hill Press for the invitation to participate in this commentary series. Special thanks goes to Alex Varughese, my editor and friend, for his editorial expertise and constant encouragement in this project.

My utmost gratitude goes to my wife, Elaine, and our two children, Stephanie and Michael. They have been colleagues, students, teachers, companions, and friends across the wonderings of my life. They have listened as their husband, father, pastor, and teacher read the Scriptures and added his own words to them, and they also have read the Scriptures and added their own words. I have seen our eyes dance with the joy of new discovery and I have noticed our eyes glaze over, perhaps because the picture painted excluded any meaningful interpretation for life. And I have also seen a tear form in our eyes, and as it was blinked away, the world appeared differently. One could say in those moments that the text was interpreting our world and each of us in it. What I am most thankful for is that we have embodied the good, gleeful, glad tidings of the gospel; we inhabit a new world that solicits wonder, love, and praise. Perhaps this is the ultimate meaning of Deuteronomy, passing the faith along in our wilderness wonderings.

Stephen G. Green

DEUTERONOMY

ABBREVIATIONS

With a few exceptions, these abbreviations follow those in *The SBL Handbook of Style* (Alexander 1999).

General

→	see the commentary at
AD	anno Domini (precedes date)
BC	before Christ (follows date)
ch	chapter
chs	chapters
ed.	edited by, edition, editor
e.g.	for example
etc.	*et cetera*, and the rest
f(f).	and the following one(s)
HB	Hebrew Bible
lit.	literally
LXX	Septuagint
NT	New Testament
OT	Old Testament
sec.	section
v	verse
vol.	volume
vv	verses

Modern English Versions

NIV	New International Version
NRSV	New Revised Standard Version

Print Conventions for Translations

Bold font	NIV (bold without quotation marks in the text under study; elsewhere in the regular font, with quotation marks and no further identification)
Bold italic font	Author's translation (without quotation marks)
Behind the Text:	Literary or historical background information average readers might not know from reading the biblical text alone
In the Text:	Comments on the biblical text, words, phrases, grammar, and so forth
From the Text:	The use of the text by later interpreters, contemporary relevance, theological and ethical implications of the text, with particular emphasis on Wesleyan concerns

Old Testament

Gen	Genesis
Exod	Exodus
Lev	Leviticus
Num	Numbers
Deut	Deuteronomy
Josh	Joshua
Judg	Judges
Ruth	Ruth
1—2 Sam	1—2 Samuel
1—2 Kgs	1—2 Kings
1—2 Chr	1—2 Chronicles
Ezra	Ezra
Neh	Nehemiah
Esth	Esther
Job	Job
Ps/Pss	Psalm/Psalms
Prov	Proverbs
Eccl	Ecclesiastes
Song	Song of Songs/ Song of Solomon
Isa	Isaiah
Jer	Jeremiah
Lam	Lamentations
Ezek	Ezekiel
Dan	Daniel
Hos	Hosea
Joel	Joel
Amos	Amos
Obad	Obadiah
Jonah	Jonah
Mic	Micah
Nah	Nahum
Hab	Habakkuk
Zeph	Zephaniah
Hag	Haggai
Zech	Zechariah
Mal	Malachi

(Note: Chapter and verse numbering in the MT and LXX often differ compared to those in English Bibles. To avoid confusion, all biblical references follow the chapter and verse numbering in English translations, even when the text in the MT and LXX is under discussion.)

New Testament

Matt	Matthew
Mark	Mark
Luke	Luke
John	John
Acts	Acts
Rom	Romans
1—2 Cor	1—2 Corinthians
Gal	Galatians
Eph	Ephesians
Phil	Philippians
Col	Colossians
1—2 Thess	1—2 Thessalonians
1—2 Tim	1—2 Timothy
Titus	Titus
Phlm	Philemon
Heb	Hebrews
Jas	James
1—2 Pet	1—2 Peter
1—2—3 John	1—2—3 John
Jude	Jude
Rev	Revelation

Apocrypha

Bar	Baruch
Add Dan	Additions to Daniel
Pr Azar	Prayer of Azariah
Bel	Bel and the Dragon
Sg Three	Song of the Three Young Men
Sus	Susanna
1—2 Esd	1—2 Esdras
Add Esth	Additions to Esther
Ep Jer	Epistle of Jeremiah
Jdt	Judith
1—2 Macc	1—2 Maccabees
3—4 Macc	3—4 Maccabees
Pr Man	Prayer of Manasseh
Ps 151	Psalm 151
Sir	Sirach/Ecclesiasticus
Tob	Tobit
Wis	Wisdom of Solomon

Dead Sea Scrolls

1QS	*Serek Hayakad* or *Rule of the Community*

Josephus

Ant.	*Jewish Antiquities*

Greek and Latin Works

C. Ar.	Athanasius, *Orations against the Arians*

Greek Transliteration

Greek	Letter	English
α	alpha	a
β	bēta	b
γ	gamma	g
γ	gamma nasal	n (before γ, κ, ξ, χ)
δ	delta	d
ε	epsilon	e
ζ	zēta	z
η	ēta	ē
θ	thēta	th
ι	iōta	i
κ	kappa	k
λ	lambda	l
μ	mu	m
ν	nu	n
ξ	xi	x
o	omicron	o
π	pi	p
ρ	rhō	r
ρ	initial rhō	rh
σ/ς	sigma	s
τ	tau	t
υ	upsilon	y
υ	upsilon	u (in diphthongs: au, eu, ēu, ou, ui)
φ	phi	ph
χ	chi	ch
ψ	psi	ps
ω	ōmega	ō
ʽ	rough breathing	h (before initial vowels or diphthongs)

Hebrew Consonant Transliteration

Hebrew/Aramaic	Letter	English
א	alef	ʼ
ב	bet	b
ג	gimel	g
ד	dalet	d
ה	he	h
ו	vav	v or w
ז	zayin	z
ח	khet	ḥ
ט	tet	ṭ
י	yod	y
כ/ך	kaf	k
ל	lamed	l
מ/ם	mem	m
נ/ן	nun	n
ס	samek	s̥
ע	ayin	ʽ
פ/ף	pe	p; f (spirant)
צ/ץ	tsade	ṣ
ק	qof	q
ר	resh	r
שׂ	sin	ś
שׁ	shin	š
ת	tav	t; th (spirant)

BIBLIOGRAPHY

Achtemeier, Elizabeth. 1978. *Deuteronomy, Jeremiah*. Proclamation Commentaries. Philadelphia: Fortress Press.

Alt, A. 1968. The Origins of Israelite Law. Pages 101-71 in *Essays on Old Testament History and Religion*. Garden City, NY: Doubleday.

Anderson, Bernhard W. 1986. *Understanding the Old Testament*. 4th ed. Englewood Cliffs, NJ: Prentice-Hall.

Barth, Karl. 1957. *Church Dogmatics II.2*. London: T&T Clark Ltd.

———. 1959. *Dogmatics in Outline*. New York: Harper & Row Publishers.

Bell, Daniel M., Jr. 2001. *Liberation Theology After the End of History: The Refusal to Cease Suffering*. London and New York: Routledge.

Biddle, Mark E. 2003. *Deuteronomy*. Smyth & Helwys Bible Commentary. Macon, GA: Smyth & Helwys Publishing Inc.

Bonhoeffer, Dietrich. 1959. *The Cost of Discipleship*. London: SCM Press.

Bratcher, Robert G., and Howard A. Hatton. 2001. *A Handbook on Deuteronomy*. New York: United Bible Societies.

Brueggemann, Walter. 1977. *The Land: Place as Gift, Promise, and Challenge in Biblical Faith*. Minneapolis: Fortress Press.

———. 1997. *Theology of the Old Testament: Testimony, Dispute, Advocacy*. Minneapolis: Fortress Press.

———. 2001. *Deuteronomy*. Abingdon Old Testament Commentaries. Nashville: Abingdon Press.

———. 2006. *The Theology of the Book of Jeremiah (Old Testament Theology)*. New York: Cambridge University Press.

———. 2008. *Old Testament Theology: An Introduction*. Nashville: Abingdon Press.

Buber, Martin. 1967. *Kingship of God*. New York: Harper & Row.

Cairns, Ian. 1992. *Deuteronomy*. International Theological Commentary. Grand Rapids: Eerdmans.

Campbell, Antony F., and Mark A. O'Brien. 2000. *Unfolding the Deuteronomistic History: Origins, Upgrades, Present Text*. Minneapolis: Augsburg Fortress.

Chaney, Marvin L. 1991. Debt Easement in Israelite History and Tradition. Pages 127-39 in *The Bible and the Politics of Exegesis*. Edited by David Jobling, Peggy L. Day, and Gerald T. Sheppard. Cleveland, OH: Pilgrim Press.

Childs, Brevard S. 1962. Memory and Tradition in Israel. London: SCM Press.

———. 1974. *The Book of Exodus: A Critical Theological Commentary*. Old Testament Library. Louisville, KY: Westminster John Knox Press.

Christensen, Duane L. 1993. *A Song of Power and the Power of Song: Essays on the Book of Deuteronomy*. Winona Lake, IN: Eisenbrauns.

———. 2001. *Deuteronomy 1—21:9*. Word Biblical Commentary, Vol. 6a. Nashville: Thomas Nelson.

———. 2002. *Deuteronomy 21:10—34:12*. Word Biblical Commentary, Vol. 6b. Nashville: Thomas Nelson.

Clements, Ronald. 1969. *God's Chosen People: A Theological Interpretation of the Book of Deuteronomy*. Valley Forge, PA: Judson Press.

———. 1998. The Book of Deuteronomy. *New Interpreter's Bible*, Vol. 7. Nashville: Abingdon Press.

Craigie, Peter C. 1976. *The Book of Deuteronomy*. New International Commentary on the Old Testament. Grand Rapids: Eerdmans.

Davies, E. W. 1991. Land: Its Rights and Privileges. Pages 349-69 in *The World of Ancient Israel: Sociological, Anthropological and Political Perspectives*. Edited by R. E. Clements. Cambridge: Cambridge University Press.

Donner, Herbert. 1990. The Separate States of Israel and Judah. *Israelite and Judaean History*. Edited by John H. Hayes and J. Maxwell Miller. London: SCM Press.

Doorly, William J. 1994. *Obsession with Justice: The Story of the Deuteronomists*. New York: Paulist Press.

Driver, S. R. 1895. *Deuteronomy*. The International Critical Commentary. Edinburgh: T&T Clark.

Fishbane, Michael. 1989. *The Garments of Torah: Essays in Biblical Hermeneutics*. Bloomington & Indianapolis: Indiana University Press.

Fretheim, Terence. 1988. "The Repentance of God: A Key to Evaluating Old Testament God-Talk." *Horizons in Biblical Theology*, 10:47-70.

———. 2005. *God and World in the Old Testament: A Relational Theology of Creation*. Nashville: Abingdon Press.

Geertz, Clifford. 1977. *The Interpretation of Cultures*. New York: Basic Books, A Member of the Perseus Book Club.

Habel, Norman C. 1995. *The Land Is Mine*. Minneapolis: Fortress Press.

Hanson, Paul. 1986. *The People Called: The Growth of Community in the Bible*. San Francisco: Harper & Row.

Harrelson, Walter. 1990. Life, Faith, and the Emergence of Tradition. Pages 11-30 in *Tradition and Theology in the Old Testament*. Edited by Douglas A. Knight. Sheffield: Sheffield Academic Press.

———. 1997. *The Ten Commandments and Human Rights*. Louisville, KY: Westminster John Knox Press.

Hauerwas, Stanley. 1981. *A Community of Character: Toward a Constructive Christian Social Ethic*. Notre Dame: Notre Dame Press.

———. 1983. *The Peaceable Kingdom: A Primer in Christian Ethics*. Notre Dame: Notre Dame Press.

Heschel, Abraham. 1951. *Man Is Not Alone: A Philosophy of Religion*. New York: Harper & Row.

High, Dallas M. 1967. *Language, Persons, and Belief*. New York: Oxford University Press.

Hobbs, T. R. 1985. *2 Kings*. Word Biblical Commentary. Waco, TX: Word Press.

Houston, Walter J. 2006. *Contending for Justice: Ideologies and Theologies of Social Justice in the Old Testament*. New York: T&T Clark.

Jenson, Robert W. 2010. *Canon and Creed*. Interpretation: Resources for the Use of Scripture in the Church. Louisville, KY: Westminster John Knox Press.

Knight, Douglas A. 2011. *Law, Power, and Justice in Ancient Israel*. Louisville, KY: Westminster John Knox Press.

Long, D. Stephen. 2008. *Theology and Culture: A Guide to the Discussion*. Eugene, OR: Cascade Companions.

———. 2009. *Speaking of God: Theology, Language, and Truth*. Grand Rapids: Eerdmans.

Lundbom, Jack R. 2013. *Deuteronomy: A Commentary*. Grand Rapids: Eerdmans.

MacIntyre, Alasdair. 1981. *After Virtue: A Study in Moral Theory*. Notre Dame: University of Notre Dame Press.

———. 1988. *Whose Justice? Which Rationality?* Notre Dame: University of Notre Dame Press.

———. 1990. *Three Rival Versions of Moral Inquiry*. Notre Dame: University of Notre Dame Press.

Mann, Thomas W. 1995. *Deuteronomy*. Westminster Bible Companion. Louisville, KY: Westminster John Knox Press.

Mayes, A. D. H. 1979. *Deuteronomy*. New Century Bible Commentary. London: Marshall, Morgan & Scott Ltd.

McBride, D. Dean. 1987. Polity of the Covenant People: The Book of Deuteronomy. *Interpretation*, 41/3:229-44.

McClendon, James Wm., Jr., and James M. Smith. 1975. *Understanding Religious Convictions*. Notre Dame: University of Notre Dame Press.

———. 1986. *Ethics: Systematic Theology, Volume 1*. Nashville: Abingdon Press.

———. 1994. *Doctrine: Systematic Theology, Volume 2*. Nashville: Abingdon Press.

———. 2000. *Witness: Systematic Theology, Volume 3*. Nashville: Abingdon Press.

McConville, J. G. 2002. *Deuteronomy*. Apollos Old Testament Commentary. Nottingham: IVP Academic.

Mendenhall, George E. 1955. *Law and Covenant in Israel and the Ancient Near East*. Pittsburgh: Biblical Colloquium.

———. 1973. *The Tenth Generation: The Origins of the Biblical Tradition*. Baltimore: Johns Hopkins University Press.

Millar, J. Gary. 1998. *Now Choose Life: Theology and Ethics in Deuteronomy*. Downers Grove, IL: InterVarsity Press.

Miller, Patrick D. 1990. *Deuteronomy*. Interpretation: A Bible Commentary for Teaching and Preaching. Atlanta: John Knox Press.

———. 2009. *The Ten Commandments*. Interpretation: Resources for the Use of Scripture in the Church. Louisville, KY: Westminster John Knox Press.

Murphy, Nancey. 1996. *Beyond Liberalism and Fundamentalism: How Modern and Postmodern Philosophy Set the Theological Agenda*. New York: Continuum International Publishing Group Inc.

———. 1997. *Anglo-American Postmodernity: Philosophical Perspectives on Science, Religion, and Ethics.* Boulder, CO: Westview Press.

Nelson, Richard D. 2002a. *First and Second Kings.* Interpretation: A Bible Commentary for Teaching and Preaching. Atlanta: John Knox Press.

———. 2002b. *Deuteronomy: A Commentary.* Old Testament Library. Louisville, KY: Westminster John Knox Press.

Niebuhr, H. Richard. 1941. *The Meaning of Revelation.* New York: Macmillan.

Nugent, John C. 2011. *The Politics of Yahweh: John Howard Yoder, the Old Testament, and the People of God.* Eugene, OR: Cascade Books.

Olson, Dennis T. 1994. *Deuteronomy and the Death of Moses: A Theological Reading.* Minneapolis: Augsburg Fortress Press.

Phillips, D. Z. 1981. *The Concept of Prayer.* New York: Seabury Press.

———. 2000. *Recovering Religious Concepts: Closing Epistemic Divides.* New York: St. Martin's Press.

Plaut, Gunther. 1981. Deuteronomy. Pages 1287-1588 in *The Torah: A Modern Commentary.* New York: Union of American Hebrew Congregations.

Polzin, Robert. 1980. *Moses and the Deuteronomist: A Literary Study of the Deuteronomic History.* New York: Seabury Press.

Pritchard, James B., ed. 1969. *Ancient Near Eastern Texts Relating to the Old Testament,* 3rd ed. Princeton: Princeton University Press.

Ricoeur, Paul. 1967. *The Symbolism of Evil.* Boston: Beacon Press.

———. 1976. *Interpretation Theory: Discourse and the Surplus of Meaning.* Fort Worth: Texas Christian University Press.

———. 1980. *Essays on Biblical Interpretation.* Philadelphia: Fortress Press.

Steck, Odil Hannes. 1990. Theological Streams of Tradition. Pages 183-214 in *Tradition and Theology in the Old Testament.* Edited by Douglas A. Knight. Sheffield: JSOT Press.

Tanner, Kathryn. 1992. *The Politics of God: Christian Theologies and Social Justice.* Minneapolis: Augsburg Fortress Press.

———. 1997. *Theories of Culture: A New Agenda for Theology.* Minneapolis: Augsburg Fortress Press.

———. 2005. *Economy of Grace.* Minneapolis: Augsburg Fortress Press.

Thiemann, Ronald F. 1985. *Revelation and Theology: The Gospel as Narrated Promise.* Notre Dame: University of Notre Dame Press.

Tigay, J. 1996. *Deuteronomy.* JPS Torah Commentary 5. Philadelphia: Jewish Publication Society.

Von Rad, Gerhard. 1962. *Old Testament Theology,* Vol. 1. New York: Harper Collins.

———. 1965. *Old Testament Theology,* Vol. 2. New York: Harper Collins.

———. 1975 (© SCM Press, 1966). *Deuteronomy: A Commentary.* Old Testament Library. Philadelphia: Westminster Press.

Ward, Graham. 2000. *Cities of God.* London and New York: Routledge.

———. 2005. *Cultural Transformation and Religious Practice.* Cambridge: Cambridge University Press.

———. 2009. *The Politics of Discipleship.* Grand Rapids: Baker Academic.

Weinfeld, Moshe. 1991. *Deuteronomy 1-11: A New Translation with Introduction and Commentary.* Anchor Bible. New York: Doubleday.

Wesley, John. 1733. "The Circumcision of the Heart." Sermon 17. The Sermons of John Wesley (1872 ed.). Wesley Center Online. Nampa, ID: Northwest Nazarene University.

———. 1736. "On Love." Sermon 139. The Sermons of John Wesley (1872 ed.). Wesley Center Online. Nampa, ID: Northwest Nazarene University.

———. 1761. "On Perfection." Sermon 76. The Sermons of John Wesley (1872 ed.). Wesley Center Online. Nampa, ID: Northwest Nazarene University.

Williams, Ronald J. 2007. *Williams' Hebrew Syntax,* 3rd ed. Toronto: University of Toronto Press.

Wittgenstein, Ludwig. 1953. *Philosophical Investigations.* Oxford: Basil Blackwell.

Wright, Nicholas Thomas. 2012. *How God Became King: The Forgotten Story of the Gospels.* New York: Harper Collins.

Yoder, John Howard. 1972. *The Politics of Jesus.* Grand Rapids: Eerdmans.

Zimmerli, Walther. 1978. *Old Testament Theology in Outline.* Louisville, KY: John Knox Press.

———. 1990. Prophetic Proclamation and Reinterpretation. Pages 69-100 in *Tradition and Theology in the Old Testament.* Edited by Douglas A. Knight. Sheffield: JSOT Press.

TABLE OF SIDEBARS

DEUTERONOMY

INTRODUCTION

It is almost impossible to overestimate the importance of Deuteronomy in the Bible. Contained within this influential book are some of the most significant passages of Scripture: the Decalogue, the Shema, the Credo of ch 26, the covenant renewal ceremony in Moab, and the song of Moses to name a few. The theological vision contained in this influential book is also used to narrate the history of Israel from the books of Joshua through 2 Kings. This same theological outlook can be seen in the writings of the prophets Hosea and Jeremiah. Deuteronomy's theology is so influential that a counterargument is made within the Bible itself against making conjectures out of its theological fervor. This corrective is witnessed to in the wisdom articulated in the book of Job. Job's so-called friends answer the question, Why? by absolutizing the theology of Deuteronomy and stock wisdom in a way that allowed them to draw conclusions on the broken life of their friend. The answer that the book of Job gives is that there are multifarious and mysterious possibilities to the question, Why? Even with this said, Deuteronomy and the tradition that forms it is so central to the scriptural formation that the Bible would be utterly lacking without its witness. Its importance to the early Christians is evident in the frequent allusions to and citations from the book in the NT. Early Christians perhaps turned to this book more frequently than any other OT book because of Jesus' own dependence on the teaching of Deuteronomy (see Matt 4:1-11; Luke 10:25-28). Clements notes that the "inwardness of faith, the emphasis on attitude beside action, and the focus on love, obedience, and gratitude" that are central to the teaching of Deuteronomy are also foundational to the Christian faith (see Clements 1998, 280-82).

The title "Deuteronomy" is derived from *deuteronomion* (meaning "second law"), the title of the book in the Septuagint, the Greek translation of the Hebrew Scriptures. This title is fitting, since it portrays the Torah given by Moses on the plains of Moab prior to crossing over into the land of promise. It is considered second law not because it is a new law or a secondary law but because it is a second giving of the Law revealed to Moses on Mount Horeb. The book itself purports to be a series of addresses by Moses to Israel at the end of the long wilderness sojourn just before his death. This perspective is reflected in the title of the book, *'ēlleh haddĕbārîm* ("These are the words"), in the Hebrew Bible. In this literary context, Moses addresses Israel with a strong covenantal/political theology, because he knows that Israel will have its fidelity and form of life challenged by perverted and contaminated forces in the new land.

The biblical canon positions Deuteronomy between Genesis—Numbers and the Former Prophets: Joshua, Judges, 1—2 Samuel, and 1—2 Kings. Deuteronomy functions as a hinge that brings together the books of Moses, which are considered the underpinning of Israel's core beliefs and practices, and the six books that narrate Israel's history. These six books are shaped by the theological tradition that composes and compiles Deuteronomy, and because of this interpretation, scholars designate this material as the Deuteronomistic History. Therefore, it can be said that Deuteronomy concludes the Torah and discloses the revelatory history of Israel.

A. Where Does Deuteronomy Come From, and Where Is It Going?

The simplistic answer to this question is that it comes from God and is going into the future with God's people. But how does Israel, as a community of memory, understand the dynamism of this astonishing influence upon her? Even though the book, in its literary structure and composition, is not historically from Moses, it is indeed a formidable statement of what Israel came to accept as the content of the Mosaic faith. They believed that this faith was ratified at Horeb, and the shapers of the tradition appear to have used long-standing recollections of Moses as an authorization for resistance to political overreach.

Scholars believe that Deuteronomy, as a book, reached its final form through a long editorial process. It is not easy to date the book or to identify its origin. Most likely Deuteronomy was formed during an amalgamated process that reached at a minimum from the time of the divided monarchy (922 BC) into the exile (587-537 BC). The book's theological similarity can be perceived in the book of Hosea and in the Elohist source of the Pentateuch. This insinuates the possibility that the tradition originated among the northern tribes. The question that interpreters need to ask is: How does this theological tradition migrate to Judah?

The tradition preserved in the north seems to have been developed by a band of Levites, who were teachers/priests. This dynamic tradition moved from the ashes of the northern kingdom, with its fall to the Assyrians, into the south as an effort to restore what remained of Yahweh's people. These Levites asked a life-and-death question: What can prevent the tragedy that occurred in the north from repeating itself in Judah? Only a return to Yahweh and his political covenant is the solution that Deuteronomy gives. This return to Yahweh and his covenant politics is traced all the way back to Horeb, which describes Israel as Yahweh's holy people.

The Deuteronomistic tradition proclaims that Israel shared in a succession of unbroken continuity all the way back to the emancipation from Egyptian bondage. It was Yahweh who liberated Israel and led her to the place where she could hear his will for the people: a vision of an intended political order. This political imagination called the people to an exclusive loyalty to Yahweh alone. The implication of this political reality is that it is to encompass all of Israel's life. Israel, who was to witness in her communal form of life to the character and purpose of Yahweh, was never to abuse power through overreaching the boundaries of the other in her life together. Kings, priests, nobles, and others who owned land and resources were not to abuse those with less resources and power. Abuses of power were understood as an attack on Yahweh's sovereignty. Therefore, this political imagination takes up the cause of the poor and the oppressed and opposes any person or group that by commission or omission contributes to the impoverishment of the land and its people.

This political interpretation of the function of Deuteronomy is not new to commentators of this grand book. McBride writes:

> In his Antiquities of the Jews (4.176-331), written toward the end of the first century A.D. for an enlightened gentile audience, Josephus concluded a review of the pentateuchal narrative with an apologetically motivated but nonetheless insightful paraphrase of Deuteronomy. The book, he averred, preserves the divinely authorized and comprehensive "polity" or national "constitution" that Moses, on the final days of his life, delivered in both oral and written testamentary forms to the tribes of Israel assembled near Abile in the Transjordan. (1987, 229)

The political motives for such a maneuver are obvious, but the theological claims behind these maneuvers carry weighty conceptual and moral significance. One could say that Deuteronomy is political theology that attempts to describe how life is to be lived in the land and why Israel was driven from the land. The claim of Deuteronomy is that the welfare of the people is dependent upon faithfulness to the political policies and practices of Yahweh and not the politics compelled by an imperial court. Covenantal politics rendered on Mount Horeb began "with Moses and not with the kingship" (Clements 1998, 292). Yahweh's people thrive when they embody Torah but deteriorate when they turn away from the covenantal politics of Yahweh.

A word needs to be said about the way this commentary employs the concept of "politics." It is utilized in a way similar to the use of John Howard Yoder's *The Politics of Jesus* (1972), Kathryn Tanner's *The Politics of God* (1992), and Alasdair MacIntyre's *After Virtue* (1981). It functions as a collection of stories, policies, and practices that shape the identity of a community-of-memory as they pursue the meaning of *the good* for the tradition itself. A communal ethos arises out of these stories, policies, and practices that influences the character of persons within the community. This means that the politics of a community molds the way individuals understand and operate in the world. It should also be remembered that *power* is always operative in human relationship, therefore politics. Language, form of life, and power are interwoven as cords in a rope.

The constant exhortation in Deuteronomy is: "Remember that you were slaves in Egypt and that the LORD . . ." (5:15; 15:15; 24:18).

> The nature of human relationships is such that they always have stronger and weaker members; they are relationships of inequality. If the inequality is pronounced enough, the weaker member loses his personality; he almost becomes an inanimate thing. This was obviously true in slavery. It was said that a man lost half his soul the day he became a slave. If a slave injured himself, he said that it was his master who had suffered injury. . . . Not surprisingly, justice becomes identified with what the strong can reasonably be expected to give, and with what the weak can reasonably expect to receive. The supernatural virtue of justice is the ability to bring equality into unequal relationships. (Phillips 1981, 104)

The covenantal politics of Deuteronomy addresses this issue of power relationships. The belief is that when Yahweh is worshipped alone, the weak and vulnerable are cared for in the land.

Placing the book of Deuteronomy into an appropriate historical setting is helpful in understanding its covenantal message. Although there are multiple historical situations that shape the formation of Deuteronomy, the reader should be aware of axiomatic circumstances that portray the theological power of its message. These instances can be perceived in answering the question: When was loyalty to Yahweh being undermined by the worship of other deities and their political policies and practices? Despite the fact that idolatry and injustice are constant threats in the history of Israel, there are at least three major episodes that speak to this question in Israel's history. The first is the period given in the book itself, the time ahead of the original takeover of the land. The temptation that the people would face is the practice of worshipping the gods in the land of Canaan. This practice would create a form of life that would be alien to the covenantal politics of Yahweh. Only the exclusive worship of Yahweh would safeguard Israel from these foreign beliefs and values.

The second historical period was the decades following the fall of the northern kingdom before the Babylonian exile. The temptation was to accommodate the beliefs and traditions of Israel to other nations and their customs, religious values, and form of life. Most of this accommodation was a result of establishing treaties with other nations out of fear and intimidation. Some of Judah's most horrific leaders reigned during this period of time, and the adaptation of foreign beliefs and values resulted in a malfunctioning form of life. It was during this time that at least a portion of Deuteronomy brought about one of the greatest theological and political transformations in Israel's history. Second Kings 22—23 narrates this remarkable story of a young king, Josiah, who comes to the throne and authorizes one of the greatest reforms in Israel's history.

The third occasion was during Judah's encounter with Yahweh's judgment in exile. The people experienced the loss of land, temple, and monarchy. Israel suffered exodus in reverse; they were captive in a land far removed from the land of promise. They were separated, once again, by a wilderness that no one could navigate. In the vagueness of possibilities, Israel was asking, Was all completely lost, or was there hope for a new deliverance, a new covenant, and a new Israel? Deuteronomy and the tradition that it embodies provided a hermeneutical lens to see why the exile took place and why hope was conceivable. Yahweh's political order gives answers to the why of judgment and the how of homecoming: Yahweh alone is God!

B. What Are the Themes of Deuteronomy?

The themes of Deuteronomy orbit around one dominant notion: *the dialectic of grace and responsibility*. Deuteronomy declares that Israel is nothing less than an elect people and at the same time their very life is contingent upon their attentive hearing and doing of the will of Yahweh. How is the reader to understand this insistent tension? Clements says it well when he writes: "Grace and law were as inseparable as promise and fulfillment. Each pointed in its own way to the central reality of a divine purpose involving the history and destiny of Israel" (1969, 49).

The concept of grace is expressed in Deuteronomy as *Yahweh's gift giving*, especially in the early narrative sections. The premise that undergirds the concept of Yahweh's gift giving is the belief that everything belongs to Yahweh alone. Nothing lies outside the realm of Yahweh's ownership; therefore, if Israel has anything, it is a gift. He "gives" land, Torah, provision, and even

Israel's own election. Yahweh is the God of grace, the one who gives and gives and gives again. Therefore, Israel lacks nothing, because everything belongs to Yahweh and he is a gift-giving God.

Yahweh's ultimate gift to Israel is his election of her. Clements explains the idea of election in Deuteronomy:

> In Deuteronomy the divine action which instituted the covenant is described for the first time as an act of election. This both emphasized the fact of divine grace, which established Israel's covenant relationship to God, and also related this to the existence of other nations. Thus Israel's privileged position before God is made the subject of careful reflection, and the consequences of this for other nations are more consciously brought to the fore. The concepts of holiness and covenant relationship are brought to focus in a doctrine of divine election in which Israel's very existence as a nation is made the subject of theological interpretation. (1969, 45)

Deuteronomy 7:7-9 declares:

> The LORD did not set his affection on you and choose you because you were more numerous than other peoples, for you were the fewest of all peoples. But it was because the LORD loved you and kept the oath he swore to your ancestors that he brought you out with a mighty hand and redeemed you from the land of slavery, from the power of Pharaoh king of Egypt. Know therefore that the LORD your God is God; he is the faithful God, keeping his covenant of love to a thousand generations of those who love him and keep his commandments.

Israel's election is founded not on the greatness of the people but on the basic fact of God's love for Israel. The electing favor of God is sheer grace.

Another central theme in Deuteronomy is *the holiness of the people*. Deuteronomy recognizes holiness not as something that is gained because of obedience or even surrender, but is in some degree already a reality for Israel. Clements writes, "The holiness of Israel of which Deuteronomy speaks is an established fact, not a spiritual ambition" (1969, 32). Holiness in Deuteronomy indicates that the people are set apart for the purpose of Yahweh by the very act of his choosing. This understanding differs from the call "to holiness" in Leviticus: "Be holy because I, the LORD your God, am holy" (19:2). To live "out of" the act of electing-holiness is to exemplify the purpose of Yahweh. This purpose is revealed in the very formation of Yahweh's covenantal politics.

A major difficulty in understanding holiness in Deuteronomy is that holiness is often coupled with violence: devoting a city and its population to the ban. The reader of Deuteronomy must ask the question: Does this mean that God is to be considered violent? This is a difficult question to answer biblically. In order to understand the ban in Deuteronomy it should be interpreted in light of the three periods of time mentioned earlier in the introduction. In at least two of the three periods of time devoting a city and its inhabitants to the ban would not have been a historical possibility. So, what does this tell the reader about the ban and violence?

Violence that is symbolized in devoting a city to the ban must be understood within the underlying milieu of false gods and ideologies that surround ancient Israel.

> The particular horror of the Deuteronomists was that vestiges of the beliefs and practices of the pre-Israelite inhabitants of Canaan should continue. These are made the object of the strictest prohibitions because of their offensive nature. (Clements 1969, 35)

Can God's people embody their special calling and identity if they are assimilated into the host culture in a syncretistic manner? Israel's unique purpose and calling would come under threat. The people would fail not only to be blessed but also to be a blessing to the rest of creation. The unmistakable difference between the holy people of Yahweh and the surrounding people groups would not be known. There would be no comprehension of Yahweh and his purpose for the world; therefore, it was understood as essential for Israel to maintain a clear and unadulterated identity as God's holy and chosen people. This included eliminating all fallacious and misleading ideologies, values, and practices of counterfeit gods.

"Christians" picture God not in holy war but in the person of Jesus Christ. Jesus' words and deeds are enacted as compassion and restoration. From a Christian viewpoint of these passages, both individuals as well as the community of faith are to understand themselves as consistent witnesses to the character and purpose of God in Jesus Christ. So what does Christian holiness mean in relation to the violence that is depicted within the text? Christians must always remember that Jesus commanded us to love our enemies, and this would at least mean to not kill them.

To be a faithful countersign to the character of God in both word and deed is to practice holiness. The question that the text poses for Christians is not so much how or when to use violence, but how to maintain an alien status to the host cultures that the church finds itself within. Reflecting the character and purpose of God, as revealed in the person of Jesus, includes not only the embrace of others in love but also the exclusion of bogus practices, values, and ideologies. If Christians are to bear truthful witness to Jesus, to be holy, then they must remove all cultural norms that would detract from their witness to the character of God in Christ. In today's culture of violence, the exclusion of violence might be the Christian meaning of "devoting to the ban."

The gift of the land is one of the major theological motifs around which Israel understands her life in covenant with Yahweh. He gives the land to whomever he chooses, because it is his to do with as he wills. The gift of the land also includes a divine decree to go in and take possession of the land. Yahweh's undertaking enables the land to be received by his people, but it is not without human participation. Israel does not have the strength to "go in" and *take* the land, but she is required to "go in" and *inherit* the land. It is because Yahweh gives the land that Israel can go in and possess it. But "go in" she must. Divine gift and human responsibility are not incompatible, but they are parts of a whole. Embodied faith is obedience.

The land is not only God's gift to Israel but also a threat to her. The story of Israel and her God vacillates between the promise and the gift of the land and the impulse to abuse and exploit it. Israel's temptation is to treat the land as a possession that she secured for herself. If she succumbs to this temptation, then she will suffer the loss of the land itself. The land is Yahweh's and Israel must always live in his gift-giving grace by worshipping him alone and practicing her life as his chosen and holy people.

Deuteronomy 6:10-15; 8:1-20; and 9:6 point out that Israel faces the inclination to "forget" that Yahweh is the one who brought her into the land and gave her the land and its gifts. Succumbing to this temptation will result in the two great sins: idolatry (6:14-15; 7:4-6; 11:13-17; 12:1 ff.; 12:29-32 [12:29—13:1 HB]; 27:15; 29:2 ff. [29:1 ff. HB]) and injustice (10:17-19; 15:1 ff.; 24:17 ff.; 27:19-20). Manipulating God and other human beings for one's own agenda and welfare seem to be the great temptations of both ancient and contemporary persons. The themes of grace and responsibility are united once again in the larger theological vision of Deuteronomy as Yahweh's saving activity to both give the land and provide for an order within the land.

This order can be observed in the *concept of law.*

Deuteronomy particularly emphasizes that the purpose of the law was not to bind Israel to a set of arbitrary restrictions, but to guide it towards the fullest enjoyment of life. Repeatedly it is stressed that the law is given "that it may go well with you," and "that you may prolong your days in the land which the Lord your God gives you." (Clements 1969, 58)

Israel did not understand her keeping of the Law as a way to motivate Yahweh to bless her. In other words, there was no understanding that virtuous conduct would earn favor with God. Laws reflect the order of the universe and therefore provided a communal way of living that produced well-being in the land. One could say that to disregard the Law was to go against the order of reality and therefore to get splinters in the psyche of the community itself. The Law is not given as a burden upon the people, but as a gift for guidance that establishes life and fruitfulness. Law allows for the blessing of Yahweh; it is amazing grace.

This amazing grace of the Law that is given is not simply for an individual to perform, but for the community to enact. Laws are policies and practices within a political framework.

> By accepting the fact of Israel's existence as national state, with all that this implied in the way of political responsibility, Deuteronomy accepted that it had to legislate for everybody . . . No citizen was permitted to excuse himself from keeping the law, and certainly no freedom of religious choice was conceded. Israel had been committed by God to obey his will. (Clements 1969, 34-35)

Responsible grace is a call to radical obedience. This obedience is demonstrated in a twofold manner: complete loyalty to Yahweh and social obligation to the community. Both of these aspects are intertwined in the covenantal politics of Yahweh, so that complete allegiance and fidelity to Yahweh demonstrates itself not only in worship but also in a just form of life. This form of life is profoundly concerned with social order that expresses itself in a communal protection of the marginal. The marginal are pictured as widows, orphans, and sojourners. These are people without land and therefore without resources. Deuteronomy repeatedly states that they are to be provided for and even given a sense of dignity in the community (see 10:18-19; 14:29; 16:11, 14; 24:17, 19-21; 26:12-13). The reader should pay close attention to the Decalogue and its exposition that is expressed in the laws found in chs 12—26 for Deuteronomy's emphasis on loyalty to Yahweh and social obligation to the community.

The problem with the ancient people of God is that they did not keep the policies and practices of the politics of Yahweh, and death rather than life ensued. The gift of the Law was disregarded in the land, and the land became polluted and toxic. Israel no longer lived as Yahweh's chosen and holy people, and the blessings that produce life evaporated like dew in the heat of the wilderness. Israel's ongoing history of infidelity and iniquity suggested that she was likely to collapse, but Yahweh's underlying fidelity would establish a new act of grace. This grace will enable the people to be responsible to the will and ways of their God. It will change the hearts of the people (30:6-10). Therefore, Deuteronomy must be considered a decisively hopeful book, because it is firmly based upon the gracious character of Yahweh who will establish a new political order, a new covenant.

C. What Is the Structure of Deuteronomy and Why?

It is only in coming to terms with the entire book of Deuteronomy that a reader is able to understand the final purpose and function of the book. The structure of this book is shaped by the genre of law. The question that is important to answer is: How does law function for a group of people? Is it by keeping the law that people are given access into a community? Or, is the law a body of material to be understood, as one understands catechesis, so that one can know what kind of community one belongs to? Perhaps, but it seems more likely that laws are a collection of communal policies and practices that constitute a political framework for a people of memory. In other words, law governs and regulates a community. If one is a part of God's people, elected, then one is ruled by these policies and practices.

This politic is both inviting and binding for the community. It functions like a political platform that invites the whole people to participate within its practices, and it is binding for all who participate. Another way of expressing what this collection of policies and practices are attempting to accomplish is that they are endeavoring to shape the identity of the people. The opening narratives provide the identity stories of the people who will then practice their life together in the way of Torah. The final collection of materials are cautions, hopes, songs, and stories that summon the community to renew its identity as a people who are intent on living out the policies and practices of the politics of Yahweh. Even the death of Moses does not derail the politics of Yahweh, but moreover functions as a way of moving forward into the newness of God's tomorrow. Perhaps the best way of understanding this political book is in answering the question: How does Israel go on without the leadership of Moses? It is by the leadership of Yahweh who presides over his people through the political order of his covenant established at Horeb.

Structure of Deuteronomy

I. Remember the Past, Do Not Forget (1:1—4:40)
   A. Introduction (1:1-5)
   B. Resume the Journey (1:6-8)
   C. Just Leaders (1:9-18)
   D. Fear and Refusal to Enter the Land (1:19-46)
   E. Journey in the Wilderness (2:1—3:22)
   F. Moses Prohibited from Going into the Land (3:23-29)
   G. Obedience (4:1-40)
II. Living as Yahweh's People (4:41—11:32)
   A. Refuge (4:41-49)
   B. The Decalogue (5:1-33 [1-30 HB])
   C. Completely Devoted to God (6:1-25)
   D. Destroy and Detach (7:1-26)
   E. Don't Forget . . . (8:1-20)
   F. Know That . . . (9:1—10:11)
   G. What Is Required? (10:12—11:32)
III. The Law Book (12:1—26:15)

A. No Other Gods: The Politics of a New Reality (12:1—13:18
[12:1—13:19 HB])
   1. The Place that Yahweh Shall Choose (12:1-32 [12:1—13:1 HB])
   2. Seduction and Hearing the Voice of God (13:1-18 [2-19 HB])
B. Honor the Holiness of God's Name (14:1-21)
   1. You Are a Holy People (14:1-2)
   2. Eating Gracefully: Clean and Unclean Foods (14:3-21)
C. Regulations Concerning the Tithe (14:22-29)
D. Liberation (15:1-18)
E. The Firstborn of the Livestock (15:19-23)
F. Religious Festivals (16:1-17)
G. Position, Power, and Privilege (16:18—18:22)
H. Life (19:1—21:23)
I. Boundaries: Social and Sacrosanct (22:1—23:18 [22:1—23:19 HB])
J. The Common Good (23:19—24:22 [23:20—24:22 HB])
K. Uprightness: Private and Public (25:1-19)
L. Stewardship (26:1-15)
IV. Blessings and Curses (26:16—30:20)
A. This Very Day . . . (26:16—27:10)
B. Keeping Boundary of Identity Safe and Secure (27:11-26)
C. Blessings and Curses (28:1-68)
D. Choose Life (29:1—30:20 [28:69—30:20 HB])
V. The Death of Moses and the Transition of Yahweh's Guidance (31:1—
34:12)
A. Moses' Successor (31:1-29)
B. Moses' Song (31:30—32:47)
C. Moses' Death Foretold (32:48-52)
D. Moses' Final Blessing on Israel (33:1-29)
E. Moses' Death (34:1-12)

COMMENTARY

I. REMEMBER THE PAST, DO NOT FORGET: 1:1—4:40

OVERVIEW

Forty years had transpired since Moses led a ragtag band of slaves out of the most powerful empire of the known world. The Egyptian empire was unable to control this group of slaves; the hand of God delivered them. This profound liberation would give voice to shouts and songs that Yahweh had triumphed gloriously by throwing the horse and the rider into the sea! But why would it take forty years to come to this place near the Jordan? The hard march of eleven days is all that is necessary to travel these 160 miles or so.

Fear and unbelief are the reasons that are given in Num 13:1—14:45 for the detour that would last forty years. The spies who were sent in to explore the land brought back a distressing description concerning the dangers that lie ahead: "The people who live there are powerful, and the cities are fortified and very large" (Num 13:28). Fear of the threat that is in front of them, and a lack of trust in the one who liberated them, would bring about a pilgrimage to nowhere. The generation that had received the Torah at Horeb would perish. Now a new generation stood before the land of promise. This new generation is a band of nomads. They survive by the gifts that each day brings. These nomads come to trust these daily gifts for nourishment and guidance.

Nomadic wanderers were about to become a settled nation. The sacred promise is within eyesight of being fulfilled. The question that hovers behind these texts is: How will a people on the move, who had depended daily on gifts to survive, live in the settled land? There will be temptations in this land of milk and honey. The great temptation will be to forget that Israel is always to be a people who live from gift. Liberation, guidance, provision, land, and Torah are all gifts to be held in memory with gratitude.

The first four chapters form an introductory narrative that prepares the reader for the gift of the Decalogue, which functions as a structure for the Law section of chs 12—26. These opening chapters of Deuteronomy look as if they are an editorial reconstruction of material that already exists elsewhere. The accounts in these chapters have parallels in the book of Numbers. There are also a few insinuations to material in the book of Joshua. The implication of this observation is that the theologians of Deuteronomy and its tradition refashion this narrative material for their own theological purposes. The intention of this opening section is to create a narrative that distinguishes and exemplifies the community's intended identity, beliefs, values, and practices. In other words, this material is used politically to set up the politics that are promoted in the Law section: the politics of Yahweh.

A. Introduction (1:1-5)

BEHIND THE TEXT

There are four observations that need to be made as one prepares to understand this pericope: structure, places, time, and wordplay. The structure is a concentric structure. Christensen and Biddle outline the pericope as follows (Christensen 2001, 60; Biddle 2003, 15):

A   (wordplay) These words Moses spoke

   B   (place) In the area near the Jordan

     C   (time) It is eleven days from Horeb

       D   (wordplay) Moses spoke what Yahweh commanded

     C1   (time) In the fortieth year after Horeb

   B1   (place) In the area near the Jordan

A1   (wordplay) Moses expounded this Torah Yahweh spoke

The places specified in this introduction are difficult to harmonize. Most scholars understand this location in the vicinity of the Jordan in Moab. Some of these places may appear as locations where one would stop on the Exodus journey (Christensen 2001, 7). Perhaps the references mean to suggest that Deuteronomy records a series of Moses' speeches delivered along the journey (Biddle 2003, 14). The precise meaning of these locations remains obscure.

Two key places are important to make a note of in this pericope. The first is Arabah (v 1). This is the depression from the southern tip of the Dead Sea to the northern shore of the Gulf of Aqabah (Biddle 2003, 16). Most translations translate this term "wilderness." The other very important place is Horeb (v 2). Horeb is commonly referred to as Sinai but is Deuteronomy's name for the location where Moses received the Law from Yahweh (see the exception to this in 33:2 where the text refers to Sinai).

There are two time references in this pericope. These references root this book in very specific ways to history. The reference, "the fortieth year, on the first day of the eleventh month," tie the book with the proceeding books and the story of the journey through the wilderness. The journey from Horeb (Sinai) to Kadesh Barnea is described as an eleven-day (v 2) walk by way of Seir (v 2). Could it be that these two time references are to point out that forty years is not needed to travel this 160 miles or so?

The wordplay is from the Hebrew *dābar*. This Hebrew root is used twice in v 1 in the translation "these . . . words" and "Moses spoke." It is also used once in v 3 in the translation "Moses proclaimed." The final use is in the early part of v 6, "The LORD our God said." Verse 6 is either the end of the first pericope or the connection to what would follow.

IN THE TEXT

■ **1-5** The context of these opening verses is the preparation of nomadic people to become a settled people. The words spoken by Moses to the people (v 1) are none other than the words Yahweh commanded him to speak (v 3). The wordplay on *dābar* is interesting. Verses 1, 3, 5, and 6 use this Hebrew word group to convey a literary and theological message: **These are the words Moses spoke . . . Moses proclaimed . . . Moses began to expound this law, saying: The LORD our God said . . .** Additional words that speak about communicating are added to this passage to highlight the movement of revelation in and through Torah and preaching. The first of these (v 3) is **The LORD had commanded . . .** The reader should notice that Moses **proclaimed** what Yahweh **commanded**. This is understood as equivalent to Yahweh putting words into Moses' mouth. The second of these concepts that describe communication (v 5) is: **Moses began to expound this law . . .** To **expound** means to make plain or clear.

The generation that Moses addresses is not the original assembly at Horeb, but they are still the covenant people of Yahweh who live from gift as gift. Deuteronomy is Moses' attempt to make clear the **law** or Torah (v 5) so that it can be understood by a new generation as Yahweh's gracious gift and themselves as the gifted ones. This Torah, in Deuteronomy, does not claim to be an additional collection of laws to supplement those given at Horeb. It is also not merely a restatement of those laws. Torah, as understood by Deuteronomy, is addressing a later generation about to encounter a new situation. It can never be woodenly spoken to a new generation. The power of Torah is always made explicit in the terms of particular circumstances of space and time (Brueggemann 2001, 26). Preaching and practice are the ways of making the old new in every generation. The expounding of the Torah by Moses is the character and purpose of the book of Deuteronomy.

Moses' preaching of Torah is a call for Israel to organize itself congruent with the past, yet relevant for the new situation they are about to enter. They are to live as the gifted ones in the settled land of promise. The subject matter of Moses' exposition of Torah is a political schema for Israel. The question that Deuteronomy's narratives and Torah answer is: How are settled farmers to live in the vein of nomads?

FROM THE TEXT

By specifically locating this introduction in time and space, the book acknowledges that the transmission of Torah is not some wooden proposition about human conduct, but it grows out of the life and experience of a people "on the way" with God. Torah is expounded in the context of human history. This does not mean that the purpose and will of God are without authority, or that they can take any direction that one may want to take them. The gift of Torah is to be carefully received and understood, so that it can be made clear to a new generation with new challenges and temptations. This introductory pericope points to the continual need to proclaim and make clear the purpose of God in the contemporary context that is called "today."

What this says about the nature of God is that God reveals himself in the concrete context of space and time. God discloses himself in history. The self-disclosure of God is a promise to an old man, a voice in a bush, a path through the sea, a guide through the wilderness, ten words on a mountain, and a man on a cross. This self-disclosure is to be cherished, understood, and expounded to each new generation. One might say that the work of theology or preaching is never finished. God continues to disclose himself through the expounding task of preaching and teaching from the deposit of faith.

Israel would face many new temptations in the context of the settled land. These temptations may be summarized as: How do we live from gift as gift? One of the great temptations for Israel would take the form of the fertility religions: a worldview where the desire for regularity and security would become ritualized. Israel was no longer on the move as a nomadic people; she now has crops to plant and harvest and flocks that are in need of guaranteed pasture. She will live among a people whose practices are an attempt to guarantee the cycle of rain and fertility. She will be tempted, as the later Deuteronomistic Historians would note, to *waver between two opinions*. The story of Elijah in 1 Kgs 18 narrates a confrontation with the prophets of Baal. The temptation of Baalism originates in the desire to secure one's own safekeeping by using the gods to shape the future. Any attempt to control nature or destiny is tied to an economic outcome.

When people forget that they live from gift, they begin to live for themselves. They fail to live as a gift for others. The second great theme of this exposition called Deuteronomy will explore the care of others. The relational network that is called covenant involves the interconnections of God and everything God has created. Torah is God's gift to his people. As they expound and practice Torah they are being formed into a people that live from gift as gift. Or to put the matter into a new context, How is Israel going to live in the settled land with the politics/practices of a nomadic people who are being led by Yahweh?

B. Resume the Journey (1:6-8)

BEHIND THE TEXT

The structure of this unit appears to be linear and in two parts. Yahweh is the speaker in the first part of the passage. The speaker changes by the early part of v 8. Moses, now the speaker, refers to Yahweh in the third person in this verse. There are some manuscripts that allow the continuance of the divine speech to take place: "I swore" rather than **Yahweh swore**. The LXX uses the first-person singular in its translation. This allows for the continuity of the divine speech. The exposition of this commentary follows the Masoretic Text. By following this reading it sets up the transmission of a prior generation's word from God to a new generation's context. Christensen has a useful discussion of the structure (Christensen 2001, 11-12).

IN THE TEXT

■ **6-8** Moses' first exposition of the Torah is not filled with laws and practices, but with story, promise, and command. Remembrance, obedience, and hope are the dynamics of Israel's journey with God. Yahweh liberated a former generation from Egyptian captivity and saved them from the horse and its rider as they passed through the sea. He sustained them with food and water and gave the precious gift of Torah on Horeb. Yahweh once again restated his promise of the land to that generation. All they have to do is trust and obey: **Go in and take possession** (v 8).

The reader of Deuteronomy recognizes that it is now the children and grandchildren of this earlier generation that stand before the land of promise. This new generation was aware of the terrifying venture that their parents and grandparents were unwilling to undertake. Therefore, their parents wandered about in the wilderness for the next forty years. Children were born to these nomadic people. In time these children developed the proficiency needed to live the life of a nomad: a people who are dependent upon the resources of each day to sustain life. They discovered how to follow the signs of providence, to gather what is needed for each day and trust in provisions for tomorrow. Their nomadic training developed the virtue of hope fashioned by the story of Yahweh.

This new generation of nomadic pilgrims realizes that remembering their ancestors' encounter with Yahweh at Horeb is not about uncovering historical information, but an open opportunity for the present (Cairns 1992, 32). Every generation in Israel stands with its ancestors, hearing the command and promise as if for the first time (v 8). The use of **us** in this passage (v 6) includes this newest generation. There is also a grammatical change in v 8 from the first person **I have given you this land** to third person in reference to Yahweh **take possession of the land the LORD swore he would give to your fathers.** The promise of the land is not simply to Abraham, Isaac, and Jacob or even to a previous generation, but it stretches out before the present generation. They could see the very location where the promise will be fulfilled. All that is needed is obedience to Yahweh's imperatives: **Go in and take possession.**

FROM THE TEXT

Stories of grace and promises of hope saturate the commands of God. Imperatives in the Christian faith are not given in a noncontextual world but are always in the framework of memory and anticipation. What God has done and what God has promised to do, meet the people of God in the present moment of their own history. God's Word summons faith and hope. The present is the milieu of grace. This is the manner in which the text describes the condition of Israel on the way to the land of promise.

What does this observation say about the character of God? In simple terms: the commands of God are given in the context of grace. The church is a pilgrim people. She, like Israel, is called within the milieu of election and promise. God chooses her and promises her that he will be her God and she will be his people. God commands his people within the context of all that God has done and will do. The command is an act of grace that enables the people of God to move from promise to fulfillment.

Deuteronomy 1:6-8 makes it clear that promise and fulfillment are not a type of determinism. Israel has a choice to make in the context of God's grace-filled command. Her response sets the course for her near future. Israel's negative response would bring disorientation, drudgery, and death. But the text also reminds the reader that one generation's choice does not derail the gracious activity of God. Israel will have another opportunity to stand before the land of promise. She will be instructed through the difficult times of disorientation, drudgery, and even death. The promise of God will lie before her once again. A Word will be spoken, filled with memory, promise, and command.

This cycle of graced-freedom is repeated again and again in the life of Israel and the church. Relentless grace is the narrative of the canonical story of God. The cycle of failure, repentance, and deliverance can be discerned in the book of Judges and bears witness to the relentless grace of God. The rise and fall of the monarchy again displays the enduring grace of God. The failure of the people of God to hear this Word embodied in Jesus, did not short-circuit this tenacious grace of God. The grace of God calls for a response but is greater than all of the fearful and faithless responses to it. Deuteronomy invites God's people to once again stand in the moment known as today. Grace will once again fill the command of God to his people who are on the way from yesterday to tomorrow, from promise to fulfillment. **I have given . . . go in . . . take possession.**

C. Just Leaders (1:9-18)

BEHIND THE TEXT

Deuteronomy 1:9-18 engages the concept of justice. This passage is framed (vv 9 and 16) by the phrase "at that time." This expression teases the reader into noticing the temporal circumstances of Israel's narrative history. "At that time" references an event recorded in Exod 18:13-23, and because it takes place prior to the giving of Torah at Horeb, it indicates that the concept of justice is an early concern of the community while it is still journeying through the wilderness.

To understand the concept of "justice" one must understand a particular world picture. Change this picture and the meaning of justice changes. In other words, the meaning of justice is tied to a belief and value system of a particular people in time. Israel's understanding of covenant is implicit in her belief and value system. There is no doubt that her understanding of covenant grows and changes across time, but covenant is at the heart of her beliefs and values. In the ancient Near East covenants are treaties between parties. In some way a covenant is a political reality. The policies and practices contained in a covenant are connected to a larger web of social practices and beliefs. Covenant agreement involves the specific obligations that belong to various relationships within a community. Two key concepts that are associated with covenant are "righteousness" and "justice." Deuteronomy 1:9-18 uses these concepts in varied ways to communicate the significance of a righteous and just community.

IN THE TEXT

■ **9** In the early stages of Israel's journey, the people came to Moses to have him settle disputes among them. But Moses was unable to execute his role as leader-judge among the people because of the sheer number of people and his own exhaustion. According to Exod 18:13-23, Jethro, Moses' father-in-law, recommended that Moses create a social structure of judges. These judges were to help Moses in the task of creating a just community by hearing the disputes within the community and judging rightly between the people. The criterion for "judging rightly" is the world picture of covenant with its policies, practices, and values. This world picture comes from the character of Yahweh, which is revealed in the narrative of his dealings with Israel.

■ **10-11** Israel's experience of deliverance from bondage and fruitfulness in the land are both implicit reminders that she lives from the gifts of Yahweh. But these gifts become not only an opportunity to flourish and increase but also a threat to exploit others in the community. The dilemma that fruitfulness brings is the overreaching of people against one another. Moses anticipates that Israel will continue to be fruitful and that Yahweh's generative promise will remain well beyond the nomadic wilderness wonderings. Into the ever-expanding community a system of adjudicating between parties must be set up and maintained. Israel's very existence is dependent upon it.

■ **12-15** Moses administered justice in the community's life as a result of his encounters with Yahweh. But, the question is presupposed, what will happen to justice in the absence of Moses? Verses 12-18 establish a community structure that enables the settling of relational disputes by setting up a social arrangement with leaders that allows for the maintenance of a just community.

Verses 13-15 set forth the structure and the criteria of leaders. The structure is concerned with the matter of governance: polity. The content of this polity is the heart of the book of Deuteronomy. This section of the passage is concerned with the positions of leadership for this governance. The functions of the leaders described in these verses are not easy to distinguish. There may be a military function or an administrative role or a judicial function. Possibly the roles will overlap in the early stages of Israel's possession of the land. What is important is that the assignment of these roles is to preserve justice and equity among the people of Yahweh.

The structure itself is not capable of securing justice and equity; it takes people to enable the politics of Yahweh to function. They need to be people of wisdom, understanding, and who garner the respect of the others (v 13). These virtues indicate those who have a reputation in making judgments acceptable to the community and the ability to know, discern, or distinguish between good and bad. In order for Israel to function as a people of justice, it will take both a particular politic and public persons who have the qualities to judge rightly.

■ **16-18** The concern in these verses is with the ultimate goal of this polity in Israel. Justice and impartiality must be the warp and woof of the people called Israel. Deuteronomy, as a whole, will in due course define the concept of justice, but the reader is given the core values of how justice is confirmed. Verse 16 refers to the necessity to **judge fairly**. This phrase is made up of two key Hebrew root words that define Israel's covenantal life. The first of these is *šāpaṭ*, which means "to judge." The word "justice" (*mišpaṭ*) comes from this root word. Various forms of *šāpaṭ* are found twice in v 16 and twice in v 17. In these verses this word is translated **judges** twice, **judging**, and **judgment**. Justice (*mišpaṭ*) is the righting of wrongs. The second word (*ṣedeq*, translated **fairly**) comes from the root form *ṣdq*, which conveys the idea of rightness; the noun *ṣĕdāqâ* means "righteousness." Those who practice and promote *ṣĕdāqâ* in the community are the righteous (*ṣadîq*). "Righteous" does not have some spiritual or disembodied meaning, but it is always understood within the context of covenant. When the requirements for being faithful in a relationship are performed by fulfilling covenant obligations, then that person or community is *righteous*. The opposite is also true. A person acts in an unrighteous way when he or she does wrongly or fails to do rightly in the specific obligations of the relationship. When judges **judge fairly**, then justice is enacted in the disputed relationship because they make judgments based upon how people behave in their relational obligations. When the system and the officials allow this fair judgment to take place, then the community is just.

The problem that a judge will face is how to see rightly. Prejudice or prejudging is a problem with all people. People of wealth, power, position, and even insider/outsider location determine the eyes one sees with and the ears one hears with. The instruction is very clear: do not let partiality cloud your judgment. Small or great, Israelite or alien cannot determine the way one judges. Justice is dependent upon right judgment and right judgment is dependent upon nonpartiality (vv 16-17).

There is a reason that a people who live from the promise of God are called to be just. God himself is just. God, not the judge at the gate or even Moses, is the ultimate judge. A community of promise is to extend Yahweh's promise of blessing to all in just and fair judgments. The promise of blessing and being a blessing is dependent upon justice, and justice is dependent upon judging rightly.

Some cases are too hard and need further examination and judgment (v 17). In these cases the judges are to bring it to Moses. No one person is able to see clearly enough or hear unmistakably enough to judge rightly all of the time. A problem arises when Moses is no longer with Israel; what will Israel do? Joshua will step into the place of Moses, and when Joshua is no longer with Israel, then the judges will step into Joshua's place. When the judges are no longer with Israel, then a king will step into their place. When the kings fail, then the prophets will speak. When the monarchy fails and Israel is judged and taken

45

into exile, then the hope of a righteous leader is born. A Messiah to judge not by what his eyes see and his ears hear, but with "righteousness" he shall "judge" (Isa 11:3b-4). God is just, and his promise is encased in right judging.

FROM THE TEXT

In the milieu of this passage it is obvious that Yahweh is just. He judges in the ways that he instructs Israel to judge: not according to partiality, but fairly. He cares for insiders and outsiders, for the great and the small. One could say, based upon the witness of this scripture, that God's moral makeup is just and right in all of God's dealings.

God's people are to live in a way that reflects his covenantal character. They are summoned to become a political reality that fosters justice and righteousness by judging fairly in the community. The prophets understood this covenantal character of God and his people. They make it clear that the righteous and just character of God requires his people, and even the nations of the world, to act justly to all. Justice and righteousness forms not only the center of the prophetic tradition but the Torah itself.

From the story of Abraham and the messengers of Yahweh who argue over Sodom and Gomorrah to the end of the NT witness, justice and righteousness have formed the center of a faith-filled community. This does not mean that justice and righteousness have been easy for the people of God to embody. Humanity is shaped by a picture of the world that fosters a competitive spirit and that believes that there is scarcity of resources rather than an abundance.

World politics demonstrate a willingness to win at all costs, even if that means cruelty and violence. Out of fear, human communities have banded together to fight off the other. Insiders and outsiders have been the environment for war, genocide, ethnic cleansing, and concentration camps. Money and position blind the eyes of judges and deafen the ears of politicians. Racism, sexism, and religion have initiated some of the greatest acts of injustice this planet has ever seen.

It is into this world of prejudice and coercive violence that a small group of people dares to keep alive the memory and hope of a world blessed by God. This hopeful memory is a world where justice and equity form the center of a politic, a world where lions and lambs can lie down together and their offspring can live without fear (Isa 11:1-9). In such a politic, there is no Jew or Gentile, slave or free, male or female (Gal 3:28). This politic enacts a kingdom where judgment is performed in such a way that the marginal are included, the outcast is embraced, and the prodigal is welcomed home.

This political vision is the seed of the world that is to come. An amazing thing happens when wise, thoughtful people dare to live as if this world is already at hand, as if the Messiah has already appeared in history. A reflection of this world begins to take place. Slavery is abolished. Women are given the dignity and equality of all humanity. Racism is exposed and repelled. The poor have hope. The rich have compassion. The neighbor is understood as everyone. The enemy becomes a friend, and *shalom* binds all things together.

D. Fear and Refusal to Enter the Land (1:19-46)

BEHIND THE TEXT

The original account of the mission of the spies is told in Num 13—14. The story found in Deuteronomy draws upon that tradition, but there are a few differences between the two descriptions. In Numbers, Moses is the one who is commanded by God to send out the spies. In Deuteronomy, it is the people who insist that the spies be sent into the land. Another major difference is found in the reason for the mission. In Num 13:17-20 the purpose of the spies is to see if the land is as good as promised and to see if it is fortified. In the account of Deuteronomy the mission is simply to find the best route into the land and the cities located within the land.

The plot line of this story progresses from the order to leave Horeb (Deut 1:19-21), through a diversion of spying out the land (vv 22-25), to the climax of sedition (vv 26-28). The story then takes up the responses to the rebellion by Moses (vv 29-33) and Yahweh (vv 34-40). The final segment of the narrative describes the audacity and defeat of Israel (vv 41-46). What is attention-grabbing in this account is that Israel begins and ends her journey in Kadesh Barnea (vv 19, 46). The narrative points to a meaningless circle that a faithless and disobedient Israel undertakes. Israel advances in such a way that she discovers herself headed back in the direction of the Red Sea to the wilderness.

One of the more confusing problems in the study of the Hebrew text of Deuteronomy is the recurrent alteration in the use of the second-person singular and plural forms in verbs and pronominal suffixes (Christensen 2001, 33-34). The first two instances of this alteration of plural and singular forms are found 1:21 and 1:31. The story uses the plural form until v 21. In this verse it moves to the singular in all instances. Verses 22 and following move the grammar back to the plural form. In v 31 the text again moves to the use of the singular: "There *you* saw how the LORD *your* God carried *you*, as a father carries his son." This verse then transitions to the plural: "all the way *you* went until *you* reached this place." These verses form a frame around the account of Israel's rebellion.

■ **19** The earlier events of Israel's journey from Mount Horeb to the banks of the Jordan are retold as a case study on fear and doubt. Verse 19 takes up the journey by introducing a key concept into the story: fear. The Hebrew word for fear (*yir'â*) is used three times in this passage (vv 19, 21, 29). In v 19 this word is used to modify the wilderness **that vast and dreadful wilderness**, which is a dangerous and threatening place. What is being confessed is that Yahweh leads his people through this kind of fear-provoking place, so the community does not need to fear when Yahweh directs them to go over into the land of promise (vv 21, 29).

■ **20-21** These verses speak of the arrival of Israel in the oasis of Kadesh Barnea. It is from there that Israel is positioned to enter the land that Yahweh promises to give to them. Within these verses another key concept is introduced: "to give." This word is used four times in this pericope (vv 20, 21, 25, 39). All of these instances indicate that the land is Yahweh's gift to his people. God, not Israel, will bring about the fulfillment of promise. Israel's responsibility is to **go up and take possession of it** (v 21).

To take the land is the reason that this section of the passage ends with: **Do not be afraid; do not be discouraged**. The concept "to take" can either mean to take by force or to inherit. In this text it very likely means both. Readers of Israel's story know that she inherits the land of promise, but she is also required to take it by force. Verse 39 of this pericope helps the reader understand the synergistic meaning of this concept: "I will give it to them, and they will take possession of it."

■ **22-25** Canaan is unknown to the people. The text implies that Moses is eager to pass over into the land to take possession of it, but the people are cautious and want to establish a strategy to take possession of the land. Moses agrees with the wisdom of the plan and chooses a representative from each of the tribes to participate in the reconnaissance mission. In the Valley of Eshkol the spies gathered samples of the land's gifts. They returned to present the bounty of the land and to give personal testimony of the land that they are to "take possession of" (v 21). The land is good!

■ **26-28** These verses witness to the reality that all is in place to take possession of the land, but fear dominates the community. This fearful response of the people is a sin against their God who offers the land. Sin is described in the use of the words **unwilling** and **rebelled** (v 26) and **grumbled** (v 27). This response of Israel takes the reader back to the idea of "take possession," which is both a gift and a risk. The fear of larger people, giants, and fortified cities causes the community to renarrate their understanding of Yahweh.

Because of the **Anakites** (v 28) Israel assumes that Yahweh hates them (v 27) and that his emancipating act from Egypt was a ploy to destroy them. **Anakites** comes from a word that means long neck or giant. They suppose that Yahweh did not act out of love but with a longing to see them destroyed. They could not see God's mighty acts of deliverance and provision, but only giant people and grand cities. What caused such a reinterpretation of Yahweh and his mighty acts of salvation? They must have interpreted "take possession" not as an inheritance to receive but as a task that is dependent upon their own might and resources. If Yahweh demands this task, then he must hate us.

■ **29-33** These verses describe Moses encouraging the community to trust Yahweh, but the immobilization of fear deconstructs Israel's faith. Moses implores the people to trust Yahweh by recalling God's mighty acts on their behalf. Israel is to remember that Yahweh fought for them in Egypt, carried them in the wilderness, and guided them with fire and cloud. He is going before them and fighting in their behalf. The land that they are to take possession of is as an inheritance and not a reward. They will not take possession of the land by their own power and might, but by the hand of God. Nevertheless, the community of Israel could not bring themselves to trust and obey. The giants are too big and the cities are too fortified.

■ **34-40** Up to this point in the story, only Moses, the spies, and the people verbalize their hopes and fears. After hearing the words of mistrust, fear, and rebellion, Yahweh becomes angry and speaks. There are three results of the anger of Yahweh. First, no adult who is alive in the community of Israel will enter into the land of promise (v 35). The only exceptions are Caleb and Joshua. God gives the reason for the exception of Caleb and Joshua in the affirmation of Caleb: **because he followed the LORD wholeheartedly** (v 36). Caleb and Joshua have complete confidence that Yahweh is faithful to his pledge and is able to accomplish what he promises. The contrast between these two and all others is the contrast between faith and faithlessness.

The second result is that Moses himself will be excluded from entry into the land (v 37). The text gives no indication of God's reason as to why Moses is prohibited from entering into the land. The implication is that Yahweh judges Moses with the people, regardless of the fact that Moses acted as God's spokesman and reminded the community of God's faithfulness to her through deliverance and providence. When one attempts to propose any reason for Moses' culpability or God's logic in this passage, it is little more than speculation. The text is silent on this matter.

The final result (v 39) of the lack of faith is a promise of hope: **your children who do not yet know good from bad—they will enter the land.** Yahweh's promise is not limited by a single generation. One generation's fear and failure does not control the purpose of God. The promise will be fulfilled, even though the people are faithless. Yahweh is faithful! The little ones, whom the faithless generation attempted to protect from the losses and anguish of defeat, would turn out to be the future for Israel. Fear must never paralyze one generation in an attempt to protect the next generation. Faith, trust, and obedience to the God of promise are the only hope for the generations that follow. The stark contrast is given between the fearful doubters and the innocent children. The ones most at risk will receive that which has been promised. Moses, in the text, reminds his community that they are the very children who did not know right from wrong. Go and take possession of the land!

■ **41-46** This is the final section of this pericope, and it articulates the response of Israel to the judgment of Yahweh. In the heat of God's judgment Israel repents! There is confession of sin (v 41) and a renewal in support of obedience, but this obedience is turned into conjecture and therefore disobedience. The people, who have twisted the meaning of Yahweh's deliverance from Egyptian slavery and providential care in the wilderness from God's love to God's hatred, cannot now engage in holy war (Miller 1990, 34). Their battle is no longer Yahweh's. Victory will not come to a people who do not trust in the God who delivers.

Israel has refused to go up and take possession of the land. Now when God announces punishment and they are told that they are to turn back, they disobey yet again. What is at stake is trust and fidelity. The God who promised to fight for them now declares: **I will not be with you. You will be defeated by your enemies** (v 42). If Israel fights without Yahweh, it is an act of disbelief and will result in defeat. They will weep, but Yahweh will not hear their cries (v 45). The irony is that Israel's new act of obedience looks a lot like an old act of disobedience.

FROM THE TEXT

This passage witnesses to God, who delivers, provides, guides, gives, and commands. The response that God is looking for is articulated by the phrase "take possession of [the land]." When taking possession is understood as receiving an inheritance, rather than winning a contest, then one responds like Caleb. This response is not simply being a person of courage but being a person who trusts in the God who promises. The problem is that fear dominates Israel's response to the call of God to go up and "take possession of [the land]." Fear surfaces when people interpret their future possibility through the lens of their resources. For ancient Israel, the size and strength of the people in the land was put side by side to their own rather limited size and strength. This understanding subjugated Israel's judgment. But neither courage nor fear is the virtue needed in this passage. *Faith-full obedience* is the virtue that is called for from the biblical witness. Trust, not courage, enables one to "go up and take possession" (v 21).

Dietrich Bonhoeffer discusses in his *The Cost of Discipleship* the synergistic relationship between faith and obedience (1959, 57 ff.). What comes first: faith or obedience? One must have faith to be obedient to the call of God, yet it is obedience that allows for faith. Karl Barth, in his *Dogmatics in Outline*, articulates faith as a threefold expression: trust, knowledge, and witness (1959, 15-34). For Barth, trust demands an existential engagement with another. Knowledge is what one trusts about the other. Witness is the embodiment of trust, *faith-filled obedience*, in the world.

The journey of the people of God is one of deliverance, providence, and realization. All along the journey there is the risky call of obedience; an obedience to go, follow, and take possession. The story of the spies bears witness to this kind of existential engagement with Yahweh. Yahweh delivers Israel out of the land of Egypt and provides and guides and promises. Now, the people are called to step out and take possession of the land, to bear witness through this risky act of *faith-full* obedience. "See, the LORD your God has given you the land. Go up and take possession of it as the LORD, the God of your fathers, told you" (v 21).

E. Journey in the Wilderness (2:1—3:22)

BEHIND THE TEXT

Chapter 2 is Moses' account of both peaceful encounters and great battles as Israel journeys from Kadesh Barnea to the border. Even though many commentators divide this pericope into multiple passages, this interpretation will account for these verses as a whole. The consistent premise of this narrative is Yahweh's ownership of the land. The outline of this pericope is:

1. The Wilderness Years (2:1-25)
   a. Passing by the Descendants of Esau (2:1-8a)
   b. Passing by the Descendants of Lot (2:8b-15)
   c. Passing by the Ammonites (2:16-23)
2. The Defeating of Two Kings (2:24—3:11)
   a. Defeat of King Sihon (2:24-37)
   b. Defeat of King Og (3:1-11)
3. Distribution of the Land East of the Jordan and a Summons to Take the Land (3:12-22)

I. The Wilderness Years (2:1-23)

a. Passing by the Descendants of Esau (2:1-8a)

■ **1-8a** These verses narrate Israel's turn northward through the land of the Edomites. The older version of this story, which is found in Num 20:14-21, is a divergent tale of a humble request to pass through the foreign land. This request was rejected twice. Deuteronomy's account is quite different. It relates a warning by Yahweh to Israel to refrain from any aggression with the Edomites because they are **relatives** (Deut 2:4). They are the descendants of Esau, and Yahweh has given them the hill country of Seir. This understanding points to Israel's conviction that the land belongs always to Yahweh.

The key to understanding this section of the passage is the word *nātan* (*to give*). This word is used repeatedly in Deuteronomy to show the act and work of Yahweh in giving the land to Israel. The Hebrew word *nātan* is used two times in v 5. The first is **I will not give you any of their land.** The second is **I have given Esau the hill country.** Yahweh not only is not giving this land to Israel, but he has given this land to the Edomites. This pattern will be used in the next two people groups that Israel is to pass over.

A basic conviction in the book of Deuteronomy is that Israel lives from the gifts of Yahweh. She has an obligation to continue to live from the gifts of Yahweh and to extend these gifts to others. **The LORD your God has blessed you in all the work of your hands. He has watched over your journey through this vast wilderness** (v 7). God's gifts to Israel are more than land but include all of his providential care. Israel does not need to confiscate food and water from the Edomites, because Yahweh is aware of her needs and is unfailing in his giving and care for Israel. This confession can be seen as Yahweh's providence toward Israel and is used to show that he also providentially cares for the Edomites.

b. Passing by the Descendants of Lot (2:8b-15)

■ **8b-15** These verses recount a second phase of Israel's journey toward the land of promise. This phase is through the land of Moab. Israel is not to engage in conflict with the Moabites, because this land is also a gift of Yahweh to them. *Nātan* is used two times in v 9. The first use points out that Yahweh will not give Israel possession of the land of the Moabites. The second use expresses the conviction that Yahweh had given Ar to Lot's descendants. Both of these instances point out the fact that it is Yahweh alone who owns the land; therefore, it is his to give. Israel's kinship with Moab is older than that with Edom; it reaches all the way back to the stories of Abraham. This relationship restrains the probability of violence with the Moabites.

Thirty-eight years passed from the time Israel left Kadesh Barnea. These years saw the entire generation of fighting men perish from the people of God. The old, disobedient generation no longer existed. A new generation of trust and obedience developed in the tough nomadic ways of the wilderness. Their guiding principles are the policies of their nomadic God, Yahweh. They follow the signs, trust in provisions, and learn to discern the will of their God who journeys with and before them. They developed the habits that would create the character and temperament of trust and hope.

c. Passing by the Ammonites (2:16-23)

■ **16-23** A third positive encounter with the people of the land is narrated in this subsection. The territory of Ammon is understood as belonging to a kinsman and is honored as a gift of Yahweh. Verse 19 has two instances of *nātan*. Both of these uses are like v 9. The first use is **I will not give you.** The second use is **I have given it as a possession to.** All three of these sections focus on the concept of Yahweh as the Giver of the land. Yahweh gives land not only to Israel but also to all of the people. It is only by permission and command that Israel is allowed to take possession of the land. The land is Yahweh's gift to give to whomever he will. He engages other people groups as well as Israel.

The advance of the people into the land of promise not only calls attention to the nonviolent encounter with the three groups of people who already occupy the land, but it also acknowledges that prior to the gift of the land to Edom, Moab, and Ammon, the land was occupied by other inhabitants. These inhabitants were strong, numerous, and tall (vv 10-12, 20-22). These threatening people went by many names: Emites, Anakites, Rephaites, Horites, and Zamzummites. These three short stories do not go into great detail in characterizing these peoples. What is important is that they were once in the land, but now they are gone. Yahweh, by his power and gifts, gave their land to a new people. Even powerful people are not able to stand against the purposes of God. Israel can be assured that with Yahweh she can possess the land. No threat is too great for God.

2. The Defeating of Two Kings (2:24—3:11)

a. Defeat of King Sihon (2:24-37)

■ **24-37** The narrative now enters a new phase, the successful military campaign east of the Jordan. These verses recount the battle that defeated Sihon, king of Heshbon. A more detailed account of this battle is preserved in Num 21:21-31. The initial word of Yahweh to Israel, **See, I have given into your hand . . .** , is an assurance of victory. Yahweh is the Giver of the land.

Deuteronomy 2:24 uses the word *nātan* ("to give") to convey the idea that Yahweh is giving Sihon and his country into the hand of Israel. In v 25 it is used to describe how Yahweh will put terror and the fear of Israel into the nations: **I will begin to put** [*tēt*; infinitive of *nātan*] **the terror and fear of you** . . . This Hebrew word is used in v 28 to point to the petition that Israel makes to Sihon to give water to them as they pass through. Verse 29 is another occasion for the use of *nātan*. It points to the completion of the request to Sihon and explains to him that Yahweh is going to give the land of promise to them. Verse 30 is another use of this term. This time the text speaks of Yahweh hardening the spirit and heart of King Sihon, in order to give him into the hands of Israel. The NIV translates *nātan* in vv 31 and 33 as **to deliver** Sihon. In this context it is deliverance that is understood as a gift to Israel. The final use of *nātan* in this section of the pericope is found in v 36. Repetition of the verb "to give" with Yahweh as the subject shows that Yahweh is in control of the events that follow. The battle is not something that Israel accomplishes in her own strength. Yahweh, not the strength of Israel, will win the battle.

Sihon embraces combat because Yahweh created in Sihon the urge to resist. The reader is left with the impression that Yahweh gives not only land and victory but also a hard heart. This is a problematic issue in this text: Yahweh **had made his spirit stubborn and his heart obstinate in order to give him** . . . (v 30). It is one thing to say that Yahweh gives strength, the victory, or even the land, but it implies something else to say that Yahweh had a role in hardening the spirit and heart of Sihon.

The issue of a hardened heart can also be seen in Exod 4:19—6:1 when Yahweh causes Pharaoh's heart to become callused. Based upon the framework of the Exodus tradition, the hardening of the heart associates Sihon with Pharaoh. Beginning in Exod 4:21 the reader is informed ten times that Yahweh intends to harden Pharaoh's heart. This is a way of saying that his intellect is going to be resistant to change. Some commentators, such as Richard D. Nelson (2002b, 47), say that this is a way to demonstrate that Yahweh is in control of even the psychological aspects of human history. The question that this commentator asks is: How can Wesleyans interpret this concept of a callused heart?

A Wesleyan might find a clue to the hardening of the heart of Sihon in his resistance to the peace negotiations. The peace negotiations were similar to the negotiations in the previous three sections within this pericope. Deuteronomy 2:27 makes the request to let Israel pass through the country. This request expands to include the payment of silver to provide food and water. But Sihon refused the peace negotiations (v 30). This reflects the typology that is found in the hardening of Pharaoh's heart. Request is made to Pharaoh, and refusal ensues. A fundamental assumption of the OT is that human beings have a choice between good and evil. Is this text a breach of this principle, or is it pointing to a reality that resistance and refusal harden the perspective of a person?

Verse 34 asserts that Israel **completely destroyed** Sihon's people and left no survivors. This is a case of *ḥerem*, the religious idea of ban or devoting or setting apart people or things to destruction. Deuteronomy 20:10-18 is a law of warfare that will spell this war doctrine out in detail. The positive side of this concept and story suggests that Israel was single-minded in its obedience to Yahweh, and in these harsh demands of obedience Israel acknowledges that the victory belonged to Yahweh alone. The concept of devoting a community to the ban also suggests that this act was an act of gratitude to Yahweh. Even though these are appropriate responses to the gracious activity of God, the act of violence is not a completely satisfactory Christian reading of holy war, and a detailed explanation will be given in the exposition of ch 20 in this commentary. It should be sufficient to say that the political and religious threat of Sihon and his people was eliminated. But, because of the teaching and life of Jesus, violence can never be affirmed as a Christian interpretation of these sacred texts.

Verse 37 of ch 2 is a report lodged between the two war stories of Sihon and Og. This report looks back to v 19 and substantiates the action. War is not all-inclusive in the gift of the land. Yahweh will win the battles, because Yahweh will give the land.

b. Defeat of King Og (3:1-11)

■ **1-11** This subsection narrates the war with Og of Bashan, which parallels the Sihon episode with a few exceptions: there are no peace negotiations and no talk of hardening the heart of the king. Recurrent themes of Yahweh *giving* and *devoting to destruction* are narrated in this section. *Nātan* is used in vv 2 and 3: **I have delivered him into your hands** and **our God also gave into our hands**. *Ḥerem* is used twice in v 6: **We completely destroyed them** and **destroying every city**. The description of the conquest includes the taking of sixty towns and their massive fortification. This detail witnesses to the act of Yahweh and his gift to Israel. Verses 8-11, which contain a summary of the victories, move mainly away from the conquered kings to the land that is given. The narrative asserts repeatedly that the land is a gift. The might and power of Israel are not the deciding factors in inheriting the land. It is Yahweh, Israel's God, who wins the battle and gives the land. Israel's response to Yahweh can only be to trust, obey, and give thanks.

A final statement about the king is made in this subsection: **Og king of Bashan was the last of the Rephaites. His bed was decorated with iron and was more than nine cubits long and four cubits wide** (v 11). He was no small adversary, but one of the fearsome population that paralyzed the people of Israel back in 1:26-33. He belonged to a people who were stronger and taller than Israel. The reader is told of this giant whose bed is made of iron and is more than thirteen feet long and six feet wide. No wonder this pericope affirms

Israel with the words of Yahweh: **Do not be afraid of him, for I have delivered him into your hands, along with his whole army and his land** (3:2).

3. Distribution of the Land East of the Jordan and a Summons to Take the Land (3:12-22)

■ **12-22** An allocation of the territory conquered in the wars with Sihon and Og is narrated in this section. These verses also bring to completion the journey of Israel to the border of the land of promise. This division of the passage is a similar account to Num 32. In Numbers the tribes of Reuben and Gad suggest to Moses that since the pastureland of Gilead would provide excellent pasturage for their large flocks that they be permitted to stay behind when Israel crosses the Jordan. Moses likens this proposal to the refusal of Israel at Kadesh Barnea to take Canaan. Reuben and Gad propose that they be allowed time to build pens for their livestock and cities for their families. They would then leave their families behind and join the conquest of Canaan. The report in Deuteronomy points to Moses' initiative and omits any reference to Reuben and Gad. It also stresses the fact that Reuben and Gad took possession of already existing cities.

Deuteronomy implies that the land and all that is within it is given as a gift from the hand of Yahweh. An example of this is expressed in the use of **we took** (from *yāraš*, which means "to take possession of" or "to inherit") in 3:12. Israel "inherited" the land from the hand of Yahweh; she did not take the land on her own. The idea of gift is also reinforced in the continued use of the Hebrew word *nātan*. Now it is Moses who is **_giving_** the land to the Reubenites and the Gadites. The uses of *nātan* are found in vv 12, 13, 15, and 16. It should be noted that this Hebrew word goes back to its most frequent subject, Yahweh, in v 18. In this verse, the land just given by Moses is understood as given by Yahweh to Israel. Verse 19 also points to this fact by referencing the gift of the cities: **in the towns I have given you.**

Moses calls Reuben and Gad to join with the other tribes, who helped to defeat Sihon and Og, in taking possession of the land. The battle is Yahweh's, but the people are one people, in one covenant, under one God. Their flocks and families may stay behind, but all of Israel is called to pass over and take possession of the land. Verse 20 makes this very powerful concluding observation: **until the LORD gives rest to your fellow Israelites as he has to you, and they too have taken over the land that the LORD your God is giving them across the Jordan. After that, each of you may go back to the possession I have given you.** This reinforces that everything is a gift from the hand of Yahweh.

Finally, Moses confesses the theme of the conquest: **Do not be afraid of them; the LORD your God himself will fight for you** (v 22). Israel is to take possession of the land by receiving it from the hand of Yahweh. It is Yahweh who is giving the land to this ragtag band of nomads. The tall and mighty people with their great cities are no match for God's people, because Yahweh fights for them. The Israelites did nothing to bring about the destruction of Sihon and Og. The appeal is for Israel to believe and obey. When they do, the seemingly overwhelming menace over them disappears. When Israel uses the sword, the victory is credited not to the ability of the warrior but to the strength of Yahweh. **Do not be afraid**; believe and obey, for the battle belongs to Yahweh!

FROM THE TEXT

The gift of the land is a major theological category around which Israel reflects on her life with God. The land is both God's gift and threat. Israel's story vacillates between the gift of the land and the temptation to misuse it. Her temptation is to treat the land as a possession that she secured for herself. Deuteronomy 6:10-15; 8:1-20; and 9:6 point out that Israel faces the temptation to "forget" that Yahweh is the one who brought her into the land and gave her the land and its gifts. Failing in this temptation will result in the two great sins: idolatry (Deut 6:14-15; 7:4-6; 11:13-17; 12:1 ff.; 12:29-32 [12:29—13:1 HB]; 27:15; 29:2 ff. [29:1 ff. HB]) and injustice (10:17-19; 15:1 ff.; 24:17 ff.; 27:19-20). Manipulating God and other human beings for one's own agenda and welfare seem to be the great temptations that contemporary persons face.

The God of Israel gives the land and everything else to whomever he chooses. In this passage Yahweh gives a portion of the land to the descendants of Esau and Lot. It is his to do as he wills, yet, Yahweh does give Og and Sihon and their land into the hands of Israel. Nothing lies outside the realm of Yahweh. He is the God of grace, the one who gives.

God's activity enables the land to be received by Israel, but this grace is not isolated from human responsibility. It takes human effort on the part of Israel; she has to wage war. Israel does not have the strength to go in and *take* the land, but she is required to go in and *inherit* the land. It is because Yahweh gives the Israelites the land that they can "go in" and possess it (1:8). But *go in* they must. Divine gift and human participation are not incompatible, but they are parts of the whole. Grace without responsibility is, in Bonhoeffer's phrase, "cheap grace" and responsibility without grace is failure. Faith for this generation as well as all of the generations that are to follow is known as faithfulness.

The second generation of Moses' people still faced the same threats; there seem to always be fortified cities and giants in the land. Nevertheless, the land of promise does not belong to giants, but to Yahweh. It is his to give and to take. The older generation forfeited its future because it believed that the land must be wrestled out of the hands of the giants. The battle seemed to be out of reach for these freed Egyptian slaves. The question of this passage is not what went wrong with the previous generation, but can a new generation trust that the land will be given? Trust is only trust if it is embodied as obedience. Promise is fulfilled when God's people do what they are told to do: "go up and take possession" (1:21).

F. Moses Prohibited from Going into the Land (3:23-29)

BEHIND THE TEXT

This text repeats the subject of Moses' exclusion from the promised land (3:23-29; see 1:37-38; 4:21-22). Here again, there is no reason given why Yahweh held Moses accountable for the disobedience and rebellion of Israel.

The structure of 3:23-29 can be organized around two wordplays: *'ābar* ("to cross over") and *rā'â* ("to see").

1. Moses asks Yahweh to let him *cross over* and **see** the land (3:23-25)
2. Yahweh becomes *cross* (*'ābar*; "angry") with Moses (3:26)
3. Moses is not permitted to *cross over* but is permitted to *see* the land from a distance (3:27)
4. Moses is commissioned to prepare Joshua to cause the people to *cross over* into the land, which Moses *sees* from a distance (3:28)
5. Israel remained in Beth Peor (3:29)

IN THE TEXT

■ **23-25** Up to this point, when Moses speaks with Yahweh he functions as a mediator for the people. His prayers on behalf of the people change God's mind (Exod 32:11-14; Num 14:13-25). In the present passage, Moses seeks Yahweh's favor for himself. Deuteronomy 1:37-38 states that Moses is informed that he will not enter the land of promise, but he resists this destiny. He pleads, once more, that Yahweh change his mind concerning his future. This request is simple and personal, **Let me go over and see the good land beyond the Jordan** (3:25). The word that is translated **pleaded** in v 23 means *to be gracious, or to show favor*. Moses is asking for the grace of God to allow him to cross over and see the land.

Moses' request does not come from any perceived weakness in Yahweh. He confesses that Yahweh's greatness and strength are demonstrated in the course of history (v 24). This reference is most probably in light of the great themes of the liberation from Egypt and the providential care of the wilderness. Yahweh is able to grant the request that is made, and he is even able to change his own mind.

Moses' request does not seem unreasonable. The reader should remember that it is Moses who led Israel to the edge of the land of promise. All that Moses asks is that he be allowed to lead the people into the land of promise.

This final act of Moses' leadership would complete the redemptive activity of Yahweh through his servant. It seems natural to want to finish the story that shapes one's life. Walter Brueggemann states it this way: "The prayer sounds like the prayer of every older generation that it be permitted one more season of leadership and control" (2001, 45). What is so terrible about seeing a project from start to finish? Readers know that the meaning of every story is discovered only in its conclusion. No wonder Moses wants to finish well.

Two wordplays are introduced in this opening request for Yahweh's gracious act toward Moses: to see and to *cross* over. In v 24 Moses confesses to Yahweh that he had **begun to show** him (lit. "caused him to see"; causative form of *rā'â*, "to see") the great and mighty acts of God. He then requests, in v 25, that Yahweh let him *cross* over (*'ābar*) and see (*rā'â*) the good land that Yahweh had promised and was about to allow Israel to cross over and possess. Yahweh commands Moses to go up to the top of Pisgah and **look** [*rā'â*] **at the land** from a distance, because he will not himself cross over into the land of promise. The final use of *rā'â* in this passage is found in v 28. Moses is instructed to command Joshua to be strong because he is going to lead the people across into the land that Moses is about to **see**. Moses' request is granted in an incomplete way. He is allowed to see the place of promise, but from a distance. This idea implies that the task that Moses is given takes more than one lifetime to complete. The fulfillment of the life task of Moses can be seen from afar, but not necessarily experienced in his lifetime.

■ **26** The second wordplay is the Hebrew word *'ābar*. Moses wants **to cross over** (*'ābar*) and **see** the land of promise. He wants to participate in the fulfillment of the promise. *'Ābar* is used twice in v 25. The first use is the request, "Let me go over." The second use is translated "beyond." The desire to "cross over" is understood to be "beyond" the Jordan, the present boundary that keeps the people and Moses from experiencing the place of promise. *'Ābar* is also used in v 26 in the translation **the LORD was angry.** This is an interesting wordplay. Moses wanted to "pass over" into the land of promise, but Yahweh "passed over" Moses. Moses' request is denied him. The text makes it clear that it is **because of** the people **(you) the LORD was angry with** Moses **(me) and would not listen to** him (v 26). What can this mean?

In 1:37 the theme of the mediator bearing the disapproval of Yahweh for the sake of the people is initiated. This theme is addressed again in this passage. Does Moses suffer for the sake of the people or by the people or with the people? The answer to this issue is clouded in mystery. God, suffering, and life itself are all oblique. To universalize every detail concerning these great themes is to miss their richness and tincture. Suffering is not flat and without nuance. Sometimes one suffers with the community because of the ills of the community. Sometimes one suffers at the hands of the community.

Sometimes one suffers for the community. Most of the time these three are intertwined in such a way that they are all true. In the richness of OT canonical story, this seems to be true of Moses. He sins, he is the object of the sin of Israel, and he is a part of Israel who reaps the fruit of her sin.

■ **27-29** The final two uses of *'ābar* are found in vv 27 and 28. In v 27 Moses is told that he can look from afar at the land of promise, since he is **not going to cross this Jordan**. In v 28 the reader discovers a new vision of who would cross over. It will be Joshua who **will lead this people across** into the land of promise. Moses is now led to a new understanding of the conclusion of his story. Following Yahweh's denial of Moses' plea, the reader is led back to the theme sounded at the beginning of the book of Deuteronomy, the relinquishment of Moses' leadership to others (1:9-18). The finale to Moses' life story is busy preparing and enabling Joshua to finish the task of Yahweh's call upon Moses.

FROM THE TEXT

A great mystery is how God works his will in spite of the unfaithfulness of people. Israel sinned a multitude of times between the promise to Abraham and the conquest of the land. She also experienced numerous difficulties and hardships. The witness of this text wrestles with the ideas of God's sovereignty and changeability. God is capable of changing his mind. Why else would Moses petition Yahweh to **let me go over and see**? Creative sovereignty does not need to rush in to bring about its intentions; often they take time because the purposes of God are achieved through history. Perhaps God's redemptive grace is his creative, sovereign, and noncoercive determination to fulfill his purpose for the world.

The present text also witnesses to the mystery of the meaning of life. Life is short. The older one gets the more one realizes that all the goals of one's early years are not going to be completed. No one lives long enough to accomplish the complete meaning of an individual life. There is always one more task to undertake no matter how long one lives. Life is also full of reversals and disappointments. Circumstances and other people often victimize an individual human being. A person is also frequently detoured by personal decisions and actions. With the shortness of life and the reversals of life, how can life be fulfilled?

This text allows the reader to contemplate the death of even Moses and the unfinished dimension of his life. It puts meaning, mentoring, and hope together. Moses would need others to bring completion to what he is given to carry out. The story of his life makes sense only in the light of the story of a community's life. Even this community's story would need others to bring completion to what they are given to accomplish. Their story will discover meaning only in light of another story: the story of God.

The meaning of life is found in the Creator of life. From the beginning of creation to its culmination, God's loving narrative is its meaning. Each person has a role to play in this grand narrative. One's role and story is never finally complete. Maybe this is what the writer of the book of Hebrews means when he writes in 11:39-40: "These were all commended for their faith, yet none of them received what had been promised, since God had planned something better for us so that only together with us would they be made perfect."

Deuteronomy 3:23-29 also explores the mystery of suffering and sin. Who sinned in this passage? The text says that it was the people, yet in other places it was Moses' sin (Num 20:12). What is the reader of Scripture to think? Can one suffer on behalf of the people? Surely the Lord Jesus demonstrates the mystery of vicarious suffering. Yet, the reader also knows that one can also suffer with a people. As this commentary is being written, the world is in a great economic downturn—a recession. People can live with responsibility, not take on too much debt, give to others and yet lose their health, jobs, and homes. The sins of a consumer culture can and do destroy the lives of many responsible people. Moses suffered with the people, for the people, and as a sinner among the people. The mystery of sin and suffering is too great for flat answers and clichés. The greatest mystery is that God is able to take suffering and by his creative sovereignty to allow it to become redemptive.

G. Obedience (4:1-40)

BEHIND THE TEXT

Commentators are uncertain as to whether 4:1-40 belongs with chs 1—3 or with ch 5 (Biddle 2003, 77; Christensen 2001, 71). It seems to form a literary connection between the narrative review of the first three chapters and Moses' delivery of Law in ch 5. This opening segment of ch 4 is a lengthy section of persuasive instruction in relation to Israel's responsibility to obey the Torah given at Horeb. It provides instruction on how to read the decrees and laws in the rest of Deuteronomy. This persuasive instruction is a genre called paraenesis. This genre reminds the hearer of required moral practices and presumes that they will install them into a belief system that they already participate within.

Some scholars argue that Deut 4 was written during the exile (Olson 1994, 29). In light of this, ch 4 may be one of the latest sections of Deuteronomy to be written. Even though ch 4 is placed in the mouth of Moses, it functions as an updated interpretation of the entire book. The primary evidence for this late dating is found in 4:26-28 with its apparent reference to an exile and scattering of the people.

The reader is confronted by two obvious internal tensions in this passage. First, the passage shifts from second-person plural to second-person singular. Verses 1-28 are primarily plural; vv 29-40 change to singular. This brings a range of critical evaluations to the literary history of this passage. These evaluations range from a complex layering of material to an overall literary unity. Second, the argument of the passage is uneven. It moves from a focus on theophany and the Ten Commandments in vv 9-14 to a prohibition on idols in vv 15-24 to a consideration of Israel's future in vv 25-31, to finally the uniqueness of Israel's God in vv 32-39. The passage is divided into three major sections: 4:1-8, 9-24, 25-40. These three sections constitute a literary whole, which displays a circular design.

IN THE TEXT

■ **1-8** The opening verse is a declaration of purpose for all that will follow in the passage as well as the remainder of the book. **Now . . . hear** (v 1) is a combination of two Hebrew words that point to a conclusion from the previous passage and an introduction to the impending section. The opening verses of the passage put forward the presupposition that controls the entire Deuteronomistic History (Joshua; Judges; 1 and 2 Samuel; 1 and 2 Kings); the land is Yahweh's free gift, but Israel's continuing occupation in it is dependent upon her obedience to the laws that Moses gives. Israel is never to forget that they were once slaves in a foreign land and that it is Yahweh who brings her into the land of promise. The land is a trust. It is never a possession of which Israel could boast as if she was responsible for making it her own. Israel's responsibility is to live with her ear attentive to the voice of God.

Hear (*šěma'*) is not only a key concept in Deuteronomy but also a virtue that Israel is to embody as she lives within the covenant politics of Yahweh. *Šěma'* is used countless times in the theological tradition of Deuteronomy to point to the loyal attention Israel is to give to Yahweh's will and purpose. Examples of this can be observed in the next two chapters. In ch 5 the Decalogue is introduced by *šěma'* in v 1. In 6:4-9, the great command to love God with one's whole being begins with this key concept.

The virtue of "hearing" the voice of Yahweh is established in a practice that includes both discernment and obedience to the **decrees and laws** (4:1) taught by Moses to Israel. Deuteronomy 12—26 constitutes the primary segment of the book that is understood as the decrees and laws that Moses teaches Israel. These decrees and laws are the policies and practices of the politics of Yahweh in the tradition. Verse 2 of ch 4 expresses the so-called canonical formula, **Do not add to what I command you and do not subtract from it** (von Rad 1975, 48). In other words, Moses is the exclusive lawgiver for the tradition. Even though these commands are canonical in their function, they do not exclude the continuing development of the tradition, but the tradition is never to depart from this central witness to Yahweh's purpose.

Decrees, laws, and **commands** are the terms used to express the perception of Yahweh's political will for the people. The clue to the meaning of these words might be implicit in the concept rendered by the NIV **laws**. The Hebrew word translated **laws**, in this passage, is from the word group *mišpāṭ*. The normal Hebrew word used for law is expressed as *tôrâ*. *Mišpāṭ* is often translated "justice." Justice means rendering a right judgment concerning a particular case. The prophets used *mišpāṭ* to make clear what is required of Israel as the covenant people of Yahweh. In the present context, *mišpāṭ* indicates a body of legal decisions resulting from the judgments of the courts. The majority of Deuteronomy is a collection of justice decisions concerning the ways in which Israel is to apply the Decalogue to her life in the land that Yahweh is giving. The implication is that these laws form a boundary to provide order for the community in the midst of the forces of chaos.

The term "law" (*tôrâ*) does appear in v 8 and is used as a gathering term for all of the words that describe the political framework witnessed to in Deuteronomy. *Tôrâ* is at least the decrees, laws, and commands that Israel is to live within as she takes possession of the land. Israel is on the brink of entering the land promised as a gift by Yahweh. She will need, in her settled existence, the political apparatus—*tôrâ*—for interpreting and applying the basic requirements of her covenant. The public life of ancient Israel is a witness to the nations. This public witness is none other than a political reality shaped by *tôrâ*.

The purpose of practicing the politics of *tôrâ* is twofold. First, if Israel practices the Law, she will live (v 1). The land is a gift of Yahweh, but Israel's survival is dependent upon her practicing the policies of the God who gives her the land. The second purpose is that in her practicing this new political reality, she is witnessing to **the nations** (v 6). The nations are to see the **wisdom and understanding** of Israel and know that God is near to her and that he gives her not only the land but also the politics for a way of life in the land. Israel's goal is not to survive but to bear witness by her very life to the God who calls, delivers, sustains, and gives.

The politics of Yahweh are challenged by the politics that were practiced with regard to the Baal Peor (vv 3-4). Numbers 25 recounts the story of how Israelite men became entwined with the women of Moab and eventually began to fall into worship of the god Baal of Peor. This false worship led to betrayal of family ties, which eventually led to the consequences of a plague that would kill twenty-four thousand Israelites. These are the dangers not only of neglecting the practice of Torah but also of practicing the alternative politics of Baal. In Num 25, Moses is told to "harass" the Midianites and defeat them, because they have "harassed" the Israelites by trickery and have caused them to practice the politics of Baal Peor (Num 25:16-18). If Israel is to live and bear truthful witness to the nations, she must participate in the politics of Yahweh.

■ **9-20** The assumption is that the reader is aware of the events that took place on Mount Horeb and has reflected upon their meaning. At least three different generations of Israelites are brought together in this text: the first generation that stood at the foot of the mountain to receive the Law, the children of those who stood at the base of Mount Horeb, and future generations who hear these words read to them. This final grouping includes the generation in Babylonian exile. The Law that is revealed on Mount Horeb is endorsed in general terms in Deut 4:9-14 and has a singular concern in vv 15-20: idolatry. The words revealed at Horeb constitute a political reality for every generation of God's people. The policies of the politics of Yahweh are an opportunity for Israel to embody a peculiar identity in and for the world. The great threat is that she may lose contact with the founding events and forget her special identity. The answer to this existential threat is that Israel is to **be careful, and watch yourselves closely so that you do not forget the things your eyes have seen or let them fade from your heart as long as you live** (v 9).

Israel never saw the face of Yahweh, but she witnessed the extraordinary outcomes of Yahweh's involvement in history. Her interpretive eye is shaped and reshaped by her story with Yahweh. The problem of long-term amnesia is addressed in this section by bringing the present generation to the defining event at Horeb (Brueggemann 2001, 54). It is not enough for one generation to remember the great event of the gift given on Mount Horeb; this memory must be passed on to each new generation. The responsibility to teach others Torah is a theme throughout the whole of the book of Deuteronomy. It also repeatedly asserts that amnesia is one of the greatest threats to Israel's long-term well-being. She is warned repeatedly that "to forget" who Yahweh is and what he has done for her will result in her ruin. She will forget who she is. Perhaps the practice of teaching the children and grandchildren what one has seen and heard Yahweh do is the way to remember grace for oneself.

Dark clouds, blazing fire, and words spoken are all a part of the event that shapes the identity of Israel as Yahweh's people (vv 11-13). This theophany has an overwhelming influence on the people called Israel. In this appearance of God, a voice is heard but no form is seen. If God is heard and his presence is interpreted from the events of history, but no physical representation or form is seen, then any attempt to represent God in a form would be totally inadequate and completely misleading. Yahweh is seen in the people who embody his words, not in stone or in wood. Therefore, no idols can be tolerated (vv 15-20).

It is in remembering the covenant-making event at Horeb that each new generation is enabled to renew what it means to be the people who have been delivered from a land of bondage and given a land of promise. The voice that speaks the **Ten Words** on the mountain will continue to sound out to the subsequent generations of Israel (v 13). Yahweh is unlike any other reality. To deal with Yahweh, Israel must remember that it is in the risky freedom of her God that she has life. No created reality can contain him. No incantation can control him. He is a God who speaks; he gives commands and makes promises.

Verses 15-20 continue detailed warnings against the dangers of idolatry. How easy it is to worship the creature when a people forget the Creator. Idolatry is the result of forgetting the words that Yahweh spoke at Horeb. Israel's overwhelming experience of the presence of Yahweh at Mount Horeb—**You saw no form of any kind the day the L**ORD **spoke to you at Horeb** (v 15)—is the primary idea of this section. Yahweh spoke from the fire and revealed himself and his purpose, through Torah. The nations will see the purpose and character of Israel's God only in the way that Israel lives her life communally. Therefore, Torah is a political document that is to take on flesh and blood by the people for the goal of truthfully witnessing to Yahweh's character and purpose.

The warning of this text is not against the worship of other gods in the form of images, but against any attempt to represent Yahweh in a physical manner. The initial admonition is against making an image in the shape of a person: male or female. Because these ancient Jews conceptualized Yahweh in personal terms, an obvious way of attempting to represent God would be in human likeness. Besides the warning against images in human form, numerous other forms are mentioned. This list of possible images mirrors other religions that may possibly influence ancient Israel. Forms of beasts can be seen in Egyptian and Canaanite religions: cats, dogs, birds, crocodiles, and bulls. There is a noteworthy distinction between the adamant enforcement of the ban of idols for Israel and the tolerance toward the worship of idols by the other nations.

In the ancient world, as well as today, people attempt to understand the mysterious forces that guide the world and they endeavor to ascertain the incantations that are necessary to secure one's own well-being. It is only natural that Israel's tendency is to forget that she once experienced Egyptian bondage and that the gracious hand of Yahweh liberated her (v 20). To forget the Creator is to also forget the Redeemer. Israel's knowledge of God is established in her own story of rescue and redemption. To forget the exodus and to replace it by the worship of anything else is to betray the truth that Yahweh's power is most truly seen in gaining freedom from oppression. The world will understand this freedom as it observes the politics of Yahweh incarnate in the social embodiment of Israel.

This purpose is once again stated in the final verse of this section of the passage: **But as for you, the L**ORD **took you and brought you out of the iron-smelting furnace, out of Egypt, to be the people of his inheritance, as you now are** (v 20). Israel is to be the possession of Yahweh. This means they are to be his people. Being the unique possession of God is to be holy, separated from all other possibilities for the use of God. To remain pure, the devoted people of God are to avoid every practice and propensity that might defile their lives and make them false witnesses in the world. Being the people of Yahweh means being a truthful witness to the character and purpose of the liberating God of the Exodus. For Israel, the practice of holiness is a political reality in the community.

■ **21-24** Moses once again expresses that he is forbidden to enter into the land of promise. These words of Moses' impending death stress the need for vigilance on the behalf of the readers in subsequent generations. How are they to live in the land without Moses? The answer, of course, is that Israel is to live according to the words that are given to Moses; they are to live in the political reality of Torah. Israel knows that **the LORD your God is a consuming fire, a jealous God** (v 24). Moses bears witness to Yahweh's judgment by testifying to judgment on himself: **I will die in this land; I will not cross the Jordan** (v 22).

This subsection does not state what **because of you** (v 21) means. Unlike the tradition found in Num 20, Deuteronomy maintains that Moses' punishment came about because **the LORD was angry with me because of you** (4:21; see also 1:37; 3:26). Numbers 20:12 explains the failure that keeps Moses out of the land of promise as his questioning whether God could effect a miracle: "Because you did not trust in me enough to honor me as holy in the sight of the Israelites, you will not bring this community into the land I give them."

This phrase in Deuteronomy seems to have two other possible interpretations of the judgment on Moses. One interpretation is that this judgment is a vicarious act on the part of Moses. Some interpreters seem to understand this passage as Moses taking Israel's place in judgment. This is an interesting expression of vicarious suffering for others. Vicarious suffering points to a pattern of moving through death to life or through judgment to promise (Olson 1994, 35).

Another possible interpretation is that Moses, along with the disobedient generation that was delivered from Egyptian bondage, is being contrasted with the new generation that now can decide to receive the land and live in it with faithful obedience to Yahweh. This might imply that the fate of each is bound to the fate of all, which is a statement concerning the politics of a group of people. Deuteronomy 4:23 warns Israel not to forget the commandments, especially in relation to idolatry. The interpretation could be made that Yahweh held Moses responsible as a leader in Israel for her involvement in idolatry. A possible example of this could be what took place at Baal Peor.

Whatever the meaning of the judgment on Moses might be, the point of the passage is that Israel must beware of the practice of idolatry (v 23). There is a great disparity between the politics of Yahweh and the idolatrous politics of the inhabitants of the land. Not only are their belief systems poles apart, but so also is their form of life. Both the politics of Yahweh and the politics of idolatry associate particular practices of a community. These practices, as a whole, mold a way of living life together. This communal way of life is a political reality. The politics of idolatry will bring the same kind of judgment that the earlier generation experienced. Yahweh **is a consuming fire** (v 24). Forgetting the ways of Yahweh leads to idolatrous practices and death.

■ **25-31** These verses appear to point to Israel's banishment and return. Moses warns Israel that if they or their children forget their covenant with Yahweh and practice idolatry, then they will be judged and taken into exile. This reaffirms what was stated in chs 2 and 3: that the land belongs to Yahweh and he can give this land as he desires. There is a basic theological grammar in Deuteronomy's tradition. It goes like this: Israel moves from faithful obedience to forgetfulness then idolatry, to judgment and defeat, to a cry for help and repentance, and finally to restoration. This cycle can be seen through the whole of the tradition, but it is very evident in the book of Judges.

The phrase **have lived** [from the verb *yāšēn*] **in the land a long time** (4:25) conveys a special meaning. The verb conveys the idea of staleness, inactivity, or sleepiness. It is easy for Israel to grow stale or sleepy in their life with Yahweh. This concept presumably refers to a lethargic taking for granted of the gifts of the land and all that is in it. God's grace calls for one overarching ethical response: gratitude. The life of gratitude is the life lived in faithful obedience to the one who gives every good gift. The politics of idolatry is based upon gaining and protecting life and all that is related to life in a world without grace.

People who make idols know that they are made with human hands. They know that the idol itself is not a god. Some ancient people may have held that the idol embodied the actual or real presence of the deity. Others believed that the deity is only symbolically present in the idol. Whatever the actual understanding of the idol is, the image is understood as the focal point of the divine presence. Once the presence of the deity is located, it could be mollified to achieve one's own objective. Yahweh will have nothing to do with being exploited. He rules his people as their sovereign; he is not going to be manipulated by Israel or any other people group.

The reference in v 26 to summon **the heavens and the earth as witnesses** is characteristic of covenant treaty texts in the ancient Near East (Christensen 2001, 93). In the ancient world the belief was that pledges were made between two parties and the gods were witnesses to these promises. By the time that Deuteronomy finally came together as a whole, Israel understood that Yahweh is not one of many gods but the totality of all that is divine. There are no uncreated witnesses to attest to the covenant promises made. Therefore, creation itself is called on to witness to the pledges made.

According to the Deuteronomistic tradition, the Assyrian conquest of the northern kingdom (eighth century BC) and the Babylonian conquest of the southern kingdom (sixth century BC) are Yahweh's act of judgment in response to the covenant failure of Israel (v 27). Ironically, when Israel is expelled for the practice of idolatry, she is reduced to the worshipping of gods that are not God in a foreign land (v 28). Gods who are merely made of wood and stone cannot see or hear; therefore, they are unable to save. Israel could not save herself, and the gods she worshipped could neither see nor hear. Israel's rescue is totally out of her control. She is not in the hands of the gods made of wood and stone that she can control; her destiny is based on the character of Yahweh (v 31).

The character of Yahweh is articulated in this passage as twofold: jealous for his people (v 24) and yet full of mercy (v 31). He wants them for his own and as his own. The theologians of Deuteronomy are cognizant that the jealous love of God consumes like an inferno. Therefore, blessing and curse is a central dimension of the theological vision of Deuteronomy. But Israel also believed that Yahweh is not a God who abandons her forever. Mercy and covenant faithfulness are at the core of the character of her God. **He will not abandon or destroy you or forget the covenant** because he is full of mercy. Yahweh's mercy is held in a dynamic tension with his jealousy.

Yahweh's promise, which is made hundreds of years prior to Moses and over a thousand years prior to the exile, still stands in spite of Israel's infidelity and waywardness. The reference in v 31 to **the covenant with your ancestors** is probably referring to the patriarchs and not to the exodus generation. The covenant that Yahweh made with the patriarchs is based exclusively on his free grace of choosing Israel as his own. God's free grace motivates him again and again to new acts of grace. It is Yahweh's character that is the hope of the covenant.

Yet, Israel is called in the midst of the consuming fire of judgment: **Seek the LORD your God, you will find him if you seek him with all your heart and with all your soul** (v 29). Judgment itself is an expression of grace. It affords an opportunity for Israel to return and obey. God's free grace is not sentimental but is directed toward blessing and life. Yahweh's people are never intended to simply survive but to thrive in the land of promise. They are called to be a blessing and a witness to all of the families of the earth. The life of Israel is to reflect Yahweh's character and purpose. Therefore, when Israel finds that she is in the inferno of judgment, she is invited to turn and hear/obey the voice of Yahweh.

■ **32-40** World histories are never narrated as Israel narrates her story. No people has ever been singled out by a god and given such special gifts: Israel hears the voice of Yahweh, is delivered from the captivity of another nation, and is given a land as an inheritance (vv 32-34). There are no parallel cases anywhere in all of the world and its history. Only Israel is given such grace!

This means that Israel is to **acknowledge and take to heart** that Yahweh is God in all of creation and that **there is no other** (v 35). Israel's special vocation is to witness in every aspect of her existence that Yahweh is the sole source of life. Her election is her vocation, and Yahweh's exclusive claim on her is conveyed in the politics of covenant. Israel is called to remember her story and to practice the political beliefs of covenant by keeping the decrees and commands that she is given (v 40). The purpose of living out the politics of Yahweh is **so that it may go well with you and your children after you and that you may live long in the land the LORD your God gives you for all time.** Israel's existence, as Yahweh's people, is a witness to all of creation that Yahweh is indeed one.

FROM THE TEXT

The major conviction of this passage is that Yahweh gives grace as well as judgment. God's grace-giving is articulated in a fourfold manner. First, God gives the land to Israel. The opening verses of this chapter express this dimension of God's grace. The land, which Israel will occupy, is a gift from the hand of Yahweh. The second dimension of God's grace can be seen in his gift of the statutes and ordinances that Moses is proclaiming to Israel. God gives the Torah to Israel: the revelation of God's will. The will of God is not persnickety or random, but for the purpose of sustaining life. Life is God's objective for the community; therefore, the Law is God's gift of grace to his people. Third, God gives God's own presence to Israel when they call on him (v 7). Finally, the giving of God is based upon the premise of his delivering the people from slavery. Verse 20 is an explicit expression of this most basic gift of Yahweh to Israel. It should be obvious to all readers of these texts that Deuteronomy is convinced that the very existence of Israel, her existence in the land and the way she is supposed to reside in the land, is a gift from God.

The implication for modern readers is that God both delivers and directs the lives of his people. Deliverance is a concept that depicts all of the ways of rescuing the lives of people. The theological language that expresses this concept describes the saving work of God in the experiences of people and uses terms such as: deliverance from sin, release from deprivation, and rescue from injustice. It should be obvious that the practices of evangelism, works of mercy, and social justice are all involved in the concept of deliverance. These practices form the spirit of the mission of God in the world through his people.

The guiding aspect of God's gifts to his people is uniquely expressed in the giving of the Torah: the revelation of his will. Teaching the Torah is not merely head knowledge, but the kind of learning that acculturates persons into the community of faith. Verse 6 points out the need for ancient Israel to observe diligently the statutes and ordinances that Moses delivers to them. It is in thoughtful adherence that the people of God become a wise and discerning community. The culture of the community and the character of individuals are to be shaped into a truthful witness to God's delivering purpose in the world.

Deuteronomy 4:1-40 is also zealous to declare Yahweh's judgment against communities that fail to establish his purpose in the world. The major temptation that Israel will encounter is to forget the things that God does. Forgetfulness is one of the great weaknesses of the people of God. There are many reasons that people forget. One of the most obvious is that the event, person, or idea to be remembered is not brought before one's consciousness in a recurrent manner. The decision to "take care and watch closely so as not to forget" is bound up in the frequent telling and retelling of the stories and the values that are contained within those stories. For the community committed to the policies of Deuteronomy this means that they are to frequently speak of and practice those values in the retelling of the stories of deliverance and direction to their children and their children's children. In other words, it is to be an ongoing way of life to pass on the faith to the next generation: this is the ongoing tradition-making process at work.

This passing on of the faith and its values from generation to generation results in intensifying faithfulness in the present. Persons become a part of a living tradition by practicing life in light of that tradition, by telling and hearing the stories that guide and describe the tradition, and by observing practitioners of the tradition. The people of God are called to take up the goal or purpose of their tradition by recalling the stories of deliverance and direction.

If a community forgets its own tradition, then they will engage in the practices of the cultures/traditions around them. By engaging in these practices they become a different people. The reference in v 3 to the Baal of Peor is a reference to a time when Israel practiced the fertility cult of her neighbors, and it destroyed the lives and homes of these ancient Jews. The practice of idolatry is within a system that is united to the worldview of alien cultures.

Ancient Israel's conceptual picture of God is contrasted with the static image that belonged to her neighbors. Human beings cannot find in the world any adequate representation of Yahweh. He can only be recognized in his story, a story that Israel shared. These storied people are a sign not at the cultic center, but in their daily life. The regularity of their life together, their politics, is to be a manifestation of their faithfulness to the commandments of God who created them. Because an idol or image is a bearer of revelation, there could only be one image that could dynamically reveal the character of Yahweh: the image expressed in the dynamism of history by a faithful human community committed to doing God's will.

II. LIVING AS YAHWEH'S PEOPLE: 4:41—11:32

OVERVIEW

Israel's journey to the border of the land of promise is completed. Deuteronomy 4:41—11:32 makes known the essential features of what it means to live in the land under Yahweh's lordship. These chapters contain the primary imperative of the entire political reality of Yahweh's covenant: his exclusive claim upon Israel.

After a brief preamble, the second discourse of Deuteronomy, which extends through the end of ch 11, calls to mind the covenant at Horeb. This sizable discourse is made up of seven subsections: Refuge (4:41-49); The Decalogue (5:1-33 [1-30 HB]); Completely Devoted to God (6:1-25); Destroy and Detach (7:1-26); Don't Forget . . . (8:1-20); Know That . . . (9:1—10:11); What Is Required? (10:12—11:32).

A. Refuge (4:41-49)

BEHIND THE TEXT

Deuteronomy 4:41-49 divides into two loosely interconnected sections. Verses 41-43 narrate Moses' establishment of three cities of refuge in the Transjordan. Verses 44-49 offer another introduction into the central section of Moses' teaching concerning the application of the practices of the politics of the covenant. In other words, it introduces the Torah.

Many scholars believe that vv 41-43, the creation of cities of refuge, are a later addition (von Rad 1975, 51). A literary expression of why this may be so is seen in the third person mention of Moses. This third person mention has not occurred since 1:5. Verses 44-49 of ch 4 form a separate subsection that consists of two headings: v 44 and vv 45-49 (ibid., 55). Both of the headings introduce the Torah proclaimed by Moses to Israel.

Verses 44-49 may be the introduction of the exposition of the law in the following chapters. If this is so, then its purpose is to place the recital of the law that follows beyond the Jordan in the valley opposite Beth Peor. This ties the geography of this legal proclamation to the conquest history. Verses 44 to the end of the chapter form an introduction of some kind, but this introduction is immediately followed by another one in 5:1, which appears to be unrelated to it. Some scholars believe that 4:44-49 belongs somewhere else, possibly at the beginning of the whole book of Deuteronomy (Plaut 1981, 1350).

IN THE TEXT

■ **41-43** It is not at all evident why this reference to cities of refuge should occur here. The cities of refuge have no connection to the exhortations of vv 1-40. The OT introduces this theme in four texts: Num 35:9-15; Deut 4:41-43; 19:1-13; Josh 20:1-9. Three of the four of these texts are a part of the Deuteronomistic tradition. The focus here is on the establishment of three cities of refuge, one each within the tribal territories of the Reubenites, the Gadites, and the Manassites.

Cities of Refuge

Cities of refuge are places to which the manslayer may flee and live. The avenger of blood is not allowed to go into these cities and take the life of the one who has killed a relative or friend. One of the problems of officially authorized justice in ancient Israel involves **the redeemer of blood** (*gō'ēl*, "the avenger of blood"; see Deut 19:6, 12), who is the nearest male kinsman of the deceased. The responsibility of **the redeemer of blood** is to avenge the victim by holding the person responsible for the death of his relative. This institution is open to misuse on the part of agitated persons who think it is their responsibility to take vengeance into their own hands. The rights of the manslayer are protected in these circumstances by setting apart the cities of refuge.

The concept of asylum is common to the ancient world in connection with temples and other religious sites, but the notion of a whole city set aside for the purpose of restricting vengeance is novel. The cities of refuge are a unique innovation of Israel. What is also of interest is that these cities are chosen on the basis of their location and not of their sacred character. This contrast with the ancient world is even more striking. Deuteronomy 19:6 explains the choice of the cities based upon the cities not being so far that **the redeemer of blood** might pursue and overtake the killer and put him to death.

The political reality of being a people in covenant with Yahweh shows itself in the protection of the neighbor from violence and revenge. ***The redeemer of blood*** is normally the nearest relative whose responsibility is to represent his kinsman, and thereby the interests of the clan. The term *gō'ēl* is used in ch 19 (see vv 6, 12), but not in this passage, though it is implied. There is no doubt that the kind of retaliation of the death of a clansman would result in blood feuds and cycles of increasing brutality.

What is worth observing is that the cities of refuge are intended for the one who did not aspire to kill his neighbor out of a sense of hatred or malice. Both of the texts in Deuteronomy designate that not intending to kill and killing not out of hate are the requirements for being able to flee into the cities of refuge. Why? The act of killing referred to in these passages is not considered murder. The difference between an accident and murder is one of intention. A problem emerges with deception. Knowing another's intention is nearly impossible. Ultimately, only the person who takes the life of another can know for sure, and perhaps even the slayer can be self-deceived. The two criteria for discovering whether the act is an accident or murder is found in premeditation and motive. Israel is to be a political reality that gives time to explore even the tragedy of the loss of the life of a friend or relative.

The policies that shape the cities of refuge suggest that Israel understood the politics of covenant as a social vocation. Her corporate witness is seen as an alternative political reality to the nations. Cycles of violence and revenge are not a part of the way she understands Yahweh. No doubt, these cities of refuge are economically a drain on Israel, but the economic interests of the rich are never to get in the way of justice and mercy. Economic inconvenience is embraced for the sake of nurturing life.

■ **44-49** These verses read like a second introduction to the book of Deuteronomy. **The law** (*tôrâ*) is the general term used in v 44 that is articulated by three other terms in v 45: **stipulations, decrees,** and **laws.** The meaning of **decrees** and **laws** is elucidated in 4:1-40. Although **decrees** and **laws** are common terms in Deuteronomy, v 45 offers the first of only three occurrences of the expression **stipulations** (see Deut 4:45; 6:17, 20). It is the declaration of these terms for the concrete detail of Israel's life that is the primary purpose of the book of Deuteronomy. **Stipulations** is a term that is regularly encountered in the context of covenant making to describe the text, emblem, or monument left behind to attest that a covenant has been made (Biddle 2003, 94). This word could also be translated *testimonies*.

In addition to the mention of the Jordan as the boundary to the land of promise, other geographical entries point to the theological significance of the story of Israel and her God. Egypt is used twice to designate the liberation and founding of Israel as a people. **Beth Peor** is a symbol for the narrative of Num 25, which functions as a remembrance of how unfaithfulness and disobedience have grave consequences. **Sihon** and **Og** and their land recall the mighty victory of Yahweh for his people. The tracing of the boundaries east of the Jordan may refer to the promise Yahweh made to the patriarchs. Finally, **Pisgah** points to the place where Moses will die. Israel will have the Torah of Yahweh through the mouth of Moses even after his death.

FROM THE TEXT

What beliefs about God are needed in order to provide places of refuge for people who have acted violently in a society? Justice is a key concept based upon the rationale that the God of Israel is just in his judgments. God will make right all of those relationships that experience abuse. What happens when the abuser accidentally participates in violence? For true justice to take place, protection must be provided beyond the immediate retort of retribution.

The rights of the individual must be protected, in modern societies, even against legitimate institutions operating within the legal limits of the law. This is especially important as it relates to matters of capital punishment. Even though modern societies do not have cities of refuge, they do have the appeal process through the courts. This process gives the community time to explore the event of violence and the circumstances that surround it. It also protects society from overreaction. If this text is taken seriously, then the judicial process in the courts should also find a way to move toward atonement. The process of reconciliation in South Africa is a prime example of how atonement can be made between victimizers and victims.

Perhaps the church itself is the place where the politics of the cities of refuge are played out. This would mean that the church functions as both a safe place and a place of atoning reconciliation. The practices that are necessary for safety and reconciliation would ultimately reflect the inclusive and transformational practices of the kingdom of God. It is crucial to bear in mind the manner in which Jesus practiced the kingdom of God in his own life and ministry through forgiveness and liberation. This narrative reality of the life of Jesus must point the way to the politics of the church in the twenty-first century.

B. The Decalogue (5:1-33 [1-30 HB])

BEHIND THE TEXT

Deuteronomy 31:26 asserts that the totality of the book of Deuteronomy is *the book of this Torah*. Deuteronomy 5 presents itself as a microcosm of the whole book, by stating in 4:44 that *this is the Torah*. Therefore, it could be said that Deut 5 provides a condensed version of the Torah of Deuteronomy. The themes as well as the structure of the book of the Torah are already contained within this chapter.

The Ten Commandments are literally "the ten words" (see Deut 4:13; 10:4) and are the source of the alternative designation "Decalogue." According to the numerical arrangement this commentary takes, the Decalogue is a compilation of divine decrees in the form of eight prohibitions and two positive commands. The earliest form of the commandments is most probably a sequence of brief, negative declarations in the form of second-person verbal statements preceded by the strong negative particle (Harrelson 1997, 24). The Decalogue appears in two places in the Bible: first in Exod 20:1-17 [1-14 HB], where Yahweh directly addresses all the people of Israel at Mount Sinai after their escape from Egypt, then in Deut 5. The imperatives are preceded by a concise self-presentation formula: "I am the LORD your God, who brought you out of Egypt, out of the land of slavery" (v 6).

Deuteronomy's Decalogue differs from the ten words in Exod 20 in a few minor ways. The most obvious difference is in the pronouncement concerning the Sabbath. These differences will be noted in the course of the commentary. Many commentaries account for the divergence as purposeful, in that the two versions together are envisaged as disclosing the full sense of the divine will (Plaut 1981, 1352).

Another concern that interpreters of the Decalogue face is the grouping and numbering of the commandments. Jews and Christians throughout the centuries have differed in the way they partition and organize the commandments. The number ten is fixed because Deut 10:4 unambiguously names the commandments the ten words. But, which are the Ten Commandments? The Jewish arrangement of the commandments is unique in that it includes the assurance or pronouncement "I am the LORD your God, who brought you out of Egypt, out of the land of slavery" as the first of the ten words. The thinking is that the first responsibility is to remember what God has already done in his act of liberation. This pronouncement seems to fall beyond the list of imperatives of the rest of the commands. It is for this reason that it seems best to begin with the first imperative: "You shall have no other gods before me." This does not mean that the indicative stating of God's act of liberating Israel from Egyptian bondage is not the basis for all of the commands, especially the first commandment: "have no other gods before me."

The Decalogue in the Christian Tradition

Within the Christian tradition there are at least two different ways of arranging the commandments: the Lutheran/Roman Catholic and the Reformed. The foremost difference between the Reformed tradition and the Lutheran/Roman Catholic is in relation to the prohibition of graven images. The Lutheran/Roman Catholic listing of the commands understands the ban on images as an extension of the first command to have no other gods. The Reformed list interprets the exclusion of graven images as a separate commandment. This difference will have a great impact on how the prohibition of graven images is understood.

In the final form of Deuteronomy, the commandments function as preamble to both the exhortations of chs 6—11 and to the law code of chs 12—26 (Nelson 2002b, 78). The drama, presented by Deuteronomy, unfolds at a decisive time of transition. Remembered revelation from Horeb is presented on the boundary line of the promised land. These laws will deal with the daily living and not cultic functions of the people when they enter into a new land. They are concerned with the daily functions of family life, property, the public square, and human dignity. The laws that concern the use of Yahweh's name and Sabbath-keeping are not even intended primarily for cultic functionaries, but for applied instruction for ordinary people. These laws imply that other people in the community have rights, and Yahweh gives these rights. They have the right to rest, to have respect in old age, to live without the threat of violence, to security in their marriage, and to property and reputation.

The structure of ch 5 is as follows:
1. The Preamble of the Decalogue (5:1-5)
2. The Decalogue (5:6-21 [6-18 HB])
    a. I Am Yahweh Your God (5:6)
    b. Three Commands Concerning the Worship and Service of Yahweh Alone (5:7-11)
        (1) No Other Gods (5:7)
        (2) No Idols (5:8-10)
        (3) No Wrongful Use of God's Name (5:11)
    c. Two Commands that Are Transitional in the Decalogue (5:12-16)
        (1) Observe the Sabbath (5:12-15)
        (2) Honor Father and Mother (5:16)
    d. Five Commands Concerning Life Together (5:17-21 [17-18 HB])
        (1) No Murder (5:17 [17a HB])

(2) No Adultery (5:18 [17*b* HB])

(3) No Stealing (5:19 [17*c* HB])

(4) No False Witness (5:20 [17*d* HB])

(5) No Coveting (5:21 [18 HB])

3. Moses as the Mediator of God's Will (5:22-33 [19-29 HB])

IN THE TEXT

I. The Preamble of the Decalogue (5:1-5)

■ **1-5** The declaration of the Law is what Moses set before the Israelites at Horeb after their deliverance from Egyptian bondage. Moses calls together all of Israel and charges them to **hear . . . learn . . . follow . . . the decrees and laws** he is about to proclaim to them. (→ 4:1-8) The people are to learn of the policies of the covenant so that they may live as the political reality of Yahweh's people.

Deuteronomy 5:4 makes a claim: **Yahweh spoke to you face to face *at Horeb*.** But, the generation who experienced the theophany at Horeb is dead. Even though the death of the Horeb generation occurred, Moses' intention is clear enough. He wants to bring the event of the covenant making into the present as an existential reality for a new generation. Yahweh enters into covenantal relationship, not only with those present at Mount Horeb, but with all who hear these words. A new time, place, and circumstance does not call for Horeb to be repeated or abandoned, but interpreted.

Moses says in v 3, **It was not with our ancestors that the LORD made this covenant, but with us, with all of us who are alive here today.** Deuteronomy, and the tradition that flows through it, will address new subjects as a way of bringing new spheres into the framework of the politics of Yahweh. However, the new times, places, and circumstances are interpreted in light of the authority given to Moses. This authority will not stop with the death of Moses, but it is passed along through the practices of Israel's faith. In other words, the theological authority is asserted in the practices preserved through the ongoing argument over the meaning and purpose of the practices themselves.

These verses convey a type of hermeneutical direction for the book of Deuteronomy. The time difference between generations collapses. The covenant is not an event of the past alone; it belongs to every present generation. The time between the original moment and the present moment is telescoped, and the two are linked. The covenant at Horeb is **with all of us who are alive here today** (v 3). The actualization of the covenant and its obligations is for the present. The hortatory nature of the text and the book cuts across all the generations and reinstates the covenant once more with all of the hearers of these words.

God's people are to **hear . . . the decrees and laws . . . learn them and . . . follow them** (v 1). These words are all concerned with Israel's active participation in response to Yahweh's covenant will and purpose. Israel is to practice the Torah in concrete social practices, and these practices witness to Yahweh's character and purpose.

Verse 5 makes it clear that God's speaking with humanity is a dangerous matter. The first generation of the exodus people knew that they dared not directly hear the word of Yahweh. Out of fear, they took safety measures. Moses is the one to meet with Yahweh. He represents the people and receives the commands of God selected for the ordering of their life together. Now the succeeding generation is to receive these words. They, too, know of the danger involved in meeting and speaking with Yahweh face-to-face. Moses, and his words, again functions as the mediator for the succeeding generations of Israel.

2. The Decalogue (5:6-21 [6-18 HB])

These verses repeat with only minor variations the Ten Commandments already set out in Exod 20:2-17 [2-14 HB]. The Decalogue functions as the foundation of Israel's national life. It forms the basic principles on which all of the further laws are to be administered by the judges and leaders of Israel. The major Law section of Deuteronomy (12:1—26:19) is an exposition of the policies and practices of these basic principles.

In Deuteronomy, God claims his people as Redeemer, not Creator. At one time Pharaoh controlled the people, now they belong to Yahweh. In the act of liberating the people, Yahweh displaced Pharaoh as Israel's lord and master (Brueggemann 2001, 66). Therefore, the God who liberates issues commands that will function as the core of the politics of liberation. Israel belongs to Yahweh, and he intends to make her into a people that reflect his character and purpose. The reader assumes that because Yahweh is the Redeemer, he is on the side of the oppressed.

Yahweh's liberating act not only demands exclusive loyalty established in the first command but also calls for obedience to all the commandments. Each of the other commandments up through the one on parents includes the expression "the LORD your God." The phrase "you were slaves in Egypt and that the LORD your God brought you out" reappears in the Sabbath commandment as the motivation for observing the Sabbath (5:15). The identification of Yahweh as the liberator from Egyptian bondage is a central theme throughout Deuteronomy. Examples of this can be found in Deuteronomy 6:12; 7:8; 8:14; 13:5, 10 [6, 11 HB].

a. I Am Yahweh Your God (5:6)

■ 6 The opening announcement of the Decalogue, **I am the LORD your God**, is the underpinning of the commandments and undeniably of the full corpus of Deuteronomic law. These words are jointly a self-disclosure of divinity and an assertion. The questions that emerge in this declaration are: Who is

Yahweh, and what does it mean for him to be Israel's God? The answer is, of course: Yahweh is the one who appeared at the sacred mountain to Moses and commanded him to go to Pharaoh and demand that the people be set free. He is the one who appeared again on that same sacred mountain to give the precious gift of Torah. The called, liberated people of Yahweh are to reveal his character and purpose in the world.

b. Three Commands Concerning the Worship and Service of Yahweh Alone (5:7-11)

(1) No Other Gods (5:7)

■ **7** Even though the first command is meant for the whole of the community, it is in the Hebrew language addressed to the individual Israelite. The one who saves Israel makes an exclusive claim on each descendant of Abraham, **You shall have no other gods before me**. What is the precise meaning of **before me**? The Hebrew word straightforwardly translates *upon my face*. There seem to be six possible meanings: "beside me," in the spatial sense; "beside me," in the figurative sense; "in addition to me," as a disadvantage to Yahweh; "before me," taking a superior position; "in my presence"; and "to spite me"—this would be an act of defiance (Weinfeld 1991, 276-77). Taken literally, the commandment may mean that no other gods are to appear at the cultic sites where Yahweh is worshipped. Some commentators believe that this would mean that the first command is prohibiting the making of images of gods other than Yahweh or of showing veneration to such gods at places where Yahweh is worshipped (Harrelson 1997, 55). Much more likely is the reading that though the ancient world is full of gods, they are not to be rivals to Yahweh.

Monotheism is not the primary concern of this commandment, but rather the fact that Yahweh is to be the only God for Israel. It assumes the existence, at least the conjectural existence, of other gods. At the same time, the instruction makes it clear that the community of Israel is not to entrust such gods with any authority or jurisdiction over their lives. Those who belong to Yahweh are claimed exclusively by and for him. All other gods are forever abolished from their worship, their obedience, and their affection. All other realms hold no ultimate control over the lives of the liberated people of God.

This radical stance of ancient Israel is a remarkable position to arrive at. Only a few generations earlier the patriarchs Abraham, Isaac, and Jacob operated under the conviction that Yahweh is understood as the chief God (Harrelson 1997, 55). He functions as the leader of the tribe or clan and accompanies the tribe in its movements to find grazing land for the flocks of this nomadic people. Now, the descendants of the patriarchs are commanded to take no account of any other god.

Israel developed her religious belief in the wilderness. Abraham lived in the Negev desert, where God made his covenant with him. Moses met God in a burning bush in the desert, where he learned the greatness of God's name and received his commission to bring the Israelites out of Egypt. God spoke to his people on Mount Horeb and reestablished his covenant with them in the Ten Commandments. Throughout the Israelites' forty-year journey in the wilderness, Yahweh accompanied them, protected them, fed them, and guided them to the land of promise.

There is no doubt that Yahweh is God of the wilderness. But when the Israelites entered Canaan, they found farmers, not shepherds. The land is fruitful beyond anything the Hebrew nomads have ever seen. The Canaanites attributed this fertility to their god Baal, and that is where the Israelites' predicament begins. Could the God who led them out of Egypt and through the wilderness also provide fertile farms in the promised land? Or would the fertility god of Canaan have to be honored? Maybe, to be safe, they should worship both Yahweh and Baal. When the way the world seems to work points to alternative sources of power and authority, it is always tempting to worship or serve these sources of power, especially when the practices that allow access to their use are a vital part of the political reality of the host culture. That is the reason that the great temptation of ancient Israel is the fertility cult.

Early in the Deuteronomistic History, the book of Judges narrates the ongoing struggle of the Israelites' attraction to, and worship of, the Canaanite gods. There is a cycle that the stories of Judges demonstrate: Israel's unfaithfulness, Yahweh's judgment, the people's repentance, and God's merciful restoration through a judge. Then the cycle would repeat itself the next time the Israelites reached for Baal instead of Yahweh. The Deuteronomistic Historians make it clear that the seductions of Baal did not cease following the judges. Under the kings of Israel, this political/spiritual crusade continues. By the time of Ahab and Jezebel, the fertility cults appear to have the official sanction of Israel's leaders. Ahab, with his wife's encouragement, builds a temple to Baal at his capital, Samaria. All the while, prophets such as Elijah, whose name means "Yahweh is God," bellowed that Yahweh alone deserves the people's total allegiance (1 Kgs 18:21). It took the Assyrian destruction of Israel and the Babylonian captivity of Judah to dissuade the Israelites from their syncretism. Israel traveled a long, hard road toward her total allegiance to the God of liberation. When the command is to have no other gods before Yahweh, it is an exclusive claim on Israel's corporate and individual life. She is to practice her life in the politics of the nomadic God whose name is a promise: Yahweh.

This commandment is not a command to acknowledge the existence of God. In biblical times the atheist was a fool. Psalms 14:1 and 53:1 [2 HB] say, "The fool says in his heart, 'There is no God.'" The atheist is understood to be misguided and even silly, but not necessarily a violator of the first commandment. Maybe the best way to understand the first commandment is with the concept "double-mindedness." Elijah says it best in 1 Kgs 18:21: "How long will you waver between two opinions? If the LORD is God, follow him; but if Baal is God, follow him." Walter Harrelson has a wonderful summary statement to the first commandment. He writes, "The first commandment, then, is the commandment that takes the reality of God seriously: as creator of the universe, as the sustainer of all beings and all being, and as the one whose purposes move forward to their consummation" (1997, 61). God will have no competitors!

(2) No Idols (5:8-10)

■ **8-10** How is one to interpret the prohibition of idols? Many Jewish, Lutheran, and Roman Catholic interpreters would group this prohibition within the margins of the first commandment. Verse 9 declares that idols are not to be bowed down to or worshipped, with the justification for this being that Yahweh is a jealous God. This gives some credence to grouping the prohibition against idols as a part of the prohibition against having other gods before Yahweh. But the question that must be asked is: Does ancient Israel really believe that idols are gods? If so, then this prohibition is just an elaboration of the first commandment. The stylistic dimensions of the literature itself seem to be concerned with a mystery different from having other gods in Yahweh's presence. For example, this prohibition represents the second imperative given in the list of commands.

In order to understand this second commandment as something other than an elaboration of the first command, one must understand what an idol is in the ancient Near East and how it functions. Ancient pagan religions did not entertain the belief that the deity is simply identical with the image set up in a temple. They knew that the gods are invisible and that they ascend above all human ability to comprehend them. They believed that the gods are pleased to disclose themselves through the image, "for the image is first and foremost the bearer of a revelation" (von Rad 1962, 214). Idolatry is a practice that allowed the gods to be approached by means of the images.

Human beings construct and venerate idols because they believe that a god can be localized and therefore reduced to the finite. Once restricted to a place, the god can be controlled to some degree through its image and incantations. This static, localized, and controllable power could never be reconciled with the revelation of Yahweh. He will not become present for Israel by means of a static earthly image. He is free "to be" what "he will be": "I AM WHO I AM" (Exod 3:14). Ancient Israel's conceptual belief is contrasted between a static image that belonged to her neighbors and the dynamic movement of historical existence.

Yahweh is a God who makes and fulfills promises. He can only be recognized in his story, a story that Israel participates in. These storied people are a sign, not at the cultic center, but in their daily life. The regularity of their life together, their politics, is a manifestation of their faithfulness to the commandments of God who created them. Because an idol or image is a bearer of revelation, there could only be one image that could dynamically reveal the character of Yahweh: the image expressed in the dynamism of history by a faithful human community committed to doing God's will (Harrelson 1997, 64). Therefore, a community that practices Torah is necessary in the formation of character that reflects truthfully the character of God.

One of the most interesting theological confessions is contained in this commandment: **For I, the LORD your God, am a jealous God, punishing the children for the sin of the parents to the third and fourth generation of those who hate me, but showing love to a thousand generations of those who love me and keep my commandments** (Deut 5:9b-10). This confession is found in roughly this form throughout the OT (see Exod 34:6-7; Num 14:18; Jer 32:18; Nah 1:2-3).

The notion of the jealousy of Yahweh, in this passage, conveys God's intolerance of the practice of idolatry. The modifier "jealous" occurs only a few times in the OT (Exod 20:5; 34:14, twice; Deut 4:24; 5:9). It is associated with the prohibition against the worship of rival deities. Jealousy is not to be considered a psychological concept when attached to God, but it points to the exclusive claim of God on the life of his people and the complete loyalty that is required of the covenantal relationship. Idolatry creates a people who lack the virtue of faithfulness and its result will last for generations.

What does this judgment upon future generations mean? There is no clear biblical example of a punishment intentionally exacted because of the sins of a previous generation. The best understanding of the statement is that the idolater's sin will have consequences that will continue to influence subsequent generations. Perhaps the idolatrous generation will never be free from the consequences of the practice of idolatry, even if they live to see their great-grandchildren. The fortunes of the individual as well as the group cohere in the judgment of God. If a community follows certain practices, the persons in that community will be impacted by those practices and experience the end to which those practices aim.

The corresponding belief in v 10 (**showing love to a thousand generations of those who love me and keep my commandments**) presupposes that those who derive benefit from the "love" of God do so because they practice their lives in a way that loves Yahweh and keeps his commandments. The first use of the word **love** is a translation of the well-known Hebrew word *ḥesed*. This word points to a combination of faithfulness and love that has an enduring quality because it is rooted in a covenantal relationship. As Israel's covenant partner, Yahweh is committed to showing *ḥesed* to Israel. It is often translated "steadfast love" (NRSV; the NIV frequently translates this word as "unfailing love"). The second word for **love** in this verse is *'ahab*, the more commonly used word for love in the OT. This word conveys love that is shown and practiced in familial relationships, such as parental love for children. There is a striking imbalance between the **fourth generation** and a **thousand generations**. This imbalance points to the conviction that the steadfast love of God outweighs all judgment and brokenness.

This commandment makes clear that making idols or images of God in any form is an attempt to depict God, which could never be adequate and therefore cannot be acceptable. These static images stand in the way of seeing Yahweh as the living God, a God who visits his people and extends to them time and again steadfast love and mercy. No idol can do justice to the living God; only human beings with a faithful story can be a representation of God on earth.

(3) No Wrongful Use of God's Name (5:11)

■ **11** The burden of the third command is attached to humanity's effort at manipulating the outcome of events. Holding sway over the power or powers that hold sway over life and destiny is constantly the quest of humanity, both ancient and modern. What are the sources of power, where do they come from, and how are they controlled? For ancient persons, a major source of power is the name of a god. God explicitly made himself known by his name. If God reveals his name, then what are people to do with "the name" of God? A great temptation is that people might take into their own possession the revealed name of God and use it insolently for their own purposes.

The Divine Name

Moses himself is responsible for the disclosure of the divine name that God revealed to him on the sacred mountain. The name, Yahweh, is given in such a way as to not reveal its ambiguous meaning. Contemporary readers should not seek to find in the words "I AM WHO I AM" (Exod 3:14) a philosophical or theological doctrine appropriate to a conceptual framework of a later epoch. Yet these words contain a very simple idea based upon the grammar itself.

The name Yahweh is a noun based upon the "to be" verb (Hebrew *hāyâ*). If this name was a verb, it would be in the "future" tense, third person, and it would be translated "He will be." The tenses of the formula indicate that more than a pointless tautology is intended. God announces that his intentions will be revealed in his future acts, which will be explained in the impending events of Israel's liberation.

When Yahweh himself gives a clarification of the name, the verb appears in the first person, "I am." The sense is: It is I who am with my people, especially in their time of trouble and need. The meaning "I will be with . . . to help and save" is what is being conveyed. This means that the name itself is a promise, and the circumstances of life provide the opportunity for fulfilling the promise. Yahweh will show himself to be near at hand and mighty to save in the circumstances of world and personal history. The name appears to be a reference to the promise of God's presence to help in time of need, but it is also a declaration that he will be the way he chooses to be. Israel will not be able to control the way Yahweh will be for them, but they can count on Yahweh being for them!

When understood in this way, the divine name has its particular significance for the historical mission of Moses. What could be of greater importance both for him and for his people than the belief of the sustaining presence of the God of the Fathers? The basis for a new communal identity is the confidence that God is discernibly and directly present and active to save. The deliverance of Israel from Pharaoh is the name fulfilling itself in Israel's own story. Therefore, the name implies the virtue of faithfulness to the character of Yahweh.

What does it mean to take the name of Yahweh in vain? The name of a person or a god, in the ancient Near East, is considered to contain inherent power. Israel could only use the name of God in its proper place: to praise him and to call upon him for help. To use the divine name in any way other than in gratitude and hope would be to take the name lightly. Gratitude and hope are stances of surrender to the lordship of Yahweh. Meaningless and empty invocation of the divine name means that one does not recognize the character and purpose of God.

The basic interpretive question of this commandment is the sense of the Hebrew term *šāv'*, which is commonly translated "in vain" (**misuses**). The basic force of the expression is *emptily* or *to no good purpose*. The term is used twice in Deut 5:11, and it appears again in the ninth commandment (v 20 [17*d* HB]) against false witness. Walter Harrelson believes that rather than being an expression for emptiness or worthlessness, the Hebrew word conveys an active power to harm (1997, 73). He translates this word "for mischief." This would indicate that using the name of Yahweh in vain entails misusing the power inherent in the personal name for God to do harm against others. Ancient Israel is prohibited from making its religion into a weapon with which it could have its way with people.

A great misuse of the divine name is false prophecy. In this instance the indication of the misuse of the divine name is perceived in two ways: when the prophet speaks and begins or ends with the messenger formula, "thus says Yahweh," and also when the prophecy is talked about. The misuse of the name is clear in these instances, for the texts regularly say that the prophets are prophesying in the name of Yahweh even though Yahweh did not send them or speak to them. This command at least means that one cannot harness God's power for empty or worthless purposes.

People who have a calling from God or a status in the community that places them in the position of declaring in some way the word of the Lord must take great care in the use of the divine name. This meaning is apparent and central: speaking in the name of Yahweh, usually in the form of "Thus says the

LORD," grounds and secures what is said so that it is presumed to be trustworthy and true. The community can count on this word because, spoken in the name of Yahweh, it is understood to be from Yahweh and therefore valid. When such words are fabrications, made up out of one's own opinion, the community that abides by the direction indicated by the words is in utter peril.

c. Two Commands that Are Transitional in the Decalogue (5:12-16)

(1) Observe the Sabbath (5:12-15)

■ **12-15** The fourth commandment is one of the most remarkable policies in the politics of Yahweh. The consistent rest from toil on the seventh day of the week is a distinctive practice by Israel in the ancient Near Eastern world. This does not mean that ancient communities did not keep time in unique ways. In antiquity, many communities practiced some days that are unique or set aside. For example, in ancient Babylonia "days of ill omen" were days unfavorable to commence important activities; on "market days" people refrained from ordinary work to devote time to bartering and exchanging goods; cultic worship was done on days linked to the different phases of the moon (Harrelson 1997, 79).

The ancient Near East practice of keeping certain days distinctive does not give adequate explanation for the origin and unique meaning of the Sabbath. Nor does the simple division of sacred time into periods of seven propose a satisfactory rationalization, although that account does have noteworthy implications. The mystery is why would an ancient people adhere to resting on one day in seven? This practice of no work every seventh day does not seem to be tied to the movement of the planets, the alternation of the seasons, or the organization of the community for the exchange of goods. As the commandment now appears, it merely levels out the days into multiples of seven and requires that the seventh in the recurring series be reserved for rest (Harrelson 1997, 79-80).

Sabbath-keeping is given a pivotal place in the Decalogue. The first three commands (found in vv 6-11) describe Israel's duties to Yahweh and the last six commands (found in vv 16-21 [16-17 HB]) express how relationships with human beings are to be handled. In Deuteronomy, the fourth commandment takes up both of these foci concurrently. The Sabbath is to be sanctified and is a Sabbath to Yahweh, but it is also a time to give rest to all. The combination of these two features of the religious tradition point out the indivisibility of worship and social justice. Sabbath keeping is a political reality of holy separation for the sake of the other, especially the other that is overloaded with extreme labor. Toil is not all that human beings are created for.

According Exod 20 God rested on the seventh day after creating heaven and earth and all that is in them. As God rested and hallowed the seventh day, so also human beings are to do the same (see Gen 2:2-3). The explanation of

Deuteronomy is very different. Human beings need rest, and especially slaves need rest. Israel is called to remember how Yahweh rescued her from the unceasing labor of Egyptian oppression. In harmony with this, she is commanded to give a break from unending toil to those who are in similar circumstances of bondage. Deuteronomy's explication draws attention to the social-ethical needs of human beings; it is political!

In the routine interactions of any society, there are significant public practices that demonstrate how power and privilege operate: some people rest while others work. The Sabbath functions as a short-term but recurrent "rising above" of public distinctions when slaves take part with masters in a new world order initiated by the great liberating God, Yahweh. The in-breaking of the new world order extends not only to the powerful but also to the powerless. As Nelson says,

> The Sabbath commandment seems to be addressed to landowners who also owned domestic animals and slaves. The alien resident within your towns is literally "your resident alien," a noncitizen who is in a patron-client relationship with the audience of this commandment . . . indicating the elevated social position of the audience. However, Sabbath means that the division between work and rest is not to be a matter of social class, gender, or even species, but an opportunity for leisure provided to all. (2002b, 83)

This commandment intends that once a week all work stop for everyone, and every difference that determines who must toil and who benefits from that toil be momentarily but regularly disrupted. The miracle of this day is that slaves and masters have common identity and common possibility in relation to toil. In Deuteronomy, the Sabbath commandment highlights the inherent contradiction between the institution of slavery and the theological implications of Yahweh's deliverance of Israel from Egyptian bondage.

Keeping Sabbath as an act of hope is a dream of the ultimate alternative reality. The fact that the work stoppage pertains not only to all members of the human community but also to nonhuman creatures indicates a recognition that the liberating desire of Yahweh extends to everyone and everything in a society. A society that does not practice some form of Sabbath inevitably takes advantage of and uses up natural resources, perhaps because it believes that more chattels can always be found. Israel's Sabbath will eventually be extended to the Sabbatical Year and finally the Year of Jubilee. It is interesting to note in Luke 4 that Jesus refers to his own message and ministry of the kingdom within the conceptual framework of the favorable year of the Lord, or Jubilee. The granting of rest to all creatures, even slaves and animals, is the foretaste of the kingdom of God.

(2) Honor Father and Mother (5:16)

■ **16** The fifth commandment, requiring honor for parents, appears to move from the religious and social synergism of the fourth commandment to narrowly focus on the social milieu. It should be remembered that the fourth and fifth commandments are pivotal and similar to each other, in that they are both the only positive commands. What is it that this commandment wished most to safeguard in the life of ancient Israel? It has in view the care of the aged, the treatment of old parents with dignity and thoughtfulness by their adult children (Harrelson 1997, 98). Therefore, the commandment would be misconstrued if it were thought of as designed to keep young children in line, to keep them well-mannered and submissive and polite toward their elders.

Just as human beings and beasts need rest from their labors, and just as grinding toil does not constitute the only reason for human life and activity, so also human beings do not cease to have value and importance when the time of their beneficial labor for the community has run its course. Parents are to be cherished and cared for in the time of their feebleness and frailty. When they enter upon their "Sabbath rest" they are to be shown honor such as they were shown in their time of active membership in society.

It should be noticed that this is the first commandment with a promise attached to it: a long and good life is connected to keeping this commandment. There is no doubt that there are children who honor their aging parents and die prematurely, and others who dishonor their parents and live long lives. It should be obvious that this is once again a practice within the political reality of how the community is to function. When placed as a promised outcome of honoring father and mother, it suggests that each generation honoring and caring for its older members creates and maintains a societal ethos that increases the prospect of a good and long life for each person in the community and for the culture as a whole. To the extent that a lack of concern for and a disregard of the older generation becomes a societal pattern, the possibilities of a long and happy life are diminished for all.

d. Five Commands Concerning Life Together (5:17-21 [17-18 HB])

(1) No Murder (5:17 [17a HB])

■ **17 [17a HB]** The sixth commandment points to a shift in the Decalogue. The elaborated commands in the first part of the ten words now give way to a series of short prohibitions. These prohibitions are joined by a conjunction following this sixth command. This portion of divine instruction begins those succinct rules that deal directly with community life and are formulated as prohibitions to safeguard the basic rights of each person.

Taking a human life is at the top of the list of an everyday awareness of the Ten Commandments. There seems to be something so central and fundamental about taking a human life that one understands this commandment as primary, universal, and without dispute; yet understanding the commandment is knotty because taking a human life is complex. All one has to do is think about the number of people who will invoke this commandment with enthusiasm against abortion and worry little about capital punishment, or be vigorously opposed to capital punishment and stand for the right of women to choose even if it means the loss of an infant's life. The simplicity of the commandment fades quickly as soon as one tries to translate it into policies to inform and shape a community. Matters become even more complex when one tries to relate the prohibition to actual acts of taking life.

Even though this commandment is made up of only two Hebrew words, it is difficult to know where to start. The interpreter of Scripture finds the first great challenge in discerning how to translate the Hebrew word for *to kill* (*rāṣaḥ*). Problems associated with the precise definition of the term are apparent, because it lacks any definitional clause. What kind of killing is implied? A literal reading of this translation obviously asserts that human life is not to be taken. But, a reading of the entire OT reveals the use of violence by the community in Yahweh's name.

The most important interpretive issue of the sixth commandment is the question: How far-reaching is the prohibition against taking life? Some translations begin to answer this question with their translation itself; **You shall not murder**. These translations would mean by this a willful and planned taking of someone's life. This translation is used by the NIV and the NRSV. But is this all that this commandment means?

This brief and straightforward commandment presents the contemporary reader with a splendid illustration of the dilemma associated with interpreting old texts. The problem is that there is no single, narrow meaning or usage of the Hebrew word. The word usage becomes more complicated as it is examined on its trajectories of meaning and usage in the Scripture itself. The verb *rāṣaḥ* is not one of the more common Hebrew terms for killing of any sort. It occurs forty-six times and in its early usage it did not refer to killing in the limited sense of murder. Problems associated with the precise definition of the term are very noticeable. This term has a broader range of meaning than simply murder; it can include accidental killing as seen in Deut 19:4 and Num 35:11. It always refers to the killing of one human being by another. Occurrences of the verb suggest that, at least in an early period of its usage, it did not refer to killing in the limited sense of murder (Num 35:6, 11, 12, 25, 26, 27, 28; Deut 4:42; 19:3, 4, 6; Josh 20:3, 5, 6; 21:13, 21, 27), but to killing that called for blood vengeance (Num 35:27, 30). If this commandment were understood in this older sense, it would prohibit vigilante justice.

Does this commandment prohibit vigilantism only, or is this text to be used to contemplate the use of aggression and brutality against people? The sixth commandment develops eventually to refer to killing with forethought and malice. Whatever the ancient use of this commandment may be, it does correspond to a concern for the promotion of human life and well-being. Members of the community are to be protected from violence. The greatest example of the development of this commandment for the protection of human life is seen in the way Jesus interprets it in Matt 5:21 ff. Jesus develops the sixth commandment to include anger against a brother or sister, and he is advocating a contrast community that embraces the commands in their greatest radical form. Nonviolence and love of the enemy are to become the hallmark of this community. When Jesus said, "Love your enemies," he at least meant, "don't kill them."

(2) No Adultery (5:18 [17*b* HB])

■ **18 [17*b* HB]** A conceptual understanding of adultery depends upon a linguistic community's definition of the institution of marriage. Ancient Israel's patriarchal social order allowed for polygamy, concubines, and prostitution. Males had considerable freedom in sexual matters. On the other hand, a betrothed or married woman committed adultery if she had sexual relations with anyone other than her husband or her engaged husband-to-be. Females were politically bound to either their fathers or later to their husbands or sons. The sexuality of Israelite women is considered the property of the significant male in their lives.

A man, by contrast, commits adultery only if he has relations with the wife or the betrothed of another man. An Israelite husband did not owe his wife fidelity. He could not, by definition, be unfaithful to his wife or wives. He could commit adultery only by having intercourse with another man's wife, in which case his crime is not against his own marriage but against his sexual partner's husband or betrothed. The disparity between the implication of adultery for the man and for the woman would in time disappear. But for ancient Israel the dissimilarity remains, because the woman is understood to depend in many ways upon the life, security, and reputation of her husband.

This command does not apply directly to modern Western culture when it is understood in its historic sense. The institution of marriage and associated sexual norms has undergone considerable development in the world that is influenced by the biblical tradition. Like attitudes toward slavery, this commandment has been overhauled since it first emerged. As a result, the definition of adultery also is changing. Clearly, the line of reasoning for monogamy must be made on grounds not limited to this commandment. Regardless of how one characterizes marriage and adultery, the commandment clearly places the sanctity of marriage, the fundamental basis of human family life, in the context of Yahweh's covenant with his people. For Christians and contemporary Jews, faithfulness in the covenant of marriage is a matter of fidelity to the God of the covenant.

A more radical understanding of this commandment is avowed in the teaching of Jesus. He said, "You have heard that it was said, 'You shall not commit adultery.' But I tell you that anyone who looks at a woman lustfully has already committed adultery with her in his heart" (Matt 5:27-28). Not only the fact of a sexual act, but also the contemplation of the sexual act, breaches the marriage vow. Consideration of the psychological complexity of adhering to Jesus' words should not lessen its moral force as a reminder of where sexual thought and action have their proper place. A reader should also notice how the teaching of Jesus places the focus on the practice of fidelity to one's marriage upon the male and not singly upon the female as the Decalogue does. It is not about having sexual relations or even thoughts about another man's betrothed or wife, but any woman. This places the focus upon the sexual imagination of the male and makes it clear that a male cannot make, even in his own mind, a female an object of his own sensual gratification.

The obvious focus of the development of this commandment is to guard the sacredness of the marriage relationship, and it acknowledges that the sexual relationship of wife and husband is the center of intimacy and assurance. Therefore, it seems totally in order to maintain that this commandment is the guideline for every marriage, expressing the commitment of the partners in marriage to treasure and preserve the unity that is called into being in marriage and in the sexual relations they engage in as marriage partners.

(3) No Stealing (5:19 [17c HB])

■ **19 [17c HB]** Conduct with respect to theft is the focus of the eighth commandment. An ostensible reading of this commandment seems to imply a simple prohibition against taking the property or possessions of another person or group of persons. Yet, many scholars believe, at the earliest stages of its history, this prohibition is to guard against the theft of another person for the purpose of enslavement. Therefore, the theft prohibited under absolute sanction of this commandment is the stealing of persons, or kidnapping, for slavery.

One of the best examples of breaking this commandment in this way is the Joseph story. Joseph, as a slave in Egypt, speaks of himself as having been "stolen out of the land of the Hebrews" (Gen 40:15 NRSV). His brothers sold him to some traveling Midianite traders and gained personal profit from the transaction. The consequence of the crime against Joseph is to cut him off completely from his family and therefore the promised future within the covenant. This crime disrupts the basic covenantal relationship that Yahweh has with his people. This active selling of Joseph into slavery dared to control not only Joseph's present-day existence but also his future. This kind of control is only to be in the purview of Israel's God.

When this commandment is understood in this way, the prohibition against theft, fundamental to Yahweh's covenant with Israel, does not concern property per se, but the worth of persons. Most of the property theft laws outside the Decalogue are treated essentially as torts, which is common law that involves a breach of a civil duty owed to some else. So, does this mean that only relationships with Yahweh and with other human beings merit treatment in the Decalogue? No, the eighth commandment would eventually develop an understanding among the people as the unlawful seizing of the property and/ or possessions of another.

The prohibition against theft comes from a tradition that recognizes Yahweh's protection of the belongings of others, based on the belief that God gives the possessions in the first place and that his gifts are sacred (Zimmerli 1978, 135). This is not a notion of the sanctity of private property for itself. The giving of gifts by Yahweh does not mean that ancient Israel supposes that it can horde possessions and property. For the people of God, such safeguards of material goods are not intended to develop into an amassing of wealth, and therefore squeeze out others from the resources within the land.

Modern readers of the sacred text have come to appreciate this commandment against theft as a broad one. The values of the eighth commandment are fundamental to community life with broad-ranging applications protecting the lives of members of the community from oppression and exploitation. For each person it provides against property being taken unlawfully and unfairly.

(4) No False Witness (5:20 [17d HB])

■ **20 [17d HB]** The ninth commandment flows naturally out of the eighth commandment. Just as one dares not steal the goods of one's neighbor, so one cannot manipulate language to serve their own ends. If they do so, they will contaminate the essence of human social existence. Language is the foundation of human community. When words can no longer be trusted, but are used for the purpose of deception, the whole community is in jeopardy (Harrelson 1997, 145).

In ancient Israel, the circumstances necessitating unhampered truth telling most frequently were those that normalized communal interactions, such as conflicts between persons or families over property, business transactions, or personal injury. When such clashes occurred, the elders or the judges or the heads of households would call for the disputants to make their presentations and bring along their witnesses. When the culpable person invalidates the truth by distorting the facts, justice is perverted. Justice can also be distorted by witnesses who perjure themselves or by judges who refuse to adjudicate fair verdicts in the appearance of the evidence. It is in these very public contexts where false accusations are devastating. The false word perverts justice; therefore, a thoughtful interpretation of this commandment understands its setting to be the courtroom or the gate, where judgments are given.

This commandment stands in a close relationship to the third commandment. These commandments prohibit the empty use of words. The third commandment banned the empty use of the divine name, the ninth commandment forbade the empty use of words in testimony. You shall not give worthless testimony against your neighbor. Literally the commandment says, *you shall not testify against your neighbor as an empty witness*. Von Rad says, "The prohibition of false witness was so important because according to the early Israelite legal usage a very great significance was attached to the testimony of the witness" (1975, 59).

In ancient Israel the burden of proof in legal proceedings is placed, to a large extent, on the accused. They are to prove their innocence in the face of accusations, and the guilt or innocence of an individual is primarily determined on the basis of witnesses (Deut 19:15-21). Israel's understanding of the centrality of the law courts for the proper function of the society and the security and protection of each member of that society is accented again here. If the courts work improperly and one is dealt with unfairly, the fabric of trust is lost in the community and anything can happen. Therefore, truth telling in the courts is no light matter. When it is discovered that a person is a false witness, they are to suffer the same penalty as would be carried out on the falsely accused (Deut 19:19).

The question that a contemporary interpreter of this commandment needs to ask is: Do we hear a more general sanction against lying? The answer to this question is yes, because the reasons for truth telling ultimately do not change from one generation to another. As with most of the commandments, the protection of the neighbor is the primary aim, and this divine principle is constantly expanding. In today's world truth telling determines the well-being of large and small covenant relationships. Covenants are dependent upon speaking honestly and not misleading the other person(s). One could say that the configuration of a culture is contingent upon a level of honesty in the communal square.

There is no doubt that it is very difficult for many roles that people play in today's society to disentangle from deception. Some roles have extraordinary pressure to misrepresent the truth. This is often the case in politics, sales, and other professions where success depends upon individuals' ability to act in ways that yield a certain desired outcome, usually economic advantage or personal advancement; yet the very fabric of a society is based upon being able to trust in all kinds of relationships. Faithfulness in relationships is a challenge for every generation, and it is a mistake to think that anyone is free from the lure of deception. Much of human existence is discolored by deceptions. The pressure to put one's views or oneself in a better light than the facts declare is a relentless pull for every human being.

(5) No Coveting (5:21 [18 HB])

■ **21 [18 HB]** The tenth commandment brings to a close the list of obligations for persons in covenant community. It draws together the protections that are found in the second tablet of the Decalogue and moves them toward an internalization that will create character in the individual. This commandment has in view a yearning after the possessions of others or the life of others. The accent of this command lies not upon the exploitation accomplished but upon the character or disposition of a person.

Israel is to demonstrate righteousness in a very public way. She believes that the internal state of affairs of the individual shows itself in action. A demonstration of faithfulness to the Torah is perceived in word and deed, not by what a person thought about doing or saying. The toil of Israel's prophets and sages is engaged with the deed rather than with emotions. Public righteousness is a matter of actual faithfulness to Yahweh and the covenant in word and action. In other words, it is embodied! Deeds display the character of a person. So what does a law dealing with attitudes and passions, rather than actual deeds, mean for ancient Israel?

Two Hebrew verbs are used for the concept of coveting in this text: *ḥāmad* and *'āvâ*. The NIV translates these two verbs **covet** and **set your desire**. *Ḥāmad* means more than the feelings of craving or longing for something. It frequently has the sense of to take steps to secure something, though it does not always represent both the desire for something and the making of plans to secure the desired object (Harrelson 1997, 148-49). *'Āvâ* means unambiguously "to desire," "long for," or "lust after." "This verb does not exclude the making of plans to realize the desire, but neither does it require such activity" (ibid., 148).

Members of the community are required to keep themselves from the power of lust for anything that belongs to the neighbor. This does not mean that temptation is not a part of the course of life, but it should not shape the character of the individual and the ethos of the community. Even though feelings cannot be legislated, there is a relationship between the inner and outer dimensions of life. The internal state of affairs of the individual shows itself in the way a person lives.

The prohibition against coveting the life or goods of others is close to the prohibition against worship of any god other than Yahweh. The first commandment requires that no other divine being or principle count for anything in the life of the Israelite. Those who have associated themselves with the God of the covenant, with the God who brought Israel out of Egypt, are now bound to this God in interior ways. The Shema says that the people are to give the allegiance of their heart to Yahweh and let no other ultimate realities in all creation exercise any rival authority over them (Deut 6:4-5). They not only do not worship other divine beings at the cult centers, but they are to give no credence to these powers, no place to such powers in their own thinking or feeling.

So just what does the tenth commandment wish to rule out? Yahweh's covenant partners are mandated to keep themselves from the power of yearning for their neighbor's wife or possessions. Not only are the faithful not to take the neighbor's wife as their own, that would be a violation of the seventh commandment, but they are also prohibited from hungering for the wife of their neighbor. The craving that is prohibited is thought of as beyond what is normal; it is a hungering for the neighbor's goods that goes well beyond the desire to have one's own life enhanced by the possession of additional goods (Harrelson 1997, 151-52). Coveting is ultimately a life lived without gratitude for the opportune gifts that are received by oneself and one's neighbor. It lacks the basic belief in the story of God's providence and benevolence.

3. Moses as the Mediator of God's Will (5:22-33 [19-29 HB])

■ **22-33 [19-29 HB]** The picture that is painted in this subsection portrays the whole people directly receiving the Decalogue as the basic political reality of their covenant with Yahweh. They react in apprehension at the overwhelming display of sights and sounds that are associated with Yahweh's disclosure on Mount Horeb. The fire, the cloud, and the thick darkness all concealed the appearance of Yahweh from sight, but Israel hears the voice of God directly. Therefore, with great trepidation Israel asks for a mediator between them and God.

A paraphrase of vv 25-26 [22-23 HB] is "we have stayed alive so far, but if we have too long of an exposure to the divine presence, it might kill us." Remaining alive in the land that Yahweh is giving to Israel is the goal of the tradition of Deuteronomy. Israel's long-term option for life in the land is also tied to obeying the Law (v 33 [29 HB]). What are they to do? Israel knows that the danger of death lies on both sides of the issue: to be exposed in the land without Yahweh's Torah is death and to be exposed to Yahweh's presence is also death.

Israel understands the necessity for, and the threat of, the presence of Yahweh. What is required is someone to mediate between God and humanity. Life is threatened if the people hear the voice of God (v 25 [22 HB]); therefore, the people need one who is willing to risk imminent death for the sake of the people. But will Moses have to die for the sake of the people, and if he does, how will God's word continue to live and work within the covenant community?

The proclamation of the Decalogue takes place before the whole assembly. The **words**, which is translated **commandments**, of v 22 [19 HB] are apparently the Decalogue. That Yahweh **added nothing more** helps separate out the partial subject matter of Horeb from what Moses would speak in Moab, and it also highlights the exclusive authority of the Decalogue. *These words* are not just proclaimed and devoted to memory, but the scene maintains that God wrote the Decalogue upon two stone tablets and gave them to Moses. This incident reinforces the uniqueness and influence of the Decalogue over all other laws. No other laws are spoken directly by God to the people. No other laws are written in stone by the divine hand. But even this giving of the Decalogue is a one-time occasion in an earlier period. How will the commandments move, with the people, into the future? Moses is to become the connection to the future as the stone tablets are handed over into his custody.

Those who speak to Moses (v 23 [20 HB]) are appropriately restricted to the leadership of ancient Israel. They request that Moses act as a go-between in all future exchanges with Yahweh. The overwhelming intensity of God's self-disclosure needs a mediator. Rather than the incapacitating horror of Exod 20:18-21 [15-18 HB], they demonstrate a reasoned and proper caution, approved by Yahweh as appropriate **fear** of the Lord (Deut 5:29 [26 HB]). The bewilderment of the people (v 24 [21 HB]) is apparent, but so is their allegiance, as reflected in the reverberation of their voices when they speak of Yahweh as **our God** (vv 24, 25, 27 [21, 22, 24 HB]).

Yahweh informs Moses that the leaders' request for him to be their mediator **was good** (v 28 [25 HB]). The assertion of this text makes it apparent that God's powerful word is communicated through human intermediaries such as Moses. But does this mean that Moses will have to die for the sake of the people as he mediates God's word to them? And if Moses does die, then how will God's word continue to live and work within the covenant community? It is in answering these questions that the text itself will allow Moses to function not only as the mediator of God's word to Israel but also as a metaphor for this mediation.

Verses 28-31 [25-28 HB] describe Yahweh giving instructions for the people to return to their tents while telling Moses to stand by him so that he might instruct him concerning **all the commands, decrees and laws you are to teach them to follow** (v 31 [28 HB]). The meaning of Israel returning to her tents is that they are no longer a formal assembly before Yahweh's presence. The personal pronoun **you** in v 31 [28 HB] emphasized the separation of Moses from the rest of Israel. The people are no longer on the scene, so Moses will pass on what they need to hear to them at a later time, and this will include the time past Moses' life. Moses is the mediator of the voice of Yahweh through the Torah. Verses 27 and 31 [24 and 28 HB] emphasize that Deuteronomy is nothing less than the authoritative voice of Yahweh mediated by Moses.

Verses 32 and 33 [29 and 30 HB] belong together in their concern to inculcate obedience as the way to life for the covenant community. The benefits of the people's obedience are established in a longer than usual list for the book of Deuteronomy. Doing the commands of God is essential for a life in the land that Yahweh is giving to Israel. Doing God's commands according to v 32 [29 HB] is like journey on a prescribed path; Moses commands Israel to **not turn aside to the right or to the left.** The pilgrimage that the nomadic people called Israel are on demands following exactly the path that Yahweh is making for them to take. Obedience is a political reality that can be understood as a metaphor for traveling through time and space with the God who leads out of Egypt, through the wilderness and into the land of promise. Israel is to live by the providence and guidance of God as nomadic settlers.

FROM THE TEXT

In contemporary American life, the commandments have become a kind of cultural code, as substantiated by the widespread concern for their public display. They are a symbol as much as a text for moral guidance. The fear of losing the commandments in the public square seems ironic when it comes from people who have eliminated the commandments in their own sacred space. The place of the commandments in catechesis and liturgy has been replaced with forms of entertainment or self-help.

An opposite argument can also be seen in twenty-first-century Christians who suppose that the Decalogue is a resource to save people. It has never functioned as a means for obtaining salvation, but its function is political; it is a political schema intended to shape the already-being-saved people of God in the world. The commandments grow out of the narrative of Israel's deliverance; they are a way of life for God's liberated people. Therefore, they are placed at a climatic point in the story of redemption. The Decalogue never answered the question: How do people become the people of God? It answers the question: How are the redeemed to live as the people of God?

The commandments deal with everyday life, not the cultic environment of religion. There is no mention of sacrifices, festivals, or offerings. The focus is on the commonplace existence of work, sex, family life, possessions, and household images. These commandments also deal with the public square: court testimony, manslaughter, curses, and magic. Even the commandments that are concerned with images, Yahweh's name, and Sabbath are not regulations for priests, but are practical guidance for the common person. An example of this can be seen in the Sabbath command. It is not a day for pilgrimage or sacrifice or even study, but it is simply a pause in ordinary daily labor. The commandments advance a social morality. The politics of living with neighbors involve their rights to rest, respect in old age, living without threat of violence, security in marriage, in property, and reputation.

These commands are also for future members of the community. They are the defining collection of practices for the ongoing narrative of the people of God. This is the reason Moses restates the commandments when Israel is poised on the boundary line of the promised land. A long time had transpired since Moses received these commands on the mountain of the Lord. Yet, the third verse states: "It was not with our ancestors that the LORD made this covenant, but with us, with all of us who are alive here today."

C. Completely Devoted to God (6:1-25)

BEHIND THE TEXT

From the perspective of a reader encountering the final form of the book, chs 6—11 constitute a third introduction to the law code, which is contained in chs 12—26. While chs 12—26 contain a wide range of circumstances relevant to Yahweh's covenant with Israel, the editors of the final form of Deuteronomy consider the Decalogue the essence of the covenant and the first commandment the quintessential declaration of Israel's relationship to Yahweh. As a result of this focus, Deut 6—11 formulates a theology that presumes Israel's fortunes are linked to her faithfulness to Yahweh. The larger Deuteronomistic vision displays this theological view of history.

The sixth chapter can be divided into four segments:
1. Introduction (6:1-3)
2. The Shema (6:4-9)
3. Warning against Disobedience (6:10-19)
4. Directive to Inculcate Later Generations (6:20-25)

IN THE TEXT

1. Introduction (6:1-3)

■ **1-3** These verses constitute the fourth time, in the book of Deuteronomy, that an introduction is used to describe what is to follow as the Torah. The other introductions are 1:4-6; 4:1; and 5:1. **Commands, decrees and laws** refer to the Decalogue, which both directs this section and the Law section found in chs 12—26. The NIV expression **commandments** is really singular, *commandment*, and most likely refers to the body of Mosaic teaching that is to be taught and embodied by the life of the people as a whole. It may also refer to a basic principle, which undergirds the whole of the Law. If it is a first principle, then the **decrees and laws** (v 1) describe the various ways that the *command* is to be embodied.

In this context, this most basic principle, which is referred to as commandment, would be the exclusive claim of Yahweh on Israel. This commandment is an exposition of the first commandment, which is articulated in chs

6—11. It also makes sense of the context of introducing the Shema. This command is not merely to be available to the community to hear, but the people are to be taught to live it out. Teaching to do the command implies the ongoing practicing of it so that it becomes habituated for generations into the community. In others words, the commandment will develop skillful practitioners who will become exemplars for the further generations. Each generation is to teach the next. Yahweh did not intend the covenant to be treated as formless doctrine, but to become a form of life, which is the basis of living life.

Verses 2-3 articulate allusions to the land and to upcoming generations fusing a connection between the land and those reading these texts. These verses also bring together a pair of similar-sounding Hebrew words that are translated **hear** and **be careful** (*šāma'* and *šāmar*). These words suggest a careful, sustained obedience. The skillful teaching and acting upon the commandment will have an outcome in ancient Israel for generations. **As long as you live** and **so that you may enjoy long life** (v 2) convey primarily the life of the whole people, continuing over generations.

Embodying the command of Yahweh will create an ethos of **fear the LORD your God** (v 2). This ethos within the community will in turn allow for a further keeping of the commands of Yahweh. **Fear**, in this context, does not describe being terrorized by divinity, but a reverence for God that will result in keeping his commands. This fear of Yahweh has a twofold connotation: fear moves one to keep the commands and by keeping the commands one persists in the fear of Yahweh. This political reality creates a culture that will for generations produce life and prosperity in the land that is given by Yahweh.

Verse 3 uses a traditional description of the land that is intended to inspire vigilant obedience: **milk and honey**. These are choice foods in the ancient Near Eastern cultures, and as a metaphor they represent the sweetness of life and fertility. This metaphor is also closely associated with the patriarchal promise; it harkens back to the promise made to Abraham concerning both the land and his offspring (Gen 12:1-3).

2. The Shema (6:4-9)

■ **4-9** The introductory exhortation, to learn to observe the statutes and ordinances of Israel's covenant with her God, gives way to the prescribed declaration that becomes the central confession of faith in Judaism. This confession is named for its first word (*šěma'*), the imperative form of the verb *šāma'* ("to hear"). There is an ambiguity in the syntax of the first clause of the Shema. It permits two possible translations and interpretations: (1) . . . *Yahweh our God is one*, which gives prominence to the unity of deity, or (2) . . . *Yahweh only is our God*, which gives importance to the exclusivity of God's claim on Israel's loyalty. The chief difference concerns whether to translate *'eḥad* as an adjective (*one*) or an adverb (*alone*). Both of these make good sense.

Even the casual reader of Scripture recognizes that the Shema is a radicalization of the first commandment: "You shall have no other gods before me" (Deut 5:7; Exod 20:3). Although it is possible that the oneness of Yahweh points in some sense to radical monotheism, the tone of Deut 6 shifts from uniqueness to unity and integrity. Yahweh is indivisible. This may mean that Yahweh may not be worshipped in a variety of manifestations, like Baal. It may also mean, in keeping with the call for the centralization of worship in Deuteronomy, that Yahweh is not to be worshipped at a variety of places. Whatever else the Shema might mean, it does not allow for a nominal attachment to Yahweh above other deities, but lays claim to total fidelity and surrender to Yahweh, who is undivided, whole, and absolute. The totality of Israel's commitment is motivated by her God's absolute uniqueness.

The second clause of the Shema extends Yahweh's claim on Israel: she is called to love God. Love, in the OT, is not understood as sentimental and emotive. To love God involves loyalty and obedience. Love in this context is the kind of loyalty and service one owes as a vassal to an overlord or as a child to a parent. Israel's love is not to be in any way disembodied, but it is to show forth in faithfulness and obedience. Loving Yahweh is demonstrated in undivided and loyal living.

Not only is Israel expected to serve Yahweh alone, but her devotion is also to claim the totality of each life. The love called for is total commitment. This undivided life is expressed in the phrase **heart**, **soul**, and **strength**. Ancient Israel understood the **heart** (*lēb*) not as the seat of emotion, like contemporary culture, but as the place where decisions are made. **Soul** could also be translated *being*. This word, *nepeš*, indicates a person's life or vitality. **Strength** (*mĕ'ōd*) implies the idea of a person's full capacity. This would include natural abilities and resources. Even though the use of these three concepts seems to describe different compartments of one's life, the intention was never to imply that one could love God with one's **heart** without loving God with one's *being* and *resources*. Human beings are not fragmented into compartments. God does not desire our disembodied wills or our interiorized souls or even our embodied resources. Human beings are whole persons who think and act and live in social networks. The force of **heart**, **soul**, and **strength** requires a devotion that is single-minded and complete.

Verses 6-9 point to the habituation of the all-encompassing love of God in the life of the community. **These commandments** are literally *these words*, and they refer to the exclusive love of Israel toward Yahweh. *These words* are to be upon the heart, but how? The heart, in this context, points to the forming of a person's character or disposition. John Wesley called this disposition "affections," and these are formed through the habituation of a person's life. The quest is to become a singly devoted lover of God. This can only happen if ***these words*** are to become a part of the living fabric of life. The Shema was to be passed on to the next generation, not by a coercive enforcement, but by making them the framework of everyday life.

Israel's undivided love for God is not simply something a radical individual is called to do, but is to be enacted by the community. Individuals are persons in social networks; therefore, to love God is to be undivided not only in one's own life but also in the life of the whole of the culture. The exclusive love of God is to comprise the whole of Israel's life; it is to become a political reality. It is interesting to notice the forceful arrangement of instructions. They move from the private **heart** outward to **children, home,** walking, sleeping, getting up, **hands, foreheads, doorframes** of the house, and finally, the public space of the **gates** (vv 6-9). These instructions are to govern daily life and activities both at home where love of God is taught and modeled, and at the gates, the centers of public assembly where justice is given out. The practice of the love of God is to permeate every sphere of life.

The Shema in Jewish Daily Worship

Recital of Deut 6:4-9 is a part of the morning and evening prayer of Judaism. In Jewish daily worship, these verses are recited along with Deut 11:13-21 and Num 15:37-41 as "Recitation of the Shema."

3. Warning against Disobedience (6:10-19)

6:10-19

■ **10-19** The mandate of fidelity to Yahweh is now developed in a particular manner. These verses use a strategy of arguing to show the benefits of obedience to the requirement as stated in the Shema. Verses 10-19 reveal an interesting structure. Verses 10 and 18-19 both speak of God's fulfillment of a promise to the patriarchs. The difference between the two is that v 10 describes the gift of God to Israel based upon his promises to the patriarchs. Verses 18-19 speak in terms of promise and responsibility: **Do what is right and good in the LORD's sight, so that it may go well with you and you may go in and take over the good land the LORD promised on oath to your ancestors, thrusting out all your enemies before you, as the LORD said.** The implication is that they also will be thrust from the land if they fail to keep covenant.

This section of the text attempts to assert the dichotomy between the blessings and curses of Yahweh. The curse of this material threatens the accursed with an ironic reversal of providence. God gives a land that is good before Israel ever lives in it. Houses, cisterns, vineyards, and olive groves are already prepared, and they are given along with the land. Israel did nothing to **build** or **plant** (vv 10-11). God's free grace is given in lavish ways. But this paragraph is also a warning of the great danger of forgetting (v 12). The threat of forgetfulness comes with the good life. God's gracious gifts become the very thing that are a threat if it is ever forgotten that they are the result of God's grace.

In v 16 the vulnerability of forgetting is counteracted by remembrance of a story that the readers are expected to know. At **Massah** Israel doubted Yahweh's generosity. Massah is a metaphor used multiple times in the OT (9:22; Exod 17:1-7; Pss 78:56; 95:8-9). The story itself is narrated in Exod 17 and states that it was only a few days after Yahweh delivered Israel from Egyptian bondage that Israel tested Yahweh at Massah. The Israelites lacked water to drink and they complained mightily about this lack of water. The narrator places a vexing question into the mouth of the ancient people of God, "Is the LORD among us or not?" (Exod 17:7). The story of Massah points profoundly to the fickle characteristic of human faithfulness. The worship of Yahweh should never depend upon a test.

The command **Do not forget the** LORD (Deut 6:12) progresses naturally into the requirement to be faithful to God. In forgetfulness, the next step is toward serving and following **other gods** (v 14). Serving other gods will bring destruction. Annihilation is the threat given in v 15 to a forgetfulness that leads to serving other gods. Yahweh will not tolerate infidelity. If Israel violates the covenant, then she will find others in possession of her cities that they did not build, her houses that they did not fill, her cisterns that they did not hew, and her vineyards and olive groves that they did not plant. Just as the Canaanites' loss will be Israel's gain, so if Israel fails to keep covenant her loss will become the gain of another.

Unearned prosperity and blessing might become a snare for Israel if she forgets her history. Israel must not walk after the other gods who are worshipped by her neighbors. She must worship and serve Yahweh alone, who delivered her from Egyptian bondage and is giving her the land of promise. The theological vision of Deuteronomy seldom moves from the basic theme of absolute loyalty to Yahweh. This loyalty is not in the disembodied minds or emotions of the people but is demonstrated in obedience to God's commandments. The irony of the passage is that the gifts of God will become the great temptation for Israel to abandon her God.

4. Directive to Inculcate Later Generations (6:20-25)

■ **20-25** The concluding verses of this chapter address the matter of teaching the children. There are a lot of references in Deuteronomy to the children, and the reason for this emphasis on the children is that Deuteronomy is always anticipating the next generation. Deuteronomy takes the present generation back to the past and brings the past in new ways into the present. The children are now the ones before whom all the choices are placed, and someday the Torah will confront their children. These verses assume that a break between the generations has taken place.

Children ask questions such as, What is this? or Why? or Why do I? These verses envision an occasion when children ask for the meaning of the practices and doctrines that shape the life of the community. The answer the father is to give is not one of the content of individual laws per se, but the foundation and objective of the practices and doctrines (vv 21 ff.): **We were slaves of Pharaoh in Egypt, but the LORD brought us out of Egypt with a mighty hand.** These questions give a father an opportunity to recite the chief items of the creedal salvation narrative. The questions that children ask are an opportunity for teaching the next generation the significance of the way they live their life in light of God's mighty deeds. The meaning of laws, practices, symbols, and doctrines are tied to the story of Yahweh's mighty deeds for Israel. The inquiry is not simply to learn what the laws and practices are, but to discover why they are to be kept. People become the stories they tell.

The story of grace is the premise of law (vv 21, 23-24): **We were slaves of Pharaoh in Egypt, but the LORD brought us out of Egypt with a mighty hand . . . to bring us in and give us the land he promised on oath to our ancestors. The LORD commanded us to obey all these decrees and to fear the LORD our God, so that we might always prosper and be kept alive, as is the case today.** Israel's story of deliverance from Egypt and the gift of the land are the foundation of the covenant. These implications are always tied to Israel's prior existence as Pharaoh's slaves. The Hebrew word order is interesting: *Slaves we were to Pharaoh in Egypt and Yahweh brought us out from Egypt by a mighty hand* (v 21). The inference is that Israel lived under the laws of Pharaoh. But Yahweh freed the people. The people now have a new Lord and a new set of laws. The reign of Yahweh and the political implications of Torah do not bring about oppression and slavery, as in the days when Pharaoh was Israel's master. The sovereignty of Yahweh is a gift to the people who have received the prior gift of liberation. These gifts are to be received and appropriated in obedience as a provision for the good life.

What the people learn from their parents is passed on to the children so that each new generation is prepared to stand before Yahweh and fear him as God (v 13). The fear of the Lord is clearly the aim of educating the next generation; the call to **fear *Yahweh*** (v 24) incorporates all that is meant by the call to "love Yahweh" (v 5) and the command "do not follow other gods" (v 14). Reverence and total commitment are the elements of **fear the LORD our God** (v 24).

The question, How does this education take place? imagines a family in energetic discussion about the meaning of their practices, doctrines, and God's expectation for them. Parental instruction and conversation is to take place at home and away from home. Parents are to teach their children in such a way that their last thoughts before falling asleep and their first thoughts upon awakening are about the Lord's command "to love him." These words are not simply to be recited or repeated, but they are to be discussed. This means talked about, studied, learned, and practiced. The practical implications for life are to be thought out and discussed with the next generation.

FROM THE TEXT

The dominant thought in Deut 6 is the singularity of God and the exclusive claim that this singularity has upon God's people. Many people believe that the exclusive claim of God is totalitarian and oppressive, but the biblical narrative does not portray God in these overbearing ways. A more helpful way of understanding the exclusive claim of God is to recognize it as an invitation to become his partner in caring for the world. This partnership is possible only within the human community that lives in such a way as to reflect God's singular purpose for creation. The premise of the biblical text is that there is a unity in the created order that embraces the material, the political, and the ethical. Creation, including human beings, is not fragmented and compartmentalized, but united and whole. Therefore, the Shema implies a connection between the character of God and the gift of his commandments. Israel is called to trust Yahweh as the Lord of creation; therefore, the commandments are his gift that brings well-being. Practicing the Torah produces wholeness.

The question that Christians must ask is: How are believers in Christ to respond to the Shema? Christians confess that God is one, whose name is Father, Son, and Holy Spirit. In light of the Trinitarian thinking of the church, the Shema has both theological and anthropological implications. The theological implication has to do with the character of God. From all eternity God is Father, Son, and Holy Spirit; he is love. Because of this, God's love is not contingent upon creation but is the presupposition of creation. God created from love as an act of love for the sake of love. God is the relational ground of all reality. This would mean that that the purpose of sovereign love is covenantal.

The unity that arises out of the claim of the oneness of God is that there is only one absolute purpose that undergirds all reality. This purpose is one and not multiple, whole and not divided, and is conveyed in the love of the Father for the Son through the Spirit, and the love of the Son for the Father through the Spirit. No wonder, when Jesus was asked in Matt 22:36: "Teacher, which is the greatest commandment in the Law?" he answered: "'Love the Lord your God with all your heart and with all your soul and with all your mind.' This is the first and greatest commandment. And the second is like it: 'Love your neighbor as yourself'" (vv 37-39). Just as God is not divided, and creation is not divided, so also love is not divided.

The relational ground of all being brings to mind the second implication: the anthropological one. It is no wonder that a loyalty to anything other than the ground of all being, the God who is love, counterfeits the meaning of life. The demand of the Shema is not just a demand but is what makes human life purposeful. All secondary claims on human life are subsumed within the total claim of God, so that the demand is ultimately God's gift of grace.

In the face of the multiple pulls and dimensions of human life, humanity is held together by this singular ultimate allegiance, the God who is love. It is possible to deal with the secondary claims only if one has a sense that ultimate and full allegiance is directed toward God alone. When a person loves God with one's whole being, one is moved to love all reality. Perhaps this is the reason that Jesus says that the second command is like unto the first: "Love your neighbor as yourself." If God is love and the ground of the universe is love, then the purpose of life is love. An undivided loyalty to the God who is love demonstrates this loyalty through a form of life that is a witness to love. Maybe Wesley was trying to say as much when he described perfect love in his sermon "On Love" as the love of God shed abroad in our hearts (Wesley 1736).

For many churchgoing people, faith is a matter of sentiment or feelings, but not of daily actions. For others, belief is a mental issue principally demanding acquiescence to certain doctrines. For a great many contemporary evangelicals, Christianity belongs to a somewhat separate sphere of life. The Shema declares that commitment to the one singular reality of God cannot be a compartmentalized matter. The mandate to love God lays claim to a person's whole life. This love issues forth in affections that produce gratitude and generosity . . . loving God and neighbor.

D. Destroy and Detach (7:1-26)

BEHIND THE TEXT

The compositional history of ch 7 is complicated. Indications of this complexity include the use of second-person plural and second-person singular interchangeably. Some scholars suggest that two separate topics have been combined: the demand to destroy the nations and the demand to remain detached from the nations, especially in relation to worship. There is no evidence that these two themes were originally developed independently or that this chapter can be divided into separate layers according to each. The connection between the destruction of the other nations and false worship appears in a number of OT texts. Examples of these connections can be seen in Josh 4—6 and 1 Sam 4.

Israel is constantly threatened, throughout her history, by the danger of foreign cultures and practices. She is required to remain separate from the alien people groups and their beliefs and practices. What is amazing in this text is that she is called to destroy not only persons but their culture and religion as well. The motivation for this complete separation is Israel's election and designation as a holy people. Yahweh's choice of Israel means that she must be a countercultural society. Deuteronomy 7 includes both a demand for the total destruction of alien people groups and a policy of social separation. Both of these policies are intended to protect Israel's distinct identity.

The text, when it is removed from the holy war context of the conquest period, becomes more of an ideology that promotes the need for total cultural separation. When it is placed in the historical setting of Josiah's reform, it addresses the need for the removal and destruction of foreign religious practices from the land. During the exile and in the postexilic historical setting, Israel was not the conquering nation but the conquered nation. During these times Israel did not have the power to destroy different people groups; so why was the text retained, and how does this text function in these new settings? The tangible dilemma is that an alien presence and ideology threatens Israel's identity, and the danger of assimilation by foreign practices is very real. The reader should bear in mind that Deuteronomy and its tradition are attempting to unify the nation, remove foreign ideologies, and reform the religion of Israel.

There seems to be a concentric structure in ch 7. Verses 1-5 and vv 25 and 26 demand that Israel wipe out the nations and their religion. Within this outer framework, vv 6 and 16 initiate topical subsections. The new subsections are election and conquest. Chapter 7 may be outlined as follows:

1. Command to Destroy the Inhabitants and Their Religion (7:1-5)
2. Yahweh's Election of Israel (7:6-15)
3. Yahweh Will Fight for Israel (7:16-24)
4. Command to Destroy the Idols of the Nations (7:25-26)

IN THE TEXT

1. Command to Destroy the Inhabitants and Their Religion (7:1-5)

■ 1-5 Chapter 7 begins by naming seven people groups who occupy the promised land: **the Hittites, Girgashites, Amorites, Canaanites, Perizzites, Hivites and Jebusites.** These nations will present a threat to Israel's life in the land. Therefore, the wording of this passage begins with a call for absolute separation from other people groups that are already in the land. The list of the seven nations is traditional and with certain changes appears frequently in the OT (Gen 15:20-21; Exod 3:8, 17; 13:5). This list of nations that Israel is to eliminate may also function as a rhetorical device to indicate all of the nations. This would have significant ideological weight for a postexilic Israel.

The belief system that undergirds this pericope is that separation is absolutely necessary for keeping Israel faithful to Yahweh in this contagious ideological environment. Three assertions are given that support this conviction, which implies that Israel must both have faith and be faithful to Yahweh. First, these other nations are **larger and stronger than you** (Deut 7:1). This term **larger**, which literally means *more numerous*, reappears throughout ch 7 (vv 1, 7, 17, and 22). The second assertion is that Yahweh, and not Israel, will be the one who will defeat the enemies (v 2). The tenets of holy war in ancient Israel clearly stand behind this declaration. Yahweh is the Divine Warrior and he fights Israel's enemies on behalf of his people. This affirmation leads to the third pronouncement: because the battle is Yahweh's, Israel may not enter into any kind of covenant relationship with these nations. In fact, the very opposite is the case. These nations must be utterly destroyed, or *devoted to the ban* (v 2). The *ban* is a kind of sacrifice of dedication. It is the final act in the ritual conduct of a holy war, the handing over of the captives and the booty to Yahweh.

In vv 2-3 there are a series of commands that make any intermingling of Israel's life with other people groups impossible. These imperatives are: **destroy them totally, make no treaty with them, show them no mercy,** and **do not intermarry with them.** To make any sort of covenant with alien people groups would be to set up a countercovenant to the one with Yahweh. Intermarriage would form attachments between families and lead Israel to worship other gods. Perhaps political alliances, which are sealed by marriage, are peculiarly in mind in this passage. Verse 4 points to the threat of worshipping foreign gods because of intermarrying: **they will turn your children away from following me to serve other gods.** The foreign father-in-law would lead the Israelites astray, so that together they would engage in unacceptable worship. This implies that an Israelite son would become acculturated into an alien community with its beliefs, practices, and values.

2. Yahweh's Election of Israel (7:6-15)

■ **6-15** Verse 6 points to the reality that Israel is a holy nation: **For you are a people holy to the LORD your God.** This means that they are a people set apart for God and must refrain from everything that might sway their surrender to Yahweh's sole authority. As a holy people, Israel is related to Yahweh in the same way that an object of holiness is related to the deity. Holiness in this and every other context derives its nuance of meaning from the way a people conceptualize deity. Therefore, Israel's holiness means that they are to reflect the character and purpose of Yahweh. Holiness, in this passage, is not a status or state of affairs that Israel must achieve but is a reality that is established by God's own choice. Israel is called to live into the reality of her holiness. Living with this holy purpose means that the people of God are called to a distinct mission, and this mission is to reflect the character or purpose of God to the world.

An understanding of why Israel is God's own now follows this statement about Israel being a holy people. Yahweh's choice of Israel is an act of his election: **The LORD your God has chosen you out of all the peoples on the face of the earth to be his people** (v 6). Yahweh does not choose Israel because of any quality that she may possess. The text makes it clear that Yahweh chooses Israel because he set his love upon her, even though she is **the fewest of all peoples** (v 7). God's people must never allow the hubris of pride to become a part of the ethos of the community or the affection of an individual. It is God's act of grace that calls and determines people as his own.

As the elect, Israel is called to obedience, which is her way of witnessing to the character and purpose of God. Being Yahweh's witness necessitates that Israel keep Torah, because to fall short of observing Torah is a catastrophe: the integrity of God's character is jeopardized in his people. Holiness, election, and obedience are intertwined in the theology of this passage.

In vv 9-10 Yahweh's character and purpose is expressed through a variety of qualities. Yahweh is acknowledged as "truly God," "a faithful God," and "a God of retribution." The similarity between God's covenant loyalty and his punishment is balanced in favor of his loyalty and mercy. Retribution seems to be directed to the liable individual or group, yet covenant loyalty is applied to a thousand generations. Israel's obedience gives Yahweh an opportunity to display his fidelity and love.

Verse 12 picks up the focus of obedience and makes it the proviso for God's covenant loyalty. The consequence of covenant faithfulness, between Israel and God, is the blessing of fertility. Yahweh's promise to the fathers and covenant faithfulness go beyond mere possession of the land to the outpouring of sumptuous blessing. Yahweh promises fruitfulness in family, field, and flock (v 13). The blessings of Yahweh are concrete and material. These blessings of fruitfulness discredit any rival claims of alien fertility gods.

There are wordplays in v 13 that would deconstruct the fertility gods. The words that are translated **grain** (*dāgān*), **wine** (*tîrôš*), and **oil** are in the consciousness of the Hebrew reader as common nouns reflecting the names of rival gods: Dagon and Tyrosh. The phrase in this verse concerning cattle and flocks also embodies a mocking allusion to the names of two of their rival gods. Shagar and Astarte are robbed of their claims by their use in the phrase **the calves [*šeger*] of your herds and the lambs [*'aštārôt*] of your flock.** The names of these gods are deconstructed by the wordplay so that the blessing of fertility is tied to Yahweh (Nelson 2002b, 102).

3. Yahweh Will Fight for Israel (7:16-24)

■ **16-24** This subsection returns to the subject matter of destroying the nations that inhabit the land and their religion. Verse 17 brings up the question that dominates the consciousness of a deficient group of people who are go-

DEUTERONOMY

7:16-24

ing to war with a highly favored opponent: **How can we drive them out?** The answer to this question is **do not be afraid of them; remember well what the** Lord **your God did to Pharaoh.** *Fear not* is a common admonition when ancient Israel is confronted by conflict or potential violence. Fear seems logical when the enemy is more powerful, but Yahweh is going to fight for Israel. A no-fear approach is based upon Yahweh's past action for Israel. Therefore, the people are called to **remember well what the** Lord **your God did to Pharaoh.** In remembering the mighty acts of God, Israel is assured that he will **do the same to all the peoples** they fear (v 19).

Israel is not alone, but Yahweh is among them. No one will be able to withstand the Divine Warrior and his holy war. *Panic* or **great confusion** is that characteristic weapon of Yahweh, yet Israel also must participate in this war (v 23). It is Yahweh who dislodges the nations **little by little,** but Israel finishes them off (v 22). It is Yahweh who gives the people over to Israel until they are destroyed (v 23). Yahweh is in the midst of his people; therefore, no one will be able to withstand Israel receiving the land from his hand.

4. Command to Destroy the Idols of the Nations (7:25-26)

■ **25-26** These two verses develop the theme of the purpose for the victories won over the inhabitants of the land. The mission is to eliminate every competing practice and material associated with idolatry. The holiness that must be embodied by Israel is seen as not only renouncing alien gods but also eliminating every opportunity for their worship in the land. Everything that is associated with divine images is to be eliminated. Even precious metals (v 25) that could be used in covering idols are assigned to the category of that which should be destroyed.

Eradication of any cause for pagan worship is the clarion call. All things related to the fertility gods must be absolutely and completely shattered. Their continued presence would bring a contamination to the land and become contagious to the people of God. It should be obvious to the reader that this is a statement countering the fertility cult in ancient Israel. Israel does not need the fertility gods for the land to be fruitful. Yahweh is the God of creation.

FROM THE TEXT

Christian readers of this passage need to always remember that they read these texts in light of "the rule of faith." The rule of faith is an early church premise that interprets the conceptual pictures of God through the lens of God's self-disclosure in Jesus Christ. When Christian readers come to difficult texts, like this passage, they must always hearken back to the Christian conviction that the character and purpose of God is seen most clearly in the person of Jesus Christ. So how are Christians to understand election, holiness, and the use of violence? A Christian investigation must take place both within both the social and historical context of the texts themselves and in light of the self-disclosure of God through the person of Jesus Christ.

Israel's election is for the purpose of God's grace for creation. This includes not only the nations but also all of the cosmos. The call of Abraham is an election not simply for the sake of being blessed, but to be a blessing to the all of the families of the earth (Gen 12:3). This understanding of election points to a narrative perception of being engaged in the mission of God for the world. Israel's participation in this mission meant that she would at least be a light to the nations, or in other words, a faithful witness of God's character and purpose. A grand illustration of ancient Israel's understanding of God's purpose is expressed in the amazing picture painted by Isa 11.

Israel's election and blessing brings the reader to the next key concept within the text: holiness. Deuteronomy's understanding of Israel's holiness is not something she attempts to gain but something she already participates within. It is because she is elected that she is also considered holy. This means that she is set apart for the purpose of God by the very act of God's electing grace. The purpose of God is not some arbitrary decision of God but is located in the very character of God.

If a reader of a religious tradition wants to understand how the concept holy is used, that reader needs to understand how the conceptual picture of God is described. A community's understanding of holiness is always tied to its understanding of God. Christians picture God not in holy war but in the person of Jesus Christ. Jesus' words and deeds are enacted as compassion and restoration. In the canonical context of this passage, both individuals as well as the community of faith are to understand themselves as consistent witnesses to the character and purpose of God revealed in Jesus Christ. To be a trustworthy witness to God in both words and deeds is to be holy.

So what does this holiness mean in relation to the violence that is depicted within the text? The brutality that is symbolized in devoting a city to the ban must be understood within the underlying milieu of false gods and ideologies. Israel's identity as the chosen and holy people of God is threatened by the practices of counterfeit systems of belief and value. The people of God are able to embody their special calling and identity only if they resist being syncretistically immersed into alien cultures. Israel's unique purpose and calling is threatened by alien belief and value systems. God's people would fail not only to be blessed but also to be a blessing to others.

The contrast between the holy people of God and the nations is eliminated if believers follow the ways of the host culture. There would be no knowledge of God and his purposes for the world; therefore, it is essential for

God's people to maintain a clear and unadulterated identity as holy and chosen. This includes eliminating all fallacious and misleading ideologies, values, and practices of counterfeit gods. This interpretation is at least one way for Christians to interpret devoting a city or a culture to the ban. But Christians must always remember that Jesus commanded us to love our enemies, and this would at least mean to not kill them.

The question that the text poses for Christians is not so much how or when to use violence, but how to maintain an alien status to the host cultures that the church finds itself within. Reflecting the character and purpose of God, as revealed in the face of Jesus, includes not only the embrace of others in love but also the exclusion of bogus practices, values, and ideologies. If Christians are to bear truthful witness to Jesus, to be holy, then they must remove all cultural norms that would detract their witness to the character of God in Christ. In today's culture of violence, the exclusion of violence might be what *devoting to the ban* means for followers of Jesus Christ.

E. Don't Forget . . . (8:1-20)

BEHIND THE TEXT

Chapter 7 warns of alien dangers lingering in the land, while ch 8 turns to the dangers inherent in the land's very goodness. The juxtaposition of two aspects of grace comprises the essential argument of the passage. First, Israel must remember her wilderness wanderings and the gifts of Torah and the land. Everything that Israel possesses is a gift. Second, Yahweh's gifts bring prosperity, and prosperity often causes people to forget that they are recipients of grace. Material comfort is one of the great temptations for the people of God. Privileged circumstances often cause Israel to overlook her reliance upon Yahweh. Prosperity can create a fraudulent outlook that fails to recognize life, in all of its dimensions, as a gift. Therefore, pride rather than gratitude becomes the disposition of a community. Moses worries that Israel may, in her new security and prosperity, forget the defining narrative of her redemption.

The complex makeup of this chapter is likely the result of a complex history of composition. Although no agreement has been reached about this history, some explanations seem fairly apparent. Verse 1 begins in the second-person singular, then quickly shifts to second-person plural. The principal argument conceives of forgetting Yahweh by taking credit for securing the land and its richness. Warnings about this attitude are included in this chapter. A secondary line of reasoning associates forgetting directly with a failure to keep the commandments of Yahweh. This chapter has the following structure:

1. Remember God's Mercy in the Past (8:1-6)
2. Look to the Future and Do Not Forget (8:7-18)
   a. Remember the Promise of the Good Land (8:7-10)

b. Do Not Forget Yahweh Your God (8:11-18)
3. Remember and Live, Forget and Die (8:19-20)

IN THE TEXT

I. Remember God's Mercy in the Past (8:1-6)

■ **I-6** The first verse is a summary of all that will follow in this chapter. Moses continues to speak to the people of Israel with an appeal to obey the commandments. It should be noticed that the second-person singular is used in the Hebrew text. This underscores the principle that keeping the commandments is an expression of singular obedience of the whole people. **Every command** (v 1) is literally *all the commandment* and is understood in a collective sense: the whole Torah as delivered by Moses. Deuteronomy 4:2 expresses a similar collective authority of the commandment of God. The Law is regarded as a complete and perfect whole, and the ancient people of God are not to add to it nor take away from it. This entire commandment is to be diligently observed so that the people may live and multiply in the land. Four expressions describe the benefits that result from Israel's careful obedience: to **live**, to **increase**, to **enter**, and to **possess** the land. Life and death are at stake for the people, and life is dependent upon a careful enactment of Yahweh's will.

The argument of this section asks the listeners to consider both the hardships and the gifts of the wilderness wanderings. The directive to **remember** (8:2) is for Israel to contemplate the significance of their forty years' experience. The wilderness makes or breaks people. It is a metaphor of insufficient resources and distorted orientation. During this period people are either refined or overcome. The convictions that shape this passage recognize the wilderness wanderings as a time when Yahweh guides and provides for Israel. Wilderness disorientation is a time of testing that clarifies what is in the **heart** of the people (v 2). The metaphor **heart** should be understood as the inner disposition of a person or the ethos of the group.

When the people are hungry, Yahweh feeds them (v 3). The provision of manna is God's grace to his people. **Manna** appears only twice in the book of Deuteronomy (8:3, 16). This concept should not be explained in some kind of natural or scientific way. The text understands manna to be a miracle of God's providence. Not only is manna a miracle of provision, but also it is designed to instruct the people in the most fundamental conviction of their existence: the source of life is Yahweh. Therefore, every word that comes from the mouth of Yahweh is more essential to Israel's existence than even food. Yahweh is Israel's life source!

The provision of manna does not mean that Israel should expect Yahweh to miraculously provide food in every situation. God has many ways of providing for the life of people; in this situation it means manna. In the texture of everyday life, ordinary ways of going about acquiring food and every other resource are normal. What this passage is attempting to communicate is that if Yahweh commands the people to do something, even if they lack the resources to do it, they are still to obey. One could say that the command of God and the provision of God are linked. When people are in full obedience to God's word, they witness God's faithful provision. Faith and obedience are two sides of the same coin.

Yahweh provides not only food for the journey but also clothing and strength. **Your clothes did not wear out and your feet did not swell during these forty years** (v 4). This miracle, during the time of Israel's nomadic dependency, is not mentioned anywhere else in the OT. The gifts in the desert and the lessons learned shape this young ragtag community. Yahweh's love for his people trains and disciplines them in the wilderness (v 5). The discipline and training of the people in the wilderness prepares them to trust and obey God in the pathway of life's journey in the settled land.

One of the better-known expressions in the book of Deuteronomy is found in v 3: **man does not live on bread alone but on every word that comes from the mouth of the LORD.** After fasting for forty days in the desert, Jesus is tempted to turn stones to bread. It is in the midst of this temptation that Jesus quotes these words from Deuteronomy to counter this temptation to use his power to satisfy his own hunger and possibly the hunger of others (Matt 4:4; Luke 4:4). The fundamental purpose of these words is not to elevate the spiritual or disembodied over the physical or embodied, but to recognize that everything is a gift from the hand of God. Life and all the provisions that make life possible are gifts from God.

The premise of Deut 8:6 is that Yahweh gives not only the land but also the commandments. He who guides Israel when they are a nomadic people is the same reality that gives the commandments for guidance when they are a settled people. Commands are not to be simply appreciated but to be enacted in the journey of life. These commands are to shape the ethos of a community and the character of an individual. When the people *walk* in obedience, they practice a form of life that conforms them to God's will (v 6). This correlation to God's will results in the fear of Yahweh, and such fear forms the virtues necessary for further obedience.

2. Look to the Future and Do Not Forget (8:7-18)

These verses point to the great temptation of the good land, the temptation to forget that all is a gift and to begin to believe that all is a result of one's own ability. It should be noticed that "land" is used multiple times in this subsection. Following the specific use of "land" is a statement in a parallel phrase describing the goodness of the land. It is a good land with incredible resources and is portrayed as a type of paradise.

a. Remember the Promise of the Good Land (8:7-10)

■ **7-10** Verses 7-9 are one sentence in the Hebrew language. This long sentence describes the land as watered and therefore full of life-giving goodness. In a desert, water is the difference between life and death, and in this land **brooks, streams, and deep springs** are a part of this "paradise" (v 7). Water allows for the produce of grains and fruit trees; therefore, the people will eat bread without scarcity and never go hungry (vv 8-9).

b. Do Not Forget Yahweh Your God (8:11-18)

■ **11-18** Moses is quick to caution Israel about forgetting Yahweh in the plethora of blessing (vv 11-13). To the ancient reader of Deuteronomy, who has grown somewhat soft in the lush land, the enormous wasteland appears as a horrendous territory. It is waterless and full of serpents and scorpions. Yahweh reveals his fidelity to the people through his provisions for them. Yahweh is the Giver of all good gifts to Israel (vv 15-19). He is the one who rescues them out of Egyptian slavery, who leads them through the vast and terrifying wilderness, and who provides manna to eat for the sustenance of life. Yahweh's guidance and provision was to humble and test Israel in order to do good for them in the end.

How is a reader of this text to understand testing that brings humility as a benefit for the people of God? Israel is intended to learn from the wilderness encounters that its sustenance comes from Yahweh, who is like an instructing parent. The problem is that she never learns this message well. Canonically, the temptations of Jesus form an alternative to Israel's failure in this test (Luke 4:1-13). The close ties between the temptations of Jesus and Deuteronomy are obvious: the testing theme, the wilderness setting, and the theme of hunger, the forty years and the forty days and nights, and finally the quotation from Deuteronomy: **Man shall not live on bread alone** (Luke 4:4). Jesus' temptations should be understood particularly in relation to this message. In contrast to Israel in the wilderness and in later times, Jesus is obedient and triumphs over the evil in his time of testing. His victory recapitulates the temptations of Israel. This recapitulation enables his victory to become the victory of his followers.

3. Remember and Live, Forget and Die (8:19-20)

■ **19-20** The grammar transitions from **you** (singular) in the opening part of Deut 8:19 to **you** (plural) in vv 19*b* and 20. Why does this take place? There is no exact answer, but some scholars believe that this points to a later addition to the original passage. Whatever it may designate, the message of these verses is a solemn warning: **you will surely be destroyed** (v 19*b*). The Hebrew grammar makes two very concentrated expressions in these verses by doubling up the words. The first is *if you forget-forget* (if you ever forget), and this points to an intensive focus on the concept of forgetting Yahweh (v 19). The second is the fourfold use of the word *'ābad* ("to perish"). The first is a doubling up that is translated: **you will surely be destroyed** (v 19). The other two uses of the term describe the perishing of the nations who inhabited the land prior to Israel and then refer to Israel perishing like those nations: **Like the nations the LORD destroyed before you, so you will be destroyed for not obeying the LORD your God** (v 20).

Forgetting Yahweh leads to the most horrible type of tragedy: walking in the ways of other gods, serving them and worshipping them. The result of this is that the people will be leaving the springs that produce life. Therefore, the result of abandoning Yahweh is death. Covenant faithfulness means life, and covenant unfaithfulness means death. If the people of promise forget Yahweh and serve and worship other gods, Yahweh will destroy them just like he is about to destroy the people who inhabit the land.

FROM THE TEXT

The argument of this chapter is pragmatic: obedience to Yahweh makes life possible; self-sufficiency leads to false gods and therefore ruin. This simple, straightforward insistence is shrewdly articulated by going back into the ancient story line that facilitates a comparison of then and now. Such an assessment elevates the reality of the past against the illusion of the present. There has always been the realization, among the people of God, that public life, and maybe life itself, is dependent upon remembering the story of communal identity and the practices that continue to keep that identity vibrant.

One of the better-known phrases of this chapter is v 3: **One does not live by bread alone, but by every word that comes from the mouth of Yahweh.** Jesus quoted these words from Deuteronomy in his encounter with the devil. After fasting forty days in the wilderness, Jesus was starving. His temptation is to use the power of God to satisfy his hunger. When Jesus quotes Deuteronomy he is not holding up a spiritual ideal over a physical world. Rather he is acknowledging that all gifts that make life possible come from God. God is the source of life; therefore, the ways of God are to be lived out. To forget God is to exist in ways that will eventually cause a person and a people to become habited by those forces that lead to devastation and death.

In the land into which Israel is going, the gods that would be a great temptation for the ancient people are bound to the fertility cult. These gods made threats on the inhabitants of the land that required faithfulness to the practices that habituate a community into a false narrative of reality. This false story line asserts that it is only by placating the gods that productiveness will take place.

The principles and doctrines of contemporary culture are similar to the gods and ideologies of the ancient fertility cult. These sirens seduce the masses of existing civilization into a similar fictive account. Money, sex, and power have become the gods that manipulate the practices of Western culture. Maybe some form of money, sex, and power have always been the spiritual authorities that drive human beings in their quest for security and abundance. These values are all seductively reliant upon the gods or ideologies of fruitfulness that embody self-reliance and free activity. After all of these millennia, potency still appears to be what compels people. Rather than Baal, it is a free market society, or a freethinking democratic state, or perhaps even a holier-than-thou religion. Israel is to understand that no system can bring about the flourishing of life. All flourishing, and therefore life, is a result of the providential gifts of God. Humanity does not live by bread alone, but by the self-disclosure of God and God's will for his creation.

F. Know That . . . (9:1—10:11)

BEHIND THE TEXT

The narrative argument developed in chs 1—11 explores the meaning of Israel as God's chosen people; 9:1—10:11 maintains this argument by asking: Why is Israel constantly unfaithful to Yahweh? The answer given is a familiar one; Israel fails to remember. Forgetfulness is a chronic problem for the people. The theme of memory is connected with Yahweh's deliverance from Egypt and Israel's failure to give recognition to Yahweh. Israel's forgetfulness even includes her failure to remember her own failure.

The themes of journey and commandment are brought together in this passage, but the narrative does not follow the Exodus account in its details. Deuteronomy varies from Exodus in its order of events following the covenant at Horeb. The Exodus text follows the covenant-making narrative event with instructions on making the tabernacle (chs 25—31), while Deuteronomy lacks those same instructions. Because of the differences between Exodus and Deuteronomy in their chronological scheme, some commentators attempt to locate this passage in Deuteronomy after 5:31 [28 HB]. Such efforts do not seem to take into account the developing arguments of Deuteronomy. Unlike Exodus, Deuteronomy uses apostasy to illustrate a general tendency in Israel's life. The narrative of apostasy is built into the movement toward occupying the land.

It is difficult to work out a chronology of the events reported in this passage. They are not cataloged in what seems to be a customary way. The chronology is eclipsed by the pattern of references to "forty days and forty nights." It has been argued that the five mentions of "forty days" structure the narrative: covenant made (9:9-11); covenant broken (9:12-17); amends made for covenant broken (9:18-21); covenant renewed (9:25—10:5); Moses continues to lead the people (10:10-11). Though the "forty days and forty nights" are very important to the passage, they do not seem to be an appropriate way to structure the passage. The following is the literary structure of the passage:

115

IN THE TEXT

1. Israel Is about to Seize the Land, but Not by Its Power or Its Own Righteousness (9:1-6)

■ **1-6** The phrase found in 5:1; 6:4; and 20:3 is stipulated at the beginning of this passage: **Hear, Israel**. This hearing is to take place before Israel moves across the river and engages the nations in a conquest for the land. But what is Israel to hear? She is to hear of the strength of her God and the stubbornness of her own history. Yahweh will fight for her even though she is weak. But he will do this not because of anything she possesses or is, but because Yahweh is judging the nations who have not acted in righteousness. The one thing Israel must do is to follow Yahweh by enacting his commands.

The nations on the other side of the river are more powerful and fortified than Israel has the capacity to overcome. The Anakites, a very large people, are in the land (v 2). There is a great disparity between the weakness of Israel and the strength of the Canaanites. How could Israel go over and seize the land? The capability of Yahweh is the only resource that can overshadow the strength of the Canaanites. Israel's hope for victory originates in Yahweh and his promise to the patriarchs.

The wherewithal of Yahweh is portrayed in three ways (v 3). First, it is Yahweh who crosses the river ahead of Israel. Second, it is Yahweh who will destroy the Canaanites who stand in the way of Israel inheriting the land. Third, it is Yahweh who will humble the Canaanites before Israel. But the people are not simply spectators. Israel must participate in the conquest. She is told that the Canaanites will be dispossessed and destroyed, but she must play a part in the endeavor (v 3). Israel's possession of the land displays the mystery of the correlation of divine and human action.

The temptation for Israel is to claim a superior righteousness as the source for God's blessing and election. Israel is warned three times (vv 4-6) that it is not because of her righteousness that Yahweh is driving out the nations. This threefold warning seems to be a parallel to Yahweh's motivation for driving out the nations: **the wickedness of these nations** (v 4). A lack of righteousness is what causes the removal of the nations from the land, and Israel should realize that it could also happen to her. The warning that she is **a stiff-necked people** (v 6) makes this threat even more vexing to the ancient

116

reader. Later readers of this story know that the unrighteousness of the nation caused its removal: Israel went into exile!

Blessing and curse are associated with righteousness and unrighteousness in the book of Deuteronomy. Because of this, many people assert that tragedy is a sign of unrighteousness, and triumph is a sign of righteousness, yet this statement should not be all-inclusive for every disaster or success. Time and again there is a much larger unknown that could explain the consequence of life. The book of Job addresses the problem of universalizing the doctrine of blessing and curse. The reader of Job knows that he is a righteous person, yet he experiences what his friends interpret as a cursed life. The interpreter of these texts must never universalize tragedy and describe it as the result of unrighteous living.

Yet, with the warning not to universalize tragedy, the interpreter of this text should recognize that unrighteousness leads to forfeiting God's gift of the land. Israel will join the Canaanites under the title "former residents" because of her unrighteous acts and unjust form of life. The gift of the land is not a reward for righteousness, but the continued possession of the land is certainly contingent upon faithful obedience to the covenant.

There is an important addition (v 5) as to why Yahweh is dispossessing the nations and giving the land to Israel: he is fulfilling the promise that he made to Abraham, Isaac, and Jacob. This text plays with an interesting theological tension between an act of judgment and an act of gracious fulfillment of promise. Readers of this passage should explore the mysteries of cause and effect. It is not a simple calculus in the narrative logic of grace. Is it judgment? Is it a fulfillment? Perhaps this passage in Deuteronomy is ultimately concerned with the mystery of providence. This text makes it clear that Israel is not going to inherit the land because of her righteousness but because of the free grace of God.

2. Remember Your Rebellions (9:7-24)

■ **7-24** The force of this section is that Israel must not forget that she is habitually obstinate toward Yahweh. This segment of the passage is an extensive recollection of rebellions that function as a paradigm for her understanding of herself and Yahweh. The warning to Israel is that she should not trust in herself. From the middle of the seventh verse, starting with the words **from the day you left Egypt until you arrived here, you have been rebellious against the** LORD, the grammar changes from an address in the singular to an address in the plural. This continues to the end of the story of the rebellion in vv 22-24. Israel has a long history of stubbornness toward Yahweh. This history stretches from the time of the exodus to the present moment on the plains of Moab.

Verses 7-21 describe Moses' climb up Horeb as the backdrop to the whole story. If ever there is a time when Israel should've been faithful to Yahweh, it is during the events connected to forming the covenant at Horeb. Yahweh's deliverance of Israel from her taskmasters in Egypt just happened. He led her through the sea on dry ground. He provided for her in the wilderness. The very finger of God writes words on two stone tablets; he is giving Israel the words of life. The narrative leaves the reader anticipating that the people would be waiting at the foot of the mountain to hear a word from their God. But, it is during the theophany on Mount Horeb that Israel turns aside from the path God commanded for her. The shocking visibility of Israel's stubbornness is seen in her entanglement with idolatry, even before a human eye had glanced at the tablets of stone, written by the finger of God. They acted defiantly by forming the image of a golden calf. How could people in the midst of these events rebel against God?

The infamous golden image is fashioned at the very moment when the covenant is being concluded. The people have already turned aside from the path that Yahweh commanded for them to follow. Israel is a stubborn and stiff-necked people. The word **stiff-necked** is used to describe the people because they refuse to hear and follow the words and ways of God. The theme of "journeying" or "proceeding in a way" dominates the vision of Deuteronomy. This concept becomes a key metaphor for a pattern of living. The reader imagines this metaphor as a way of life or a political reality for the people of God. Even when Israel becomes a settled people, they are to remain in the way of Yahweh. The politics of this nomadic people depend upon the guidance of their God for all of their needs in both the wilderness and in the settled land.

These verses also put into words God's threat to destroy the people and eradicate the memory of them from world history. Israel's very existence is at stake. She broke the covenant. Yahweh would have been justified to conclude that he is no longer bound by the covenant. If "self-righteousness" is the benchmark for the relationship between Yahweh and the people of Israel, then there is no reason for the people not to be crushed. But Yahweh has a different way of dealing with his people. Yahweh calls on the human partnership of Moses in an outlandish way. He both entices and invites Moses in these verses.

Yahweh entices Moses by telling him that he will make a nation out of him and that this nation will be mightier and greater than the one that is gathered at the foot of the mountain (vv 13-14). This appeal invites Moses in the phrase **let me alone**. In these words the reader can also recognize that Yahweh, by this very invitation, gives the impression of appealing to Moses to intercede for the people. Why else would Yahweh need for Moses to not interfere? The reader is left to wonder if in fact the threat of judgment is always for the purpose of intervention and restoration. The book of Jonah, and his judgment oracle, is a prime example of how this kind of threat is understood.

Verses 15-21 recount Moses' descent from the mountain. The story is told in the first person from Moses' point of view. This is a contrast to the report of the event in Exodus 32 where the event is narrated from the viewpoint of the people and Aaron. Deuteronomy's version is also an abbreviated divergence from the Exodus description. It does not contain any intervention before the descent, and there is no description of the clamor of the feasting that the Exodus version provides.

Verses 16-17 make it clear that the deeds of Israel are to be interpreted as "sin." This sin, and maybe all sin, is understood in the words: **You had turned aside quickly from the way that the LORD had commanded you** (v 16). To sin, in the OT, does not always mean a conscious and willful turning from the way of God, but it always means any turning or veering from the path of God whether or not known. The narrative itself implies that Israel veered from the path of exclusively serving Yahweh as God before she received the Decalogue.

The molded calf is the focal point of Israel's sin in this passage (v 21). She turns away from the path of Yahweh's purpose and will to another. The calf may represent another god, or it could simply be a physical representation of Yahweh. In either case, it is breaking one or both of the first two commands. Israel is a covenant breaker before she even reads the covenant words written on tablets of stone. These tablets are still in the hands of Moses, but Israel has already shattered these covenant words. What else is Moses to do but hurl these tablets to the ground and smash them before the eyes of Israel? Broken covenant and broken tablets go together. It should be obvious to the reader that the smashing of the tablets is more than an act of emotional disturbance. Moses, who is the mediator of the covenant, regards the covenant as crushed. Therefore, the tablets handed to him from God are meaningless.

Having shattered the tablets, Moses immediately begins interceding for the shattered people of Israel. Verse 18 shifts to the ministry of Moses, presenting him as praying for the people during his fast of forty days and nights. This is a second reference in this passage to Moses not eating or drinking for the sake of the people. The first reference is found in v 9 when he went up to the mountain to receive the commandments from the hand of God. Now he positions himself **prostrate before *Yahweh*** (v 18) with the commandments broken by the people and also by his own hand. When one is prostrate before God, it implies submission and humility. No self-righteousness, not even Moses', is able to save the people. Their salvation is totally at the mercy of Yahweh, and yet Moses is invited to participate in this act of mercy and grace for the people.

Moses' fear for the people is acknowledged in v 19: **I feared the anger and wrath of the LORD, for he was angry enough with you to destroy you.** The covenant is based upon the fundamental belief that Israel is God's people just as Yahweh is their God. Israel's capricious and impulsive choice led to one of the most grotesque forms of sin, idolatry. Yahweh has every right to visit the sin of the people upon them in both the present generation and even subsequent generations. Israel will learn that she is a people bent on turning away from the path of Yahweh, and she will also learn that she is in need of a mediator to intercede for her. The problem for Israel is that her priest, Aaron, is at least partially responsible for this great sin. The very people who hold the office of mediation between God and his people are culpable for the moral and theological failure of the people. Moses will also need to intercede for Aaron (v 20), on whom the immediate responsibility for the sin of the people rests.

Verses 22-24 maintain the argument that Israel is habitually rebellious. These verses appear to disrupt the flow of the passage from the report of the content of Moses' intercession in vv 25-29, by reporting the rebellion of Israel in addition to the golden calf mayhem. Israel's persistent waywardness is seen in her resistance of Yahweh time after time in her journey in the wilderness. Each of the places mentioned—**Taberah, Massah,** and **Kibroth Hattaavah** (v 22)—are scenes of complaint against Yahweh, and they are practically the same as a rejection of his whole purpose for liberating them.

Numbers 11:1-3 narrates the rebellion at Taberah. It is at Taberah that Israel unexpectedly erupted into a general complaint about her meager conditions, to which Yahweh responds with fiery anger. It should be noted that the name of the place, Taberah, means fire, and that fire is often coupled with God's anger and punishment (Lev 10:2). Massah is taken from an earlier episode in the journey of Israel. Exodus 17:1-7 recites the story of the quarrelsome people when they lacked water and accused Moses of poor leadership. Moses cries to Yahweh concerning this matter and Yahweh says that Moses should take the staff and strike the rock, from which water then gushed. Because the people put Moses and therefore Yahweh to the test, the place is named Massah and Meribah. These names mean "proof" and "contention."

Soon after the Taberah incident the people cried out because they craved meat. It was at **Kibroth Hattaavah,** which means "graves of craving," that Yahweh gave meat to the people to eat. Numbers 11 recounts this interesting story. The Israelites are weary of a never-ending diet of manna, and voice their longing for fish, cucumbers, melons, leeks, onions, garlic, and meat. Moses takes the matter to Yahweh who decides to supply the people with meat in abundance for a brief period. A wind blows quail to Israel, who gathers them in great measure. But God is angry with them for their ungratefulness, and he sends an affliction upon them. Many of the people die and are buried in Kibroth Hattaavah: graves of craving.

These are not examples of out-and-out defiance to Yahweh's commandments like the golden calf incident, but of Israel's small-minded lack of trust and gratitude. On the other hand, Israel deliberately and defiantly violates

Yahweh's direct and unmistakable order to move out from Kadesh Barnea to take possession of the promised land. The final episode that Moses recalls in this section is the story of the spies found in Num 13—14. Yahweh orders Moses to select twelve spies, one from each of the twelve tribes, in order to investigate and assess the land of Canaan. The spies search out the land and return with a description that it is fertile but is occupied by powerful warriors in effectively fortified towns. One of the spies, Caleb, encourages the Israelites to go with confidence in Yahweh and take the land, but the other spies embellish the hazards of the land and the stature of the populace and implore the people against any incursion on Canaan.

This story is a pivotal narrative that sets the stage for the overall movement from the death of the old wilderness generation to the birth of a new generation of hope on the border of the promised land. The people refuse to enter Canaan and yearn for a return to Egypt after hearing the spies' report of the terrifying land and giant warriors in Canaan. God appears and vows to obliterate Israel and disinherit her, but Moses once again pleads with Yahweh to forgive the people. What is interesting in this story is that judgment and salvation both take place in the act of God toward the people. The old generation is condemned to wander forty years and die in the wilderness, but a new generation of Israelites will be allowed to inherit the promised land.

This story is understood as part of this cycle of revolts, which is emblematic of the habitual rebellion of Israel. The incessant narrating of incident after incident gives a description of the rebellious features of Israel's entire history. Israel is not a righteous people, but stiff-necked and stubborn. Israel is small-minded, ungrateful, fearful, and disobedient. Clearly, Yahweh did not choose them for their exemplary righteousness.

3. Covenant Renewal and the Journey Resumed (9:25—10:11)

■ **9:25—10:11** Moses refuses to agree with Yahweh's request to make him a great nation. In its place, he prays that God's anger will be tempered and that his gracious character would revitalize the people of covenant. Moses' intercession in these verses differs from the Exodus account by eliminating the idea of substitution. He said, "Please forgive their sin—but if not, then blot me out of the book you have written" (Exod 32:32). His intervention is based upon Yahweh's prior undertakings (Deut 9:25-28): his deliverance of Israel from Egyptian bondage and his promise to the patriarchs. Moses also indicates that Yahweh's honor is jeopardized, since the nations will explain the destruction of Israel quite differently than Yahweh or Moses describes it.

The result of Moses' intercession indicates a startling fact about Yahweh: he can revise his decision. Clearly, the beliefs that shape this passage point to an open future, even for God. This seems to cut through what many evangelicals believe about God—that he never changes his mind. But the Bible tirelessly bears witness that the persistent prayers of saints and other servants move the heart of God. It should be noticed that Moses' prayer is not that Yahweh would change his own character, but that he would be consistent to who he is: the one who is faithful, redemptive, and forgiving. Yahweh is the God of grace who will withhold judgment in favor of mercy. What is clear from the motivating appeals of Moses is that the prayer is not asking for a whimsical action on God's part, but for the divine will and purpose to be manifested in the open future of God's journey with his people.

Deuteronomy 10:1-5 narrates the story of making the ark and two new tablets. After the failure of the first attempt to guarantee the covenant with its authorizing sign of the stone tablets, Yahweh allows for the construction of new tablets that point to a new opportunity. The construction of the ark also serves this new purpose. It is not mentioned in relation to the first tablets, but it is at this moment presented as part of the preparations for sustaining the covenant forever. Its purpose is to hold the tablets of the covenant, in the conventional practice whereby treaties are placed in religious shrines.

The ark is commonly thought to portray the place where God is present for Israel. The ark is often characterized as the throne, or even the footstool, of Yahweh. When Moses turns and descends from the mountain for the second time, his endeavor makes a contrast with his first turning to go down. On the first occasion he comes down to find the likeness of the calf, and he shatters the tablets; now he comes with the new tablets and houses them in the ark. A new basis is arranged for the covenant. It is now firmly established.

Many interpreters regard 10:6-9 as an inclusion into the main narrative. It should be noted that many translations, including the NIV, use a parentheses around these verses to point out this insertion. When the reader of Scripture compares the route Israel takes in these verses with Num 33:30 ff., it becomes apparent that the Deuteronomy account is at best a partial travel record. Perhaps this portion of text is chosen because it mentions **Moserah**, the place where Aaron is said to have died, which differs from the Numbers account (see Mount Hor in Num 20:22-29). Either Deuteronomy has discovered a different tradition about the death of Aaron, or it is less concerned with the precise location than with displaying the provision for worship in the context of the continuing journey to the land. The contrast between the false worship of the golden calf and the true worship of Yahweh becomes clear to the reader. Not only will Yahweh be worshipped, but he is also the one who institutes the arrangements for true worship. In any case the inclusion of these verses is most likely not muddled editing, but a desire to show that Moses' prayer is heard and answered for both Aaron and Israel.

The reference that is made to the ark of the covenant in Deut 10:1-5 is commented on again in vv 8-9. It is referred to in these verses as **the ark of the covenant of *Yahweh***, and it is the location for the tablets of the Decalogue. They are placed within the ark and this specifies the essential subject matter of the social relationships between Yahweh and his people. In this context it also may be a symbol of covenant renewal. It should also be noticed that **the tribe of Levi** is **set apart** for the service of Yahweh as bearers of the ark and tablet, which means they will function as the mediators for Israel with Yahweh, and **pronounce blessings** in Yahweh's name (v 8). The phrase **as they still do today** implies a historical setting much later than the thirteenth century for the final shaping of the traditions preserved in Deuteronomy.

Deuteronomy does not systematically distinguish separate roles and privileges for priest and Levites, even though there are hints of such distinctions within 10:6-9. The tribe of Levi's vocation to serve Yahweh in the official worship of the people entails a disqualification from having its own tribal territory. This is most probably the reason for the significance of the statement that *Yahweh* **is their inheritance**. The priests' entitlements in return for their duties are elaborated in 18:1-8, which assumes that they live throughout the tribal territories of Israel, are entitled to serve at the main place of worship, and have their living both from such service and from certain private lands that they may hold. The notion of privilege gained from serving Yahweh in the cult to compensate for tribal territory is maintained in Num 18.

Deuteronomy 10:10 is a shift from the literary context of the passage. Moses slips back to his own role in the narrative. This signals a change of subject syntactically, and it begins with the forceful pronoun I rather than using the normal narrative sequence. This implies that vv 6-9 are not a straightforward interruption but are fully developed into the discourse. Moses refers to the second period on the mountain, when he prayed for Israel and received the new tablet, with an allusion to the first period. The expression **at this time also** matches the last words of 9:19, which referred to other later intercessions of Moses.

Israel's repeated failure to be faithful to the covenant is apparent, but even her unfaithfulness cannot keep her out of the land. A renewed advance toward the land is indicated in v 11: **Go . . . and lead the people on their way, so that they may enter and possess the land I swore to their ancestors to give them.** The covenant is intact, in spite of the unfaithfulness of the people, because Yahweh is a promise keeper. He made a promise to the fathers; because of Moses' intercession, the gracious fulfillment of promise will take place.

FROM THE TEXT

Many interpreters of Deuteronomy consider it to be a mechanical and moralistic view of reality. They suppose that embedded in its theological vision is a blessing-and-curse judiciousness that always manipulates the outcome of human life. If you obey, then you will be blessed; but if you disobey, then you will be cursed. This passage makes it clear that this mechanical and moralistic view cannot be absolutized in its application. Yet, this passage is a reminder that something is at stake. Even though Israel is elected as Yahweh's people, their election does not mean that righteousness is inconsequential; unrighteousness does lead to judgment. A prime example of this is the people of Canaan. The major reason for their displacement is their unrighteous form of life.

What does this mean for the present generation of God's people who are about to enter the land? It means that they go into the land as a people of promise always aware of their tendency to practice unrighteousness. Israel is not by nature faithful to Yahweh or each other. They will have to be formed into a faithful and righteous people. This righteous formation can only take place by the habits formed in the grace of God. God's gracious activity is perceived in acts of emancipation, providence, and the imparting of the Torah. Israel is to become by grace what God is by nature: faithful.

But what happens when communities of faith become unfaithful and therefore unrighteous? They are judged in their unrighteousness, even though they have a promised future with and for God. The juxtaposition of this answer is revealed in the numerous ways that Moses is described as an intercessor for the community of faith. One of the most interesting convictions of this passage is that God allows human beings to assist with the redemption of people. The theological vision of this passage discloses that even though people are by nature rebellious and stubborn, people are also the instruments God uses to redeem and restore.

Moses is Israel's mediator. This means that he is equally serving as a priest, a prophet, and a ruler. These roles point to a go-between responsibility for Moses. Perhaps these are the roles assigned to spiritual leadership: to both speak for God to the people and to speak to God on behalf of the people. The role of the mediator is costly to Moses; the people misunderstood him and he also shared the destiny of the people. It seems that the role of mediating between God and God's creation is always a costly enterprise.

G. What Is Required? (10:12—11:32)

BEHIND THE TEXT

The focus of this passage attempts to answer the question: What is required of Israel as she lives in the land of promise? In order to answer this central question, the pericope asserts a sequence of imperatives. These commands are supported by a rich diversity of motivational clauses. Some of these motivational clauses are fixed staunchly to the imperatives themselves: the divine intent for good, Israel's ability to conquer the occupied nations, and long life in the land. Other incentives form longer sections intermingled among the commands. This line of reasoning focuses on Yahweh's character as evidenced in election and redemption, his greatness as reflected in a concern for the marginalized, his unfolding of history, the fertility of the well-watered land, and the promise of an effortless conquest.

Beginning with 11:13-17, blessing and curse become the dominant themes. This passage also prepares the reader for the upcoming law code that is contained in chs 12—26. The law code, functioning politically, will determine whether Israel is blessed or cursed. The reader, along with ancient Israel, is required to make a simple choice (11:26-28). The structure of the passage is as follows:

1. What Does Yahweh Require? (10:12-22)
2. Love Yahweh and Remember His Grace (11:1-7)
3. Keep the Commandments, Serve Yahweh, and You Will Be Blessed (11:8-21)
4. Blessing or Curse Is Before You Today: Choose . . . (11:22-32)

IN THE TEXT

I. What Does Yahweh Require? (10:12-22)

■ **12-22** These verses begin with **and now,** which is a strong section marker and refers generally to what has gone before. This phrase marks a turn from the historical survey of 9:7—10:11 to its implications for behavior and loyalty. History and morality are not separated in this passage, but the account of Israel's story forms the framework for her ethics. Moral obligations, and the words and concepts that define them, are tied to a historical narrative that substantiates them.

Verse 12 asks a question that ultimately is answered in the remainder of the passage: *What does Yahweh your God require of you?* The rhetorical device of question and response implies that Yahweh's requirements are not difficult to understand but are well within the grasp of God's people to comprehend and perform. The answer is expanded in the verses that follow, and these verses bring together the concepts of love and law in a way that is not in contradiction to each another. Instead, they create a new social order fashioned as a response to Yahweh's love and care for Israel. Therefore, there can be no excuse for disobedience if Israel is to reflect the character and purpose of Yahweh. It should be obvious to the reader that what Yahweh commands is both Israel's obligation to carry out and within Israel's capacity to accomplish.

The obedience required by Yahweh is not obscure but straightforward even though there are a variety of commands that described it. A list of infinitives is taken up in vv 12-13 of Moses' admonition: **to fear, to walk, to love,** to serve, and to observe. This ethical response can be compared to Mic 6:8, where the prophet asks, "What does **Yahweh** require of you?" The answer is: "To act justly and to love mercy and to walk humbly with your God." Although the answers are somewhat different, the substance of the answers is the same. Deuteronomy 10:18-19 describe Yahweh as doing justice and loving the weak and marginalized. This text makes it very clear that the people of God are to imitate Yahweh.

In v 13 the purpose of Israel's obedience is basic and clear. It is for Israel's **own good** that Yahweh gives the commandment. He does not desire the obedience of his people for his own well-being but for theirs. God does not need the obedience of people; people need to be obedient for their own sake. This means that the Torah is not an obligation placed upon the people of God for God's sake but is a gift given by God for his people's sake. Law is the gracious gift of God for the purpose of the well-being of the people.

Biblical faith recognizes that the world is created and designed in a particular way, a way that expresses the character and purpose of God. Proverbs 8:22-36 is a poem about Wisdom's role in creation, and it instructs the people of God to hear and keep the ways of Yahweh or Wisdom so that they might be blessed and find life. Ultimately, the commandments of Yahweh enable the people of God to live in the intended framework of creation. The will of God never intends to make life more problematic for God's creation, but to enable all of creation to live within the divine rhythm of life. All of this suggests that the commandments are concerned with the well-being of creation and therefore with the order and purpose of creation.

Deuteronomy 10:14-15 use poetic language to declare Yahweh's role as cosmic Lord. The distinctions between **heavens, even the highest heavens** are uncertain. The sky may be implied by **heavens**, but that which is beyond would most probably be implied by **highest heavens**. The most important connotation of the text is that Yahweh is over the whole of creation. Yahweh, as Creator, rules over the whole of the created order. His rule is directed toward life. This rhythm of life forms a relational/covenantal framework for the whole community of creation. Israel is to participate within this great rhythm that Yahweh has purposed for the sake of life. This is the political reality that Israel is to take with her as she enters the land of promise.

The contrast between vv 14 and 15 is between Yahweh's greatness and his choice in electing Israel's ancestors. Verse 15 sets forth a contrasting observation; notwithstanding Yahweh's lordship over the whole of the cosmos, he has set his heart on Israel. The election of Israel is based on God's affection for an identifiable people. Israel did nothing to procure the electing grace of God, but it is Yahweh's sovereign love that establishes the choice of ancient Israel. It is the God of the entire universe that freely chooses Israel, not a regional god of some ethnic tribe. The reader is once again confronted by the past gracious act of God upon the present. God's past action also applies to the present audience: **as it is today**. This phrase is translated literally *like this day*. The events of the past and the present moment are grounded in the love of Yahweh. God's love for the fathers and his promise to them is finding expression in the people who are gathered on the plains of Moab. It is the character of this electing God that forms the core for the responsibility of the covenant; therefore, love is to be expressed in the social reality of the people called Israel.

The besetting problem of Israel's stubbornness is the focus of this section of the passage and the practice of circumcision is used to explore what Israel is to do to overcome this stubbornness. Yahweh's covenant with the fathers is conveyed through the outward sign of circumcision. Genesis 17:9-12 narrates the story of this original outward sign of covenant loyalty: Yahweh is the God of Abraham and his descendants, and they are his people. This covenantal practice eventually becomes a metaphor that indicates an internalized fidelity to God.

Figuratively, **circumcise** implies the outward sign of Yahweh's ownership. This ownership is to be applied to the interior volition of a person: **Circumcise your hearts, therefore, and do not be stiff-necked any longer** (Deut 10:16). This implies not only a detachment from any hindrance to obedience but also an attachment to radical obedience. To love God entails a suitable disposition or heart. The metaphors of circumcision, heart, being stiff-necked, and stubbornness all involve an attitude. This attitude is what John Wesley describes in his sermon "On Perfection" as "affections" (Wesley 1761). These affections are not disembodied but are embodied in the way people live with others in God's world. The verses that immediately follow v 16 imply that the uncircumcised heart shows itself in a lack of justice and a failure to love and care for the vulnerable in the community.

For the LORD **your God is God of gods and Lord of lords, the great God, mighty and awesome, who shows no partiality and accepts no bribes. He defends the cause of the fatherless and the widow, and loves the foreigner residing among you, giving them food and clothing** (vv 17-18). The three classifications of socially disadvantaged people—orphans, widows, and sojourners—function as a metaphor for people who are in powerless and marginalized social contexts. The story-formed people of God are witnesses not only to the provision of God for them but also by their conduct as a political reality of providential care by providing for those in need. The Hebrew for **shows no partiality** is literally *does not lift up faces*. This phrase means that one does not show favor to one person over another. Partiality is usually associated with some form of **bribe**. This concept usually indicates favoritism toward the rich, powerful, and insiders of a culture and is used as a political reminder of a just and fair community.

Deuteronomy insists that Yahweh has specific concern for those in the community whose social and economic status is not secure. The will of Yahweh for the marginal is that they should receive just and appropriate treatment. The doctrine of Yahweh's fairness and justice stands at the heart of Israel's legal system. The law code section in 16:18-20 articulates the interrelation among justice, power, and leadership. Yahweh's justice for Israel, when she was powerless and marginalized, is the framework for Israel's justice in the land. Yahweh is the one who enacts justice for the orphan and the widow. The insignificant must receive proper treatment and dignity, which makes them significant.

Israel knew what it is like to be resident aliens: **You are to love those who are foreigners, for you yourselves were foreigners in Egypt** (v 19). Their communal memory reminded them that they were aliens in Egypt and that they were treated harshly and unjustly without any sense of dignity. Yahweh desires to provide food and clothing for the resident alien, just as he provided these resources for his own people. The way he does this is through the politics indicated in this passage. Israel's political reality demonstrates that Yahweh provides bread and clothing for the vulnerable through his people. To love Yahweh and love the neighbor/stranger is undeniably the greatest commandment. Israel is Yahweh's storied witness to the world. They are to embody justice and mercy, which reflects Yahweh's character in the manner in which they conduct their lives.

Verses 20-22 bring to a close this first part of the passage with renewed exhortations to fear and worship Yahweh alone.

Events are understood as God's work because God enables his people to recognize that these events are God's doings. Therefore, it is not merely God's deeds but God's self that becomes the focus of gratitude. Every generation is enabled to see the work of God on their behalf. Such recognition allows lives to be changed and gratitude to be offered up in words and deeds. The people experienced the power of Yahweh on their behalf, from the exodus to the present moment, and in gratefulness they are to praise and worship him. Israel understands that Yahweh has a claim upon them as their God, which makes them his people. The claim of Yahweh on Israel is understood as: **Fear the LORD your God and serve him** (v 20). To fear God means to know oneself as a creature, which is dependent and vulnerable. Therefore, to fear God is to know God as the source of all life and purpose. What is interesting in this context is that **the LORD your God** is further defined in terms of practical compassion for the vulnerable.

Not only is Yahweh going to give the land to his people, but also the people are going to be made capable of being Yahweh's own possession. The singular worship of Yahweh is to have a transforming result: it is to produce a community that is a sign of God's character. In other words, the transformation of the nature of Israel is a political reality. When worship does not mould a people to be a symbol of God, one is left to imagine what is actually being worshipped. These verses give the impression that worshipping Yahweh and caring for the vulnerable cohere in a way that is a sign of the covenant. One cannot love God and disregard one's neighbor. Being at home in the land first and foremost means that Israel must be a social embodiment that witnesses to the purpose of Yahweh. She would inhabit the land as a people habituated to love Yahweh by keeping his commandments always.

2. Love Yahweh and Remember His Grace (11:1-7)

■ **1-7** Verses 1-21 delineate two reasons that Israel should love and obey Yahweh: memory and hope. Verses 1-2 make clear that love for God and obedience to his laws are integrally linked to one's memory of the past. The past is narrated as Yahweh's gracious deliverance and guidance for his people, which the present generation is commanded to **remember today** (v 2). The first incentive begins by remembering Yahweh's stunning liberation of Israel from Egyptian oppression. This act confirms his sovereign benevolence for Israel. The incalculable power of Yahweh is demonstrated to the full for those Hebrew slaves who experienced a miraculous deliverance from Egypt and who observed the overthrow of the pursuing Egyptian army by Yahweh's strong arm (vv 3-5).

Yahweh's graciousness is also demonstrated in his continual guidance of Israel through the wilderness (vv 5-7). The reader of Deuteronomy perceives divine activity within both the flow of history and the forces of nature. The phenomena of moving out of Egypt and moving through the wilderness are interpreted in a confessional manner; Yahweh is responsible for both movements. This gives the impression that Yahweh uses secondary causes to bring about his will. Later, Israel will interpret her own history through secondary causes in the context of exile. Yahweh uses the Babylonian Empire to judge Judah, and he uses the Persian Empire as an instrument of salvation for his people. Yahweh integrates the historical and the natural forces of the world as he acts through them to accomplish his purpose.

More threatening and dangerous than the foes of Israel is the threat that the people would forget the greatness of Yahweh's gracious action in the past. The lessons of the past need to be learned by each generation all over again. The discernment and courage of the few also must be passed on and habituated in the present generation. Verse 7 makes a case for passing on the faith so that it becomes an existential reality for the next generation: **But it was your own eyes that saw all these great things the LORD has done.** Salvation is viewed as concrete events that also have consequences for succeeding generations.

Since there are many who have never witnessed the episodes of Egyptian liberation and guidance in the wilderness, those who experienced such salvation have a duty to make clear to future generations the power of Yahweh to save. The community's sacred discernment is necessary for her future.

3. Keep the Commandments, Serve Yahweh, and You Will Be Blessed (11:8-21)

■ **8-21** The people are exhorted once again (v 8) to perform the commandments of Yahweh, but now the motivation shifts from memory to hope. The people are to observe the Law, soon to be declared to them, because without such observance they will not find **the strength to go in and take over the land**. In this second incentive for loving Yahweh, Israel is to envision the future achievement of God in the future conquest of the land and the ongoing care and blessing of the people once they take possession of the land. Both of these accomplishments are understood as achievements of Yahweh. Israel is called to hope.

The promised land—**a land flowing with milk and honey** (v 9) that does not depend on human methods—is contrasted with Egypt in v 10. The Egyptians irrigated the land like a person irrigates a vegetable garden, but Yahweh himself cares for the land flowing with milk and honey. It is watered directly by the rain of heaven; therefore, the people are not to be dependent upon human systems but on the provision of God. The years of wandering in the wilderness prepared Israel for this type of dependency. The people developed a nomadic political culture; they receive what each day brings from the hand of God. When they cross over into the land of promise, they will still need to be dependent upon the hand of Yahweh to provide for them. Yahweh is who makes the land flow with milk and honey.

Yahweh's promise to provide for Israel ends with a warning: **Be careful, or you will be enticed to turn away and worship other gods and bow down to them** (v 16). The Hebrew word translated **enticed** is *pātâ*, which is defined by words such as *gullibility* or even *openness to deception*. This implies, especially in this setting, a turn to other gods to secure rain and therefore fertility in this desert place. Enticement is a subtle action. It involves almost not noticing what is going on around oneself. In the case of the fertility cult, it involves the regular way that life is conducted and therefore how life is interpreted.

The reference to the danger of turning to foreign gods is common in the Deuteronomistic tradition. The ancient Canaanite culture believes that the gift of rain stems from the power of the god Baal. The Israelites are to be careful to recognize Yahweh as the Giver of rain and all fertility. Life in abundance comes from the hand of the God who led a ragtag band of slaves out of the land of bondage and the house of slavery. The one who liberates is the one who provides. Israel must never forget that the one who sends the rains can also seal off the heavens so that there is no rain. There is no survival, no life, in the land that is Yahweh's gift to them if they fail to remember the Giver of gifts.

Verses 18-21 repeat many of the commands and the images that are employed in 6:6-9. Israel, as a community, is to place these words in her heart and soul. The reader of the text is left to ponder just how these words are to become internalized, so that they form the very character of the individual and the ethos of the community. The solution to this query is answered in the text itself, these inward realities are to be habituated into the lives of persons and into the community itself. Words such as **Fix these words of mine in your hearts and minds; tie them as symbols on your hands and bind them on your foreheads. Teach them to your children, talking about them when you sit at home and when you walk along the road, when you lie down and when you get up. Write them on the doorframes of your houses and on your gates** (11:18-20) point to the all-pervasive dimension of how these words of the covenant are to shape the very life of the community and the individuals within the community. What seems to be implied by these practices is that the entirety of the life of Israel is to be engaged in habituating these words in the present and for the sake of future generations.

The motivation given for Israel's habituation is **so that your days and the days of your children may be many in the land the LORD swore to give your ancestors** (v 21). Moses is not discussing the length of an individual's life span but is speaking to Israel's permanent possession of the promised land. This concept suggests that the manner in which a community practices its life determines the durability of the community. History narrates the stories of many people groups that are swept into the dustbin of history because they lost their unique identity and value system. Only the habituation that is brought about by consistent practices and witnessed to by compelling exemplars will survive the onslaught of syncretism.

4. Blessing or Curse Is Before You Today: Choose . . . (11:22-32)

■ **22-32** This subsection rearticulates the deep-seated assurance of the conquest. Within the framework of this assurance, an equilibrium is maintained between the command of Yahweh and his promise of the land: **If you carefully observe all these commands I am giving you to follow—to love the LORD your God, to walk in obedience to him and to hold fast to him—then the LORD will drive out all these nations before you, and you will dispossess nations larger and stronger than you** (vv 22-23). This theological tension of binding blessings with obedience pervades the entire Deuteronomistic tradition. The mysterious tension between divine action and human engagement is played out in the **If . . . then . . .** phrase of these verses. It should also be noticed that v 25 portrays the two aspects of the promise once again: no one will be able to stand against Israel because Yahweh will put terror of the Israelites into the people of the whole land.

Chapter 11 closes with an open future placed before Israel: **See, I am setting before you today a blessing and a curse** (v 26). Moses vocalizes blessing and curse, not like Abraham conferred upon Isaac or Jacob upon his sons, but with covenant boundaries. A choice must be made by Israel between obedience and disobedience, blessing and curse, life and death. The implication is that obedience to Yahweh is what it means to love him (v 22), and disobedience to God ultimately indicates **following other gods, which you have not known** (v 28). Every generation is called to love God by obeying him; if they do, then they will walk in the way of life. But if they refuse, then they will walk the pathway of destruction.

One of the most interesting literary observations of this last section of the pericope is the use of the concept of Yahweh's giving to Israel. The verb *nātan* ("to give") is used three times in these verses: vv 26, 31, and 32. In v 26 the NIV translates the participle form of the verb as **setting (before)** . . . In this verse the gift is the possibility of both blessing and curse. What an interesting gift. This could imply that the true gift of God to the people is their freedom to make a choice in the moment. In v 31, Yahweh is **giving** (*nātan)* the land to his people. In this verse the gift given is the land itself. This would seem to be the most expected employment of the concept of the gift of God to the people. Yahweh gives the gift of the land of promise. In v 32, Yahweh is **setting** [*nātan*] **before** Israel his **decrees and laws**, his gifts to Israel. These three categories of gifts are very interesting: the freedom to choose, the fulfillment of promise, and the revelation of God's purpose. Israel does nothing apart from the grace of God, yet she does not do anything in a robotic or mechanical way. The purpose of God is known, possible, and promised. What a mystery.

Moses instructs the people to institute an obvious reminder of the two alternatives that lie before them. They are to establish **Mount Gerizim** as a symbol of blessing and **Mount Ebal** as a sign of curse (v 29). The two mountains in the middle of the land of Canaan near the town of Shechem are topographically distinct: Gerizim is a mountain green with vegetation, a sign of God's blessing; and Ebal is a starkly barren and dry mountain, a sign of a curse and death. The two mountains are visible reminders of the alternative ways that Israel could walk. Disobedience leads to curse and death. Obedience leads to blessing and life.

Whenever the people of God hear the commands of the covenant of life, they are presented with a choice: they will either choose life or they will choose death. Communities and individuals always stand at the boundary jammed between landlessness and land, flanked by blessing and curse, sandwiched between life and death. No generation is free from this choice that will bring life or death; they are all carried back to that moment when all possibilities lay before them. The future is open . . . There is a mystery that exists between God's electing call and the people's response. The God who promises is also the God who is in partnership with humanity for the immediate future. God's people will collaborate in shaping their future as they resolve to act in the open space that is created for obedience or disobedience. The consequence of their choice is a life-or-death matter!

FROM THE TEXT

What makes this section of Deuteronomy so fascinating theologically is the dynamic manner in which the issue of divine purpose and human responsibility dance with one another. Deuteronomy appears disinclined to accept as true a world where God preordains the outcome of even God's purposes. No one, not even Israel, will be made to do God's will. There is a freedom that is created for people to partner with God in accomplishing his will. Yet, the convictional milieu within which Deuteronomy emerges is unwilling to declare that human beings are eager to do God's will. They are not; the very opposite is true, as their history shows and as the imploring of Moses implies. The result of not doing the will of God is to suffer destruction. Human culpability is a part of the theological matrix within which Deuteronomy's vision is articulated. A strong interplay can be noticed between God's purpose and the culpability of people to perform the will of God.

Yet, does this mean that God's promises will not be achieved for his covenant partner? This is the mystery that the text is constantly wrestling with. God will keep the promises to the ancestors and their descendants. Grace will not give up, but it will also not be coercive. The assortment of gifts—blessing and curse, the land, and the statutes and judgments to his people—conveyed through the threefold use of *nātan* implies that God's gifts (grace) are working with his covenant partner to accomplish his purpose for his people and his creation. But the people must receive the grace of God. They must receive not only his will and the land but also the "now" of their decision. God gives freedom in the moments of the journey of a life or the life of a people. Freedom is a wonderful and terrifying gift of grace.

The people who are alive at Moab are characterized as living between blessing and curse. The implication is that people are always living in "the now" between blessing and curse. A decision is perpetually at hand in the present moment. The decision sets the path for either blessing or curse, for life or death. Moab may be the ultimate metaphor for a people or a person. It is the place where the gracious acts of God are remembered and where the will of God is given in a fresh way. In this "place between," which is called "now," the gift of freedom will tip the scale toward life or death, blessing or curse.

133

Because life is always lived *on the way*, one could say that the life of faith is the nomadic life, the life that hears a call to leave and cleave to the place that is also a gift.

It should be obvious that something must happen to the people; their character must change. God's command to Israel **to circumcise the foreskin of your heart** (10:16) is out of the ordinary. This decree has not occurred to this point in Deuteronomy, but the image is important elsewhere in the OT. The meaning of this metaphor is apparently the internalization of faithfulness to God and his covenant. Simply being willing to rehearse and support God's covenant authority is not enough for the theological vision of this passage. The formation of the character of God's people is what the covenant is longing to accomplish. The metaphor of a circumcised heart eventually will entail the conceptual framework of the new covenant. Because of this, the metaphor became one of Paul's important images, which he makes use of in Rom 2:25-29. He writes:

> Circumcision has value if you observe the law, but if you break the law, you have become as though you had not been circumcised. So then, if those who are not circumcised keep the law's requirements, will they not be regarded as though they were circumcised? The one who is not circumcised physically and yet obeys the law will condemn you who, even though you have the written code and circumcision, are a lawbreaker. A person is not a Jew who is one only outwardly, nor is circumcision merely outward and physical. No, a person is a Jew who is one inwardly; and circumcision is circumcision of the heart, by the Spirit, not by the written code. Such a person's praise is not from other people, but from God.

III. THE LAW BOOK: 12:1—26:15

OVERVIEW

Old Testament scholars refer to Deut 12—26 as the Deuteronomic Code. This collection of material consists of laws that modern persons would consider both secular and sacred. Ancient communities did not recognize a separation between the secular and the sacred; therefore, everything was considered sacrosanct. The Deuteronomic Code is not the only self-contained collection of legal material in the Pentateuch. Exodus 20—23 is a collection that is designated the Covenant Code and Lev 17—26 is a compilation that is named the Holiness Code. These three codes repeat a substantial corpus of ideas and very likely point to a preserved tradition that is expressed in different periods of time in Israel's history with fairly distinctive interests.

These fifteen chapters make up almost half of the book of Deuteronomy and set the framework for the political implications of the Deuteronomistic tradition itself. It should be noted that a great many scholars believe that some form of this law code was discovered in the seventh century, which brought on Josiah's reformation. Second Kings 22—23 narrates the discovery of the book of the law in the temple and the subsequent reform. Stipulations of the covenantal polity are arranged to signal a collective course of action that embodies the Decalogue. Israel did not understand Torah as something that makes her Yahweh's people, but as a social order given by God for the sake of his people. Torah is the politic of Yahweh. An inexact correlation can be perceived between the order of themes touched on in the law code and the structure of the Decalogue. This can be discerned as:

"No other gods" (12:1—13:18 [12:1—13:19 HB])
"Misuse of God's name" (14:1-21)
"Keep the Sabbath" (14:22—16:17)
"Honor father and mother" (16:18—18:22)
"Do not kill" (19:1—22:8)
"Do not commit adultery" (22:9—23:18)
"Do not steal" (23:19—24:7)
"Do not bear false witness" (24:8—25:4)
"Do not covet neighbor's wife" (25:5-12)
"Do not covet anything" (25:13—26:15)

The above arrangement of the Decalogue is Jewish; therefore, the prohibition to other gods and idols is understood as the first command. The ninth and tenth commands are two forms of coveting. This commentary does not follow this inexact structure of the law code but interprets the code in a thematic way:

A. No Other Gods: The Politics of a New Reality (12:1—13:18 [12:1—13:19 HB])
B. Honor the Holiness of God's Name (14:1-21)
C. Regulations Concerning the Tithe (14:22-29)
D. Liberation (15:1-18)
E. The Firstborn of the Livestock (15:19-23)
F. Religious Festivals (16:1-17)
G. Position, Power, and Privilege (16:18—18:22)
H. Life (19:1—21:23)
I. Boundaries: Social and Sacrosanct (22:1—23:18 [22:1--23:19 HB])
J. The Common Good (23:19—24:22 [23:20--24:22 HB])
K. Uprightness: Private and Public (25:1-19)
L. Stewardship (26:1-15)

A. No Other Gods: The Politics of a New Reality (12:1—13:18 [12:1—13:19 HB])

BEHIND THE TEXT

Deuteronomy 12—13 interprets the first commandment, "You shall have no other gods before me." It is tempting to read these chapters against the historical backdrop of Josiah's reform as recounted in 2 Kgs 22—23. The centralization of all worship of Yahweh, in this context, would take place in Jerusalem. The reader should notice that there is no reference to Jerusalem in the text. Therefore, the passage ought to be read in light of a larger theological theme: the exclusive claim of Yahweh as God. This larger theme can then be read into the reform of King Josiah.

In addition to understanding the larger theological theme of this pericope, 12:29-32 [12:29—13:1 HB] introduces a reminder that there is great harm to pagan practices that so easily habituate the people into a form of life with its beliefs and values. These verses are a bridge section that connects 12:1-28 to 13:1-18 [2-19 HB].

Structure:
1. The Place that Yahweh Shall Choose (12:1-32 [12:1—13:1 HB])
    a. Destroy Their Places of Worship (12:1-7)
    b. When You Live in the Land . . . (12:8-12)
    c. Worship Only at the Place Yahweh Chooses (12:13-19)
    d. When Yahweh Enlarges Your Territory . . . (12:20-28)
    e. Do Not Imitate the People of the Land (12:29-32 [12:29—13:1 HB])
2. Seduction and Hearing the Voice of God (13:1-18 [2-19 HB])
    a. Seduction by False Prophets (13:1-5 [2-6 HB])
    b. Seduction by Friend or Family (13:6-11 [7-12 HB])
    c. Seduction by Another City (13:12-18 [13-19 HB])

IN THE TEXT

1. The Place that Yahweh Shall Choose (12:1-32 [12:1—13:1 HB])

The regulation to centralize the cult at *the place that Yahweh shall choose* (v 14) may be the most noticeable element in all of Deuteronomy's contributions for ordering Israel's life. There can be no doubt that this centralization profoundly changes the life of the people of Israel, especially the rural population. This centralizing regulation appears in a triple form: vv 2-7, 8-12, 13-19. Each of these descriptions is developed based on the statement that Israel be allowed to offer sacrifices just in *the place that Yahweh shall choose* to make his name dwell. This assertion is developed in different ways within individual situations. Although the city of Jerusalem indubitably came to be equated with *the place that Yahweh your God shall choose*, the emphasis of Deuteronomy is on the insistence that the central worship place be the one that God chooses. Yahweh will choose where his presence will be offered; human beings, even Israel, cannot control or confine the presence and power of God.

Verses 2-7 explore the centralization of worship in terms of the purging of foreign religious practices. Verses 8-12 call attention to the difference in proper behavior before and after the settlement in the land. Verses 13-19 draw a distinction between human discernment of holy places and divine election of those places. It also explores some functional concerns for eating nonsacrificed meat. Verses 20-28 are a reiteration of the last section of the passage and put emphasis on the significance of distinguishing what could be eaten only at the place of worship and what could be eaten anywhere else. The development of this section anticipates expansion in the land area controlled by the ancient people of God. Verses 29-32 [12:29—13:1 HB] lead the reader to focus upon the assumption that shapes the composition of the passage to this point, unequivocally the threat of foreign gods. Israel will likely be tempted to comport themselves in the same manner as the former populace of the land.

a. Destroy Their Places of Worship (12:1-7)

■ **1-7** These verses convey the policy of the politics of Deuteronomy to destroy the places that are used to worship other gods. Verse 1 provides an introductory description of the content of the law code. The **decrees and laws** refer to the section of laws/practices found in chs 12—26. The wording is similar to the wording in the introductory portions previously in Deuteronomy (4:44-45; 5:1; 6:1-2). These texts imply that the laws/practices are designed with the future inhabitants of Israel in mind. The word translated **laws** is not the Hebrew word *tôrâ* but *mišpāṭ* ("justice" or "judgment"), derived from the verb *šāpaṭ* ("to judge"). The doctrine of Yahweh's fairness and justice stands at the heart of Israel's legal system. Yahweh's justice for Israel, when she was powerless and marginalized, is the framework for Israel's justice in the land. Laws, in this context, connect with judicial matters and that means they are policies for the life of the community. The policies of Israel's laws are not simply a matter of having good beliefs about the way the community is to view itself, but the people are to **be careful to follow** these policies (12:1).

In addition to the command to carefully follow the decrees and laws, three other themes reappear in v 1: Yahweh as the God of the fathers, the gift of the land, and life/prosperity in the land. These themes have already occurred numerous times in the first eleven chapters. The theme of Yahweh as the God of the fathers reminds the hearers that they are a people of promise. Yahweh keeps his promise. The gift of the land refers to the land as an act of grace for Israel. Israel did not by her strength or righteousness possess the land, but it is given to her. The final theme is one of living in the land. Watchful doing of the commandments is essential for life and vitality in the land. One could say that this theme is concerned with the responsibility of Israel for the gift/grace of God.

Verses 2-4 are concerned with the destruction of foreign places and objects of worship. The ancient people of Canaan believed that **high mountains** and **hills** were the home of gods; they also thought that sanctuaries built on these sacred locations allowed them to have access to their deity. These ancient neighbors of Israel also believed that under certain trees the gods could be approached. Some of the trees are considered by the Canaanites as symbols of fertility, which was the dominant theme of Canaanite religion.

The command to destroy the Canaanite sacred places includes objects used in worship by the Canaanites: **altars, sacred stones, Asherah poles**, and **idols**. The underlying rationale is that these objects and the places associated with them would influence and shape Israel's religious life if they were left in the land as Israel took possession of the land. People become habituated through their practices and value systems. Therefore, the elimination of these places and objects would also eliminate the practices associated with these places. The act of destruction not only removed the temptation for Israel to lapse into Canaanite forms of worship, but it eradicated the name of the gods from that place. Only one name can be associated with the land, and it is the name of the God who fulfilled his promises to the people. The name of Yahweh is to be glorified in the whole of the land.

Verse 4 addresses a very interesting topic. Not only is Israel not to worship the gods associated with the Canaanite culture, but they also are not to worship Yahweh in ways that the Canaanites worshipped their gods. It should be obvious to the reader that the opposition between the tradition of Yahweh and the traditions that belong to the inhabitants of the land has broad social and cultural differences. Israel is not allowed to worship Yahweh like the Canaanites worshipped Baal. The practices and the values that form the people of promise are to form a people who reflect the character of Yahweh.

Verse 5 sets up an antithesis to the places mentioned in v 2. The people are commanded to **seek the place** that Yahweh their God elects **to put his Name**. The idea of placing one's name in a place suggests the custom of rulers immortalizing their names on cities or shrines in order to demonstrate ownership and sovereignty (2 Sam 12:28). The divine name appears as a type of mediating power through which God remains accessible without being localized. In this way the symbol of identity brings together the earthly and heavenly dwelling places of God. This means that the transcendence belonging to Yahweh could be maintained without forfeiting the belief in the importance of a special sanctuary with all of its symbols.

Even though this command has a unique historical significance during the time of Josiah's reform, it also leaves room for the divine choice to continually designate a place to bear the name of God. The centralization formula asserts that the selection of the central place is a matter of divine choice, not the result of some type of sacredness implied in the site itself. The text does not designate a particular name for the place where Yahweh is placing his name. It does not need to be mentioned, for it is only Yahweh's name that is important.

A fundamental purpose for the sanctuary, chosen by Yahweh, is that it serves as the location to which Israel is to bring all of her offerings (Deut 12:6). The list of offerings to be brought to the central place is wide-ranging in character. This wide-ranging list (**burnt offerings, sacrifices, tithes, special gifts, what you have vowed to give, freewill offerings, the firstborn of . . . herds and flocks**) would preclude the presentation of blasphemous offerings elsewhere. These offerings would arise out of the bounty that Yahweh provides for Israel in the land of promise. Thus, the very possibility of Israel bringing these offerings exists only by the fulfillment of Yahweh's promise. These offerings allow for an emphasis on eating together and rejoicing in **the presence of Yahweh** (v 7). A joyful environment is implied in this list of offerings. The atmosphere of rejoicing takes place within the context of family and friends in the presence of Yahweh. This celebration creates the ambiance for a profound awareness that Yahweh provides success and fruitfulness. God blesses Israel.

b. When You Live in the Land . . . (12:8-12)

■ **8-12** Just as v 4 is a contrast with the worship practices of the Canaanites, so also the command **not to do as we do here today** (v 8) focuses upon the period before entry into the land of promise. Not only is Israel to denounce and destroy the worship places and practices of the Canaanites, but they are also to pattern their own lives and worship for a constructive outcome. This desired outcome is the singular worship of Yahweh. The singular worship of Yahweh is not for the sake of worship itself, but in order to become a people singularly devoted to Yahweh.

The assembly of wilderness pilgrims is portrayed as disorderly, because they are acting according to their own desires (**everyone doing as they see fit**). The contrast is made between the unstructured practices of the period of wilderness wanderings and the later practices of the settled people. Verse 9 recognizes that the people are engaged in disorderly worship because they **have not yet reached** their **resting place**. Yahweh promises that they are on the way and that they will enter the land by crossing **the Jordan**; Yahweh will give them **rest** from their enemies and they will **live in safety** by giving them the land as an inheritance. The lack of structure also indicates the lack of a centralized place to worship Yahweh their God. The purpose of this passage is not to identify this place but to compel Israel to match up her worship to the divine command. Yahweh's name sets apart the central place that he chooses to be identified with, and it achieves both orthodoxy and orthopraxis. What a community accepts as true habituates the way a community conducts itself and also vice versa.

The centrality of the first commandment and the centrality of the place of worship are tied together in this pericope. Doing what seems good according to one's own desires moves the people away from the singular claim of God on the lives of the people of promise. When Israel settles into the land, people will predictably find themselves a long way from the new place of God's choice. Distance itself will become a temptation to use the adjacent revered places for the sake of convenience. But the temptation to convenient worship will not only violate God's commands but also form a people incapable of reflecting God's purpose in the world.

There is a common theme in this section of the passage: it is all too easy to practice worship in a way that will not honor God and therefore will make the people other than the kind of people that reflect God's purpose and character in the world. True worship can take place only in the presence of the one true God, sharing the enjoyment of the sacrificial meals in the sanctuary. Israel must not stop at any place but must travel on to the place that Yahweh chooses. Verse 11 repeats the list of offerings mentioned in v 6.

Verse 12 gives a specific list of those sharing in the celebration, mentioned briefly in v 7 as "you and your families." The list includes one's sons and daughters, male and females servants, and the Levites who reside in the towns without an inheritance. It should be noticed that there is no noticeable role for the priests in this passage, even though there is the insistence upon the centrality of worship. Why? Chapter 26 does describe the care and resourcing of the priest, but this passage points to the particular care that one is to extend for those who are dependent upon the resources that God makes available. The Levites are included in the passage itself, because they are without an inheritance. It should also be remembered that the Levites most probably are the ones who kept the tradition of Deuteronomy alive in ancient Israel.

c. Worship Only at the Place Yahweh Chooses (12:13-19)

■ 13-19 Deuteronomy never names "the place that Yahweh will choose," but most scholars identify this particular site as Jerusalem. Whatever the site, in the opinion of this ancient tradition, it does not exclude the blessing of Yahweh upon the local communities and families. These verses point to the local context of celebration and feasts. The people are not to use for sacrifice any place other than the one Yahweh chooses, but they are to feast in their local settings. There is a distinction that is being made between the sacrifice of an animal and the slaughter of an animal. The blessing of a meal together with friends and the needy can be enjoyed in every town. The blessings of Yahweh remain local, even if the undertaking of sacrifice must be at the faraway place that Yahweh elects.

This section is attempting to convey that both the local community and the centralized sanctuary are legitimate spheres of sacred significance. It is not so much that what is on one occasion holy becomes secular, but rather that a great deal of daily life is also located in Yahweh's dominion. **The blessing the LORD your God gives you** (v 15) may be enjoyed in the local setting, but the implication is that it should not be horded but shared. It is interesting to notice again in this section that the Levite is not to be neglected as long as the people live in the land. From the call of Abraham onward, blessing is never understood as something to be amassed at the deprivation of the needy. "I will make you into a great nation, and I will bless you; I will make your name great, and you will be a blessing. I will bless those who bless you, and whoever curses you I will curse; and all peoples on earth will be blessed through you" (Gen 12:2-3).

d. When Yahweh Enlarges Your Territory . . . (12:20-28)

■ **20-28** The opening words of this segment of the passage express the confidence that Yahweh will enlarge the territory of Israel. **The place where** Yahweh **chooses to put his Name** (v 21) will be too far for the greater part of the population to travel every time they wish to eat meat. Consequently, the significance of distinguishing what could be eaten only at the place of worship and what could be eaten anywhere else becomes the subject of this section of the passage.

It is interesting to notice that herds and flocks are mentioned as meat for the people to eat both in the place of worship and in their local settings. Beef and mutton are eaten in both the local setting as well as at the place of worship. They are permissible both for common consumption as well as sacrifice. It should also be noticed that gazelle and deer could also be consumed, but not sacrificed (vv 15, 22). Wild meat is permissible to eat, but it is not acceptable to sacrifice. Yahweh's blessing can be enjoyed everywhere, even though the enactment of sacrifice is to be at the place where he would designate.

What is also interesting is the fourfold repetition of the theme **do not eat the blood** in vv 23-25. What does this imply in the value system of these ancient people of God? Verse 23 gives the explanation on why the people are not to eat the blood, **because the blood is the life, and you must not eat the life with the meat.** There is sacredness to **life** (*nepeš*).

The *nephesh* in all creatures is in some sense an inflow of the vital force of God, who is the living God. Belief that the *nephesh* resides essentially in the blood arose no doubt from the observation that the ebbing of life coincides with the flow of blood from the body . . . the blood, then, as the vehicle of *nephesh* is regarded as peculiarly close to God and within the sphere of the holy. (Cairns 1992, 131-32)

e. Do Not Imitate the People of the Land (12:29-32 [12:29—13:1 HB])

■ **29-32 [12:29—13:1 HB]** The reader is led to focus upon the premise that shapes the composition for the passage to this point, explicitly the jeopardy of foreign gods and the practices related to these gods. Verse 29 envisions an immense threat for the people of God: to practice their religion like the former residents of the land. Israel will be tempted to function in the same way as the former populace of the land. She must resist these foreign values and practices not simply as a political necessity but as a religious obligation.

Verse 31 makes it clear that they are not to worship Yahweh their God in a way that reflects the practices of these other nations **because in worshiping their gods, they do all kinds of detestable things the LORD hates. They even burn their sons and daughters in the fire as sacrifices to their gods.** The history of Israel points to the fact that she is not always innocent of this type of hideous act, for children are murdered for alleged religious intentions as can be seen in the reigns of both King Ahaz (2 Chr 28:3) and King Manasseh (2 Kgs 17:17-18). God alone has the authority over life and death. Yahweh is the Giver and Sustainer of life. Life and not death is the purpose and meaning of creation. The crime of sacrificing human life leads to the complete deterioration of a people and their eviction from the land.

FROM THE TEXT

Orthodoxy, right thinking, is not the only concern with the people of God; they must also concern themselves with orthopraxy, right living. This is the central concern of Deut 12. The way a people practice their life together will shape what they value and ultimately believe. To worship Yahweh in a way that other gods are worshipped is dreadfully iniquitous, even if the name of Yahweh is attached to the false practice. This should be a warning regarding profane practices for the people of God throughout history. To claim a false practice as belonging to Yahweh or Jesus does not make the practice acceptable. The people of God are to have a recognizable form of life; they are to reflect the character and purpose of God. Therefore, the people of God must ask not only what is necessary to believe (orthodoxy) but also what is essential to do (orthopraxy).

2. Seduction and Hearing the Voice of God (13:1-18 [2-19 HB])

This subdivision directs the reader's attention to the problem of seduction. The readers are instructed to "do all I command you; do not add to it or take away from it" (12:32 [13:1 HB]). These commands are difficult to distinguish within the cacophony of voices in the land that they will inhabit. Israel must discern the voice of God in the unmarked occasions of time. The either/or of the ethical and theological vision of the tradition of Deuteronomy is harshly stated in this passage. If they fail to discern the voice of God, they will lose the favorable possibilities that stretch out across their future.

God's people must not tolerate the powerful dissonance of the misleading voices of false prophets, mistaken friends or family members, and even the erroneous ideologies of whole communities. These deceptive voices, with their misguided beliefs and values, will entice Israel into following the practices that are associated with other gods. These dissonant intonations must not be tolerated in any way. They must be destroyed completely, or Israel will risk her own devastation. The complete destruction of these seductive enemies poses a problem when one reads these texts through the lens of the Christian faith. How can a Christian reader understand the power of this passage without resorting to a violence that the Lord Jesus prohibited? This problem will be addressed in the final section of the exposition, but first a reader must hear what the text is addressing.

This section consists of three types of seductive stimuli: religious leaders that proclaim an alternative god, close associations that witness to an alternative deity, and alluring alien cultures with their false spiritual realities. A recurring model addresses each of these seductive impetuses. This design is made up of four elements: (1) a seductive invitation to an alternative ultimate concern, (2) an assertion that Yahweh alone is to be served, (3) a call to purge the seductive power, and (4) a closing saying concerning the ending of the refusal to go along with the seductive voices.

a. Seduction by False Prophets (13:1-5 [2-6 HB])

■ **1-5 [2-6 HB]** Those persons who are recognized as religious leaders receive the opening warning concerning the seduction of the people of Israel. These leaders are described as **prophets** or **dreamers**. Most probably these people enjoy a unique status within the community as religious authorities. Prophecy and dreams are acceptable channels of receiving revelation in ancient Israel. There is no hint within the text that these religious authorities are from an alien culture or religion; therefore, they become a great source of influence for the people of Israel.

What makes their influence even greater is that they are said to declare signs or wonders that take place within the immediate account of the people's lives. The coming to pass of a predicted event would normally be an indication of the validity of the messenger (see 18:21-22). What are the people to do? The predictive words of a religious leader ignite faith and passion. The community would suppose, "They must know what the rest of us do not know." In this

144

particular case, the prophet or dreamer would solicit the people to follow after other gods. No prophet of the true God could speak in such a way that would contradict the first commandment. Only false prophets speak in such a way.

Events like this are nothing less than a test to see if the people of God will love and serve God alone. This temptation occurs often in the course of human history. What are people to do when the predictive persons, instruments, and methods tell them to follow something else in an ultimate way? Predictive fulfillment seems so right. What makes this predictive fulfillment so frightening is when the very religious leaders of the people of God are the ones who envisage what is about to take place and then draw the attention of the people to sources other than the God of creation and redemption.

The penalty for these false religious leaders is capital punishment because of the gravity of the transgression. Of course, today, this penalty cannot be carried out in a literal way. It must be remembered that Jesus himself is accused of being a false religious leader. This accusation cost him his life. It should also be remembered that the ethical policy that he announced and embodied insisted upon loving even one's enemies. So what can this policy mean when a Christian is reading this text? It at least means that the community must disassociate with a religious leader who directs the adherents to worship and serve another god. This disassociation is described as a "purging" in the passage under consideration. But, it must be remembered, that what counts as a false prophet or leader in this passage is calling the people to follow after another god. This "purging" is not to be enacted because of a doctrinal argument, or even over how to interpret texts or historical events, but is to take place because the religious leader calls the people of God to follow and serve something as ultimate other than the God of creation and redemption. No matter how successful or even supposedly "right" a religious leader may be in predicting a future state of affairs, the criteria of the sole sovereignty of God is to determine the allegiance of the people who are redeemed from the land of bondage and given a place of promise.

b. Seduction by Friend or Family (13:6-11 [7-12 HB])

■ **6-11 [7-12 HB]** The second set of circumstances, concerning the seduction of people to serve other gods, is elucidated in an analogous manner to the earlier segment of the passage. The enticement to infidelity with Yahweh is expressed in the same terms as before with only a further qualification of the gods, namely that they might be gods worshipped anywhere, near or far. In this situation the person responsible for the seduction is not a religious leader within the religious/theological tradition but is someone who is close to the individual follower of Yahweh, a member of one's own household.

The temptation from the false prophet or dreamer would most likely be made in the presence of others, based on a sign or wonder. This second inducement would likely have transpired behind closed doors and would be launched by a cherished relationship in the veiled places of life. An example of worship of false gods and idolatry done in these surreptitious places can be seen in Deut 27:15: **Cursed is anyone who makes an idol—a thing detestable to the LORD, the work of skilled hands—and sets it up in secret.**

The closest relationships in life's web of interactions could very well be culpable in attempting to seduce fellow covenant companions to desert the worship of Yahweh and turn to other gods. The quandary is that these relationships are where one's greatest loyalty is established. The warning is that seduction could very likely come from among one's most cherished friends. It should be noticed that the seductive voice might perhaps come not simply from your wife, but *the wife of your bosom*, or not simply from your friend, but from *your friend who is like your own life*. A corrupt person is always in a position to exert the strongest influence on those who are in a close, intimate relationship with him or her.

In order to shield against the obstacle of alien sacred influences, Deuteronomy embraces dreadfully ruthless decrees. These declarations are to function as a horrifying prevention. The action prescribed for the person with whom the enticement begins is in essence the same as that for the false religious leader, but it is declared in a fuller fashion. It just may be that this is so, not only for reasons of consequence, but also to take away any pretext that might develop on the basis of the intimacy of the relationship. What is amazing is that the tempter is to be treated with the same severity as the previous inhabitants of the land; they are to be utterly destroyed. Verses 8*b*-10 [9*b*-11 HB] make this very clear: **Show them no pity. Do not spare them or shield them. You must certainly put them to death. Your hand must be the first in putting them to death, and then the hands of all the people. Stone them to death, because they tried to turn you away from the LORD your God, who brought you out of Egypt, out of the land of slavery.** The closeness of the relationship is not to be taken into account in the way the tempter is to be confronted. Those that make the accusations, the close friend or family member, are to take a leading role in carrying out the punishment. To give in to the temptation or to even cover up for it would fail to deal with the source of malevolence in the community. If their verdicts were wrong, then they would bear the guilt.

c. Seduction by Another City (13:12-18 [13-19 HB])

■ **12-18 [13-19 HB]** In the third instance the threat is a community that is full of troublemakers. These are not people that one may disagree with about a variety of issues, but people who go about advocating a sacred substitute for Yahweh. Israel is called to take excessive action against such insolent advocacy because they are a threat to the entire community of God's people. After *inquiring, probing, and investigating* the matter thoroughly, and finding the truth, Israel **must destroy it completely, both its people and its livestock** (v 15 [16 HB]). Verse 15 [16 HB] makes it clear that the brutality of the punishment is so severe that a judicious examination would have to be carried out to authenticate if indeed the matter is true. If the proof is beyond question, then the severest measures are to be taken.

Verse 16 [17 HB] uses the Hebrew word *herem* to describe what should take place with such a city. The penalization for this apostasy of a city is for all intents and purposes the same as the approach taken with the Canaanite cities. Narrative examples of this castigation can be seen in the stories of the defeat of Kings Sihon and Og in Deut 2:26—3:22. Israel "completely destroyed" (3:6) these people and left no survivors. This is a case of *herem*, devoting a community to the ban. This story suggests that Israel is single-minded in its obedience to Yahweh.

Dual themes of Yahweh giving the land and requiring the *herem*, to destroy without survivor, persist in the stories of conquest. The description of the conquest includes the taking of sixty towns and their massive fortification. This detail witnesses to the act of Yahweh and his gift to Israel. A summary of the victories found in Deut 3:8-11 moves primarily away from the kings that are conquered to the land that is given. The narrative asserts that the land is a gift. The might and power of Israel are not the deciding factor in the gift of the land. It is Yahweh, Israel's God, who wins the battle and gives the land. Israel's response to her God can only be to trust, obey, and give thanks. The implication in ch 13 is that an Israelite city has become a Canaanite city in its beliefs, values, and practices.

Everything in such a deviant apostate community is infected by their impure actions. Therefore, **You are to gather all the plunder of the town into the middle of the public square and completely burn the town and all its plunder as a whole burnt offering to the L**ORD **your God. That town is to remain a ruin forever, never to be rebuilt, and none of the condemned things are to be found in your hands** (13:16-17 [17-18 HB]). Even though these are responses within the ancient texts, the act of violence is not a completely satisfactory Christian reading. It should be appropriate to declare that the political and religious threat of foreign cultures with their beliefs and values are to be eliminated. But, because of the teaching and life of Jesus, violence can never be affirmed as an appropriate rejoinder in a Christian interpretation of these sacred texts.

FROM THE TEXT

How are followers of Christ to interpret and exemplify the significance of this passage? Are they to use violence because the text not only encourages them to do so but also commands them to do so? In fact, they are to annihilate religious leaders, family and friends, and even whole cities. Are they to act as secret police, watching their own families and friends? Or, are they to ignore the passage altogether, because Christ tells his followers to love their enemies? Surely loving one's enemies would mean at least don't kill them. One would presume that this would include the enemies of God. Surely God is powerful enough to take care of God's own enemies. It should be obvious that an interpretive lens is necessary for Christian readers of this challenging passage.

For the Christian reader to begin to grapple with the theological and ethical dimensions of this passage there must be recognition of the threat being addressed. The apparent danger is associated with the possibility of violating the first commandment, "You shall have no other gods before me." The two major divisions of this pericope describe the context for the threat of infidelity. Multiple places for worship concede multiple voices and practices in relation to that worship. Therefore, one place that Yahweh designates for his presence becomes essential for a people determined to be acceptable in beliefs and practices (12:1-32 [12:1—13:1 HB]). Orthodoxy and orthopraxy are necessary if the integrity of a tradition is to be maintained. Alien cultic sites, with their interpretations and rituals, are to be eliminated if communal identity is to be sustained over time.

Deuteronomy 12:29-32 [12:29—13:1 HB] is introduced as a reminder that there is great harm with pagan practices that could so easily habituate the people of God. This section is a type of bridge section that connects the next part of the passage. Hearing and following the voice of Yahweh is necessary if Israel is to be the people of God. Therefore, all other voices claiming to speak for something that is an ultimate concern other than the voice of God must be resisted and even destroyed (13:1-18 [2-19 HB]). Not only is seduction to serve other gods prohibited, but also the very seductive voices must not even be tolerated. Israel is duty-bound to hear and follow the voice of Yahweh alone; all other voices claiming priority over the voice of their God are to be resisted and destroyed.

Infidelity to Yahweh is a danger that is brought on by a lack of both orthodoxy and orthopraxy. A people believe what they "do" and do what they "believe." Walter Brueggemann's contemporary equivalents to the challenges of sustained loyalty to God are interesting. He understands these as religious people who do not have regard for the faith tradition, because they see it as narrow, harsh, and exclusivist. He also sees those who threaten the identity of the faith community as those who are willing to compromise the beliefs and practices of the community of memory based upon the cultural norms of the surrounding culture. He finally understands the final group to be those who are outside the faith tradition who lack any understanding of the faith itself (2001, 154-55).

It is all too easy to cast off any person or group that disagrees with one's own hermeneutical position. All too often they are labeled as alien or even removed from their place within the community because of a differing interpretation. This text seems to be a warrant for such coercive activity, but it must be remembered that Jesus and the prophets before him, as well as reformers down through the heritage of the church, have all been persecuted by the very people of God that are claiming to speak for God. Many times the "new voice" is an old voice that only seems new because it hasn't been heard for a long time.

The question that should prompt the thoughtful Christian reader is: How can the faith community remain faithful to its historic convictions without resorting to violence? The church historically understands canon, creed, and apostolic secession or history of interpretation to be resources in the exclusive worship of the triune God. What is of greatest importance in this passage is securing the witness to the true identity of God. Who is the God that the Christian community is to worship in praise and practice? The canon can be read from a variety of interpretative places; each place will mold a conceptual picture of God for the reader.

The church developed a reading strategy that is her "rule of faith." That rule infuses her historical confession: God's name is Father, Son, and Holy Spirit. This hermeneutical strategy can be traced through the heritage of the church. Sometimes it is well used, and other times it is abandoned. The God of the OT and NT, for Christians, is not different from the one who is revealed to believers in Jesus. His name is Father, Son, and Holy Spirit. God is eternal, relational love. This picture of God must be the centrality of worship and the unity of belief and practice if orthodoxy and orthopraxy are to shape the community of memory known as the church.

B. Honor the Holiness of God's Name (14:1-21)

BEHIND THE TEXT

The laws of Deuteronomy are absorbed in an argument over religious loyalty, which has a very public face that will ultimately shape the identity of the community. In this particular passage, these laws are primarily concerned with dietary practices that differentiate between clean and unclean animals. Are these practices random and arbitrary, or are they related to the exclusive claim of Yahweh upon his people? The dietary bans on certain categories of animals and the permission for other types of animals are framed by a foundational theological pronouncement, "you are a people holy to the LORD your God" (14:2, 21); this declaration describes Israel as holy in her relationship to God. This declaration means that the community of Israel is to reflect the identity of her God, Yahweh. The question that ancient Israel or even contemporary readers will naturally ask is: What does it mean to be a people who are to reflect the character and purpose of God? This passage addressed, at least in part, this very question by putting forward a series of practices that contain both prohibitions and authorizations.

It should also be noted that a similar list of clean and unclean food is found in Lev 11. Because of this and other likenesses, it is probable that this is not a free arrangement of dietary practices but a redacted composition assembled from lists of older dietary practices that already constituted part of a tradition. The listing may have been originally assembled as instruction for priests and then incorporated by the writers of Deuteronomy as appropriate for the whole of Israel. That would make this list an alternative adaptation of a common original source of clean and unclean animals. The purpose of the whole people of Israel would be similar to the role of the priests in Israel. Holiness would define them both. It should also be noted that Deut 14:3-21 is in the grammatical plural "you." This may indicate a later addition to the earliest draft of the text (Cairns 1992, 230). Chapter 14 may be outlined as follows:

1. You Are a Holy People (14:1-2)
2. Eating Gracefully: Clean and Unclean Foods (14:3-21)

IN THE TEXT

1. You Are a Holy People (14:1-2)

■ **1-2** The first two verses of this chapter contain three pronouncements concerning Israel's identity as it relates to her God. She is described as: **children of the LORD your God, a people holy to the LORD your God,** and finally **the LORD has chosen you to be his treasured possession.** What these three statements concerning Israel's identity point to is a unique separation that she enjoys and undertakes in relation to God and from all other people. What should be of special note in these pronouncements is that they are not stated as something that Israel is to accomplish, but as something that is already accomplished by the free grace of God. Israel's status as Yahweh's holy, treasured children is a direct result of the mystery of God's gracious choice. Israel does not achieve her status by any merit of her own.

Deuteronomy takes an important position about Israel, holiness, and the Law; she is commanded to keep the Law because she is holy and not because she hoped to grow into being a holy people. This implies a self-evident characteristic of the concept of holiness in Deuteronomy: it is a fact based upon the free grace of God. Other traditions within the OT understand holiness as an attainment to be achieved. A wonderful example of this can be found in Lev 19:2: "Be holy because I, the LORD your God, am holy." In Leviticus, the people of God are called to be like Yahweh. Deuteronomy is describing the actuality of Israel's holiness because of its special relationship to God, which it cannot evade, because it has been accomplished out of the unique circumstances of the selecting pursuit of Yahweh in her history. It should be very clear that in Deuteronomy, holiness is an act of God's free grace. This does not mean that Israel is free to do what she wanted because of God's free grace, but that her status as the holy people of God is to have a momentous authority upon its social, political, and religious life.

The peculiarity of God's act of free grace necessitated the requirement of unique identity-forming practices. Yahweh's generous act of electing a people is to be enfleshed by the people whose very identity is created by grace. Israel understands that she must practice the habituation of being God's holy, treasured children. Embodiment through consistent obedience to God's gracious commands is the form of life that the people of God are to take. Israel is to reflect her identity as God's own people. The separation that is announced regarding Israel is to be safeguarded within her.

The remainder of the pericope describes a variety of practices that the people of God are to participate in, yet there are two practices within these first two verses that are attended to. These practices are associated with mourning customs of alien religious convictions. Craigie believes that these practices may relate to the mourning of El following Baal's death, the myths and practices of the fertility cult. The ancient text seem to describe El as lacerating himself; therefore, the laceration of the body with the consequent flow of blood is a part of the mourning practices utilized by religions that are in proximity to ancient Israel. In addition to mourning customs, the cuts may have also been a part of the seasonal ritual within the Canaanite fertility cult. In this context this practice may have been a type of magic designed to revitalize the god Baal on whom the fertility of the land is believed to be dependent (Craigie 1976, 229-30). Because Israel is the unique possession of Yahweh, she is prohibited from participating in any practice that is tied to the gods of other people. Yahweh alone is her God, and she is to serve him in unreserved allegiance. Israel is separate from all the people groups of the world; therefore, she must be separate from all of the practices to foreign gods.

2. Eating Gracefully: Clean and Unclean Foods (14:3-21)

■ **3-21** These verses put into words the practices that are connected to the theological claim that is articulated in the first two verses of this chapter as well as v 21: that the people belong to Yahweh and therefore they are holy. The practices found in vv 3-21 are concerned primarily with dietary procedures. The inventory of impure animals (vv 3-8) is followed by declarations regarding those fish and birds that are permissible for consumption (vv 9-10, 20) and a list of those that are not (vv 12-20). Anything not acceptable for utilization is declared a **detestable thing** (v 3). Verses 3-21 do not give explicit explanations concerning the significance of these kosher practices, but it does link them to the theological claim in the first two verses as well as v 21.

Some readers of these dietary practices understand them to have reference to public health concern. They rationalize that they are threats of a variety of bacterial contaminants linked with shellfish, pork, and other prohibited meats. The argument would be that kosher regulations are ancient Israel's parallel to public health regulations today. This interpretation would make these dietary practices primarily concerned with hygiene issues.

Other readers explain these laws in relation to pagan religions. It is clear that the regulations in the first two verses are connected to the pagan practices of the fertility cult, and this should point as a possible clue to the purpose of the other practices found in the remaining verses, especially since they end in v 21 with another reference to the holiness of the people of God. Many of the animals that are categorized as unclean have an important role in pagan cults. An obvious example of this is the prospect of swine used as a cult animal in Canaanite culture (Biddle 2003, 243). All animals that are used by pagan worship practices are not eliminated however, and the best example of this is the bull, which is considered clean by ancient Israel and yet is notably linked to the worship of Baal.

The reader will notice that some of the creatures that are considered unclean are flesh eaters. This might imply some sort of taboo that is associated with the boundary between life and death, which has already been addressed in v 1 as it banned self-mutilation practices in relation to the dead. It should also be observed that some organisms are regarded as unclean because they are presumed to violate the law of the orderliness of nature. "Four-footed animals are normal to the pattern of creation if they are cloven-hoofed and cud-chewing. Animals that do not conform to this dual condition seem somehow to threaten the orderliness of creation as appointed by God" (Cairns 1992, 141). This would seem to connect with the creation images of the priestly tradition that understood separation as the means by which chaos is kept at bay.

So, what is the ultimate purpose of these practices in ancient Israel? There may have been multiple reasons by the time these were collected into this list by the theologians of this tradition, but a hint to its purpose may be found in the use of the Hebrew word that is translated **detestable thing** (*tô'ēbâ*) in v 3 (see also 7:25; 12:31). In 7:25 and 12:31 this word is applied to the worship of foreign gods, a matter that is repugnant to Yahweh. Given the literary and theological context of ch 14, it seems likely that the ultimate purpose of the dietary restrictions is to determine and preserve the communal identity of the people named Israel. Israel is to reflect the character and purpose of her God, which is an orderly separation within creation for the sake of life. Because Israel is a holy people to her God, she is to rehearse the whole of her life as an alternative to the people groups around her, and this includes how she eats. One could say she is to eat gracefully.

FROM THE TEXT

In Deuteronomy, the holiness of Israel is understood as a gracious gift of Yahweh to Israel. This gift, however, is to be embodied in a particular form of life among the people of God. Holy people are to organize their daily lives as a way of maintaining the distinctive separation of clean and unclean, of sacred and profane. The mixing of these elements brings on the destructive powers of chaos and death. A great example of this can be observed in the opening chapters of Genesis where the act of creation is seen in a series of separations (darkness from light, water from water, day from night, land from water, etc.) that eventually lead to the separation of the Sabbath. The powers of chaos and death ensue as these areas of separation are transgressed and the ultimate chaotic waters engulf the biosphere in the great flood. The purpose of Yahweh for his creation is life, and life is impossible when the lines of separation are crossed. Dietary practices are a daily routine of habituating the people of God to the realization of God's purpose for creation.

What might this possibly mean for Christian communities in the twenty-first century? Does it mean that they must refrain from eating these particular unclean creatures, or is something else at stake in this list of dietary practices for contemporary Christian readers? The NT begins to give the Christian reader an interpretive lens through which to interpret this passage.

Dietary practices and the issue of clean and unclean confronted early followers of Jesus. Peter's dream in Acts 10:10-16 is concerned with these practices. Peter has a vision and is instructed to eat indiscriminately from unclean and clean animals, but he refuses. The heavenly voice instructs Peter, in v 15, not to pollute what God cleanses. The point of this command should be understood in light of the quandary of involvement with the Gentiles, not necessarily unclean food. Although it is unlawful for a Jew to associate with non-Jews because of their uncleanness, God removes this obstacle. God shows Peter that Gentiles can no longer be regarded as unclean, which frees Peter to come to Cornelius' home.

Jesus also addresses this matter of defilement in Mark 7. This passage has three expressions of Jesus' teaching on the subject of defilement and purity. The first is a confrontation with the Pharisees and some of the scribes, when they noticed that some of Jesus' disciples are eating with defiled hands. The second setting is when Jesus addresses the crowd beginning with v 14. The final occurrence is Jesus explaining the issue to his disciples. The same word group that is used in Acts 10 for unclean food is used in Mark 7 in both noun and verb forms. Jesus appears to summarize his clarification of clean and unclean in v 15. He says: "Nothing outside a person can defile them by going into them. Rather, it is what comes out of a person that defiles them." This comment of Jesus makes the observation that at the very least adherence to the dietary laws, for followers of Jesus, is not mandatory.

Does this mean that earlier Christians are not concerned with the practices of purity? Of course early Christians are concerned with purity. The apostle Paul expresses this multiple times in his writings. Two great examples are found in the book of Romans. In ch 6 the apostle uses the practice of baptism to describe the alternative life of the new reality in Christ. He writes,

> What shall we say, then? Shall we go on sinning so that grace may increase? By no means! We are those who have died to sin; how can we live in it any longer? Or don't you know that all of us who were baptized into Christ Jesus were baptized into his death? We were therefore buried with him through baptism into death in order that, just as Christ was raised from the dead through the glory of the Father, we too may live a new life. (Vv 1-4)

The remainder of the chapter argues for the life of holiness based upon the alternative reality brought about by baptism. Baptism is a participation in Christ's death, burial, and resurrection, "so we too might walk in newness of life" (6:4 NRSV). "Walk" implies distinct ethical behavior. It means the life of holiness.

The apostle Paul also makes use of the language of holiness in Rom 12. In the opening two verses he calls on believers to present their embodied lives to God as holy and acceptable. He then goes on in v 2 to implore the Roman believers to resist conforming to this present age, but he calls them to be transformed habitually by the renewal of their minds. He writes: "Do not conform to the pattern of this world, but be transformed by the renewing of your mind. Then you will be able to test and approve what God's will is—his good, pleasing and perfect will." The transformation of the mind into the new age brought about by Christ is to be habituated not by dietary practices but by the gifts and practices of the kingdom. Humility and cooperation will be hallmark practices of the participants in the new age brought about by Christ. Even though these kinds of practices are very different from dietary practices, they still function to differentiate the followers of Christ from the culture around them.

Detectable practices are indispensable to preserve and reveal the uniqueness of the community of faith in the work of upholding God's purpose for creation. The people of God are called to live in a particular way, guarding the life of the community and individual from uncleanness and pollution that not only will threaten its own existence but will endanger the coherent fabric of the entire creation. This passage articulates the distinctiveness of God and the

154

resulting distinctiveness of his people. The essential question the people of God must ask today is: What does that distinctiveness look like in the twenty-first century? For Christians, the answer must begin with Jesus.

C. Regulations Concerning the Tithe (14:22-29)

BEHIND THE TEXT

This segment can either be considered with ch 14 or the ensuing sections through 16:17. The focus of this section is on the cyclic observances that Israel is to practice once she successfully inhabits the land. It appears that this small segment is a transitional or hinge section. Statutes having to do with the tithe do not seem to signify a coherent arrangement of practices. It is difficult to determine whether the tithe every third year is the customary tithe or a supplementary offering for the needy in the community. Legislation regarding the offering of the firstborn male of the flocks is the subject of 15:19-23. Chapter 26 gives detailed instructions on the offering of the firstfruits (see vv 1-15). Biddle points out that the relationship between the offerings of firstfruits, the sacrifice of the firstborn in the flocks, and tithes is unclear in Deuteronomy (2003, 251). Ian Cairns writes:

> It is striking that the Book of the Covenant makes no mention of the tithe, but does discuss the offering of the first fruits. It may be surmised, that in the course of historical development the "first fruits" came to be interpreted and calculated as 10 percent of the total produce. (1992, 143)

All of this points to the probability that Deuteronomy did not have a fixed understanding of this practice in the life of the community.

The centralization of worship is used as an occasion to alter the people's social experience and also to provide an income that advances the joy of worshipping Yahweh and a social safety net for those without needed resources. Israelites are instructed in this passage "to set aside a tenth of all that your fields produce each year" (v 22). This practice, in Deuteronomy, integrates both a religious and a secular dimension of life. This would mean that the secular couldn't be separated from the theological facet of the community's life. The way a people live and the way a people believe are not separate issues, but aspects of one another.

Deuteronomy 14:22-29 is divided into two major sections. The first section (vv 22-27) deals with the individual celebration with the tithe for the Israelite, his family, and the Levite. The second section (vv 28-29) deals with the tithe on the third year. This tithe is specifically designated for the economically marginalized in the community.

I. The Individual Celebration with the Tithe for the Israelite, His Family, and the Levite (14:22-27)

■ **22-27** The tithe, in this passage, is a jubilant celebration of the fulfillment of Yahweh's promise of a land flowing with milk and honey. All of the harvest as well as the firstlings of the flocks and herds are to be marked off as a tithe to Yahweh. The firstborn offspring of the flocks and herds signified the new life and provision that Yahweh bequeaths. It is as it should be that the firstlings would be designated for a celebratory meal of thanksgiving. Yahweh's blessings are the means for life.

On the face of it, this practice seems like a heavy levy placed upon the people, yet life's provision is acknowledged as a divine gift. Verses 22-27 attend to the unique celebration that an individual Israelite and his family are to have in the company of Yahweh. The family's enjoyment of a meal in Yahweh's presence is a unique contribution to the sacramental regulations that the book of Deuteronomy provides.

Israel assumes that Yahweh gives the gift of the land and its produce; therefore, she is to remember these gracious gifts with joyfulness. Yahweh is the definitive owner of the land, and his gift of the land to Israel did not mean that he stopped holding the title to it. The ancient worshipper acknowledged God's ownership and provision by eating the tithe jubilantly in the presence of God. To practice the tithe reminded the member of the congregation of Israel that even though there is collaboration with God, the harvest of crops and flocks is ultimately an act of receiving and not predominantly producing. The celebrant cooperates in a life-sustaining cycle, but only God has definitive influence. The practice of tithing reaffirmed that the people of God live from gift.

A part of the purpose of the tithe is tutorial. The yearly trek of giving and receiving is used to inculcate the people on the subject of the character of their God. Yahweh is the true Owner of the land and Giver of life. In addition to the virtue of gratitude, Israel learns to fear Yahweh (**revere**), as is articulated in v 23. The fear of God is not to take the shape of panic, as one has when one anticipates tragedy, but to recognize that God is the one who gives and gives again. "Reverence" would be the best word to describe the fear of the Lord. The tithe helps the people not only recognize the gifts of God in their own lives but also witness God taking the gifts of the tithe and turning them back again as gifts to those in need. This is apparent in vv 27 and 29. This virtue of the fear of God must be habituated within the very ethos of the community and the character of the individual. Tithing habituates the virtues of gratitude, reverence, and generosity.

Verse 24 points to a difficulty created **because the place where the LORD will choose to put his Name is so far away**. The fruitage had to be transported to the place where Yahweh chooses to place his name. To relocate the foodstuffs became problematic because of geography. Consequently, a different decree, dealing with this convention, is made for the benefit of those who live a long way from the central sanctuary and might have had to transport their tithes this distance. Israel is told to **exchange your tithe for silver, and take the silver with you and go to the place the LORD your God will choose. Use the silver to buy whatever you like: cattle, sheep, wine or other fermented drink, or anything you wish. Then you and your household shall eat there in the presence of the LORD your God and rejoice** (vv 25-26). By this instruction the people obtained authorization to sell their tithe where they lived and to use the earnings to buy at the sanctuary what they needed for the sacrificial celebration.

Narcissism can have no place in the life of the people of God. Enjoyment of the land leads to appreciation of the persons at the sanctuary, which in turn necessitates a derivative reaction of openhandedness and generosity to those who have no direct approach to the good things of the land. The special provision for the Levites in vv 27-29 is peculiar to the tradition of Deuteronomy. The Levite is listed with the poor, because Levites have no land allotment of their own.

2. The Tithe on the Third Year (14:28-29)

■ **28-29** These verses deal with the tithe on the third year. The correlation of the cultic tithe proper to the tithe disbursed every three years for the poor at the local level is by no means easy to understand. The reader asks: Is this to be an extra tithe for the poor, or is the tithe of the third year designated for the poor? Literarily, the passage itself implies that it is one and the same tithe that is being discussed; it is only the implementation of it that is modified.

Many facets of the usual practice of the tithe are continued in the third year with two new features. The first feature is that the tithe is not brought to the place where Yahweh places his name but is kept within the local community of the worshipper. This would have a significant impact upon the landless in a local community. The second facet is that the practice is intensely material. The sacramental practice is transformed into an act that is concerned with the poor in a local village. One can imagine what a ten percent infusion of extra resources into the local community for the sake of the poor could accomplish. People with land, who reap the blessing of the land, bring an offering for the landless, which has no resource for the blessing that the land provides.

This specification for the tithe is significant because it provides for the use of the tithe without its coming to the sanctuary. Every third year, instead, the goods allocated as tithe are put in safekeeping in the localities as part of

14:28-29

an arrangement for the well-being of everyone in the community. The aim of the decree is to bestow an alternative means of access to Israel's wealth, in the absence of their control of land. The land is Yahweh's gift to the people. This gift gives gifts of provision; it is a land flowing with milk and honey. But what are people to do who do not have access to the blessing of the land? This social ritual is intended to prevent the impoverishment of the marginal within the local community.

The ruling that the tithe of every third year is to be wholly given for the benefit of the Levites, the aliens, the fatherless, and the widows marks a regulation that recognized that these people groups are in special need of support. An indicator of Israel's obedience can be detected by her response to the directives of caring for the Levites, aliens, orphans, and widows. As she cares for those who have the least, she demonstrates the gracious character of her God. One might say that in Deuteronomy the Levites, aliens, widows, and orphans represent Yahweh to Israel the way the least of these represented Jesus in Matt 25:34-46.

FROM THE TEXT

The theological vision of Deuteronomy makes it clear that God does not have need of anything, including the tithe. The land already belongs to God, and all that is produced from the land is his. Israel is warned to never forget that it is Yahweh who leads her out of the land of bondage into the land flowing with milk and honey. Israel is not an owner but a steward of the land. It is Yahweh who causes the land to be fruitful. The gods may need to be manipulated by gifts and sacrifices, but Yahweh is not a needy God who depends upon gifts. God has no needs to be tended to or satisfied.

Any time giving is tied to a needy God or a way of manipulating him, it should be obvious that this is not the God that the sacred Scriptures testify to as the Creator, Sustainer, and Redeemer of the world. If God does not need the resources produced from the land, then what is a faithful reading of this passage concerning the tithe? It should be apparent that the tithe is tied to the gift of the land. It is from the produce of the land that one gives a tithe, and it is for the sake of those who do not participate in the immediate bounty of the land that the tithe will also benefit. The tithe is bound to the gift of the land, which means that in a contemporary setting the tithe is joined to those who benefit from the resources that providence provides. God, through external circumstances, gives and gives again.

There are two major virtues that the practice of tithing is intended to habituate: gratitude and generosity. The opening section of this passage describes the joy of communing with family and friends in the presence of God. To bring the offering and to eat in the presence of God is to joy-

14:22-29

fully acknowledge that the bounty of life comes from the hidden hand of God's providential care. All that one has is a gift; therefore, there is ultimately only one response to grace and it is gratitude. The tithe is a practice whereby people are enabled to recognize the immensity of the gift that sustains life.

From such a grateful heart, generosity flows. One does not give in order to receive, even if that reception is nothing other than a sense of self-righteousness. One gives as an act of gratitude, and God takes the act of gratitude and gives again. Grace is not bottled, but flows through the conduit of gratitude. The stipulations within the practice of tithing in Deuteronomy allow for what might be described as a new social reality. It is interesting that in the Greek language of the NT, the word group that describes giving is also the word group for grace, thanksgiving, and joy. To acknowledge the grace that is given in the provisions of life brings not only gratitude but also plenteous grace for all in the providence of God.

D. Liberation (15:1-18)

BEHIND THE TEXT

A straightforward reading of the text, in the storied context of Deuteronomy, describes the challenge to those who are moving from a nomadic way of life to a settled way of life. This challenging form of life also is transformative on an economic level. As Israel moved into the land the economic structure begins to shift from an egalitarian pattern of life that operated in the social arrangement of extended families and clan, where property, if it is owned, is largely held in trust throughout the group, to a land-owning economy. In this type of economic arrangement the acquiring of more and more land and the capital that comes with it are prominent features. The amassing of wealth and the acquisition of influence and power are given to the few; for the less fortunate who make up the bulk of the population, the path to economic ruin and destitution is the way forward. These circumstances are entwined in a changing economic model that allows for the accrual of debt. Debt is the new Pharaoh in a land-owning economy.

Deuteronomy 15 is dominated by a Sabbatical pattern. The narrative implies that the people, who have successfully arrived in the land of promise, are to go beyond the Sabbath practice to simply rest one day a week. They are also to enact a Sabbath policy that would allow each person in Israel to be emancipated to experience Yahweh's gift of rest and the renewal of life in the land. This is not the only text in the OT that addresses the issues of the poor and indebtedness in relation to the Sabbath. This directive for the year of debt release is similar to the laws located in Exod 21 and 23. It should be noticed that in Exod 23 the Sabbath has a vigorous social-political component. This stipulation for the seventh year matches other regulations in ancient Israel of not farming the land every seventh year. The harvest, which grows of itself in the Sabbath Year, is for the poor. It appears that the law of the fallow year is formulated into a policy relating to the debt that has crippled the poor and needy.

The Sabbatical Year is linked to the Sabbath day. It should be remembered that the Sabbath is a celebration of God's authority over time and space. The priestly tradition states unambiguously that it is God who creates the world (Gen 1—2), and the Deuteronomistic tradition makes it unmistakable that it is Yahweh who emancipates Israel from Egyptian bondage (Deut 5). Rest from the bondage of Pharaoh, and ultimately chaos, allows for life. Therefore, Israel is to keep the Sabbath and the Sabbath Year holy. The Sabbath and life and its renewal belong to God.

The concept of emancipation is not limited to the Bible in the ancient world.

> It was a common practice for kings, soon after their accession, to issue decrees of "justice," proclaiming "freedom" . . . by annulling debts and freeing debt slaves. Hammurabi's law code apparently tried to bring some system into this practice by requiring the release of debt slaves after three years' service. (McConville 2002, 257)

For the biblical community, Sabbatical release is performed on an ordered basis as a component of a larger political system. The community alleviates debt and want, not by arbitrary acts of generosity, but through political policy and practice. Sabbath political policies are designed to provide for persons in need.

Deuteronomy 15:1-18 may be outlined as follows:
1. Regulations Concerning the Remission of Debts (15:1-6)
2. Disposition of Those Who Own the Debt Owed (15:7-11)
3. Liberation from Slavery (15:12-18)

IN THE TEXT

1. Regulations Concerning the Remission of Debts (15:1-6)

■ 1-6 These verses are controlled by the idea of canceling debt. The guiding principle of the cancelation of debt is not some self-help plan that individuals are to undertake on their own behalf; neither is it an act of individual charity demonstrated by a person who has a soft spot for the poor, but this practice is to be a civic policy that is to be implemented for the sake of social justice within the community. The modern reader must realize that this civic practice is not a call to be more generous on simply a personal level but is a civic policy to redistribute resources and opportunity at a public level.

In v 1, the word that is translated **cancel** (*šĕmiṭṭâ*; from *šāmaṭ*) literally means *let fall*, and it occurs in Exod 23:11 in relation to the cultivation of the land. The interpretation of *šĕmiṭṭâ*, in this setting, as cancelation of debts is drawn from the literary context. *Šĕmiṭṭâ* and its derivatives are used five times in these opening three verses: once in Deut 15:1, three times in v 2, and once in v 3. When a word group is used repeatedly in ancient texts it is attempting to covey the importance of the concept. Release is critical to the meaning of this passage. So what is released? Is it the insolvent person or the promise to repay that is discharged? Most likely it is the creditor who gives up a certain right in respect to the loan, which ultimately liberates the person in bondage of the situation caused by debt. This is not to be done occasionally, based upon the subjective decisions of an individual, but is to be enacted regularly within the political reality of the community.

Proclamation of Yahweh's remission suggests a public declaration as a religious occasion. This religious event is to shape the social-political fabric of the community. One could say that the political practice of remission is a war on poverty. There is no separation between the religious framework and the social milieu, and there is also no private enactment that is to take place; this practice is visible and public. Yet, just how much of this law is ever enacted in Israel's history is not clear.

Verse 3 allows debt to remain against a **foreigner** (*nēkar*), but the Law precludes the retention of debt against a **fellow Israelite** (*'āḥ*, usually translated "brother"). The oneness of Israel is emphasized by the sevenfold occurrence of the term *'āḥ* in this passage, which conveys the close solitary within the covenant community. Nelson suggests that the "foreigner" in this text is not a disadvantaged resident alien but most likely a merchant. In that case, the "relationship would be commercial, not familial or neighborly" (2002b, 195). The contrast between a foreigner and kindred is a characteristic concern of Deuteronomy and strengthens the motivation.

15:1-6

Verses 4-5 are one sentence. This means that these two verses convey a singular thought. The announcement in v 4 is that **there need be no poor people among you.** For this announcement to be understood it should be interpreted as an appeal. This initial exhortation is clarified by two further elucidations: **he will richly bless you, if only you fully obey the Lord your God and are careful to follow all these commands.** This conditional declaration is governed by the response of the people to the commands of God. Careful obedience to Yahweh's command would effectively eliminate poverty. How is this so? Is this a guarantee based upon the idea that Yahweh can trust those who are munificent with more to be charitable, or is it that the openhandedness of people results in creating a culture where greater blessing is extended to all?

161

This conditional appeal, which is governed by the substance of v 5, is countered by v 11, **There will always be poor people in the land.** The fact that the poor shall never cease from the midst of the land points to the failure of character in human beings and the failure of communities to enact the just politics of Yahweh. The fullness of Yahweh's blessing is contingent upon the completeness of Israel's obedience; thus vv 4-5 are an encouragement and enticement to strive for the abundance of the provision of Yahweh that is in the very gift of the promised land. These words point to the close connection that exists between the external affairs in the future and the acts of fidelity and obedience in the present. The prosperity, described in v 6, is a result of the blessing of God, but God's blessing is contingent upon the inner health of the nation, to which the requirements stated in this chapter are directed.

Verse 6 makes a powerful claim, that Israel shall have power over many nations and that they will not be governed over by them. The assurance of this passage is that Israel's place among the nations is one of preeminence. Yahweh's blessing of the people who are obedient to this command will allow for them to prosper and flourish and even rule other nations. The pattern of no brother accumulating permanent debt is extended to the nation. This will permit Israel to realize the standing of an independent world supply of resources.

The manner of ruling that is described as economic supremacy is not necessarily domination achieved through force of arms. Lending and borrowing are financial nomenclatures. Israel is advised that she will **lend to many nations** (v 6) but that she will not **borrow** from any of them. Israel will become a major economic power in the region and thus be able to exert influence over other nations. Financial autonomy will allow for Israel's supremacy in international relations. The people of God will operate as a lord and never as a slave. This claim is not based upon the industriousness of Israel but upon their being obedient to the economic policies of Yahweh as they relate to the poor and needy.

2. Disposition of Those Who Own the Debt Owed (15:7-11)

■ **7-11** This subsection expands the social practice expressed in the opening verses of ch 15 by seeking to shape not only the behavior of the community but also the affections of the people within the community. The metaphors **hand** and **heart** (v 10) for the outer embodied actions and the internal dispositions are connected in these verses. The social practice of the year of release is not to be something that is grudgingly complied with but is to be an expression of the ethos of the community and also the character of persons within the community. Generosity must be habituated within the very nature of the people.

The major problem that many people with resources have with public policies like this is the improbability of recovering the full value of the loan.

The loan's value is diminished progressively by the proximity of the Sabbatical Year to the time the debt is incurred. Cancellation of the debt would not involve the loss of the whole loan, but only what remained outstanding. If the debt is incurred in proximity to the year of release, then the value is lost to the person who is in the position of loaning the resource. This could easily cause resentment and selfish behavior.

Verse 7 addresses this very real possibility and the ensuing attitude that is involved. It states: *Do not harden your heart or close your hand toward your needy neighbor.* The subsequent two verses advocate the contrasting response in both external deed: **be openhanded and freely lend them whatever they need**, and internal thinking: **be careful not to harbor this wicked thought**. Finally, v 10 sustains the appeal to the whole person when it says: **Give generously to them and do so without a grudging heart**. This portion of the passage finishes with the desired action: **be openhanded toward your fellow Israelites who are poor and needy in your land.**

The argument of this passage is strengthened by the incentive that Yahweh is **giving** the land to Israel (v 7). This is a major theological concept in Deuteronomy. The land and the resources that come from it are gifts that people receive from Yahweh, not a proprietorship that they earned. God freely gives to Israel, so Israel should give freely. Gift or grace implies responsibility within the biblical tradition. The responsibility of the people, for the gifts that Yahweh gives, is that these gifts be used for the well-being of all persons within the covenantal community.

A clear warning is given to those who have resources: if one refuses to help the poor, then the needy neighbor might cry to Yahweh and culpability ensues (v 9). The cry of the poor provokes Yahweh to find the oppressor **guilty of sin**. The presupposition of this passage is that all dealings are never between two parties, but that they are covenantal, and therefore they take place in the presence of Yahweh.

A final motivation is given to the Israelite who has the ability to liberate through generosity. Yahweh will bless them in all of their work and in all that they undertake. Since assistance to the needy is like God's help to the needy and demonstrates grateful appreciation for the blessing of Yahweh, Yahweh will reward generosity with blessing on all the lender's undertakings (v 10). This is most probably not a motivational promise that is attempting to appeal to the greed of individuals in order to get them to be generous. Most likely this motivational clause is stating a fact that in a generous community, where the blessings of some are extended to all, the blessings of all are poured out upon the whole of the community. This seems to be the economic way with families and smaller communities; perhaps this is also the way with the whole of Israel, and perhaps even the world.

3. Liberation from Slavery (15:12-18)

■ **12-18** This section of the passage has to do with men and women who become slaves because they are unable to pay their debts. Once exchange of goods through a monetary system is used, debt could lead a person and/or a family into severe need and bondage. If a person's debt becomes extreme, the consequence might well be that the debtor and/or the debtor's family members would be forced to enter into servitude.

In ancient communities a person who amasses debt is required to work it off as a bondservant. Many times people would build up so much debt that they would never be able to pay off the obligation. In some way these people became servants without end, or in other words, they became slaves. The practice revealed in this passage considers debt as something that must not hold a person or a family captive in perpetuity. Seven years, no matter how great the debt, is the limit of this form of enslavement. The obligation of this social order safeguards persons from the vicious cycle of continuing servitude. The policy of openhandedness is to symbolize the values of the politics of Yahweh.

Apparently, this generosity is because the landless workers as well as the landowners enjoy the status of brother. Verse 12 shuns the term "slave" and uses the term ***brother*** for the impoverished person. This seems to establish the equal standing of all people within the community of Israel. The phrase is literally ***your brother, whether a Hebrew or a Hebress.*** The term ***Hebrew/ Hebress*** is thought to refer to a landless class with Israel, echoing an older sociological meaning. However, it is likelier that the term itself is picked up from Exod 21:2, where the word may indeed retain a sociological nuance, and is used here as part of the concern to establish the equality of men and women in terms of the law of release (McConville 2002, 262).

In keeping with the radicalization of the Sabbath principle observed in the units immediately preceding, Deuteronomy adds the requirement that freedmen be sent out with liberal provision (v 14). This is a significant expansion of the Sabbatical legislation concerning the manumission of slaves in Exod 21:1-6. The rationale or motivation for this manner of release reminds the householder that, in essence, he, too, is a freedman. The landowner is to **remember that you were slaves in Egypt and the Lord your God redeemed you. That is why I give you this command today** (Deut 15:15). In addition to this positive injunction, Deuteronomy warns against begrudging the gifts of freedom and stake to begin a new life.

Verses 13-14 instruct the landowners to give the freed servant, man or woman, many sheep and abundant grain. They are not to go out empty-handed, because that would only exacerbate their circumstances, since they did not receive any income during their time of servitude. The paradigm for this may be the provisions that were provided by the Egyptians, when they released the

Hebrews from slavery (see Exod 12:35-36). The provision in Deut 15 is not jewelry but produce from the land of promise. This provision does not demonstrate that the person being released is landless, but it implies that the person has someplace to go.

Once again, in Deut 15:15, the exodus from Egypt is used as an incentive for a landlord to be a generous and liberating benefactor. The identity narrative of the people's origin arises out of slavery. Israel is not a bona fide people until Yahweh acts on their behalf. The practice of liberating people in the Sabbatical Year is both a fitting response to God's generous act of liberation and an extension of that same liberating grace. Life in the land should be marked by freedom, which has its roots in Israel's exodus experience.

Verses 16-17 are one sentence, with v 16 providing the setting for the action described in v 17. Verse 16 begins with a circumstantial clause, which points to a possibility that may occur. This postscript sanctions the possibility that a bondservant may renounce freedom and remain in servitude permanently. These verses describe an emergency measure that could allow an option for a Hebrew to stay in service if he or she so chooses. In these cases, he or she is free to make a choice and become a permanent servant in the master's household. The symbol of this choice is the piercing of the ear, and this becomes an enduring insignia of this preference.

The motivations mentioned for refusing emancipation reflect a more benevolent state of affairs than those pictured in Exod 21:3-4. In Exodus, the fundamental incentive for continued servitude is that the wife and children continued in bondage as the master's possessions. The dilemma requires that the released slave must choose between his freedom and his family. In Deut 15 this dilemma is not mentioned. It could also entail a variety of other circumstances. For a female slave the likelihood that she could prefer to remain in slavery may be more deep-seated for a couple of reasons. First, her husband or family may not be free to go with her or she may not have a family to go to. This would make her vulnerable economically in a way that a male would not be. Though the reasons for this choice may be many, Deut 15 names but one: love.

The final verse of this passage refers back to the other example of a bondservant who chooses to leave the household and is now a free person (Deut 15:18). Owners are not to be resentful of the discharged servant. In fact, they are not even to grumble about the matter. What is interesting about this verse is that it entreats the rich beyond the strict requirements of the Law. Their affections are to be of such a nature that the very way they perceive is shaped by the care for the needy. Meager legalistic conventionality is not the goal of the people of God. God aspires for an honorable people who are habituated in the virtues of righteousness and justice.

There are circumstances that are so overwhelming that they produce bondage in both groups of people and individuals. These forms of captivity take a variety of expressions in the course of history. Israel's historical experience of Egyptian slavery is the prototype for all manifestations of oppression. Likewise, her mass departure from Egypt is a mysterious triumph that characterizes each and every escape from the clutches of domination. Over and over again, Israel pictures emancipation coming by way of the veiled presence of the one who sets her free from Egypt.

For whatever reason, God does not choose to act in the world in autonomous ways, but he works through partnership with people. Moses is Yahweh's collaborator in the liberation of Israel from Egypt, and Yahweh utilizes these same unfettered people and their descendants in freeing others from further assortments of captivity. Deuteronomy 15:1-18 is a set of policies and practices that organize the descendants of slaves into the ongoing mission of liberation. These descendants of slaves believed that the purpose of God was to bless people in order to be a blessing to others. Israel would tell stories that reinforced the value of generosity and buttress the belief that blessings are not to be horded, but extended to the needy. Yahweh offered blessing not simply through random acts of kindness but through the structural practices of the community.

The misfortune of being sold into bondage, either by one's own miscarriages or the hardship that befalls a family through the accidents of history, is not to become a perpetual condemnation to hopelessness. God's people have an alternative political reality, the political reality of the year of release. It could be said that Sabbath, in all of its forms, is at the heart of the politics of Yahweh. The Sabbath Year trains a community in practices that display God's own character and purpose for his people and the world. Debt cancellation is not an isolated claim that a sovereign might declare, but it is to be the centerpiece of an alternative vision for a community formed by the politics of Yahweh. When a community conforms to the policy and practice of the Sabbath Year, it becomes a community of hope; it carries out the very mission of Yahweh whose name signifies promise.

This moral vision brings hope to the hopeless and helps the helpless. If the vision of Deut 15 has its way, there will never be a permanent class of people who are hopelessly and perpetually in debt. One cannot overemphasize how extreme and yet how vital this practice is in the larger pattern of Israel's moral values. When Cain asked, "Am I my brother's keeper?" (Gen 4:9), the overwhelming answer of the biblical tradition is "Yes, you are!" People, with their hopes and dreams and fears and dreads, in the covenant community are their "brother's keeper." Neighborly love is the purpose of a community shaped by the policies and practices of the God who blesses and liberates.

But neighbor love is not first and foremost an emotion, but a political course of action. In the seventh year, when the land is metaphorically returned to its true proprietor, the economy established on that land is also surrendered again to God's jurisdiction. The creditors acknowledge that their right to their wealth is not unlimited but always within the context of another's needs. They are therefore expected to join forces in the restoration of economic equilibrium by relinquishing some of their wealth in support of those who have need. The Sabbatical release indicates that the people of God are to normalize their economy with the highest attention given to the needs and rights of the poor and disadvantaged.

So how does the church begin to embody this text? There are a few key assumptions that many contemporary evangelicals hold that initially must be addressed. First, the church must take on the issue of spiritualizing every text or religious practice. This passage is not addressed predominantly to anything that is disembodied, but to embodiment. People are to do something about the issue of debt and poverty, not just "feel" differently. There is no question that individual affections are called into question with reference to resentment and greed, but they are subsequent issues to the subject matter of reallocation of resources.

Second, the people of God must also realize that this text is primarily addressed to the community and only secondarily to the individual. Individuals are shaped as they participate in the community that practices release and redemption. Persons develop their character within a community of memory as it envisions the "good" and instigates practices that move people toward that ideal. Practices must first and foremost be understood as a political reality for the community. These laws or policies are not simply a legalistic decree but a collection of planned forms of life embodied in a community.

Finally this text is written to the community of faith who receive these ancient words as their Scripture. This means that they have an authority in the community. These words do not have an authority in the larger secular communities that contemporary persons reside. Yet, a very important question must be asked: What impact should these practices have on the larger host culture? The passage seems to imply that Israel will *govern* the nations in a nonmilitaristic way. Perhaps the community of faith is intended to be a shaping factor in the host culture. This influence happens because of the faithful obedience that is enacted within the community, not because of coercive activity outside the community in the host culture. What this may look like for God's people today is to discern who the needy and enslaved are in the host culture, and then to move toward transforming the systemic structures and policies that hold these people captive.

So who are the needy in the twenty-first century? Would mentally and physically challenged persons, single parents, poor children, the elderly, and untrained workers be considered "the needy" in today's world? Lack of education, money, time, and vision enslave entire classes of people, and they condemn them to the captivity of a system of indebtedness. These categories of people, all too often, are surrendered to the bondage of perpetual poverty. In this cycle of poverty, substance abuse, violence, and hopelessness regulate the affections of such people. The balance of the society has their affections normalized as apathy. It seems that people who take seriously the biblical witness should give thoughtful consideration to the ways their community of faith functions and to the wider political issues, such as public education, health care, unemployment resources, and tax policies.

E. The Firstborn of the Livestock (15:19-23)

BEHIND THE TEXT

Instructions pertaining to the sacrifice of firstborn males of the herds and flocks seem isolated to the longer section that is attending to forms of liberation based upon the Sabbath commandment. The crucial expression in respect to Sabbath-keeping is: "Do not put the firstborn of your cows to work, and do not shear the firstborn of your sheep" (v 19). This expression probably indicates the requirements that are associated with keeping the Sabbath. If these regulations belong together, then offerings to God of the firstlings, and acts of justice in the social order of Sabbath liberation belong together. Consequently, a law concerning the dedication of the firstborn domestic animals to Yahweh follows the laws about liberating slaves and caring for the poor.

The literary structure of the passage is in some sense concentric. The outer stratum states that the firstlings are to be consecrated to Yahweh. The later part of this stratum is that blood is not to be eaten, but poured on the ground. This stratum points to the view that life itself belongs to God. The next layer of the structure is that they are to bring the flawless firstlings to the place where Yahweh chooses, and the backend of the structure is that they may eat flawed firstlings in their towns. The center of this structure is that they must not sacrifice firstlings with defects.

1. Sanctify the Firstlings to Yahweh (15:19)
2. Consume the Flawless Firstlings in the Place Yahweh Chooses (15:20)
3. Do Not Sacrifice Firstlings with Flaws (15:21)
4. Consume the Blemished Firstlings in Local Settings (15:22)
5. Never Eat the Blood, but Pour It on the Land (15:23)

168

1. Sanctify the Firstlings to Yahweh (15:19)

■ **19** Verse 19 begins the description of the sacrifice of the firstborn as a festive meal consumed annually. This sacrifice gives the impression that it is connected to Passover. This practice, the offering the firstborn of the flock, links together the ideas of deliverance and fruitfulness. This correlation is described in Exod 13:11-16, which lies in the background of Deut 15:19-23. Yahweh is the God who is both the Redeemer and the Creator. His deliverance from the land of slavery and his providence in the agricultural cycle of fruitfulness are interrelated deeds of gift giving. The people are to offer the firstborn from their flocks and herds to Yahweh as a sign that everything belongs to Yahweh, the one who redeems them when the firstborn of the Egyptians are slaughtered and the firstborn of the Hebrew people are passed over. The practice of offering the firstborn of the flock to Yahweh is a sign that the power of the past, which liberates and provides, can be counted on in the future.

The firstling is the first offspring of an animal that is produced during the life-bearing period of that animal. These animals are not used for their normal economic function within the social context of Israel. For example, a male firstling calf could not be put to work in tilling the ground, and a firstling ram could not be sheared for its wool. The normal economic function of those animals is prohibited. To be more precise, the firstlings would be sacrificed annually and the presenter would take part in the sacrificial meal of thanksgiving. They signified the new life and provision that Yahweh bestows. These firstlings also signal that all fruitfulness that follows also comes from the hand of Yahweh. It is as it should be, that the firstlings are designated for a celebratory meal of thanksgiving. Yahweh's blessings are the means for life.

The firstling male is not simply slaughtered, but **set apart** to Yahweh. The word translated **set apart** is from the Hebrew word group *qādaš* ("to make holy"). In this context, it means to treat the animal as belonging to Yahweh. The true Owner of the land and all that is in the land is the God who promises to the ancestors this land flowing with milk and honey.

2. Consume the Flawless Firstlings in the Place Yahweh Chooses (15:20)

■ **20** These animals are to be eaten in the central sanctuary where Yahweh chooses. So what is the difference between eating meat consecrated to Yahweh and eating meat that has not been consecrated? Another way of saying this is: What is the purpose of the sacrifice itself? The sacrifice **set apart** to Yahweh at the place of Yahweh's choosing is not because of a privation in Yahweh. God does not need meat to survive. God is self-sufficient and depends on nothing. Eating consecrated meat functions as an opportunity to share the meal of friendship with God. This meal is the jubilant feasting of the people of God because God redeems them through the exodus and provides for them in the land of promise. Their worship and feasting is an opportunity for fellowship, thanksgiving, and unreserved joy.

3. Do Not Sacrifice Firstlings with Flaws (15:21)

■ **21** These verses appear to be a criterion that shields the people from offering unsuitable sacrifices. It is possible that a firstling may be less than perfect, but this firstborn should never be offered to Yahweh. Such an animal is unlike Yahweh who gives munificently to Israel and who cannot receive back from Israel an offering not fit for that generosity. Leviticus 22:20-25 describes these unacceptable offerings as blemished. It states clearly that the offering to Yahweh must be perfect and without flaw. This means that blind, injured, maimed, or afflicted animals are outside of the criteria that are suitable to offer to Yahweh.

4. Consume the Blemished Firstlings in Local Settings (15:22)

■ **22** To present blemished animals in sacrifice is considered disrespectful to Yahweh. As food, the disfigured animal may be nourishing and acceptable, but it is to be butchered in accordance with Deuteronomy's provisions for commonplace slaughter of animals. These animals need not be slain at the sanctuary. Instead, they are handled **as if it were gazelle or deer**. A blemished animal is to be eaten in an everyday setting, but not as part of a sanctified meal within the framework of worship. Trust and gratitude are the underpinning of a sacred meal with the provider God. These affections bring forth the confidence to act in just ways with the needy and poor. If Yahweh is the source of all provisions, then one can trust future necessities from Yahweh's hand. Life and blessing are gifts; therefore, life is to be revered and celebrated.

5. Never Eat the Blood, but Pour It on the Land (15:23)

■ **23** It should be noticed that regardless of the profane character of the animal its lifeblood must be regarded with the astonishment due all of life.

FROM THE TEXT

Contemporary readers should realize that this sacrificial feast does not meet a need in God. In like manner, a sacrifice is also not demanded because God needs to see how much the worshipper is willing to give up or forfeit. This jubilant feast day originates out of the lavished free grace of God. God is the one who liberates and also gives provisions for life. These two great affirmations come together in the practice of firstlings. God is the Redeemer and Creator.

It is because God gives the best, liberation from bondage and the gift of a land flowing with milk and honey, that God should receive the first and best. This is the explanation for why there is a prohibition on defective animals. Imperfect animals do not correspond to the gifts of Yahweh; accordingly they are not to be set aside for Yahweh. Yahweh is not a God to be allocated scraps, because he does not give scraps. Israel belongs to Yahweh, and Yahweh belongs to Israel. Thus, Yahweh comes first not only in the confessions of Israel but also in the whole of her life. For this belief to become habituated into the ethos of the people it will take the regularity of practices. The practice of firstlings assists in the habituation of the supremacy of Yahweh in the social and ethical fabric of Israel.

This statement should not be misconstrued to mean that the God of ancient Israel does not care for the needy and marginalized. The opposite is the case. The story of Israel and her God constantly point to the fact that the poor, widow, orphan, and resident alien are uniquely cared for and protected. The practice of offering the firstborn simply means that God expects the best from a people who are given the best from God.

The first commandment authorizes the exclusive claim of Yahweh upon the people. They are to have no other gods before him, and they are to love him with the whole of their being. In other words, they are to give not only their best, but their all to the God who called them, redeemed them, led them, instructed them, and gave them a land. They are to be his people as he is their God.

15:19-23

This text gives the contemporary reader the opportunity to take into account the free grace of God in liberating and provisional ways. What must be thought through are not simply the stories of liberation and provision, but the various ways that gratitude and trust can become habituated through ongoing practices of giving and receiving. How do twenty-first century Christians practice the celebrative joy of firstlings? It must be remembered that it is only through concrete practices that the affections of gratitude, trust, and joy are developed. A person cannot "will" to be grateful or trusting or even joyful. These affections become a part of the character of people through the systematic ways a person participates in life.

The practice of firstlings is not a way to pay for the ministries of a church or the duty that enables one to be justified before God. This practice and various other practices are means of grace whereby people become partners in the divine dance of grace. The dance of God's grace is not primarily giving something to God but receiving, recognizing, rejoicing, and returning to the Lord!

F. Religious Festivals (16:1-17)

BEHIND THE TEXT

The Pentateuch proposes the observance of holy days in six other places: three times in Exodus (chs 12—13; 23:14-18; and 34:18-25); twice in Leviticus (chs 16 and 23); and once in Numbers (28:1—30:1). What is interesting is that in Deuteronomy neither the New Year nor the Day of Atonement are mentioned. All of the emphasis is on the three festivals that require a pilgrimage: Passover, Pentecost, and Tabernacles. In Deuteronomy, all three of these pilgrim celebrations require a visit to the central sanctuary. This centralizing practice is an effort to generate the practices and language that form a people in a very precise way. The purpose of this correctness of doctrine and custom is to move the populaces away from the relative beliefs and forms of life that surrounded them.

Ancient people characterize the passage of time by the progression of seasons associated with the agricultural schedule. They understand that there is a time for sowing and a time for reaping, a time for preparing the soil and a time for harvesting the crops. Because of this, it should not take a modern reader by surprise to discover that religious festivals are also associated with the agricultural year. Ancient people imagine that the gods safeguarded the endeavors of humanity in their toil for survival, and this includes the provisions of food. Therefore, there is a synergism between food production and theology.

The Canaanites, whose land Israel is to take over, also design their religious celebrations after cyclical agrarian interests. These festivals are intimately connected to beliefs that the gods acutely influence the fertility or infertility of every living thing. Narrating the exploits of the gods elucidates these festivals. This correlation between religious convictions and the agricultural year is the principal explanation for the earliest theological interpretation of the cycle of time.

When Israel entered the land, the people already had their ways of habituating their lives though a story-formed world. They would rehearse their religious beliefs and values in the rhythm of the agricultural cycle. But Israel is to be a different kind of people; they are the chosen and holy people of Yahweh. Because of this, the beliefs and practices of the people in the land must be rehabilitated in the sequence of cyclical seasons. Yahweh's people are to keep time differently. The stories and sacred sites that are deeply ingrained in the ethos of the existing culture required transformation. The holy places, practices, and stories of the Canaanite gods not only are to be eradicated from the land but are to be replaced with rituals that habituate the people into a different story-formed world.

172

Transforming beliefs and values is not something that can be decided in a moment, as if choosing a flavor of ice cream. Unwillingness on the part of people to forsake the beliefs and practices upon which they lived their lives is understandable. People continuously resist these changes, because communal beliefs are the way a people understand the world. In order to change these beliefs and values, Israel is required to reinterpret the pivotal moments in the seasonal movement of time. If Yahweh is to be the Lord over all, then Yahweh must be understood through the flow of time.

Israel's timetable of sacred celebrations is based upon the three major turning points of the agricultural calendar; each of these calls for proper public practices of worship. These three commemorations connect the bringing of gifts to Yahweh with thanksgiving for the yield of the land. Deuteronomy's theologians bring together the festivals observed in the spring and the fall with the story of Yahweh's deliverance of Israel. The first celebration is Passover and the Festival of Unleavened Bread in the spring. The second celebration is the Festival of Weeks. The final event is the Festival of Booths in the fall. The customs expressed in these three festivals are practiced by Israel. The theological themes coupled to the festivals are typical themes in Deuteronomy. They include the place that Yahweh chooses, provision for the disregarded groups of people, the inspiration and incentive of Yahweh's blessing, and the remembrance of liberation from slavery. The history of Israel's salvation shapes the viewpoint of these three celebrations in the book of Deuteronomy.

The structure of this passage of Scripture is divided between the three festivals and a concluding section that demands that the worshipper come before Yahweh with a gift. The opening section, which covers Passover, has a concentric structure. The outer layer of this structure instructs the people to keep the Passover in the month of Aviv, and at that time, to eat unleavened bread for six days followed by a coming together for celebration. The next level in the concentric structure is that the Passover sacrifice is offered at the place of Yahweh's choosing. The next stratum of the circular structure is that no leaven is to be found during these seven days. At the center of this concentric structure is the motivation for the celebration: the people are to remember their hurried departure from the land of Egyptian bondage.

Even though this commentary is going to explain this passage in a manner that addresses the Festivals of Weeks and Booths and the concluding summary individually, it can be presumed that the final two feasts and the summary form a concentric structure. The outer layer of the circular structure invites the worshipper to bring gifts to the festivals. The next level of the structure is to rejoice/celebrate at the place where Yahweh chooses. The center stratum is, like vv 1-8, a reminder that the people were once slaves in Egypt. It should be obvious that the center of both of these structures develop

16:1-17

173

the central motivation for the festivals: the gracious undertaking of Yahweh to liberate the Hebrew slaves from Egyptian bondage.

The following is the detailed structure of 16:1-17:

1. The Passover Sacrifice and the Festival of Unleavened Bread (16:1-8)
   a. Observe the Passover in the Month of Aviv (16:1)
   b. Present Passover Sacrifice in the Place Yahweh Chooses (16:2)
   c. No Leaven Is to Be in the Midst of You for Seven Days; Remember the Exodus from Egypt (16:3-4a)
   d. Present Passover Sacrifices in the Place Yahweh Chooses (16:4b-7)
   e. Consume Unleavened Bread for Six Days, and Convene on the Seventh Day (16:8)
2. The Festival of Weeks (16:9-12)
   a. Keep the Festival of Weeks by Bringing an Offering as Yahweh Has Blessed You (16:9-10)
   b. Rejoice Before Yahweh in the Place He Chooses (16:11)
   c. Remember You Were Slaves in Egypt and Obey These Statutes (16:12)
3. The Festival of Booths (16:13-17)
   a. Celebrate Seven Days Before Yahweh in the Place He Chooses (16:13-15)
   b. Do Not Come Before Yahweh in the Three Festivals Empty-handed (16:16-17)

IN THE TEXT

I. The Passover Sacrifice and the Festival of Unleavened Bread (16:1-8)

These verses speak to the Passover and the Festival of Unleavened Bread. Passover and the Festival of Unleavened Bread are much more detailed than the Festivals of Weeks and Booths. Deuteronomy centralizes the celebration of Passover and also designates a common date for the festival, thus creating a synchronized gathering of the whole of Yahweh's people. Passover and Unleavened Bread combine two major themes: the deliverance from Egypt and the provisions of Yahweh. Deuteronomy's interpretation of Israel's religious festivals stresses the importance of remembering the formative events of national life in the deliverance from Egyptian bondage. The community makes its worship a means of instruction and celebration of the fact that its very existence as a people is established by Yahweh's gracious intervention. The worshippers are allowed an opportunity to both experience gratification and express gratitude in the festival.

The Passover regulations contain numerous reverberations of the Sabbath syntax. These festivals are under the canopy of Sabbath in the larger literary context, and the word translated **observe** is the same word used in 5:12 ("observe the Sabbath"). The celebrations of Passover and Unleavened Bread are the primary occasions for remembering the exodus out of Egypt. The exodus is the central concern of Deuteronomy's Sabbath commandment, which differentiates it from the Exodus 20 Sabbath commandment that focuses on God's rest on the seventh day of creation. It should also be noticed that the Passover is a seven-day festival; **on the seventh day hold an assembly to the Lord your God and do no work** (v 8). Passover and Sabbath are intricately connected. One could say that the practice of Sabbath and a theology of liberation come together in the great celebration of Passover.

a. Observe the Passover in the Month of Aviv (16:1)

■ **1** Verse 1 identifies the month of **Aviv** (or, **Abib**), which is March-April, as the moment in time for the celebration of Passover. This is a period when a transition to fresh pastureland takes place in the spring of the year. In the old customs of the land, the people prepare to move the flocks from their winter holdings to the highland pastures by slaughtering "a lamb and sprinkl[ing] its blood on flock and tent poles to ward off malign influences on the journey" (Cairns 1992, 153). This time is also a period too early for a harvest celebration, for the barley is not fully ripe. The barley is developing, but it is still before the ingathering is ready to begin. The waving of the first sheaf of barley is the sign that the harvest is coming. Aviv is the interval when the supply of grain is most likely used up by the long dry season. A fresh start with the new grain is needed. It is fascinating to notice the conjoining of an agricultural season of newness and the newness brought on by the story of Israel's redemption from Egyptian bondage.

b. Present Passover Sacrifice in the Place Yahweh Chooses (16:2)

■ **2** The word that is translated **Passover** (*pesah*) is used again in v 2 to designate the animal taken from the flock or herd to be used in the great Passover festival. It should be remembered that Passover is a celebration of the event on which the covenant community of God is established. The liberation from slavery in the exodus became feasible on the night of Passover. In Exod 12:29-39 the function of Passover is recognized as a ritual of safekeeping. It narrates the protection of the Hebrew slaves when the visitation came upon Egypt that resulted in slaying the firstborn.

Verse 2 says: *You may sacrifice a Passover to Yahweh your God from your flock or herd.* This would indicate that the sacrifice could be either sheep and goats (flock) or cattle (herd). What is of interest to those reading Deuteronomy is that Exod 12:3 explicitly instructs the worshipper to take a lamb, but it says nothing about cattle. The difference between these two texts points to an enlargement of the custom from an earlier practice as reflected in Exodus. This verse also indicates that the Passover meal is eaten at the central place where Yahweh chooses. Eating the Passover meal at the central place is a unique feature of Deuteronomy, since in other places the local nature of the ritual made it appropriate for the celebration to be observed at home. This overriding of the family character of Passover in the appeals of its centralizing ideology presupposes that it belongs to the whole community of Israel. Centralization is a way to control both policy and practice. Orthodoxy and orthopraxy are its goals. Deuteronomy's ideology overshadows this aspect of the family character of Passover, but its later practice is once again located in private homes. A great example of this can be seen in the Gospels' account of the Last Supper.

c. No Leaven Is to Be in the Midst of You for Seven Days; Remember the Exodus from Egypt (16:3-4a)

■ **3-4a** Verse 3 instructs ancient worshippers that they must not eat leaven for seven days. Unleavened bread is suitable in a twofold fashion: as a means of indicating the move to the first cereal produce of the new agricultural year and as the description of the hasty flight from Egypt, for unlike leavened bread it could be prepared rapidly. It may have also implied the staple diet of the Hebrew slaves in Egyptian bondage. Whatever the case, it is clear that Israel is called to remember her deliverance from Egyptian captivity.

Therefore, the bread of affliction becomes the exuberance of joy. In the darkest of days the unleavened bread reminds the young and old alike that the new waits. There is the leaving of the old and the embracing the new. The people of God are not stuck, but they live in the hope of a God who promises and makes good on those promises. This depiction calls succeeding generations to renounce their old disobedience to Yahweh and renew their loyalty to him. Passover and the Festival of Unleavened Bread are opportunities not only to remember who Israel is but also to renew that identity through ceremonial enactment.

d. Present Passover Sacrifices in the Place Yahweh Chooses (16:4b-7)

■ **4b-7** Verses 4b-7 give further instruction on how the worshipper is to conduct oneself during the festival. Israel is prohibited from sacrificing the Passover animal in any place other than the place of Yahweh's choosing. The animal is sacrificed in the evening, when the sun goes down. This is to replicate the accomplishment that took place during the first Passover. Yet, the prohibition against leavened bread pertains to the whole land, even though the passage is concerned with the celebration of the festival at the place that Yahweh chooses. Because of this, the aura of the festival affects the lives of all those in Israel, and not simply the males who are present at the central place Yahweh chooses.

There are a couple of ways to interpret the **tents** of v 7. Return to tents sometimes denotes a departure for home. This would indicate that vv 7 and 8 expect the people to go back to their homes after the Passover sacrifice in order to eat unleavened bread and observe the final day of rest from work that is performed at the central place. Indeed, forbidding work while away from one's daily tasks at the central sanctuary would not make much sense. One would then interpret v 8 as a call to assemble in one's local setting.

e. Consume Unleavened Bread for Six Days, and Convene on the Seventh Day (16:8)

■ **8** The term **assembly** in v 8 does not inevitably indicate that the people gather in their hometowns, but it does mean something different from the term "festival," which is used in all three of the pilgrimage festivals. Only in the Festival of Unleavened Bread is the assembly described as taking place. This is to happen on **the seventh day**.

On the other hand, Deuteronomy always presumes that Israel will enjoy a settled existence in houses. This suggests that tents could indicate a temporary residence in pilgrim encampments. Israel becomes nomadic again in the pilgrimage that is made for the festival. The virtue of nomadic dependency is reinforced if this is the situation. The people of God live by the providential guidance and care of Yahweh. The meaning of **assembly** that is used in v 8 would then be a calling of the pilgrims to come corporately before God. Remaining at the central location allows for the people to assemble as a collective.

Verse 8 addresses the practice of Sabbath again. It underscores the opening six days of the total festival of eating unleavened bread and then places special prominence on the seventh day. The people are to eat unleavened bread for six days and assemble on the seventh day. As an interruption to work, this is a confirmation that the time belongs to Yahweh and that it should be surrendered to him. Precisely, the inactivity of the seventh day is a symbolic identification that the release from Egypt is a form of Sabbath. The political/theological ramifications of the practice of Sabbath and Passover are liberation and renewal.

2. The Festival of Weeks (16:9-12)

a. Keep the Festival of Weeks by Bringing an Offering as Yahweh Has Blessed You (16:9-10)

■ **9-10** The Festival of Weeks is known in the early code as the Festival of Harvest (Exod 23:16), but it is most commonly named as is recorded here in Deut 16 (Exod 34:22; Num 28:26). In all the codes, except Deuteronomy itself, the festival is specifically connected with the firstfruits of the barley harvest. Leviticus 23:9-21 goes into the greatest detail concerning this festival.

It specifies an offering of a sheaf of the first nature grain. Then seven weeks to allow for its full ripening and harvesting, which is followed by the celebration of harvest itself in the early summer. Instead of itemizing in detail the offerings due at the feast, as Leviticus does, Deuteronomy requires a freewill offering in proportion to the amount harvested.

b. Rejoice Before Yahweh in the Place He Chooses (16:11)

■ 11 The Festival of Weeks is a pause after the frenetic activity of the harvest. Seven weeks from the time the sickle is first put to the standing grain, this festival begins. Deuteronomy 16:11 is clear that this festival makes specific provisions for the community's most exposed and needy members: children, slaves, Levites, strangers, orphans, and widows. This is a recurring theme in the book of Deuteronomy and the larger Sabbath grammar that regulates the life of ancient Israel. Just as the Sabbath commandment's primary concern is to give rest to the dependent and powerless people of the community (5:12-15), so the Festival of Weeks carries out this political/theological agenda. Not only is Israel to remember their slavery in Egypt, but also they are commanded to diligently observe the statutes.

This offering appears to be an articulation of a theology of blessing where the worshipper is brought to a place of gratitude and generosity based upon Yahweh's gift giving. The festival is depicted as a joyful celebration for the whole people without distinction. Once more, it is celebrated at the place of Yahweh's choosing.

c. Remember You Were Slaves in Egypt and Obey These Statutes (16:12)

■ 12 The festival reminds the people of Yahweh's supreme gift of liberation from Egyptian bondage. It is only in Deuteronomy that the festival expressly makes a memorial of the deliverance from Egypt.

3. The Festival of Booths (16:13-17)

a. Celebrate Seven Days Before Yahweh in the Place He Chooses (16:13-15)

■ 13-15 The Festival of Booths is identified as the Festival of Ingathering in the earlier codes found in Exod 23:16 and Exod 34:22. It celebrates the harvesting of all the crops that ripen during the summer months (such as grapes, dates, and olives) and is thus, in an agricultural sense, the end of the year. The exact scheduling is indicated in Lev 23:33-34 as beginning on the fifteenth day of the seventh month, shortly following the Day of Atonement.

Tabernacles corresponds to Lev 23, as does the seven-day interval of the celebration. Both passages of scripture also specify that the feast is to take place at the place of God's choice. The Festival of Booths is joyful above all other occasions and is a link with the deliverance from Egypt in Lev 23:40. The Festival of Tabernacles is referred to a number of times in the OT simply as "the feast," suggesting it is considered to be the most important of the three annual pilgrimage festivals (e.g., 1 Kgs 8:2, 65; 12:32; Ps 81:3). Deuteronomy 31:9-13 conveys that it is this feast that is singled out for the solemn seven-yearly reading of the book of the law.

This festival also makes particular requirements for the community's care for needy members of the community. The list is similar to the Festival of Weeks and it includes children, slaves, Levites, strangers, orphans, and widows. It should be obvious that this care for the vulnerable is a recurring theme in the book of Deuteronomy and the larger Sabbath syntax that regulates the life of the people of God.

b. Do Not Come Before Yahweh in the Three Festivals Empty-handed (16:16-17)

■ 16-17 The final section is a summarizing segment reiterating the obligation of the three annual pilgrimages. At each of these festivals gifts are presented. Deuteronomy describes these gifts as being proportionate to the blessing and gift that the worshipper receives from the providential care of Yahweh. The need to appear not empty-handed is a reiteration of the deeper grammar of Deut 15:13, recalling that the released slave has both the right and the obligation to participate in the feast. Blessing comes from Yahweh and is intended to extend through the blessed to those in need. Gratitude and generosity are the virtues that are being habituated into the fabric of Israel and into the character of the individuals who make up the community.

FROM THE TEXT

Ludwig Wittgenstein might be of assistance to a current reader of these practices. He believed that when one understood the "depth grammar" of the language usage one could go on in the same way, yet beyond the usage itself (1953, §143). So how is a contemporary Christian to carry out these festive practices? Are they to keep them in strict agreement to the way that ancient Israel prescribes them, or is there a syntactical depth within their social fabric that invites the Christian community to "go on"? These three festivals describe the ritualization of a people who are endeavoring to maintain an alternative identity within the larger social order that encompass them. In a religious sense, these practices are designed to habituate people into the holy otherness that the Wholly Other desires for them. This habituation is accomplished for ancient Israel as the celebrations invite the participants to enact an alternative narrative to the way life is regulated. Keeping time becomes the story of Yahweh and his people.

By consecrating the special festival periods, time itself becomes story-formed. In the flow of time a people begin to see a meaningful course of history. A story is revealed through these festive celebrations, as the people enact a point of view that affirms survival and identity as a gift. Not only does time come to be story-formed and therefore history, but also the people become story-formed and gain an identity with a purpose. Their story is none other than God with them. They are Yahweh's people with a nonsubstitutional origin and an irreplaceable purpose.

It should be apparent to the contemporary reader that observing time through a religious narrative means that incidents are converted into history and history becomes sacred. Therefore, this way of ordering time provides an interpretative lens for one's experience. Discernment itself becomes sanctified. Occasions become episodes in a drama with a beginning and an end. This argument presupposes that a community of memory is capable of acculturating persons into a particular moral view of reality. In other words, a community is necessary for influencing the moral development toward becoming peculiar types of people. Storied personhood is fashioned out of God's act of liberation and providential care. People who discern the meaning of their lives by means of these beliefs acquire the virtues of gratitude and generosity. The people of God are an alternative community; the *communio sanctorum*.

Can Christians in concrete ways embody what it means to be the communion of saints? Is it possible, with all of the pervasive values and practices of the host society, to embody a belief system that is so alternative that this community can only be described as resident aliens? If the beliefs and values of self-rule, self-sufficiency, and self-indulgence are to be resisted, then sacred time must be rediscovered and dramatically enacted. Relentless festivals of Super Bowls and March-madness, national holidays and market seasonal movements cannot have the ultimate say in the forming of character. The story of redemption and providence must find a way to recapture Christian imagination and recapitulate life.

G. Position, Power, and Privilege (16:18—18:22)

BEHIND THE TEXT

The policies and practices of setting up public institutions is the concern of this passage. It explores the values attached to positions of authority and power. The positions of authority that are addressed include judges, kings, priests, and prophets. It is interesting that power is not centralized in one leadership category. There is a distribution of power through a number of diverse institutions and leadership responsibilities. The limitations on human authority protect the community from the tendency of an oligarchy. Perhaps this is because human beings have the propensity to worship themselves and their leaders.

Human beings, both ancient and contemporary, realize that life is ordered through various institutions. These institutions, in the biblical communities, are not given absolute power; the concept of justice limits their role. The responsibility of the institutions is to keep chaos at bay, not use power because it is possible. Specific practices associated with power are assigned unique leadership roles.

The structure of this passage is straightforward. The themes and categories of the positions of authority constitute the structure itself. Deuteronomy 16:21—17:7 seems to be one exception in this larger passage. In this section specific behaviors and practices of the people are addressed. The rest of the passage addresses the judgments rendered by a variety of leaders and institutions in ancient Israel. The text has the following structure:

1. The Pursuit of Justice (16:18-20)
2. Law on Idolatry and False Worship (16:21—17:7)
3. Law of the Central Tribunal (17:8-13)
4. Law of the King (17:14-20)
5. Law of the Levitical Priests (18:1-8)
6. Law of the Prophets (18:9-22)

IN THE TEXT

I. The Pursuit of Justice (16:18-20)

■ **18-20** This section acts as a heading for all the diverse offices that exercise authority and power within the community of God's people. Judges function as a paradigm for the implementation of governance and influence on behalf of the community; they are to **judge the people fairly** (v 18). The covenant and its policies and practices are to regulate the life of Israel through her leaders. The word *nātan* ("to give") governs the sense of this passage. The preceding verses describe how Yahweh has *given* to the people all the produce of the land; therefore the Hebrew worshipper is called upon to return in proportion to what Yahweh *gives* them. Now this text instructs the people to **appoint** [*nātan*] **judges and officials** for each tribe **in every town** Yahweh is giving (*nātan*) them; everything is done as a response to Yahweh's giving of the land to his people.

The axiomatic meaning of **justice** that the judges are to pursue when they settle disputes between people and groups is perceived in what the judges are not to do: **Do not pervert justice or show partiality. Do not accept a bribe, for a bribe blinds the eyes of the wise and twists the words of the *righteous*** (v 19). The responsibility of the judge is clearly described as meting out justice

181

and preserving righteousness in the land. These two words govern the purpose of these verses.

Justice (*mišpāṭ*) occurs in Deuteronomy in 1:17; 17:8-11; 18:3; 19:6; 21:17, 22; and 25:1. In each case the concept of fairness in judgment controls the function of the word. Justice is not a disembodied attitude, but an action that makes sense only in the context of a political reality. Justice always requires some sort of power within a relationship/politic. An example of this is that a slave cannot be unjust to a master, unless the slave moves into a position of power over the master. A slave can be unrighteous to a master, but not unjust.

Righteousness denotes doing the right thing in a relationship or covenant, but not necessarily using power in the relationship. The word group for righteous (*ṣĕdāqâ*) occurs four times in this short section: once at the end of 16:18 translated **fairly**; once, in the plural, at the end of v 19 translated **innocent**; and twice at the beginning of v 20 translated **follow justice and justice alone**. *Ṣĕdāqâ* always means to do the right act. Right action is based upon criteria within a covenant's rationality. Examples of this are: a woman is a righteous wife based upon the covenant role of a wife; a person is a righteous judge, based upon the covenant role of a judge; a righteous king, likewise, is based upon the covenant role of a king. Covenant roles determine the meaning of righteousness.

Verse 19 addresses judges in the second-person singular (**you**), and therefore the individual member of the covenant community. The second-person singular is used in all three of the probations in this verse. This decree makes justice not only a communal responsibility but also a personal and covenantal responsibility. The whole community and as a result each individual is responsible for the entire matter of justice. Yahweh judges both individuals and the community in the question of justice. Exile is proof of the result of a people who fall short of justice. The nation, and therefore individuals within the nation, are judged and thrust into exile.

Verse 20 proclaims to the judges: **Follow justice and justice alone.** The Hebrew word *ṣĕdāqâ* is used again in this context. This should be translated *righteous and only righteous action you shall pursue*. In the context of early Israelite society and Deuteronomy's world, judges did not mechanically and legalistically apply laws. Rather, they sought to determine the righteous action in resolving the dispute, based upon the covenant understanding of the relationship being litigated. Careful discernment is necessary in settling disputes, especially if the restoration of relationships in community is the goal.

2. Law on Idolatry and False Worship (16:21—17:7)

■ **16:21—17:7** The law pertaining to the judges is immediately followed by a series of laws concerning forbidden forms of worship, particularly the worship of other gods. Many scholars understand these verses as intrusive into the larger collection of laws that address the use of authority and justice in the society. But perhaps there are at least two reasons for the inclusion of these laws in this passage: first, religious crimes must be adjudicated; and second, there must be a rationality that determines right action in all other covenant relationships. Perhaps justice is defined, not by some general theory that all rationalities agree upon, but by the specificity of each tradition that uses the concept of justice. In other words, justice is defined by a communal rationality. If this is so, then Yahweh alone defines righteousness and justice for ancient Israel. These concepts have their meaning only in the context of Israel's understanding of covenant with Yahweh. Israel's covenant understanding is dependent upon acknowledging Yahweh alone as God.

Earlier, in Deut 7:5 and 12:3, the people are instructed to tear down the poles and pillars of the Canaanite cultic centers. Now, in 16:21-22, they are unequivocally prohibited to erect comparable cult objects beside the altar of Yahweh. Any kind of syncretism with foreign religion is an abomination to Yahweh. In relation to vv 21 and 22, the presenting of an imperfect sacrifice is similar in result to defiling God's sanctuary (17:1). Nelson describes **wooden Asherah pole** (16:21) as either a wooden artifact prepared and set up, or a stylized tree (2002b, 218). The prohibition of a sacred pole beside the altar of Yahweh indicates the people's practice of the worship of Yahweh in a manner approximating the Canaanites' worship of their gods. This sacred pole would amount to a Yahwistic Asherah, in distinction from an Asherah of the original people of the land. Asherah would function very similar to an idol, a way of localizing and manipulating deity.

The premise of vv 21-22 is the concept of covenant. Not only does covenant signify the bond that unites Israel to Yahweh, but it is also the association of relationships and roles connecting people to people. To worship other gods is to cause not only a withdrawal from Yahweh but also to abandon the political understanding that their loyal bond to Yahweh produced their social relationships and roles. Thus, a break in covenant with Yahweh caused a break in covenant with each other. A community comprehends the right action to perform in the various roles and relationships based upon shared identity narratives and practices.

Alasdair MacIntyre argues in a very similar manner when he asserts that justice is determined by the specificity of a rationality that is narrated by a tradition (1988). The Decalogue and the various laws that are reverberations of it are grounded in the first two commandments. Covenantal social arrangements are derived from and guaranteed by the singular understanding of the God who makes and keeps covenant. Yahweh alone is God, and he determines for the covenantal community what defines justice, righteousness, and the proper use of power. This would mean that any analysis of justice in a Yahwistic community would be contingent upon fidelity to Yahweh.

The theologians in the tradition of Deuteronomy narrate Israel's history as one abuse of power after another. This shapes the central concern of the Deuteronomistic History. Most of Israel's kings acted in unjust ways frequently when they allow the nation to be influenced by other gods and idolatrous practices. Solomon is one of the supreme examples of the synergistic reality of revering other gods and failing to practice justice consistently (see 1 Kgs 11:4, 11).

Justice must also be meted out to those who are accused of false worship (Deut 17:1-7). Deuteronomy confesses that Yahweh will guarantee justice in this case also. It is interesting to notice that a Yahwistic rationality is used as criteria to judge if one worships Yahweh alone. A quandary could crop up with the emphasis upon proper worship of Yahweh alone; one might be falsely accused of worshipping false gods. What is Israel to do? Does anyone's testimony bring about the death penalty? Are there safeguards to keep someone from falsely accusing someone who happens to be a rival or an enemy?

Particular steps are taken as a safeguard against injustice on the part of fraudulent or misguided witnesses, by requiring the authentication of two or more observers. Yahweh insisted that one witness is insufficient to convict a person of false worship; it takes adequate evidence from two or three witnesses. This is comparable to indictments like murder or rape where the death penalty is also imposed (Deut 19:15-21). Verse 7 of ch 17 insists that these witnesses cannot be left in an untainted position to the verdict; they must cast the first stones in order to affirm the truth of their testimony. They are responsible for their testimony. The death penalty is not some act of vengeance, but a purging of the evil from the midst of the people. In other words, it is for the sake of maintaining a Yahwistic rationality.

3. Law of the Central Tribunal (17:8-13)

■ **8-13** It will take unique leadership in the community if Israel is to live in radical obedience to Yahweh. The Levites are not only to instruct leadership in the covenantal rationality of justice, but they are to function as the ultimate arbitrators of adjudicating cases. The delivery of judgment is relocated, in this passage, from the **gate** in v 5 to **the place where Yahweh chooses** in v 8. This rearrangement indicates a change in the theme. Inevitably circumstances would occur where there are too few witnesses. How is a verdict to be reached in such cases? These situations could involve a variety of issues from homicide to disputes over property and possessions. For this reason, a court of appeals is established, at the place that Yahweh chooses. This court's purpose is to settle the matters of justice that are too difficult to adjudicate in the local settings.

Levitical priests make up this court, under the direction of a chief justice. Once brought together, this ruling body functions as an appeals court, whose judgment is final and binding. Cultic and civil policies and practices are intertwined in the land that Yahweh gives, and this reaffirms the interpretation above that a particular rationality determines the conceptual definitions of justice and righteousness. The irrevocability of the judgment pronounced by the court is unchangeable; death is the punishment for refusing to receive a verdict. Definitive judgments are essential to avoid disputes that could lead to personal or community vendettas.

Deuteronomy's interest in establishing an agenda for the worship of Yahweh at only one central place encompasses a number of rival, and often conflicting, assertions relating to the history of the priesthood. The expression in v 9 **Go to the Levitical priests** suggests that at the time of Deuteronomy not all priests were Levites; this text also suggests a power struggle that in time led to the unquestioned assumption of priestly responsibilities and privileges by the Zadokite priesthood. After the division of the kingdom, religion in the southern tribe of Judah centered on ritual sacrifice in the temple. The priests known as the Zadokites controlled temple worship. The Zadokites descended from Zadok the priest, who was appointed as high priest by Solomon after he dismissed Abiathar, the high priest during the reign of David (see 1 Kgs 2:26-27, 35). The Levites were a lower group of religious officials who were not permitted to perform sacrifices and were restricted in their functions.

17:8-13

Power Struggle in Israelite Priesthood

According to Exod 40:12-16, Moses (as instructed by God) anointed Aaron and his sons (Nadab, Abihu, Eleazar, Ithamar) to a perpetual priesthood in Israel. However, various texts indicate struggle for power and prominence within the house of Aaron. Nadab and Abihu suffered the judgment of death for offering an unauthorized fire before the Lord (see Lev 10:1-7). Of the two remaining sons of Aaron, God elevated Eleazar to prominence and gave him perpetual priesthood for his decisive action against an Israelite man who brought into the camp a Midianite woman at the time when Moses and Israel were weeping over God's anger against the nation for its participation in the fertility cult and worship of Baal of Peor (see Num 25:1-13). Solomon elevated Zadok, a descendant of Eleazar who supported Solomon's claim to the throne, as the high priest after he banished Abiathar, David's priest, who supported Adonijah's claim as legal heir to David. It is likely that Abiathar descended from the house of Eli that served the sanctuary at Shiloh (1 Sam 22:20; see also 1 Sam 14:3). Some traditions link the house of Eli with the family of Ithamar. Since the days of Solomon, the family of Zadok enjoyed prominence in Jerusalem. Ithamar's descendants seem to have lost influence over the course of history; they were made up of only eight families compared to the sixteen families of the descendants of Eleazar (see 1 Chr 24:4).

The events of the sixth century BC produced not only stoppage to the activities of the priesthood in Jerusalem but also serious divisions within the priesthood itself. Subsequent to the defeat of Jerusalem, the Babylonians demolished the temple and took most of the Zadokite priesthood into exile, leaving behind the Levites, who were too poor and marginalized to represent a threat to Babylon. A very important role in the religious life of the remaining inhabitants of Judah came under the influence of the priests who called themselves sons of Aaron to distinguish themselves from the sons of Zadok. When the Zadokite priests returned from exile and began reestablishing the temple in Jerusalem, they came into conflict with the Aaronite priests. The Zadokites prevailed in this conflict but assumed the Aaronite name. The Zadokites simultaneously found themselves in conflict with the Levites, who objected to their subordinate position. The priests also triumphed over this dispute and were able to develop the ideological framework that declared any challenge to the priestly privilege as an unholy argument. The Sadducees mentioned in the NT belonged to the Zadokite priesthood.

4. Law of the King (17:14-20)

■ **14-20** With the exception of Exod 22:28, this is the only Mosaic edict on the monarchy in the Pentateuch. In light of the dominant existence of the monarchy, such a dearth of references is noteworthy. Deuteronomy's prearrangement for the installation of a king is unique to this tradition and instructive in respect of the restraints it places on the monarchy. Deuteronomy 17:14 states the primary motive for the popular request for a king when the people settle down in the land: **Let us set a king over us like all the nations around us.** The desire of the people expressed here is sharply opposed to Yahweh's desire for them to be a holy people whom he has chosen "out of all the peoples on the face of the earth to be his people, his treasured possession" (7:6). Yahweh is not only God for the people but also king of Israel. The cult as well as the court is fashioned by God.

Two Views on Monarchy in Israel

Deuteronomy and Deuteronomistic History cast two perspectives on monarchy that indicate Israel was divided early in its national life over whether they should be governed by a king like the other nations around them. Those who resisted human kingship held the view of Yahweh's direct rule over Israel; a human king would only be a substitute for God. The other side of the argument maintained a more pragmatic view; a human structure of nationalized control was necessary to unify the nation against outside enemies.

There are obvious points of similarity between 17:14-20 and the anti-kingship tradition of northern Israel . . . scholars on the whole agree that the anti-kingship strand originates in northern Israel, and the pro-kingship strand in the south . . . the Deuteronomic school, on moving south after the fall of Samaria, accommodated their somewhat anti-kingship tradition to the pro-kingship ethos of Jerusalem theology. One of the basic Deuter-

186

onomic convictions is that it was the sins of the royal house which caused Israel's exile. (Cairns 1992, 165)

In the Deuteronomistic tradition, 1 Sam 8 is one of the most fascinating stories in the Bible that describes this tension. It portrays a major dispute in ancient Israel over the whether the people should have a king. The problem arose, according to the story, when Samuel became old and appointed his sons as judges. The sons did not follow the ways of Samuel, and they were greedy for gain and therefore lost their way. These offspring of Samuel took bribes and perverted justice. Israel demanded a king so that they might be like the other nations. Though Samuel interpreted the popular demand as a rejection of Yahweh's kingship, Yahweh instructed Samuel to listen to the people, and at the same time to warn them about the burden they will bear if they have a king like the nations. The people were not persuaded, and Samuel anointed Saul as king over Israel. The law of the king, in this passage, suggests a concession to this rancorous quarrel. A king was allowed, but rigorous restrictions were set up to limit the powers and functions of the ruler (1 Sam 8:1-22).

Deuteronomy allows kingship but with important qualifying conditions. First, Yahweh reserves the right to choose the king. This signifies that the king is to submit to Yahweh. Second, the king must be a member of the covenant nation Israel. While the custom of kingship may be appropriated from the other nations, the person inhabiting the throne may not come from an alien country. Outsiders would bring other gods, other traditions, and other regulations that would deplete Israel of its true identity. Third, the Israelite monarch must not behave like the despotic and self-aggrandizing monarchs of other nations.

17:14-20

Deuteronomy 17:14-15 allows for the authorization of a king in Israel. The primary interest of Deuteronomy is how to administer the land covenantally. Deuteronomy implies that Moses anticipated Israel's desire to be **like all the nations**. Deuteronomy suggests that desire for security and prosperity is the motivation behind idolatrous worship practices and governance through kingship. **Like all the nations** is not what Israel ought to yearn for, because she is to be a people unlike all the nations. She is holy to Yahweh. But, if the people are to have a king, the king will have to be of Yahweh's own choosing. This king is to be governed by the covenant with its policies and practices.

Verses 16-17 articulate negatively three fervent appeals as major conditions for a king: he must not have many **horses**, he must not multiply **wives**, and he must not multiply **silver and gold**. The mention of not multiplying horses is in direct relation to a large military establishment. Horses are a metaphor for such power. Israel is here presented with two alternative ways: to trust in horses and chariots or to trust in Yahweh. Even for the prophets, this became a symptom of not trusting in Yahweh. A large standing army would also be a return to slavery for Israel. An army would require the sons of the people and also their resources to underwrite the horses and chariots of the king. Israel would suffer a fate similar to Egyptian bondage; they would become dependent upon the power of the king to protect them, and in some way the people would be returning to slavery.

The king is also not to have many wives. This is not a statement about the sexual practices of a king, but about the political alliances that take place through marriages. Solomon is the great example of how "many wives" brings about the destruction of the nation by introducing false gods and alternative values into the kingdom. Solomon's heart was turned away from Yahweh (see 1 Kgs 11). As the heart of the king turns so the people turn into something other than the holy people of Yahweh. Identity of the people is the issue that is at stake.

The king is also not to multiply silver and gold. "Silver and gold in large quantities signal a state that is committed to opulence and self-aggrandizement, an achievement possible only by the transfer of tax moneys in exploitative ways" (Brueggemann 2001, 185). With such heavy taxation the regime becomes completely self-serving. Neglecting the poor and needy, which is at the heart of the covenant, is something that can be expected. The king is the ultimate judge within the nation. If the king is concerned with royal acquisition, then the needy will remain in need.

Deuteronomy 17:18-20 makes it clear that the essential duty of the king is not merely to abstain from certain procurements, and to be from the people, but to constantly examine and consider the Torah. This instruction is made available by the Levitical priests. The monarchy is never intended to be autonomous but constantly compliant to the Torah. The durability of the monarchy depends upon the king being habituated by Torah. The accounts of the kings in the Deuteronomic History narrate the failure of the kings to live up to the policies and practices of the covenantal politics of Yahweh. The guidelines of this passage do not set out to defend or expound the king's rights, but rather they limit the role and power of the monarchy. The overall tone is not one of enthusiasm for kingship but reluctant acknowledgment that it is a historical given. Deuteronomy seeks to ensure that the king will not discourage or obstruct the people's responsibility to the will of the great king, Yahweh.

5. Law of the Levitical Priests (18:1-8)

■ 1-8 These verses deal with the legislative provisions for the **Levitical priests** as well as **the whole tribe of Levi**.

Priests and Levites

The term "Levite" is applied to anyone who belonged to the tribe of Levi. In Israel's early tradition, a distinction was drawn between those within the tribe of Levi who were privileged to serve as priests (i.e., the family of Aaron), and other members of the tribe of Levi who served in noncultic tasks, primarily as assistants to priests. The distinction between priests and Levites is somewhat arbitrary since all priests were Levites, though not all Levites were priests. It is likely that in Israel's later history, the nonpriestly group of Levites may have assumed a larger role in the temple worship.

Deuteronomy 18:1-2 deals with the tribe of Levi (Levites) as a whole, but shifts emphasis to legislation that relates specifically to the Levitical priests (vv 3-5) and then back again to the Levites as a whole (vv 6-8). The tribe of Levi did not receive a portion of the land as its tribal territory, but provisions were made for the allocation of forty-eight towns as Levitical towns within the territories of other tribes of Israel (see Num 35:1-8). Deuteronomy makes clear that the whole tribe of Levi was completely dependent on Yahweh and the generosity of the people: **They shall have no inheritance among their fellow Israelites; the** LORD **is their inheritance, as he promised them** (Deut 18:2). Deuteronomy presents the Levites as a physical symbol of Israel's dependence on God. They are highly esteemed for their religious service to God, but they are in need of the gifts of the community for provisions. The specific provisions for the Levitical priests are listed in vv 3-5, which include portions of the offering that supplied the priestly families with meat, corn, wine, oil, and wool. The legislation in vv 6-8 makes the provision for the Levites who live in Levitical towns anywhere in Israel who might wish to relocate to **the place the** LORD **will choose** (v 7) in order to **serve there in the presence of the** LORD (v 8). This provision seems to apply for both the Levitical priests and the Levites in general. They are to have an equal share in the offerings that are brought by the people to the sanctuary.

The geographical distance of the Levitical towns from the central sanctuary (Jerusalem) would have made it difficult for all Levites to be involved with the cultic functions and equally benefit from the offerings that came from the people. Deuteronomy intends for the Levites to become more fully included in Israel's cultic affairs. Two particular themes concerning the Levites are suggested in Deuteronomy. The first is the recognition that the Levites are wholly dependent upon the gifts and tithe offerings of the people. Since they possess no substantial tribal territory of their own, the Levites' allegiance to Yahweh as God is their title deed to a role in Israel's life. It is interesting that Deut 14 allocates the special third-year tithe to help the Levites as well as the poor.

The second theme is the recognition that Israel is dependent upon the Levites and their theological vision for a right understanding of Yahweh and his ways. His ways are the ways of justice, and justice is defined by a rationality that Yahweh gives through Torah (see 17:18-20). Moreover, they are ministers who serve in the name of the Lord and mediators between God and Israel. This synergism of the people needing the Levites and the Levites needing the people may testify to a similar synergism found between Yahweh and his

18:1-8

people. They need Yahweh to survive and experience blessing, and he needs them as partners to extend blessing.

6. Law of the Prophets (18:9-22)

■ **9-22** This section is organized around the aspiration to ascertain God's will for the community. The yearning for this discovery is obvious; it is to secure and safeguard one's life and possessions. In the ancient Near East, many possible channels existed for such discernment. This text begins with a strong warning to Israel not to engage in **the detestable ways of the nations** (v 9) and is followed by a list of the banned practices, which include causing *a son or daughter to pass through fire* (v 10) and attempting to communicate with dead ancestors (v 11). The list contains the most common pagan practices to discern the future and to manipulate the situation to one's own advantage. Israel's destiny is to be a people shaped by Yahweh, who liberates and provides, so that their character expresses gratitude and generosity. The temptation to engage in syncretistic ways with the beliefs and practices of Israel's neighbors would constantly be near her. She must resist the temptation; Yahweh cautions Israel to avoid the pagan practices with the implicit warning that Israel's practice of these customs would result in her expulsion from the land. Verse 12 contains the theological rationale for the expulsion of the pagan inhabitants of the promised land.

Verse 13 declares, **you must be blameless before the LORD your God.** There are two observations that should be made in this verse: the first is that the word **you** is in the second-person singular. This would indicate both that Israel is understood as a singular reality and that the individual in the community is under obligation to obey this command. The second observation is the location and the meaning of the word *tāmîm* (**blameless**). This word does not mean that a person is to live without making mistakes, but it means complete and whole. This is the first word in the Hebrew text. Literally the verse reads: *Completely whole you will be with Yahweh your God.* In this context, this would imply that the practices of the other people groups within which Israel lives are not to divide their lives. Yahweh and his covenantal promises and politics must shape them wholly and completely. Israel must know Yahweh's will not in order to control her fate, but in order to obey.

Judges, kings, and priests all have relatively secure and institutionalized bases of power and authority, but Deuteronomy is also aware that there is one other group with amazing power and influence. This group is an untidy and undomesticated faction, which often arises from the borders of Israel's culture and therefore is not obligated to anyone but Yahweh. **The LORD your God will raise up for you a prophet like me from among you, from your fellow Israelites** (v 15). A prophet did not see the future like a fortune-teller, but forthtold the word of God. The power of the prophets' words is in the creative power of God to fulfill his word, not in seeing beforehand what is in store.

Although God raises the prophet up, the prophet is still chosen from among the people. The Hebrew emphatically highlights this dimension by placing it first in the sequence of the sentence. Verse 15 reads literally as follows: *A prophet from among you, from your brethren, like me, Yahweh your God will raise up for you.* Like Moses, this prophet will not have superhuman strength but will have the promissory presence of Yahweh: "I will be with you. And this will be the sign to you that it is I who have sent you: When you have brought the people out of Egypt, you will worship God on this mountain" (Exod 3:12). The future prophets are like Moses. Moses refers back to what happens at the mountain of God where he receives both his commission and the Decalogue. Moses is commissioned to stand in for both Yahweh and the people. He speaks the word of Yahweh and he takes risks on the people's behalf. To mediate between God and the people is the inference of what a prophet like Moses will be. The consequence of this kind of life that stands between God and the people also has a negative effect; the prophet will most likely die because of this calling.

The rest of the passage, Deut 18:20-22, tackles the difficulty intrinsic to the noninstitutional office of prophecy. How is the community to tell a true prophet like Moses from a false prophet claiming to speak a word from Yahweh? First, any prophet that speaks a word in the name of any god but Yahweh is false. But this is not enough to guarantee that a prophet is speaking Yahweh's word. The definitive guideline is that the word is false **if what a prophet proclaims in the name of the LORD does not take place or come true** (v 22). Unfortunately, this guideline is not always self-evident in the immediate circumstance; the community must wait and see whether the prophet's words come true. It should be remembered that the prophet does not see the future and predict it, but speaks God's creative word, which creates the future.

18:9-22

True and False Prophecy

Though Deuteronomy sets forth the guidelines that distinguish between true and false prophets, two cases in the OT illustrate the ambiguity and uncertainty about the nature of prophecy in Israel. In the first case, though Jonah spoke about the destruction of Nineveh as commanded by Yahweh, it did not come to pass. Jonah spoke a true word from Yahweh, yet Yahweh repented when the Ninevites repented. Jonah was angry because Yahweh did not do what Jonah announced as the word from Yahweh. Jonah may also have been concerned about the loss of his own credibility as a true prophet. Is Jonah a true prophet? This is a question that the Hebrew people would ask again and again in relation to the judgment oracles. The answer that the book of Jonah gives is obvious: of course Jonah is a true prophet because it is the character of Yahweh that causes God to change his mind.

Jonah says, "I knew that you are a gracious and compassionate God, slow to anger and abounding in love, a God who relents from sending calamity" (4:2). Knowing a true prophet from a false prophet takes some discernment itself.

Jeremiah's confrontation with Hananiah in Jer 28:1-9 illustrates another difficulty about the claims of those who speak on behalf of Yahweh. Hananiah also spoke in the name of Yahweh, a message of peace that contradicted Jeremiah's message of Yahweh's judgment. In this text, Jeremiah neither affirms nor rejects the words of Hananiah but simply hopes for an immediate end of the Babylonian crisis, though he himself called for Judah's submission to Babylon. In his response to Hananiah, Jeremiah uses the Deuteronomic criteria and reminds the people and Hananiah that they will have to wait and see the fulfillment of Hananiah's claim of peace before recognizing his claim as an authentic prophecy of Yahweh (Jer 29:9).

FROM THE TEXT

The policies of Deut 16:18—18:22 tackle the responsibilities of public power. They disclose vital criteria with reference to the purpose and meaning of authority. This passage's particular viewpoint is that power should be utilized in the interest of justice. The premise that shapes this view of the Scriptures is that all reality is tied to a larger covenantal framework. There is no doubt that Israel is in a unique covenantal relationship with Yahweh, but the covenant with Israel is understood to be for the sake of the nations. The ancient people of God believe that all life comes from the creativity of Yahweh; therefore, all life is in the end answerable to Yahweh. The opening chapters of Deuteronomy narrate that the nations are to be removed from the land because they have behaved in ways that destroy the relational condition of life. A similar view to this is also seen in the wisdom tradition of ancient Israel.

Even though the wisdom tradition and Deuteronomy differ, they may share a common worldview that allows a reader to see the larger function of justice and righteousness in the context of covenant relationships in all of creation. Proverbs 8 is an aphoristic sonnet that speaks of creation being ordered by God through wisdom. This means that creation has a proper order and it is supposed to function in a particular way. This proper order is portrayed as a covenant order in the Deuteronomic tradition. Deuteronomy understands that this order is revealed in the gift of Torah. Each part of creation has a role if cosmic harmony is to happen. When it does function properly, *shalom* is the result. Right actions within this order are what the wise do, and in the Deuteronomic tradition they are called righteous actions. As soon as people fail to live righteously, they disrupt the order of creation or they break covenant. The restoration of covenant, the order of creation, is the harmony created by right judgment. The sufferance of judgment, which is itself justice, reestablishes the ordered world, which produces blessing and life.

Prophets, priests, kings, and judges are the offices within the institutions that shape human communities. What are these positions of authority to do within the context of their particular institutions? Are they to safeguard their own positions and privileges, or are they to safeguard the institutions, where they discover their own role, and the power and privileges of the institutions? Prophets speak words that shape destiny. Priests perform rituals that produce confidence. Kings enact policies that create stability. Judges adjudicate cases that determine orderliness. So, what are the goals of these offices within the larger framework of the people of God?

The multiple offices within ancient Israel have a singular goal within the vision of this passage—to establish and maintain justice. The opening section of this passage, 16:18-20, addresses the appointment of judges and officials throughout the tribes and towns and affirms that there is to be one purpose, *justice and only justice* (16:20). The next section of the passage, 16:21—17:7, addresses laws concerned with idolatry and false worship. This passage seems out of place, as it relates to the theme of justice, except for two issues: judgments need to be made concerning false worship, and judgments are made within a particular covenantal view of the world. The next section, 17:8-13, speaks to the highest court in ancient Israel. The purpose of this court is to adjudicate cases that are too difficult for the local judiciary to determine. This court is to observe everything that Israel is instructed in the Torah. It should be noted that the adjudicating based upon Torah is to produce justice.

The passage then shifts to the limitations of authority within the monarchy in 17:14-20. The criteria and purpose for the monarchy is clearly stated, to diligently observe all the words of this law and these statutes. In other words, to enact justice within the land based upon the rationality of the covenant. The next unit within this passage, 18:1-8, addresses the care that is to be given the Levitical priests. This seems almost out of place relating to the theme of justice, except that the Levites are to be cared for so that they can care for the purposes of Yahweh within the covenant of Israel. The final section of this passage, 18:9-22, addresses the issue of the prophets. False ways of determining the direction that Israel is to take are rejected. Acknowledgment and obedience to the prophets of Yahweh is necessary, because they speak for God. Prophets are to speak only what they are commanded by Yahweh to declare; therefore, a Yahwistic covenant polity is proclaimed. Justice is the major concern for this pericope.

If justice is the primary concern of the institutions within ancient Israel, then how are justice and righteousness defined? The definitions of these terms are determined by and within the social syntax in which these words are practiced. This social syntax is covenant. A covenant is the social arrangement of a specific relationship. If a person does what is agreed upon within this social ar-

16:18—18:22

rangement, then a person is righteous. Even though there are many covenants within the social fabric of all cultures, for ancient Israel the covenant with Yahweh defined all other covenant relationships within the community. The law defines the particular covenantal obligations within the larger covenant in which the people of Israel participate.

When covenants are broken, then making things right is the responsibility of the covenant community. "Justice" is the term that is used to define the righting of things. A lack of justice is discerned in a community where victims of broken covenants are allowed to languish and where victimizers are allowed to continue in their destructive ways. Wholeness is impossible in these relationships because all covenants were within the milieu of the overarching covenant with Yahweh.

This covenant was established in the exodus from Egyptian bondage and was countersigned in the endorsement that was given at Horeb. Israel is shaped by life-giving liberation and is to continue this life-giving liberation in her various binding relationships. These relational obligations are described by the covenantal politics of Yahweh. Because Yahweh is a God who cares for the needy and marginal, Israel is to be a people who care for the needy and marginal. The widow, orphan, sojourner, and poor define the threshold for the covenant community. If the least of these are taken advantage of, or disregarded, then unrighteousness and injustice take place. Institutions with power and authority are to guarantee the covenant rights of all people in relationships within Israel, especially the needy and weak.

Even though Israel's relationship to Yahweh is described as a covenant within the social structure of the community, it is more than simply one of many covenants. It is the defining reality of all covenants; therefore, it is *the* covenant. Rationality is determined by the narrative history of Israel and her God; therefore, pure devotion to Yahweh is essential for the community to maintain the covenantal politics of Yahweh. Yahweh and Yahweh alone defines the covenant and therefore the covenants for ancient Israel. When false gods and worship practices are introduced into Israel, it is impossible to maintain covenant faithfulness and justice. Yahweh, and his story with Israel, circumscribes covenant.

What are the implications to these observations for contemporary Christian readers? For example, are the readers of these texts to work toward a monarchy? This would be a reading strategy that would credit the scripture with a picturelike correspondence to the way the world is to work. Perhaps these ancient texts picture something like a grammar for the way life is to work in covenant. Maybe power and authority in the various roles within institutions are to bring about justice in the community. This would at least mean that power should not be exploited for one's own security and advancement, nor for the security and advancement of the institutions that the power stems from. A Christian reader may want to ponder these four fundamental topics: the purpose of power and authority, the rationality that defines justice and righteousness, the obligations described by the covenant, and the singular devotion to Yahweh as an essential aspect for the covenantal politics of Yahweh.

Hypothetically, power and authority can be divided into two aspects: the community of faith and the larger host society. When addressing the context of the community of faith, practitioners of the faith are obliged to ask various questions concerning the use of power and authority. Examples of some of these questions are: How must the church use power within its community? What does justice and righteousness look like in various covenantal relationships within the church? How are clerical offices to operate inside the community of faith? These questions and many more should occupy the discerning Christian reader of these texts.

There is also the issue of the host society within which the church is located. Is the church to use power to coerce the host culture to believe the way the people of God believe? In other words, is the church called to attempt to create a theocracy? If so, then whose version of the faith is the church called to enforce? Again it seems that the issue should be justice. How do the people of God attempt to witness in the public forum to justice for the least of these? Dialogue and civil argument should be a function of the church's witness to the host culture. How this civil argument takes place must be achieved in behavior exemplary of the self-disclosure of God in Christ Jesus. Much more must be attended to in correlation to the church's role and responsibility with civil justice, but this should at least be a starting point in the discussion.

H. Life (19:1—21:23)

BEHIND THE TEXT

Chapters 16—18 introduce the offices of power and authority in ancient Israel. The purpose of these positions of influence is to mediate social and cultic affairs. Chapters 19—21 detail the laws governing the functions of the judges, priests, elders, and other leaders. These laws include a series of policies in seemingly random arrangement, yet a closer look will reveal that they all share a common framework: the protection of life in the community. Even the laws concerning violation of property markers, witnesses, female captives, and the rights of the firstborn are construed with a linkage to the sixth commandment.

A gray area exists in the line of reasoning between two social obligations: the priority of life-giving compassion and the necessary but ambiguous limits of death. The tug is between protecting the innocent so that "you may live long" (22:7 NRSV) and **show no pity: life for life, eye for eye, tooth for tooth, hand for hand, foot for foot** (19:21). The decrees in this passage orbit

195

around a collection of circumstances where the boundary lines are complex and thorny. The primary assumption of this commentary is that the literary context should inform the meaning of the passages in question. Glancing at the structure of the passage suggests a depiction of this encompassing theme:

1. The Protection of the Innocent (19:1-21)
   a. Cities of Refuge (19:1-13)
   b. Boundary Markers (19:14)
   c. Witness Laws (19:15-21)
2. Intentional Killing, Warfare, and Military Deferments (20:1-20)
3. Possibilities and Limits in the Clashes between Life and Death (21:1-23)
   a. Unsolved Murder and the Role of Elders and Judges (21:1-9)
   b. Female Captives of War (21:10-14)
   c. The Right of the Firstborn (21:15-17)
   d. Rebellious Children (21:18-21)
   e. The Rights of the Executed (21:22-23)

I. The Protection of the Innocent (19:1-21)

This chapter divides into three parts: a policy pertaining to the cities of refuge (vv 1-13), a policy with regards to ancient landmarks (v 14), and a policy pertaining to witnesses in legal cases (vv 15-21). Judicial process is the connection that brings together these three subsections. What is of interest is that the focus of these three policies is in relation to process and procedure.

a. Cities of Refuge (19:1-13)

■ **1-13** Verses 1-13 are concerned with the danger of manslaughter and an ensuing cycle of vengeance. The issue of vengeance is a substantial matter for any community's political framework. If retribution is allowed to proceed unrestrained, then it can render any society unlivable. The cycle of retaliation is an ever-spiraling development that enlarges to more and more hostility, rather than contracts to less and less violence. Restraining the savage advance of bloodshed is in the end what these cities are designed to short-circuit.

The opening three verses designate the **three cities** (v 2) of refuge as an asylum to be quickly available for anyone who takes the life of another. What is fascinating about this initial section is that the cities of asylum are to be available to anyone who takes the life of another. The question of innocence or guilt in the matter of killing another person is taken up later in this section, but initially the only thing that seems to matter is a place of safety to flee from the avenger of blood. This place of safety discloses a bit about the people as well as their God. A natural human tendency is revenge, especially in a society made up of tribes and clans. The avenger of blood is the next of kin, and the natural tendency is that revenge could spark a blood feud that could make the land unlivable. The establishment of the cities of refuge also points to an understanding of deity that reflects an extraordinary value placed upon life and peace. Yahweh is a God who liberates and blesses his people in the land.

Accidental death is the concern of vv 4-7. If the loss of life is a result of an accident, then the avenger of blood will be shedding innocent blood. For this reason, the cities must not be too far for the fleeing person to arrive in safety. Former bad blood or even family or clan honor could be used as a motivation for the pursuing of a killer. If a person is subsequently killed, who is innocent of malice, this would be an unjust action and it could also escalate into full-scale feud between clans. A remedy for blood feuds and their endless retribution is a place of refuge where time would allow heads to cool and facts to come forth. Therefore, cities must be reachable, and three cities are needed in the beginning of Israel's occupation of the land.

Verses 8-10 form a supplementary expansion of the law that makes accommodation for **three more cities** (v 9) as the territory of ancient Israel expands. The motive for additional cities is to have ease of access for people on the run. If the cities are spread too far apart, then a person may never make it to a place of sanctuary. The motivation for these cities is ultimately Israel's love for and obedience to Yahweh. Cities of refuge keep the bloodguilt of killing the innocent from defiling the land that Yahweh is giving Israel. Yahweh is the motive for these additional cities, and ultimately for the whole of the cities of asylum.

Premeditated murderers are not to be protected. Verses 11-13 specify that if a person is judged guilty of premeditated murder, then the avenger of blood is allowed to take the life of the murderer. When the conditions of culpability are satisfied, then the process of family justice is allowed to take its course. If innocent people are killed, it often leads to further blame and hostility. But when justice is enacted, even through execution, it brings an end to further bloodshed and leads to peace. It should be apparent that not only are the innocent protected but also the land is purged.

b. Boundary Markers (19:14)

■ **14** Verse 14 deals with repositioning the boundary markers and thereby seizing someone else's land. This regulation shifts from authorized boundaries set around cities of refuge to assigned boundaries set around parcels of inherited land that belong to each family or clan. There are various commentators who consider this law to be misplaced as an intrusion into the section that deals primarily with the taking of life. But, numerous other scholars consider that this law fits into the larger section (19:1—21:23) and is relevant to the pragmatic application of the commandment to not kill. If this is so, then this verse suggests that the decree to not reposition boundary markers would fall under the theme of killing. To reposition the boundary indicators of that inherited land is at the very least the diminishing of the life of one's neighbor. It can also cause a feud.

Taking away a boundary indicator is deliberately sinful, since embezzlement of the land deprives families of blessing and hope. It should not be forgotten that the land is Yahweh's gift to be distributed among the tribes. Life and blessing are conferred on people by means of the land; therefore, to embezzle the land is a form of taking life. What makes this crime so complicated is that satisfactory proof is difficult to acquire. When boundary markers are moved, it could very well cause controversy that would result in violence and hostility. The introduction of the ruling at this point in the passage provided a notice that evidence would require painstaking impartial examination.

c. Witness Laws (19:15-21)

■ 15-21 Verses 15-18*a* tackle the problem of a malicious witness. Because deceitful witnesses can lead to the devastation of innocent life and therefore the inability to enact justice within community, the question must be asked: How are judgments to be made? The need for at least two witnesses raised the quandary of fabrication of evidence either in making of false charges or through convincing an additional individual to serve as a corroborator with no real warrant for doing so.

The Hebrew word for **crime** in v 16 is *sārâ*, which means "defection" or "turning aside." In 13:5 [6 HB] it conveys the idea of apostasy or "rebellion" against God. It also has a similar meaning in Jer 28:16 and 29:32. It should be remembered that Jeremiah is a part of the tradition that shapes and is shaped by Deuteronomy. On the basis of the meaning of this word in these passages, the meaning is probably more than an overall wrongdoing, but most probably means some form of rebellion against Yahweh.

Both the accuser and the accused are required to appear before Yahweh. If rebellion against God is the accusation of the malicious witness, then this would imply that God is both the plaintiff and the judge. This appearing before Yahweh is accomplished by appearing before the priests or judges. The correlation of mentioning Yahweh with the public officials points to the conviction that bearing witness has everything to do with the kind of people Israel is to embody both individually and corporately. They are to reflect God and the covenant. A lack of truthfulness hurts not only the person being accused but also the entire community. Reliance and responsibility are annihilated, and the fabric of community is in jeopardy. Due process is necessary in a community that pursues justice, especially a justice that is defined by the logic of the Mosaic covenant. Judges are to investigate the matter thoroughly. This means that they are to interrogate the two people closely. Wisdom and discernment are necessary for

19:15-21

these positions of authority. Implied in the statement of standing before Yahweh is that there is help to be had by the hand of God.

A distortion of justice is the result of a community that allows fallacious evidence. What happens to an unreliable witness that deliberately misleads the judicial system? This is the question that occupies the remainder of this section. False witnesses create a great danger to a covenantal community shaped by the liberating and life-giving activity of Yahweh. Firm penalties are imposed on anyone who bears false witness. The false witness is to receive the same punishment that the accused would have received. A crucial conviction of this passage is that punitive punishment serves as a prevention to further violations. Evil is purged from the midst of the people when this type of retributive sentencing is administered. The purging of evil, and this implies more than simply settling accounts, implies that there is something at stake for the whole community. The "evil" that this leaves, if unchecked, would destroy the very fabric of the people. They would become something other than what Yahweh purposes for them to become.

According to this passage, pity should not control the outcome of those who bear false witness. If the likely outcome of the verdict for the accused would involve the death penalty, then a life for a life should be enacted. If the penalty would occasion some other form of punishment, then in like manner those that bear false witness would experience the same. If it is to remove sight, then an eye for an eye; if it is to mutilate a person in an alternative way, then a tooth for a tooth or a hand for a hand or a foot for a foot. Justice administered this way would surely create not only a truthful community but also a blind, toothless, lame, and dead community. However, the "eye for an eye" law also means that even the false witness receives protection from excessive and unjust punishment. Punishment should not exceed the degree of damage **intended to do** to an innocent person by a false witness (v 19).

The Christian community cannot read these words unmediated by the gospel. The words of Jesus, in Matt 5:38-42, must be heard in this context:

You have heard that it was said, "Eye for eye, and tooth for tooth." But I tell you, do not resist an evil person. If anyone slaps you on the right cheek, turn to them the other cheek also. And if anyone wants to sue you and take your shirt, hand over your coat as well. If anyone forces you to go one mile, go with them two miles. Give to the one who asks you, and do not turn away from the one who wants to borrow from you.

2. Intentional Killing, Warfare, and Military Deferments (20:1-20)

■ **1-20** Inquiries of manslaughter and accountability for the loss of life predictably lead to questions of combat and the massacre that ensues. In view of the fact that the taking of human life is a deed accountable to Yahweh, warfare

199

is surrounded with the questions of accountability. This reality leads many readers of Deuteronomy to describe the regulations of comportment in war, as a policy of "holy war." Concerns of culpability and holiness envelop this passage of Scripture. Deuteronomy has to do with blessing and life; therefore, when any human life is taken, it becomes a theological issue within the politics of Yahweh. This section is divided into two major segments: vv 1-9 describe the policies of who may possibly go to war, and also it contains inspiration to go to war without fear; vv 10-20 speak to regulations that presume policies and strategies for going to war.

The first set of instructions (vv 1-9) beckons Israel to go to war with both courage and discrimination. These verses articulate the policy of who may possibly go to war, and they also encourage bravery. The chapter begins with a declaration that is theological through and through: **the LORD your God, who brought you up out of Egypt, will be with you**. Israel's battles are deemed to be Yahweh's war against his enemies. The land that is conquered belongs to Yahweh. If the war, the land and the people belong to Yahweh, then the conquest is a "holy war." Not only are the beliefs regarding the conquest attached to Yahweh, but also Yahweh determined the practices inside the invasion. The conquest is not a campaign for Yahweh, but Yahweh's crusade.

The opening verses of this chapter focus on how to overcome fear, the greatest enemy that Israel will battle. Fear ascends when the people catch a glimpse of horses, chariots, and superior military power, because they fail to perceive that Yahweh is with them. The Egyptians and the Assyrians, because of the success they brought to battles, used horses and chariots. Israel also desired to have these weapons of horrendous destruction, for they perceived themselves as small and weak. But Israel is not to rely on anything other than her God. Yahweh is not just any god or defense system, but the God who brought the Hebrew slaves from the land of Egyptian bondage. It is Yahweh who delivers his covenant people from the most powerful force upon the planet.

Yahweh, who delivered them and led them in the past, is the one who goes with them into battle. Verses 2-4 clearly convey that the battle belongs to Yahweh, for the priests are to **come forward and address** the troops (v 2). Warriors and generals are not to give the speeches, for these battles are a particular sort. The battle belongs to God. Therefore, servants of God, the priests, are to address the troops in the name of God. Sermons from these clerics are simple and to the point: **Do not be fainthearted or afraid; do not panic or be terrified by them. For the LORD your God is the one who goes with you to fight for you against your enemies to give you victory** (vv 3b-4). Even though Israel is portrayed as going out to war against the enemies, the matter is not that these people groups are a threat to their survival, but that they are enemies of Yahweh. The battle is sacred because it belongs to him. Therefore, courageous faith is the essential virtue that is necessary for the people to carry out to battle.

The mustering of the troops for battle is described in vv 5-9. The official, who is a priest, gives exemptions to certain classes of people: new homeowners, landlords of newly planted vineyards, those who are engaged, and the terrified. The first three exemptions are reiterated in a reverse manner in Deut 28:30, where the people are warned against disobedience and what would be the result of such disobedience: they would not enjoy the blessings promised in the land. Exemption to a battle implies the belief that if one is a new homeowner or a new vineyard owner or a husband-to-be, then the blessings that go with these basic fruitful activities are to be enjoyed. Israel, like the whole of life in creation, is to be fruitful and multiply in the land that Yahweh is giving them. They are to experience rest in the land of promise (Deut 12:9). This at least means that they are to have the blessings of the land, without the threat of enemies.

If courage is the virtue that Israel is to embody, then faith in Yahweh's providence becomes a necessary element to the character of those who will go out into battle. In light of the thesis of fearlessness in the face of a powerful adversary, the passage makes clear that the discharging of the fearful is aimed at preventing fear from dispersion through the combatants like a disease. The historians of the tradition of Deuteronomy narrate a wonderful story to illustrate this line of reasoning. In Judg 7:2-3, when Gideon is summoned to battle the Midianites, a criterion is given for those who should go to battle. The purpose of the story is to demonstrate that the battle and its victory belong to Yahweh. It is only after the sacred officials mustered the troops that the **commanders** are to take charge of them (Deut 20:9). The battle belongs to Yahweh. Other justification for discharge hardly seems related to this interest in maintaining courage among the troops.

Verses 10-20 develop policies and strategies for going to war. Combat is brutal, malicious, and destructive; therefore, rules must be in place for a covenant community if they are to engage in this devastating endeavor. Formulating rules to regulate warfare begins with asking the question: Who should be saved in this savage pursuit? For the covenant people, the offering of terms of surrender is the first step taken in reducing war's devastating consequences. If they respond compliantly, then all of the people in that town are to be spared. A part of the agreement to spare the lives of the people in the town is that they would serve Israel.

This offer of surrender has qualifications that surround it. First, it is given to those towns that are far away. In other words, these towns did not offer an ideological threat. Second, the towns are offered **peace**, but with a price to the town. *Shalom*, in v 10, does not mean wholeness or tranquillity for the residents of the town, but life with submission and servitude to Israel. Even

201

though peace did not mean that the town would be spared from submission, it is a promise to the residents that their lives would be spared. If they do not responded compliantly, but join the battle against Israel, then all the males would be put to the sword. There are many ethical issues that Christian readers of this text need to sort out, but at the very least one can recognize that life itself is held to be of great enough value that wholesale slaughter is not the order of the day for everyone. Israel could have neighbors.

Rebuffing the terms of submission would result in brutal action as a consequence of Israel's victory in battle (vv 12-15). Israel is to put all males to the sword, and they are to take as the spoils of war the women, children, livestock, and everything else in the town. The slaughter of all the males is not devoting the town to the ban but is to make ineffective any further threat that the town may offer in the future. This is permitted only to those towns that are far from the settlements of the Hebrew people. The towns that are near are to be devoted to the ban. Universal rules for warfare do not pertain to the special situation of the imminent conquest of the promised land. To devote to the ban means that the complete destruction of an enemy as a type of sacrifice to Yahweh is required. This word literally means to remove something from common use and to set apart for a special purpose. The policy of the "ban" is that nothing is to be left alive. Everything that breathes is to be destroyed: both people and animals.

20:1-20 The most significant motive for these battles, as articulated in v 18, is that **they will teach you to follow all the detestable things they do in worshiping their gods, and you will sin against the LORD your God.** The driving force for unmitigated annihilation is not national security or even acquiring resources, but for theological and ethical reasons: false beliefs would lead to false forms of life. The previous occupants of the land of Canaan are to be exterminated because of the religious temptation to Israel would be too great if they survive with their beliefs, practices, and values. The politics of Yahweh require an alternative belief system with its own way of life. Israel's continuance in the land is dependent upon fidelity to Yahweh.

What is fascinating in the theological vision of Deuteronomy is the ownership of the land: it belonged to Yahweh. The Hebrew people are only stewards of the land, not owners. Earlier in Deuteronomy, a theological rationale is given for Israel's dislocation of the Canaanites; their form of life is abhorrent in both idolatry and injustice. They lost the land, according to Deut 2 and 3, because of their way of life. Later in Israel's story, the historians of the tradition of Deuteronomy would narrate that it is the Assyrians and the Babylonians that would be the instruments for judging abhorrent Israel in the land. Idolatry and injustice dominate the land once again. The land would throw up its inhabitants.

One of the most problematic questions, in regard to the commandment against murder, is the wide-ranging carnage that transpires in the OT, some of which God purportedly directs in the holy war conquest of the Canaanites. A Christian reader of these texts is befuddled with all of this violence. How is a Christian to understand God and violence? The early church started interpreting the texts of the Bible by the analogy of faith, or in other words, with God who is revealed in Jesus Christ. These policies and practices must be interpreted in light of the policies of the kingdom of God proclaimed and embodied in Jesus Christ. It must be remembered that when Jesus said, "Love your enemies," he at least means, "Don't kill them."

Verses 19-20 signal an interesting consideration; Israel is to protect the land, even as they endeavored to purge the land of false forms of life. The premise of this passage is that the primary impact of warfare is to be upon the participants within the battles themselves. The predicament is that damage would inevitably be inflicted upon the land in the course of purging it. Crops would be needed as provision for the troops; therefore, Israel's army would plunder them. And, whatever crops are not needed for Israel's combatants, these crops would be destroyed in order to deny them to besiege cities and their armies. It is a widespread procedure, in the ancient world, to cut off and destroy the enemy's sources of supply. The destruction of crops went hand in hand with the cutting down of trees, which are used to build ramparts and assault ramps for assailing fortified cities. As a result, military maneuvers time after time lead to the devastation of precious resources in an area where produce is always exposed and trees, far from plentiful, are of great worth. Israel is charged, as far as is feasible, to avoid harm to the natural environment and its future value for the Hebrew people.

3. Possibilities and Limits in the Clashes between Life and Death (21:1-23)

These verses address the possibilities and limits in the clashes between life and death. The laws relate to the directive against killing and force the reader into a whole series of obscurities in dealing with the boundary issues of life and death. There are five seemingly unrelated laws in this chapter. The question that any reader should first ask is: Is there a rationality and congruence within this diverse collection of laws and practices? These five laws are:

a. Unsolved Murder and the Role of Elders and Judges (21:1-9)
b. Female Captives of War (21:10-14)
c. The Right of the Firstborn (21:15-17)
d. Rebellious Children (21:18-21)
e. The Rights of the Executed (21:22-23)

The passage is bracketed by two decrees that address the subject of the community's involvement in the judicial response to murder. The first ad-

203

dresses unsolved murder and the dilemma of bloodguilt. The last speaks to concerns for the dignity that must be displayed toward even those who are executed. The middle three policies address family stipulations. The first of these three addresses the question of how to deal with female captives who have lost their father or husband in battle. The last of the three policies addresses the problem of rebellious children and the capital punishment that the community imposes upon them. The central law is the only law that does not address the issue of the loss of life directly. The connection to the loss of life has to do with the inheritance that will come as a result of the loss of life of the father, and the possible violence that could ensue if the issue of inheritance is not settled before the fact of the father's death.

The system for distinguishing between deliberate murder and manslaughter (19:1-21) supposes that a criminal is captured and that a reliable tribunal has assembled. Yet, this is not always achievable when a dead body is discovered, with no way of determining the perpetrator. How are the people to deal with a murder by an unknown hand? The contemporary reader must understand the problem that arises when such a crime is realized, a murder involves the community in bloodguilt, and the ideas of the ancients are very realistic about the consequences of such a crime. They believe that this crime is of such a nature that the capacity of the community to worship Yahweh and to continue to enact the covenant is hindered. If the murderer is caught, this damage could be avoided by his execution. But what is the arrangement if the killer remains unidentified? Could the community ever purge itself of the bloodguilt?

For ancient Israel, the shedding of blood is virtually the same as an assault on Yahweh. Israel's tradition informs her that humanity is formed in God's own image. "Blood," as is the case of Abel in Gen 4:10, "cries . . . from the ground" for justice. Israel realizes that the community is "under a curse and driven from the ground" (Gen 4:11-12). The curse on the land as well as its inhabitants remains if nothing is done. The questions that besiege her are: How can harmony be reestablished when the murderer is hidden, and must the land remain infected forever? Ancient Israel fostered a ritual to deal with these specific questions of injustice.

a. Unsolved Murder and the Role of Elders and Judges (21:1-9)

■ **1-9** Verses 1-2 provide detail regarding the first action to be taken in such a situation where no known culprit is found. Since the body is discovered in the open country, the leadership of the two nearest towns gathers to determine which town is closest to the body. This is in all probability functioning under the belief that the specific murderer is most likely a resident in the closest town. Therefore, the responsibility for justice rests with that group of people. The leaders of that town are given responsibility for reparations.

Verses 3-4 describe a prearranged procedure to comply with the community's requirements for justice. The leaders of the community are to choose a heifer that has never been used for work. It is to be a proxy for the unidentified offender. The neck of the heifer is broken in a location where the land is unutilized and where there is running water. Symbolically, this ritual allows for the guilt of the unknown murderer to be removed from the land.

Verses 5-7 introduce the Levites into the proceedings. They are to openly pronounce that the elders of the town nearest to where the corpse is discovered have no connection in the death. This is important in at least two ways: it affirmed that legal proceedings would have taken place and it also acknowledges that the shedding of innocent blood is an illicit deed that dishonors and corrupts the land. By the elders of the town asserting the blamelessness of the town and its people, and by the ceremonial enactment, the bloodguilt is washed away with the running water.

The removal of guilt from the land is achieved through the ritualistic acts of confession and death of the heifer (v 9). What could this mean? Does this mean that God needs blood from the innocent heifer, or does this ritual shape the ethos of the community? Is this ritual a sacrifice or something else? If it is a sacrifice, then is Yahweh expiated? Von Rad interprets this ritual as a sacrifice mainly because it includes a supplemental prayer to take away the bloodguilt (1975, 136-37). But he also understood that this is a sacrifice that is unlike any other sacrifice offered to Yahweh. He points out that the animal is not killed at a place of worship, but at a place that is the exact opposite, a place that is not cultivated. The animal is also killed in a way that is not used in sacrificing; its neck is broken. The washing of hands and the declaration by the leaders of innocence (vv 6-8) make it obvious that it is not Yahweh that receives the expiation; but he is the mediator who presides over reparations. It is Yahweh, through the policies and practices of a political order, who turns away the curse caused by the murder. The ritual changes Israel, therefore they are the recipients of the reparation.

What then is the function of this ritual? Von Rad assumed that this ritual is tied to an older pre-Yahwistic magical procedure for getting rid of sin (1975, 136-37). It should be remembered that sin or iniquity has the power to be perpetuated within a family system or a community. But is magic or even appeasing the deity the major function of this ritual? Perhaps there are traces of both magic and placation of the deity in this ancient ritual, but it seems to have another function that may have significance for contemporary readers. Ritual is a social convention that transmits the values of a culture from one generation to the next with the power to maintain those values over time. Ritual or practices produce an ethos in a community and character in individuals.

The question that contemporary readers should ask is: What are the values that this ritual transmits? Clearly, there are at least two values that are transmitted through this ritual practice. The first is that life is a precious gift that God bestows. When this gift is taken, it has great implications for all persons related to the taking of life. These implications include, second, the responsibility of the community for safeguarding life and executing justice when the covenant of life is broken. If the murder takes place near a town, the murderer most probably resides in the town. This ritual is another way of displaying that everyone in community is their brother's or sister's keeper.

How are modern readers to account for the convictions that inform this passage? This law is permeated by a preconscious certainty of communal accountability for what happens among and to persons within the community. This ritual of amends includes the harsh death of a heifer, as it becomes a replacement for the unknown guilty party. The awfulness of murder is stressed, so that everyone within the community will realize that there is no escape from justice, the guilt of innocent blood rests upon the land and therefore the community. This law is framed in such a way as to avert murder by escalating the revulsion of this evil. This is not a way of placating divinity so that a community can continue in its murderous ways. All who will live in a manner that reflects the covenantal stipulations of Yahweh must be vigilant.

b. Female Captives of War (21:10-14)

■ **10-14** The law pertaining to a female captive during war (vv 10-14) is arranged together with two other laws that also deal with the questions of family law through most of the remaining portion of ch 21. This particular edict is shaped from a motive of human dignity. Even a female taken captive in battle may not be maltreated; the bond with her must be an authorized one. If it is dissolved, the woman's public status, which is given to her in the intervening time, must not worsen.

The opening law in Deut 20 deals with warfare, and the opening verse of this section equally addresses the issue of war, but the principal concern is on marital relations that could ensue following battles. This is not the first time the law material addresses the issue of war and marriage, the first occasion concerned who might receive a deferment on going into battle.

Verses 12-13 of ch 21 address the appearance of the woman captured in battle. The Israelite man is told to **bring her into your home and have her shave her head, trim her nails and put aside the clothes she was wearing when captured**. These instructions could possibly be interpreted as part of the woman's mourning process, as the next phrase would suggest: **after she has lived in your house and mourned her father and mother for a full month, then you may go to her and be her husband and she shall be your wife**. The first phrase could also focus on how to acculturate the woman into Hebrew customs, practices, and beliefs. She is taking off the old and subsequently taking on the new. There is a change of status and a new life in another society.

The change in status into a new culture brought with it the values and ethos of the covenant people of Yahweh. Verse 14 articulates an extraordinary command: the Hebrew male may not treat the woman like merchandise, but as a covenantal human being. The primary interest of this course of action is that the woman must be treated as a wife and not as a slave. She cannot be sold as one would sell commodities. As a married woman and likely mother, she could be divorced and set free, but she could not be turned into a slave.

c. The Right of the Firstborn (21:15-17)

■ **15-17** A grammatical change takes place between the regulation in vv 15-17 and the earlier directive concerning female captives. The change is a move from the second-person singular to the third-person singular. The question that is addressed in this regulation is: Which offspring of a man, with more than one wife, is to receive the right of the firstborn? It should be noticed that this law does not imply that daughters are beneficiaries of an inheritance, but only the sons. Polygamy was accepted in ancient Israel, but it gives an opportunity for domestic disruption. The course of action of this law is imparted for the purpose of restraining this unrest. The contention that exists between wives extends to the siblings, particularly regarding the subject of the allocation of property. The quandary involves a man having two wives, who both have a son. This state of affairs becomes problematic by the possibility that the man may love one of his wives more than the other. Whatever answer is given to the question of who receives what in the inheritance will have implications for the mother as well as her child.

21:15-17

If the wife, who gives birth to a younger sibling, is the one most loved, then the question posed is: Can the man give that child the right of the firstborn? This law intends to protect against a subjective action that might occur. Deuteronomy makes the notion of the firstborn, in the biological sense, an absolute one and guarantees it against any arbitrary attempt to make it a relative one. The edict, in this passage, maintains that when a man allocates his property to his sons, he must give a double portion to the firstborn son regardless of who the mother is. A double portion is not an undertaking of favoritism, but a legal right of the firstborn. The position is reinforced rhetorically by placing the directive in the center of the structure. Even if a Hebrew man has a favorite son by the wife he loves the most, he must recognize the firstborn son as his primary heir.

Biblical examples of this dilemma can be noticed in Jacob's wives Rachel and Leah, found in Gen 29:30-32; and also in Elkanah's wives Hannah and Penninah, found in 1 Sam 1:5. It is also seen in the rivalry that occurs between Abraham's wives Hagar and Sarah in Gen 21:8 ff. The concept of an inheritance of the firstborn is indicated in 2 Kgs 2:9, where Elisha is asking Elijah to declare him to be his spiritual heir or firstborn. This issue also plays out in the story of the prodigal son in Luke 15:11 ff. The purpose of this law is to uphold the economic viability of the household and the right of the firstborn son to the inheritance of the land, which Yahweh gives to the tribes and families.

d. Rebellious Children (21:18-21)

■ **18-21** The decree concerning a rebellious son (Deut 21:18-21) comes right after the regulation concerning the rights of inheritance for the firstborn. Literally, this decree merges the topics of both family relations and capital punishment. The problem is that this law is unconscionable to the modern reader. Why would conflicts within a family necessitate such a ruthless ruling?

The central function of this law is not to prescribe a way to keep children in line, but to take away disciplinary action from the family head and to place it upon the elders of the community. The elders are to examine and probe the allegations, and only with their ruling could brutal punishment be carried out. The town's menfolk are to carry out the verdict. Their participation demonstrates their approval of the judgment. In this way discord within a family is yielded to judicious public examination, and capricious parental brutality is summoned to a wider communal justification. This law is not to give the parent of a child the opportunity to enact violence upon the child, but to ultimately place violence and capital punishment within the framework of the covenant people of Yahweh. Only the community, acting in accord with Yahweh's purposes, can take life. The head of the family does not have jurisdiction, on his own, over the adult members of his family. He must hand the case over to those who administer justice, namely, the elders of the city. Nor is it unimportant that the mother has to appear as a competent plaintiff. Evidently the lawgiver insists on both parents acting in agreement when they decide upon this final step.

It should be noticed that in v 20 the rebellious child is described as a glutton and a drunkard. These are the accusations that Jesus received from the religious leaders of his time. They are using Deuteronomy as a way of describing Jesus as a rebellious child, and therefore a nominee for execution. This detail alone should cause the reader of Scripture to hesitate. The tragedy is that even persons steeped in piety and theological erudition failed to recognize the revelation of God. Interpretation, even by the community at large, is a dangerous and tricky proposition.

e. The Rights of the Executed (21:22-23)

■ **22-23** In the ancient world, the public display of executed criminals is a common practice. The motivation for this is a public form of terrorism with the aspiration to dissuade any future unlawful activity. The sequence in v 22 implies that "hanging was not a method used in execution, but something done after the death of a criminal, on the same day" (Craigie 1976, 285). When a person is dead, the public display of the body is draped on a tree or post to notify everyone that the results of being a particular kind of criminal brings about a similar consequence.

Deuteronomy permits the practice a public execution, but there is a threshold to the public display that the executed body of a criminal has to endure. The practice of not allowing a person to hang on a tree overnight is a way of imposing limitations to the use of public display. By sundown, the body must be buried. This would even apply to those persons who committed repulsive transgressions. Allowing a body to suspend overnight defiles the land, not only through decay, but because the land belongs to Yahweh.

These chapters of Deuteronomy clearly state that the land is Yahweh's gift to Israel. The land not only yields produce but also, through its fertility, gives blessing and life. Israel is tempted to trust other sources for fertility, but Yahweh insists that he and he alone is responsible for the productivity of the land. Reverence for Yahweh means regard for the land, and regard for the land means respect for life. Cherishing life means respecting all life. Human beings are created in the God's image, and this includes even villains. They must be given an appropriate burial and the dignity it authorizes.

Deuteronomy believes that defilement of the land is the great threat to Israel's ongoing sustainability. The residents of Canaan are driven from the land because they defiled it, and Israel would later be taken into exile because she would defile the land once again. To protect the land not only from idolatrous practices but also from forms of life that did not recognize and encourage the gift of life is the task of Israel's witness. If Yahweh creates all life and calls it good, then God's covenant people, who are to reflect his character and purpose, are to revere life.

The Christian reader should notice that this reference is later made regarding Jesus. Galatians 3:13 states: "Christ redeemed us from the curse of the law by becoming a curse for us, for it is written: 'Cursed is everyone who is hung on a pole.'" The text in Deuteronomy does not mean that a body is accursed of God because it is hanging on a tree, but that it is hanging on a tree because it is accursed of God. In other words, the body is not accursed by God because it is dead, but being accursed is the reason one is put to death. This would mean, in this text, that the community rightly discerns the nature of the crime and administers the curse of Yahweh upon the criminal.

FROM THE TEXT

The guiding rubric of this collection of laws is the sixth command: "You shall not murder." This commandment sets in motion a different rhetorical rhythm from the preceding commands; it is short and simple. Only two words make up the Hebrew of this commandment: a negative marker and a verb. What does it mean to not kill? The purpose of Deuteronomy 19—21 is to give examples of how the sixth commandment applies to concrete life-and-death situations. These examples are in the form of practices that the community is to enact, but they also allow readers to further ponder the implication of the sixth commandment. The premise of this section of laws is that life is a gift from the Creator and it is to be cherished. The question posed by this premise is: How should community relationships be organized in order to sustain the precious gift of life itself? What is of interest to the contemporary reader is not how to practice life in exactly the same way as ancient Israel, but to ask: What kind of value system do these practices form and does that value system still operate for the community of Christ?

So, what kind of value system would hold these ancient Hebrews if they practice these laws? A quick look at the general laws should point to the system of values that is generated from the observance of these practices. The first collection of practices involves the protection of innocent people. The reason for creating cities of refuge and stipulation for not removing boundary markers and the laws concerning what constitutes a valid witness is that to take advantage of the innocent through an act of revenge or false witness or even moving markers that are to last from generation to generation constitutes an absence of valuing the gift of life. The collection in ch 19 ends with a communal practice of imposing judgment on those who disregard life: "Show no pity: life for life, eye for eye, tooth for tooth, hand for hand, foot for foot" (v 21). This is not to demonstrate that life can be taken easily, but that the disregard for life is the very loss of life. Life is a precious gift from God.

The second collection of legal practices, located in ch 20, includes military deferments and intentional killing resulting from warfare. A community cannot think of the preciousness of life without considering the carnage that results from warfare. Because ancient Israel believed that the taking of human life was an action answerable to Yahweh, warfare was encompassed with the questions of accountability before God. This certainty has led many to describe these policies of conduct in war, as a policy of "holy war." Accountability and holiness encase these practices. Blessing and life are a theological concern of the politics of Yahweh. War is to be enacted only by and for Yahweh; therefore, the policies of who may go to war are coupled with the inspiration of going to war without fear.

The final collection of practices is located in ch 21. These laws again address the issue of the preciousness of life. What is the community to do when a murder takes place and the guilty party is not discovered? How are female captives of war to be treated? Are they to be allowed to mourn and are they to be given the status of persons and not objects? What is the right of the life of the future generations, which includes the firstborn? How are rebellious children to be handled? And finally, how are the bodies of executed criminals to be treated? These questions and the policies and practices of this section all point to the respect that ancient Israel maintained for life.

Life is vulnerable and fleeting, yet it is precious and amazing. Christian readers of these laws should go beyond a referential enactment of these laws to their principled embodiment. These policies should be read through the lens of the policies and practices of Jesus, where he addresses some of these same issues but with complete nonviolence. Matthew records the words of Jesus:

> You have heard that it was said, "Eye for eye, and tooth for tooth." But I tell you, do not resist an evil person. If anyone slaps you on the right cheek, turn to them the other cheek also. And if anyone wants to sue you and take your shirt, hand over your coat as well. If anyone forces you to go one mile, go with them two miles. Give to the one who asks you, and do not turn away from the one who wants to borrow from you. You have heard that it was said, "Love your neighbor and hate your enemy." But I tell you, love your enemies and pray for those who persecute you, that you may be children of your Father in heaven. He causes his sun to rise on the evil and the good, and sends rain on the righteous and the unrighteous. If you love those who love you, what reward will you get? Are not even the tax collectors doing that? And if you greet only your own people, what are you doing more than others? Do not even pagans do that? Be perfect, therefore, as your heavenly Father is perfect. (5:38-48)

Ancient Israel and followers of Jesus believe that life is a gift of God. This basic belief moves these communities to cherish and nurture the life of one's neighbor. A value system is fostered through the practice of these policies and the expansion of these policies in the life and teaching of Jesus. This value structure is one where all life is cherished. The biblical mandate of loving one's neighbor appears to correspond with these practices and their expansion in the ministry of Jesus. It could be said of the community that reflects the nature of the God revealed in the person of Jesus and anticipated in the OT scriptures, that it is its brother's and sister's keeper.

I. Boundaries: Social and Sacrosanct (22:1—23:18 [22:1—23:19 HB])

BEHIND THE TEXT

The policies and practices in this section of Deuteronomy are concerned with boundary markers. These markers are for the sake of protecting both Israel's unique identity as Yahweh's chosen and holy people, and the protection of life itself. Bringing these two themes together specifies the purpose of what it means to be Yahweh's chosen and holy people.

IN THE TEXT

■ **1-8** This chapter appears to have no ordering principle for its laws. The regulations seem random and obscure. Yet, the protection of the neighbor dominates these regulations. Safeguarding the neighbor is involved in caring for the neighbor's possessions, especially animals. Building code rulings, found in 22:8, are concerned with the neighbor's safety. The environmental care for wildlife in providing an ongoing resource for flocks of birds, and the male and female apparel are more difficult to fit within the larger confines of the category of protecting the neighbor's life. Perhaps the meanings of the care for a flock of birds is motivated by the care for the ongoing resource of meat for the entire community, and male and female clothing might be connected to Canaanite customs.

Verses 1-4 involve a series of decrees that reflect a hospitable and cooperative responsibility for the possessions, especially the animals, of other persons within the covenant community. The stipulations suggest the concerns of a community that depend on agriculture as its primary means for support and sustenance. Such a community is composed of landowners who are daily dependent upon the cooperation and assistance of each other. The first four statutes involve the loss of property and the duty of the neighbor to take back what is lost when it is found. Neighbors, in this covenant community, are bound together in mutual care and protection.

The NIV does not indicate the reference to *your brother*, which appears five times in the opening four verses of this chapter. This Hebrew word ('*āḥîkā*) denotes kinship with the person in need. Within the context of these laws, *your brother* does not necessarily indicate blood relationships, but the relationships within covenant community. The kinship affinity is to apply to all covenantal relationships within ancient Israel.

These declarations render neighbor care unambiguous, in that a person is responsible to assist another person in need. When a Hebrew witnesses an apparent injury developing, he or she may not **ignore** the event (v 1). Instead, a person must intervene and be willing to restore the property of the owner (v 3). In fact, a person must take action whenever there is a need, and not wait until one is called upon to do so (v 4). One of the most remarkable characteristics of this ruling on neighbor care is in the last imperative, which insists that persons within the covenant community not withhold help. The meaning of this text is that covenant neighbors may not withdraw from one another. They cannot hide from one another, but they must engage with neighbor care even in the most mundane aspects of their lives. This regulation could nearly be regarded as Israel's "Good Samaritan Law."

Verse 5 is one of the better-known stipulations in the tradition of Deuteronomy. This verse is a prohibition against cross-dressing: **A woman must not wear men's clothing, nor a man wear women's clothing.** This law would prohibit cross-dressing and would suggest an analysis relating it to some pagan ritual or some sexual perversion; most likely it is associated with rituals within the fertility cult. Deuteronomy is concerned with a censure of Canaanite practices and behavior, and it is the likely insinuation of this law. Some readers consider this regulation out of place in this context, especially when the benevolent handling of animals is the next decree. What must be considered, in this context, is that the regulation comes under the general rubric of mixing things that must be kept apart. The prohibition clearly intends that everything, including male and female, shall be kept distinct.

The creation account, in Gen 1:24, points to this principle: "each according to its kind." The mixing of even the slightest matter is apparently taken to be an act that has a huge ripple effect that will eventually result in chaos and the destabilization of creation. The great example of this is seen in Gen 6:1-4. In this text, the daughters of humanity and the sons of God copulated; the result is that there are Nephilim upon the earth. The story of the flood (Gen 6:5—8:19) follows this event of mixing diverse realities. It is interesting to notice that the other mention of the Nephilim is in the land of Canaan. Because of the Nephilim (Num 13:33) Israel is too frightened to go over and take possession of the land that Yahweh promised.

The premise of Deut 22:6-7 is practical; to prevent the depletion of birds in the vicinity, a person must not take both the mother hen and the young chicks at the same time. To harvest the mother only, before the young have arrived at maturity, would also be disastrous. It would have the same effect as taking both together. The law does state, however, that the young birds may be garnered, which would leave the hen to rear other offspring in the future and assuring the continuation of the species. This law sounds almost like contemporary hunting and fishing regulations. Conservation, evidently, is not a new thing.

It should be kept in mind that the OT views animals as part of God's good creation. They are bestowed, like human beings, with the breath of life (Gen 1:30). Animals are also charged, like human beings, to be fruitful and multiply and fill the earth (Gen 1:22, 28). Human beings have a responsibility for the rest of created life, to care for it as partners with the Creator. Humanity is assured long life and prosperity only when it values the balance of life in God's creation.

Deuteronomy 22:8 articulates the potential of bloodguilt that results from negligence in building a house. Homicide falls under two major groupings: voluntary and involuntary manslaughter. Voluntary manslaughter is the intentional killing of someone, whether in the fervor of rage or with deliberate, premeditated, cold revenge. Included in this group would also be capital punishment and war. Involuntary manslaughter involves a variety of forms of negligence. These could include everything from disregard for safety to indifference for the plight of others. A **parapet** is a low wall built around the edge of the roof as a safety precaution. The reference to bringing **the guilt of bloodshed on your house** suggests that failure to provide a parapet amounts to criminal negligence.

Human life is endangered by neglect. Therefore, every housetop is to have a parapet, as a protection to those using it for any purpose. This rule seems like a building code of some sort. The code requirement here is linked to an apprehension concerning bloodguilt and shedding innocent blood, a key concern of Deuteronomy, as indicated in the establishment of the cities of refuge (see Deut 19:10). Innocent blood corrupts and desecrates the land; therefore, bloodguilt must be guarded against from both the hastiness of retribution and reckless endangerment.

■ **9-12** The laws in this section seem to bear little relation to their context. The first three laws appear to belong together, although it is hard to discern the connection. Three conspicuous sayings, having been placed together, may mean that their primary function is structural. The three laws prohibit the combination of unnatural mixtures (vv 9-11), and they reflect concern about the destructive power of mixing different categories within nature. The implication is that corruption would infect life in the land.

This subdivision concerns itself with specific exclusions: planting mixed crops, plowing with a mixed pair of animals, and wearing clothing made of mixed fabric. These cases are also treated in Lev 19:19. A fourth case in this subdivision involves a positive command about wearing tassels on the fringes of the outer garment (Deut 22:12). This command does not find a parallel in Lev 19. One should also recognize that these prohibitions do not include explanatory material. Therefore, reasons for avoiding such admixtures must be inferred by the reader. Most likely the ancient reader understood the rationality involved with these instructions. Whatever the unique beginning of these individual practices may be, the fact that they are collected together without explanation must be given credibility.

Deuteronomy 22:9 addresses planting a vineyard with two kinds of seed. This practice of sowing refers to mixed cropping, a procedure used in farming on limited amounts of agricultural land when human survival is the goal. The space between the vines is used for other crops. Scholars suggest various reasons for the prohibition of mixed cropping. The law may well have originated in a desire to avoid foreign practices, which possess some magical or cultic association. It could also have a functional reason: the inappropriate and wasteful use of crops and land. The exact motivation for this practice is lost to the modern reader because of a shortage of descriptive texts.

The translation **will be defiled** is an attempt to understand a technical phrase: literally *lest you make sacred* (from the root *qādaš*). The Hebrew word group means "holy" or "to make holy." The unusual requirement that any crops sewn together must be surrendered to the sanctuary signifies that experimenting in unnatural practice did not result in punishing the transgressor but in the disruption of gladness in the land of promise. The crops are not defiled by the behavior of the farmer, but the implication is that in using the mixed seeds it would make the crops unavailable for common use. The question is why?

Verse 10 seems fairly straightforward; the command is not to plow with an ox and a donkey together. Again, the reader is not given the motivation for this law. This directive could be put forward as a way to save from harm animals of uneven vigor. However, it should be noted that there are instances when a donkey and an ox are yoked together for plowing (Driver 1895, 253). This command may be to make the reader aware of the fact that the ox is a clean animal and the ass is unclean. This would be in keeping with Deut 14:1-8.

Verse 11 of ch 22 is a law against dressing in garments made of mixed materials, wool and linen woven together. This law does not forbid combining wool and linen as such, but only wearing an article of clothing made from that combination. Josephus suggested that the prohibition applies only to the laity, because officiating priests did wear garments made of such mixtures (*Ant.* 4:8.11). Christensen believes that the text apparently refers not to mixed materials as such but to a luxurious linen garment that a prostitute might wear (2002, 508). What should be obvious with both of these explanations is that the issues of holy and profane are at stake; mixing that which is holy with that which is profane is the concern expressed here.

Verse 12 is a policy that is not like the earlier commands. What distinguishes it is that it is positive and not negative. It is possible that tassels, like "signs and emblems," specified a distinctive Israelite identity. They are worn as a distinguishing symbol, upon the four corners of their mantles. This practice likely prompts the Hebrew people to conform to Yahweh's distinctive polity, and to help them when they are tempted to pursue the ways of mixing their life with the customs and policies close to them. If this is the case, then all of these commands are intended to reinforce the unique quality of Israel's identity as Yahweh's chosen and holy people.

Even though it is difficult to perceive any controlling rationale in the arrangement of the laws, it must be kept in mind that Deuteronomy is unmistakably the work of a deliberate theological community. This section lays down parameters for dealing with the ordered life in the land. Ordered life keeps chaos at bay in the laws of both society and nature. In other words, this section is concerned with the protection of life, which would include keeping the laws of separation. The opening eleven chapters of Genesis detail how crossing over the barriers of separation, which God establishes in creation, brings about chaos and ultimately death. This is illustrated in both the escalation of violence from Cain to Lamech in Gen 4, to the exhalation of cosmic disruption from the copulation of the sons of God with the daughters of Adam in ch 6, to the great collapse of creation in the flood in ch 7. Refraining from impurity and the gift of life go hand in hand in the vision of Deuteronomy.

Deuteronomy 22:13—23:18 forms a subdivision that takes up aspects of sexual ethics and very likely is linked to the seventh commandment. The cases developed in this passage are for the most radical circumstances. After the boundary between life and death, the boundary between the sexes is the most significant for the establishment and organization of community life. It is fundamental that sexual delineation be valued and safeguarded. When a sexual bond is formed, it is to be molded within a prescribed covenant of marriage. Only so could it be recognized and protected by the covenant community. Most marriages in ancient Israel took place after negotiations between the two families. The bridegroom paid a suitable fiscal compensation to the bride's family, believing that she is a virgin.

■ **13-30 [13—23:1 HB]** Deuteronomy 22:13-21 addresses the situation of a husband who accuses his wife of previous sexual misconduct. This law first attempts to provide wives protection from unscrupulous husbands and then, in vv 20-21, deals with a wife if such allegations are proven true. The premise behind this regulation is that a husband is entitled to a virgin wife, and that the wife is duty-bound to be a virgin at the time of her marriage. It also implies that the parents of the young woman are to guarantee the virginity of their daughter.

From a contemporary standpoint, these decrees are profoundly incomplete in terms of gender equality. Women are reliant upon the power and privilege of either their husband or father. The presupposition that encompasses these laws does not seem fair-minded to contemporary readers; men are in charge of both adjudicating the cases and carrying out the punishments. It is obvious that this is a patriarchal system of male dominance.

It should be noted that mothers are involved in the proceedings of discovering if the charge is true. They joined their husbands in defending their daughters against false accusations by providing evidence to the elders of the town. But, fathers and husbands are the principal participants in the indictments that relate to this regulation.

The mere accusation by the husband that she is not a virgin could not be used against a woman or her family. A condemning husband is required to prove his indictment. If his allegation is demonstrated as false, he is required to compensate his wife's father for damages perpetrated upon his daughter. The remuneration takes place because the husband maligned a virgin in Israel. Also, if adequate evidence is brought to the elders, any later divorce between the husband and the woman is ruled out. Even though this law sounds narrow and biased toward males, it did attempt to protect the woman's honor. Protecting a woman's honor is unusual in the ancient world.

If the girl is found to be guilty, she is put to death in order to preserve Israel's purity. This verdict is to take place in front of her father's house, in her own village, by all the men in the community. The end result of her sin is a dishonoring of her father's house and the release of an evil influence through her impure life. Evil, it is understood, penetrates the entire community through the acts of individuals. Even though modern persons do not believe that evil is a magical power that mesmerizes a community, there is conviction that evil has systemic power to shape and control human existence. For ancient Israel, the girl's execution is construed as an act of purifying the village of evil.

Today, the brutal execution of the young woman would be understood as an act of uninhibited male brutality against a woman who disturbs the communal stability of the social structure and values of the village. Violence against women still takes place too often in the world. When Christian readers interpret this text, the narrative of Jesus must take center stage. Mary, the mother of Jesus, would have been accused as an offender of this very decree. Matthew 1:19 describes Joseph's response to this reality: "Because Joseph her husband was faithful to the law, and yet did not want to expose her to public disgrace, he had in mind to divorce her quietly." Joseph operates from the premise that a husband is entitled to a virgin wife, and that the wife is duty-bound to be a virgin at the time of her marriage. The Gospel of Matthew also describes Joseph as not wanting to expose her to public disgrace, which means he would not bring this matter before the elders of the village. Grace and duty are a part of Joseph's first response. It is only after a revelation through a dream that Joseph embraces the pregnancy of Mary and places himself in solidarity with her situation.

Deuteronomy 22:22 articulates a second decree in relation to sexual intercourse that takes place outside of the boundaries of Israel's Mosaic covenant. The seventh commandment makes it clear that adultery is emphatically forbidden in Israel. If it is discovered that a man committed adultery with a married woman, then both are executed. It is conceded that adultery, which is carried out in secret, is challenging to prove. Because the punishment is so brutal and irrevocable, clear evidence is necessary. No verification is as compelling as discovering the couple in the sexual act. This sentence is in conformity with the decree established in Lev 20:10: "If a man commits adultery with another man's wife—with the wife of his neighbor—both the adulterer and the adulteress are to be put to death." The method of putting the couple to death is not stipulated in this text or in Leviticus, but stoning is often the specified way. This is described in Ezek 16:38-40:

> I will sentence you to the punishment of women who commit adultery and who shed blood; I will bring on you the blood vengeance of my wrath and jealous anger. Then I will deliver you into the hands of your lovers, and they will tear down your mounds and destroy your lofty shrines. They will strip you of your clothes and take your fine jewelry and leave you stark naked. They will bring a mob against you, who will stone you and hack you to pieces with their swords.

Purging evil from the midst of the community is the outcome of the couple's execution. **Purge the evil from Israel** (Deut 22:22) is an interesting phrase. What could this possibly imply? It at least means that adultery not only is an immoral act that disrupts the bond between husband and wife but also is a threat to the entire covenant community. The ethos of the community, with its multiple relationships, is disregarded and put at risk. Social fabric is fashioned by policies, persons, promises, and practices. A community of memory shapes countless relationships of promise, and relationships of promise influence the community.

The premise of the law in v 22 is that marital infidelity endangers covenant relationships. The breakdown of covenant relationships will ultimately result in the breakdown of community. Yet, a Christian reader of this violent text must remember the gospel. What does Jesus do with this very serious sin? A wonderful glimpse of early Christian convictions is described in the story that recalls the confrontation between Jesus and the teachers of the Law in John 8:3-11. It reads:

> The teachers of the law and the Pharisees brought in a woman caught in adultery. They made her stand before the group and said to Jesus, "Teacher, this woman was caught in the act of adultery. In the Law Moses commanded us to stone such women. Now what do you say?" They were using this question as a trap, in order to have a basis for accusing him.
>
> But Jesus bent down and started to write on the ground with his finger. When they kept on questioning him, he straightened up and said to them, "Let any one of you who is without sin be the first to throw a stone at her." Again he stooped down and wrote on the ground.

At this, those who heard began to go away one at a time, the older ones first, until only Jesus was left, with the woman still standing there. Jesus straightened up and asked her, "Woman, where are they? Has no one condemned you?"

"No one, sir," she said.

"Then neither do I condemn you," Jesus declared. "Go now and leave your life of sin."

This passage makes a couple of interesting remarks. First, only the woman is brought to Jesus for stoning. Where is the man? Second, they are testing Jesus to see what his interpretation of this situation would be. This implies that there is a premise of mercy already operating in the way that they believe Jesus will respond. Jesus does finally respond by not condemning the woman. Liberation and restoration is the goal of the ministry of Jesus. Christian readers must read texts like Deut 22:22 from the horizon of the Christian gospel.

Verses 23-29 address the possibility that a young woman might be a victim of rape. There are three different sets of laws that address different circumstances where rape might take place. These situations of sexual aggression are: sex in the town, sex outside of populated areas, and forceful sex with an unengaged young woman. All three of these circumstances have varying legal resolutions for those involved. The sentence differs according to the context. What should be noted is the motivation of the response to the first case of rape. It is the same as for the man who is caught in adultery with the wife of another, so that Israel may **purge the evil.** 22:13-30

The first context (vv 23-25) recounts the potential of forced intercourse within the setting of a town. The underlying narrative is: a man has sex with a betrothed virgin, possibly under her protest. What is important in this law is that the sexual encounter takes place in the setting of a town. What is Israel to do in this setting? The decree specifies that both the man and the woman be brought to the gate of that town and stoned to death. It should be remembered that the gate is the place and position where the community enacts justice. The man is to be executed **because he violated another man's wife.** The motive is not the pain and shame that is put on the young woman, but that she apparently belonged to a man, her betrothed, and it is a violation of his rights that is at stake. It is difficult for a contemporary reader to sympathize with this law, but it should be remembered that ancient Israel is a patriarchal culture.

Is stoning the woman just? Because the act is in a town, the law considers the woman also culpable. A verdict that she is to be stoned seems to be based upon the notion that she did not cry out for help. The only rationale that separates this act from the next law (vv 25-27) is that she is around people in the town and not so in the country. The argument would be that she must have consented, because she did not cry out, or at least cry out enough. Evil is once again purged from the community, but in a cruel and merciless way. But is evil purged from the community if the circumstances are of such a nature that the premises of this law are not correct? Maybe evil, in the form of male dominance, is allowed a systemic place in the community.

Verses 25-27 articulate a second context for rape. The situation is located in the open country—in other words, outside of earshot for someone to help the woman. Most of the text is similar to the preceding one, with the exceptions of the location of the act and the addition of a word translated **rape**. This word is translated **to seize** in most contexts, and the implication is that force is used upon the young woman and she has no one to come to her rescue. Therefore, the only person sentenced to stoning is the man who coerced the young woman. The woman is presumed innocent and acquitted of any wrongdoing. The great tragedy in this case is that she is not remunerated or sheltered for her future. In this patriarchal culture she is devastated, without a redeemer.

Verses 28-29 express a third circumstance of sexual intercourse between two persons not married to each other. In this instance the woman is identified as a virgin who is not engaged. Whether the intercourse is consensual or forced is not articulated in this law. The man is considered the guilty party in this context, and the assumption is that he seduced the young woman. It also may not be important in this patriarchal culture if the sexual encounter is consensual, forced, or seduced; she and her father would have an economic solution. The father of the young woman is given fifty shekels of silver. Because the young woman's future is shattered, the perpetrator is required to guarantee her economic well-being by taking her into his house as a wife. He is never allowed to divorce her for as long as he lives.

Verse 30 [23:1 HB] continues the sexual theme of the passage but changes the focus to the boundaries of who may become a wife. This decree articulates a policy that prohibits a man from marrying the wife of his father. The word translated **to marry**, literally indicates **to take**. Therefore, this law assumes that the woman is not the man's mother but another wife or possibly the concubine of his father. If the woman is the wife of his father, then the inference is that the woman would be a widow. Marriage to this woman crosses a boundary that cannot be changed once a relationship is in a different covenant category.

A very similar ban appears in Lev 18:8, though somewhat differently worded. In Lev 18 it states, "Do not have sexual relations with your father's wife; that would dishonor your father." This does not necessarily imply that one's father is dead, but it could be a form of adultery within the larger household. It should be remembered that ancient Israel is a polygamous culture. This law prohibits a man from marrying a woman divorced by his father or marrying his father's wives and concubines after his death. Taking a monarch's wives or concubines is a way of making a claim to the royal family on the part of a would-be seizing the throne.

Boundaries determine the scope and limits of covenant relationships. The limitations are not only to the average Hebrew man but also especially to the one who would succeed to the throne. The story of Absalom in 2 Sam 16:20-22, speaks to this very issue.

Absalom said to Ahithophel, "Give us your advice. What should we do?"

Ahithophel answered, "Sleep with your father's concubines whom he left to take care of the palace. Then all Israel will hear that you have made yourself obnoxious to your father, and the hands of everyone with you will be more resolute." So they pitched a tent for Absalom on the roof, and he slept with his father's concubines in the sight of all Israel.

He goes into his father's concubines and this act crosses the boundary in two covenantal ways: he uncovers his father and he grasps for his father's throne.

Deuteronomy 12—26 sets forth regulations that take for granted that they are valid for anyone in the covenant community. Therefore, it is imperative to delineate the boundaries of the community itself. Boundaries for the covenantal community define collective and individual identity. However, the restrictive biases in ch 23 are a bit unsettling to contemporary readers. What are the Christian readers to do with these policies when they read 23:1-18 [2-19 HB] through the lens of Gal 3:28? "There is neither Jew nor Gentile, neither slave nor free, nor is there male nor female, for you are all one in Christ Jesus." Before we answer this question, we must attempt to understand the text in light of its own context. This subsection is divided into four smaller portions: Deut 23:1-8, "Composition of the Community"; vv 9-14, "Purity in the Community"; vv 15-16, "Boundaries in Society"; and vv 17-18, "Purity in the Sanctuary Treasury." Deuteronomy 23:1-25 is numbered 23:2-26 in the Hebrew Bible [HB].

■ **23:1-8 [2-9 HB]** Verse 1 [2 HB] develops the policy that membership in the assembly of Yahweh is comprised of males who have not been **emasculated by crushing or cutting**. The emasculated may not enter the assembly of Yahweh. Why are these people excluded from the assembly? The crushing of the testicles is a procedure executed on young boys in a variety of situations in the ancient Near East. This procedure prepared them as eunuchs for service at holy places or in palaces as keepers of a royal harem. Is debarring of eunuchs from Yahweh's assembly because this maiming is a result of some foreign religious practice or is it because it violated the very command of the Creator: to "be fruitful and increase in number" (Gen 1:28), or is it because the very sign of the covenant is circumcision? Even though the law's driving force is unknown, by beginning the catalog of segregation from the community with a

221

male whose genitals are ruined, the magnitude of sexual potency as a mark of Yahweh's life-giving power is accentuated.

What is of interest to Christian readers of this text is the story found in Acts 8 of Philip and the Ethiopian eunuch. This story is a story of the inclusion of an outsider both by race and nationality, and by being a eunuch. The eunuch "had gone to Jerusalem to worship" (Acts 8:27). This is an interesting phrase given the law here in Deuteronomy. The narrative goes on to describe the conversion of the eunuch and his baptism. This story does not mean that the power of communal identity is eliminated, but the criterion becomes the gospel of the Lord Jesus Christ.

Deuteronomy 23:2 [3 HB] articulates a different policy of exclusion: Those **born of a forbidden marriage nor any of their descendants may enter the assembly of the LORD, not even in the tenth generation.** The words translated **a forbidden marriage** may be better understood as those born out of an illicit union. The Hebrew word *mamzēr* literally means **bastard**. The other use of this word is found in Zech 9:6, which states: "A mongrel people will occupy Ashdod." *Mamzēr* means here in Zechariah a mixed race of people. The motivation for this exclusion in Deuteronomy is to prevent pagan practice and beliefs from infiltrating Israel's worship and civic life. This would refer to any child born out of a relationship that was not permitted in the covenant order of society.

Deuteronomy 23:3-8 [4-9 HB] forms a subunit of thought concerning very specific groups of people: the Ammonites, Moabites, Edomites, and Egyptians. Though the Ammonites and the Moabites are mentioned together, in v 4 [5 HB], the first clause deals with the Ammonites and the second clause deals with the Moabites. Both are forbidden entry into the assembly of Yahweh for different reasons: the Ammonites did not display hospitality, kindness, and care to the Israelites during their wilderness crossing; the Moabites made persistent endeavors to destroy Israel through the prophetic oracles of Balaam (see Num 22—24). Though not stated, the text also implies another reason for the prohibition of the Ammonites and the Moabites, descendants of the illicit sexual relationships between Lot and his two daughters (Gen 19:30-38). The prohibition here may be linked to the prohibition of *mamzēr* in Deut 23:2 [3 HB]. When dealing with the Moabites, Deuteronomy reiterates a controlling theological conviction present in the narrative in Numbers: what is intended for evil, God turns into a blessing. **God would not listen to Balaam but turned the curse into a blessing for you, because the LORD your God loves you** (v 5 [6 HB]). This theological conviction can be seen in a number of texts, not the least of which is the Joseph story. God is not bound by what people do but has the creativity to transform even curse into blessing. Perhaps even the cross should be understood as the ultimate symbol of this theological conviction. It is all based upon God's great love for his people: **God loves you**. It

23:1-8

is worth mentioning that the ineligibility of Moab is not put into operation historically, for King David's grandmother is a widow from Moab. She is held up as a model of redemption.

Verses 7-8 [8-9 HB], on the other hand, declare that the Edomites and Egyptians are not to be rejected. That these groups, who are habitually Israel's enemies, are to be looked upon approvingly is astonishing. The Edomite is to be regarded as a brother. This kinship relationship between the Edomites and the Israelites suggests the identification of Edom with Esau, the brother of Jacob/Israel. The Egyptian inclusion reflects a relationship, even though historically heartbreaking, that helps to define Israel. Perhaps it is because of the earlier role that Egypt performs in Israel's story, which is one where Israel is originally delivered during a time of great deprivation and starvation. The confession in Deut 26:5 [6 HB] expresses it well: "My father was a wandering Aramean, and he went down into Egypt with a few people and lived there and became a great nation, powerful and numerous." The children of the third generation of Edomites and Egyptians could be given access to the assembly of Yahweh.

■ **9-18 [10-19 HB]** Concerns involving personal sanitation could also create a hazard that might require sanction from the community (23:9-14 [10-15 HB]). Impurity in a military camp would destabilize the holiness of the site and people. In the theological vision of Deuteronomy, the crusade is Yahweh's campaign; therefore, the battle must be conducted not only in the power of Yahweh but also in his presence. This means that the practices, people, and place are holy.

Verse 9 [10 HB] is concerned with the broader issue of purity of the encampment when Israel goes to battle. They are to **keep away from everything impure**. The Hebrew word that is translated **impure** is *rā'*, and it literally means *evil*. Evil covers a wide range of meaning in the Hebrew Bible: natural evil, moral evil, and woe. Here it most likely means anything that would deviate from the covenant with Yahweh. It clearly has a moral angle to its meaning. Morality is not simply something that an individual is accountable for, but it impinges on the entire community. What is of interest in these policies is that "evil" and "holiness" are tied to mundane activities.

Verses 10-11 [11-12 HB] address an interesting state of affairs: a man can be considered **unclean because of a nocturnal emission**, literally: *an accident of the night*. Nocturnal emission is described in Lev 15:16 as "an emission of semen." There are many explanations to why this is problematic, but OT scholars give no consensus interpretation. Is this law because of a magical belief that body fluids carried some spiritual force that could infiltrate the camp, or is there a belief that these fluids implied that potency is lost, and the battle would not go well, or is this tied to sexuality and therefore a loss of covenant boundaries? None of these explanations seem convincing enough. All the reader knows is that uncleanness is not permanent in this context.

The war camp is a place where Yahweh moves about, and his presence makes the camp holy. Functional practices are necessary for the encampment of Yahweh's people. Verses 12-14 [13-15 HB] stipulate practices for suitable toilet facilities. In these verses the word **camp** indicates that the people are on the move; they are going to war. Ancient Israel believes that Yahweh moves in the midst of his people, and the concern of the people is that he might come into contact with defilement by human excrement. How to care for the physical needs of the camp without bringing defilement is the point of this custom. The custom of purifying the camp, even with mundane matters, implies that this custom has the status of ritual. Defiling the camp poses an even greater danger for the people who depend upon a holy God in conducting holy war. The holiness of both the land and the people establish confidence for military endeavors.

Another command (vv 15-16 [16-17 HB]), based upon Yahweh's holiness, follows the previous sanction. Aspects of holiness include not only purity but also mercy. In the ancient world, a person was required to return a runaway slave to the slave's master. A collection of laws from the eighteenth century BC, the Hammurabi texts, states that runaway slaves must be sent back to their master. The law held the threat of death over the inhabitants if they did not comply with the regulation (see Code of Hammurabi, laws 15-20).

23:9-18   Ancient Israel maintained a very different understanding of vulnerable people. They were to care for the marginal, and this included the widow, the orphan, and even the outsider, called the sojourners. The person pictured in Deuteronomy is probably a refugee who is fleeing from another land. The law in v 16 [17 HB] implies that the escapee is considered a sojourner and designated a resident alien. A runaway slave is offered security and sanctuary like any sojourner. The slave is not to be frightened, subjugated, or extradited and is never to be sold again into slavery. He or she is to be given the prospect of living life in liberty and peace. Not only is the slave not to be placed back into servitude, but he or she is also to be allowed to reside in any Hebrew settlement. The community's awareness that they were once a group of slaves delivered by the mercy of Yahweh shapes their beliefs and values. Their experience of Yahweh's care is extended to those like them, the oppressed.

Verses 17-18 [18-19 HB] address the issue of prostitution in two different ways: daughters and sons of Israel must not be temple prostitutes, and the fee for the wages of prostitution is never to be given in the house of Yahweh as payment for vows. The practice of religious prostitution was widespread in the ancient Near East. This practice was not simply dealing with a sexual encounter but was connected to the worship of other gods. The boundary of the holiness derived from Yahweh forbids any holy act or ritual in relation to another god. The Hebrew word used for male or female—**shrine prostitute** (*qĕdēšâ*)—comes from the word group for "holy"; therefore, in this setting it refers to religious prostitution. Holiness defined by Yahweh prohibits holiness defined by any other god.

The ritualized practice of sacred prostitution defiles Yahweh's people. The history written by the tradition of Deuteronomy addresses this issue often. Examples of "male cultic prostitutes" are narrated in the stories found in 1 Kgs 14:24; 15:12; 22:46 [47 HB]; 2 Kgs 23:7. Female prostitution was most probably even more widespread in the ancient world. It is very likely that Hosea's wife, Gomer, was a cult prostitute. Her story not only is one of reclaiming a broken and lost life but also is a picture of broken and lost practices that do not produce the holy people of Yahweh. The offspring of these practices result in *"not mercy"* and "not my people" (Hos 1:6, 8).

In the ancient Canaanite culture, sacred prostitution was considered a holy practice. The conundrum is that this holiness belongs to a god other than Yahweh. Religious practitioners must realize that not all holy acts are the same; some pervert and pollute the people who are to reflect the God of Abraham, Isaac, Jacob, and the God who is specifically revealed in the person of Jesus the Messiah. Simply being fully submitted to a god and participating in the practices of the politics of that god does not produce a holiness that reflects the God of the Scripture. Biblical holiness has very specific qualities that reflect the character of the Lord.

23:9-18

The second part of this law concerning prostitution is directed toward disbursement of gifts into the temple treasury. Fees paid for prostitution may not be used for payment into the temple funds. This law makes it clear that there is a boundary line that cannot be crossed between money earned in holy prostitution and money given for the sanctified purposes of Yahweh. Again it should be noted that all holiness is not equal. This law also states that transgressing this policy is more than simply individual defilement, but communal defilement is a possibility if the people use ill-gotten gain for the purpose of Yahweh. Many people deem that if resources can be given for a good cause, even if those resources come from defiled practices, then the end justifies the means. But this type of thinking misunderstands both the purpose of Yahweh and the political implications for the community. Yahweh's chosen people are to recognize that the means is the goal. Israel's purpose is to faithfully witness to the world the character and purpose of Yahweh. This means that she is to reflect Yahweh in all her words and deeds. The policies and practices of Israel are to reflect Yahweh, the source and goal of those associations.

The implication is obvious: the politics of Yahweh demand that communal relationships be a reflection of Yahweh and his purposes. No amount of ill-gotten resource can be given for the positive purposes of Yahweh. To disregard the policies and practices that form a people politically is to become something other than the people who are shaped by the God of the Bible. Followers of Jesus will also need to examine the resources that they possess and give. How money is earned is at least as important as the money given. Evil money can never accomplish the purposes of God. God does not need the resources of people; he desires a people, which includes their resources. The end never justifies the means. The means is the end!

FROM THE TEXT

What do all of these laws have in common? They all point to what a community is to look like when that community is chosen by Yahweh. There is a common line of reasoning that delineates the boundary lines for the people of God. These people are to reflect God's care for the life and well-being of one another. This reflection is what is meant by holiness. Holiness is lived out in a way that allows God to be the defining reality of the community; his character defines holiness for both the individual and the community.

These boundary practices do not create a people, but they form an already chosen people into a form of life. The implication of these laws is that God's people are to represent God as a peculiar people; therefore, the form of life reflects the character and purpose of God. This symbolization of God's holiness is clearly demonstrated in a twofold dimension: the care one has toward one's neighbor and abstaining from practices that resemble the people groups and ideologies surrounding God's people.

The care for the neighbor includes the neighbor's possessions, marriage, and resources. The well-being and life of the neighbor forms the largest part of these laws. It is impossible to care in the ways that Yahweh cares if one accommodates the practices and values of foreign cultures. Therefore, the boundary lines also include restraining from all practices that resemble the people groups and ideologies that surround ancient Israel. Israel is a particular people: Yahweh is their God and they are his people.

Christian readers of this text are not summoned to practice all of these laws in the precise extent that their Jewish forefathers were, but they are called to be a peculiar people. For Christians, the conceptual image of God is none other than the person of Jesus. Colossians 1:15-19 says:

The Son is the image of the invisible God, the firstborn over all creation. For in him all things were created: things in heaven and on earth, visible and invisible, whether thrones or powers or rulers or authorities; all things have been created through him and for him. He is before all things, and in him all things hold together. And he is the head of the body, the church; he is the beginning and the firstborn from among the dead, so that in everything he might have the supremacy. For God was pleased to have all his fullness dwell in him.

This means that God is revealed in Jesus and that the politics of Jesus shapes his people, the church.

Christian preachers and teachers should explore the cultural and historical contexts of these laws. They should also notice how important abstaining from participation in the host cultures is to both ancient Israel and the early followers of Jesus. A Christian reader must also be aware that holiness is not something that an individual carries out in his or her own mind or will, but it is carried out in community and with one's body. Holiness in a community is a political reality, a form of life. This community can rightly be called the communion of saints. Only in a covenantal community of saints is it possible for saints to be formed. A saint is not first a saint in a disembodied way, but in a recognizable fashion. The inward disposition of holy people is not the primary beginning point of sainthood but is a result of the bodily practice of the kingdom of God. Jesus did not call people to feel something, but to leave and follow. Mark 10:21 states, "Go, sell everything you have and give to the poor, and you will have treasure in heaven. Then come, follow me."

J. The Common Good (23:19—24:22 [23:20—24:22 HB])

BEHIND THE TEXT

This section of the laws is loosely connected. The opening regulations in 23:19-25 [20-26 HB] are concerned with the eighth commandment, stealing. Chapter 24 moves back toward the issue of marital fidelity in the opening verses. Verses 6-9 are not necessarily thematic in relation to the whole of the passage. Beginning with v 10 the theme of resources needed to survive resumes. The exception to this is the law articulated in v 16, parents not being put to death for the crimes of their children and children are not being put to death for the crimes of their parents. Beginning with v 17 the theme moves to justice for the marginal: alien, orphan, and widow. This section contains a number of practices involving resources and theft. If the interpreter is attempting to read these laws in light of the Decalogue, then this section may be categorized under the eighth commandment. The other option is thematic:

1. Don't Steal from the Poor and Yahweh (23:19-25 [20-26 HB])
2. Don't Commit Adultery, Even with Your Former Wife (24:1-4)
3. Be Happy and Blessed in Your New Marriage (24:5)
4. Don't Take Millstones in Pledge (24:6)
5. Don't Kidnap Another Israelite (24:7)
6. Be Careful with Leprosy (24:8-9)

7. Be Careful How the Poor Are Treated with Loans that Are Made (24:10-13)
8. Pay the Poor What They Are Due in a Timely Manner (24:14-15)
9. Don't Punish Others, Even Parents or Children, for the Evil of Others (24:16)
10. Justice for Even the Most Vulnerable (24:17-18)
11. Leave Resources for the Most Vulnerable (24:19-22)

IN THE TEXT

I. Don't Steal from the Poor and Yahweh (23:19-25 [20-26 HB])

■ **19-25 [20-26 HB]** There are three laws articulated in these verses: banning interest among members of the community (vv 19-20 [20-21 HB]); keeping vows made to Yahweh (vv 21-23 [22-24 HB]); and access and limitation to resources for consumption (vv 24-25 [25-26 HB]). Laws against charging interest on loans are naively read against the horizon of the contemporary reader's own world picture. Bank and commercial loans have become a fundamental element within the economic web of institutions that shape the world today. In the ancient world, loans were normally made in an attempt to ease destitution in an instance of calamity. The wealthy often took advantage of these moments of calamity and charged high interest rates on loans. The difficulty of emerging from a spiral of debt became all but impossible. A far-reaching and alternative understanding of economic life is envisioned in the covenantal community of Israel.

Vows made to Yahweh are to be carried out quickly and completely. To use a vow as merely a way of affirming one's agreement or gratitude is to not take seriously the type of language usage a vow expresses. Therefore, people should be careful in their use of words and in the sorts of commitments they make. A vow is only completed as a speech act when it is fulfilled through the actions of an individual. To fulfill a vow is to be a person of integrity; to fail to fulfill a vow is to be a person of insincerity or dishonesty. Israel understands faithfulness in the way she perceives Yahweh across time. Yahweh makes vows in the language game of promise, and the fulfillment of these promises is what forms the reliability of the community of promise as well as describes the character of God.

The situation envisioned in vv 24-25 [25-26 HB] is neighborly admission to provisions. This law both sanctions and limits what one can have for the sustenance of life. One may go into the vineyard or field of another and consume what is grown there. The prohibition is that one is not allowed to use containers to harvest produce beyond what one can take by hand. Fences

228

are not necessary in keeping people out or produce in. The premise of the covenantal politics is that there is a social bond in the community between landowners and needy neighbors.

This practice reflects a value system where the virtues of gratitude, generosity, and respect are habituated into the ethos of the community. The contemporary reader should contemplate the practices necessary to habituate this ethos of grace and responsibility in the current community of faith. These three economic practices with reference to debt, interest, and open generosity are vital elements in shaping an ethos where people participate in neighbor love.

2. Don't Commit Adultery, Even with Your Former Wife (24:1-4)

■ **24:1-4** This matrimonial law is concerned with the forfeiture of the right to divorce in a patriarchal culture. The assumption is that the male can easily embark upon divorce. All that seems necessary is that the male not *find favor* with his wife. This lack of favor means that there is something deprecatory in his wife. This same word is used in 23:14 [15 HB] where it refers to something indecent among the people in the camp, where Yahweh is traveling along with them. It could include even a physical deficiency, even the inability to conceive and bear children. The exact meaning of the word is unclear and therefore open to numerous interpretations.

If the woman marries a second man and this marriage ends in divorce or widowhood, then the first husband is not allowed to take her as his wife again. The issue is not the status of the woman or even the marriage itself, but the status of the land. The second marriage makes the woman a used woman as far as the first husband is concerned. If the first husband relates to the woman sexually, it could contaminate the community and the land. "The law operates on the assumption that anything out of order will threaten the order of everything else; a sequel of sexual interactions that is not normal is a disruption and a threat" (Brueggemann 2001, 236).

Some of the most interesting uses of this legal practice are found in both Jeremiah and Hosea. They seem to address this issue in the relationship between Israel and Yahweh. It should be remembered that both of these books share a common tradition with Deuteronomy. In Jer 3:1-5 Israel is married to her first husband, Yahweh, but then she leaves him to attach herself to a second husband, Baal. After discovering that Baal is inadequate, she wants to return to her first husband. Israel cries out, "My Father, my friend from my youth, will you always be angry? Will your wrath continue forever?" (Jer 3:4-5). The hopefulness of Hosea narrates that the first husband is more than willing to pursue the wayward wife. Yahweh will not give her up, for he is God and not humanity (ch 11). The tradition itself implies hope beyond defilement. What must be held in tension is how the land and community are protected

24:1-4

229

from defilement and yet how there is hope beyond what seems to be a lost future. Perhaps forgiving seventy times seven is the ultimate canonical conclusion to this practice.

3. Be Happy and Blessed in Your New Marriage (24:5)

■ **5** This law resembles the exemption laws for military service found in 20:5-7. Marriage is affirmed in this ruling, which places it in a contrasting position to the law concerning remarrying a former wife. A man who is just married is exempt for one year from military service. This practice is intended to protect the marriage against the untimely death of the new husband, which would result in the bride becoming a widow so soon in her new marriage. Marriage, as a joyful expression of God's blessing, seems to be the sole purpose of the law. A man is not intended to die without the opportunity to be fruitful and multiply. Children are Yahweh's blessing, and all are intended this happiness.

4. Don't Take Millstones in Pledge (24:6)

■ **6** Millstones, for the milling of flour, symbolize the most indispensable and essential of household tools for preserving autonomy in preparing bread for one's household. Prohibiting the taking of a millstone as collateral to corroborate a loan is intended to guard the household's freedom. There is a limit to what can be taken as collateral for a loan. Impoverished people use millstones in unskilled and tedious labor to provide for the sustenance of life. Most likely, this law was designed to protect the poor and their means of making a living. Loans are not to take away the capacity to live and produce. Those who have resources must practice limits. The needy and the poor are also a part of Yahweh's covenant community.

5. Don't Kidnap Another Israelite (24:7)

■ **7** Kidnapping is considered by ancient Israel as stealing a man. This law implies that selling people in slave trade is a practice that ancient societies participated in. Clearly, transactions of this nature regarded people as property. This kind of economic practice is not accidental in this context, but fits the line of thought. People, not economic interest, are the focus of the covenant community. No practice that reduces human beings to function as a means to an economic end is permitted. The dignity of a person is of such a nature that the community must purge itself of this level of evil. A community cannot stand the course of history if people are only a means to an economic end.

The story of Joseph in Gen 37 is particularly illuminating as it deals with the issue of selling a person into slavery. Even though the story is concerned with living a life of integrity in the direst circumstances, it should also be perceived that it is the disregard to the humanity of Joseph that creates the narrative drama that sustains the story. Contemporary readers of this statute would do well to ponder the value of a human life in the community of humanity. How does this law shape the way a community is to value people? What does this law have to say about the way economic systems function? Can a believer compartmentalize life? Is it just business, or is the business of humanity . . . humanity?

6. Be Careful with Leprosy (24:8-9)

■ **8-9** The law concerning leprosy is brief and mysterious. It almost seems to function as a riddle in the middle of the laws about protecting vulnerable people. The people are instructed to be very careful with a defiling skin disease. How does this law function in this context? Is it just random or does it fit into the larger theme of protecting the needy and vulnerable? It is interesting to note that the people are told to do according to all the Levitical priests teach them, but details of this teaching are not spelled out.

Instead of spelling out the content of what the people are to do with leprosy, the law simply reminds Israel to **Remember what the LORD your God did to Miriam along the way after you came out of Egypt** (v 9). Miriam's leprosy is understood as Yahweh's judgment because of her hubris in challenging Moses' unique role in ancient Israel as leader of the people and mediator between God and the people. Does this law refer to this kind of hubris of a leader in Israel that brings its own level of defilement to the community? Or, does this law refer to a contaminating skin disease, which is also a threat to the community? Could it mean both? What is for sure is that this law is aimed at protecting the community from a contaminating condition that an individual brings to it. The afflicted person is to be excluded from the camp for a season, until such time as the proper rites of purification have removed the pollution from the community.

7. Be Careful How the Poor Are Treated with Loans that Are Made (24:10-13)

■ **10-13** Protecting the poor is the purpose of this legislation. Arduous conditions often determine the path of the impoverished. The poor often take on obligations that under better conditions they would never consider. Many times the only way to survive is to take a loan and give a pledge for repayment. This law states that the person making the loan may never enter the house of the recipient of the loan, but he must wait outside, where the pledge will be brought to him. This seems to allow for the item given as collateral to be the choice of the needy person. Making use of a loan does not have to take away the borrower's dignity.

The very poor would not have a house to enter to retrieve an item of collateral. In this case the poor would only have an outer garment, which is worn and slept in. This garment is a cover by day and a bed by night. A person who gives all that is owned is not to be deprived of this blanket at night. The pledge is to be returned when the sun goes down. A value system is shaping this legislation: even the poor and needy are not to be deprived of their dignity and humanity. The people of God are always to err on the side of kindness, compassion, and benevolence. Policies like these will not necessarily eradicate poverty from a group of people, but they will alleviate much hardship and allow for the humanity and dignity of every member within the community. As a people practice this political agenda, they reflect the character and purpose of the covenant God of Israel. Amos cites the violation of this covenantal policy by the wealthy citizens of northern Israel as one of the reasons for Yahweh's impending judgment on the nation (Amos 2:8).

8. Pay the Poor What They Are Due in a Timely Manner (24:14-15)

■ **14-15** Hired laborers are to be paid at the end of their day's work, whether they are Israelite brethren or resident aliens. These verses are policies directed toward the welfare of the poor and are linked to the previous section. The premise of this legislation is that the working poor are dependent upon daily wages to survive. Implied is that survival is dependent upon receiving enough to purchase food. A daily wage is needed each day to feed oneself and one's family each day. Again, it should be noticed that the protection of the poor expresses humanitarian concerns for all who are in the community. "The point is that the poor employee is a neighbor and not an economic pawn" (Brueggemann 2001, 239).

The well-being of the least of these determines the well-being of the community. If there is a failure to care for the working poor, then God hears their cries of misery and judges the inhabitants of the land. Yahweh heard the cry of Israel when they were slaves in Egypt; though the political powers were responsible for the hardship of the Hebrew slaves, the entire population of Egypt experienced Yahweh's judgment. God's rescue of the exploited is also the context for his judgment of the oppressors and the systems that promote oppression. The text reminds all who take advantage of their hired workers that they are **guilty of sin** and liable to Yahweh's judgment (v 15).

9. Don't Punish Others, Even Parents or Children, for the Evil of Others (24:16)

■ **16** There is not a uniform belief in the OT toward intergenerational guilt and responsibility. Clearly, the commandment found in Exod 20:5 and Deut 5:9 state that Yahweh's judgment on those who hate him would be for three and four generations. Yet, the legislation found in this text unambiguously prohibits executing members of one generation in a family for the crimes of another. The context of the commandment in Exod 20 and Deut 5 is against idolatry. To practice idolatry as a family or clan is to have the form of life of the communal assemblage shaped by the practice itself; therefore, the character and behavior of the children becomes habituated.

This text is clearly not addressing the issue of the malformation of character, but the curbing of vengeful retaliation and retribution. In some cultures revenge can inflame lopsided reprisal to the extent that entire families or even a village can be crushed. This law attempts to break the cycle of revenge and move toward justice for both victim and victimizer. What is notable is that individuals, and not others, are responsible for what they do. Israel is not to draw a conclusion concerning the character of one generation from the behavior of another. To do this is to pass judgment on the basis of the most uncertain proof. If a community practices this policy, then it will give every generation a freedom from the past failures of the generations that surround it. This community will be a community of both justice and hope.

10. Justice for Even the Most Vulnerable (24:17-18)

■ **17-18** The policy expressed in these verses is to protect the rights of the weak in the community. The weak are those who are economically distressed, vulnerable, landless, and poor; Deuteronomy identifies them as **the foreigner** or alien, **the fatherless** or the orphan, and **the widow** (v 17). The poor referenced in the policy of vv 10-13 are given the dignity of having their pledge garment returned to them in the evening, but this text goes a step further; no collateral is to be taken at all.

What is of interest is that the care for the vulnerable in this policy is tied to **justice**. To pervert justice is to become subject to the curse of Yahweh (27:19). A perversion of justice is incongruous with the character and purpose of Israel's God. When covenant with Yahweh is broken, *shalom* ceases to exist. This perversion of justice is on par with a judge taking a bribe, and it hinders the most basic rights of a person to be a part of the common good.

This course of action is not simply social policy, but social policy shaped by theological memory (**Remember that you were slaves in Egypt and *Yahweh* your God redeemed you from there** [24:18]). Israel's story begins with an act of Yahweh's liberating grace. This grace is to take embodied social form in the way the people of God seek the common good of their life together. The politics of Yahweh reflect the character and purpose of Yahweh for his creation. One might say that this political imagination is nothing less than bearing witness to God. Holiness must be socially embodied in God's people!

11. Leave Resources for the Most Vulnerable (24:19-22)

■ **19-22** This policy reflects a similarity to the former policy found in vv 17-18; Israel must care for the most vulnerable in the community. These public policies concern ownership, work, and food. Without food people die; therefore, Israel is called to eat graciously. Because aliens, orphans, and widows are landless, they will struggle for the provisions of life. The thrice-repeated citation of the groups of people who are the most disadvantaged reinforces an

233

awareness of their particular misfortunes. They will perish without assistance from the community. These needy people must not rely upon the subjective generosity of a few in the community, but the public itself must be organized to vouchsafe their care. This is clearly political policy.

Eating and working go together from the beginning of human history. Humankind is fated because of its separation from God to toil in order to live. This is apparent in the curse pronounced upon the first man in Gen 3:19. But, is this the way the blessed people are to live? Why is it that people take the curses placed upon humanity as the norm for humanity? Perhaps blessing is placed upon the graced community as the norm. The politics of Yahweh do not point to blessing as a magic incantation, but as a way of life for the common good.

Clearly, hard times come to good people. The story of Job undoubtedly points this out. But the community formed by the politics of Yahweh is created for the common good. The results of hard work are not to be hoarded for oneself, but shared with the vulnerable and needy. The policy of this text is crafted in such a way as to reflect the grace of God and the graciousness of the people of God. The politics of Yahweh insist that ownership is not simply self-serving, but ultimately for the common good. An owner must leave part of the harvest for the needy.

Once again these laws are given a narrative reminder: **Remember that you were slaves in Egypt. That is why I command you to do this** (Deut 24:22). These policies are based upon theological convictions: the land belongs to God, blessing is a gift of God, and blessing results in being fruitful and multiplying. Life is the goal of the community that is formed to eat gracefully. Politics, not magic, allow all to participate in the bounty of God's gift of life.

FROM THE TEXT

The laws in this portion of Deuteronomy appear disjointed, yet the reader looks for a cohesive theme. These regulations are concerned with stealing, marital fidelity, pledges for loans, kidnapping for profit, leprosy caused by the hubris of a leader, punishment for one's own crimes, and justice for the marginal: alien, orphan, and widow. Is there a theme for all of these various laws? Are they expositions of the concluding commandments of the Decalogue? Maybe the way to explore the theme is not to look at the specific laws but to explore the convictions of Israel concerning Yahweh himself.

So the question is: Who is Yahweh? It seems fair to say that Israel's conceptual picture of Yahweh is one that is painted with concern for the common good. The people are given the land in order to experience the blessings that result in life. Life is the goal of Yahweh's blessings. When people are placed in situations that ravage them with debt and poverty, the blessings of Yahweh are frustrated in the land. But, when the people organize their life together for the common good, life flows to all. Even marriage is considered a gift of Yahweh's grace. It is to be celebrated and is not to be used as a casual and frivolous relationship. Life for all is a result of covenant fidelity.

Well-being is at stake with the care or lack of care given to those who live on the margins of life. This segment of the book describes justice as the common good, which always includes the poor and needy. So who is this God that commands these laws? He is Yahweh, who cares uniquely for those who are weak and on the margins. Therefore, he constantly reminds Israel that she is needy and poor, a slave in the land of Egypt. He lets his people know that he hears the cries of the wretched and moves to care for their needs. His principal way to care is through a community that witnesses to his character and purpose, which is committed to the common good. Who is Yahweh? He is the one who gives blessing, hope, and life to even the least of these. Who is he? He is the one who is seen in the social embodiment of his people: the politics of Yahweh.

K. Uprightness: Private and Public (25:1-19)

BEHIND THE TEXT

The regulations contained in ch 25 seem to be arbitrary and disorganized. These directives address matters as varied as punishing criminals, caring for animals, Levirate law, intervention in a fight, commercial honesty, and remembering Amalek. Perhaps the final subdivision of the Law section (chs 12—26) is not as disorganized as it seems but is ordered around the premise of what is required for a community to be one of integrity. Each of the laws describes a community of integrity from a distinctive context. Therefore, paying attention to the laws themselves will describe the syntax of integrity and the form of life that integrity is to take.

The laws in this chapter appear to be in two sections: a collection of five regulations whose major concern is some sort of societal morals, and the concluding command to commit to memory the atrocity of Amalek. The rhetorical features of the passage include the placing of limitations upon the behavior of the people of Israel. The second of these limitations has a history of interpretation that is both literal and symbolic. The principle of the Levirate marriage is not legislated but is brought about by public pressure. The law concerning intervening in a fight seems to rely on a judicial system to adjudicate. The regulation concerning weights and measures is ultimately tied to uprightness in the character of the people. The final decree is similar to a parable, which attempts to convey a principle or value. The structure of the directives is as follows:

<h2>IN THE  TEXT</h2>

1. Limits Placed on Flogging (25:1-3)

■ **1-3** This first directive gives restrictions on legitimate punishment. Stipulations are given to establish an evenhanded procedure for retribution that protects the offender from possible excesses. The punishment must be appropriate to the offense. The punishment is to be carried out in the presence of the judge, and it shall be in proportion to the crime. What is also of interest is that no matter what the wrongdoing, the whipping cannot exceed forty blows.

A key to understanding this law is discovered in the opening verse with the Hebrew word group *šāpaṭ*. It is used two times in v 1 and the NIV translates them **court** and **the judges**. It is literally *to judge*, which implies justice. Justice is the theme of this law. Judgment is never to cross the limits of what is deserved, and what is deserved can never cross the boundary of human dignity. People cannot be whipped over forty lashes.

The rationale given in this limitation of punishment is because **your fellow Israelite will be degraded in your eyes** (v 3). The word that the NIV translates **your fellow Israelite** is literally *your brother*. This motive clause is based upon a conviction that the criminal is still a brother, a neighbor. One is not to look upon a brother in a way that degrades or shames him, even if he is a villain. This law is concerned as much about the way people view each other as it is with limitations placed upon punishment. It must be remembered that capital punishment is permitted in the OT, but even this punishment is administered to human beings. Human dignity is in the eye of the beholder, and the community of faith is to view people always with a level of dignity. When a community fails to view people this way, then people become categories and the community itself sanctions atrocities.

What does this command reveal about the conceptual picture of Yahweh? Clearly, Yahweh is committed to justice. Not only is justice used to mean adjudicating rightly, but this adjudication always holds that human beings have a God-given dignity that must not be degraded. Public humiliation even applies in the act of castigating criminals for transgressions that they perpetrate. This does not imply that punishment is not to be administered, but that the limit of its administration is on the border between dignity and degradation.

This conviction is given full voice in the words of Jesus when he says in Matt 5:43-48:

> You have heard that it was said, "Love your neighbor and hate your enemy." But I tell you, love your enemies and pray for those who persecute you, that you may be children of your Father in heaven. He causes his sun to rise on the evil and the good, and sends rain on the righteous and the unrighteous. If you love those who love you, what reward will you get? Are not even the tax collectors doing that? And if you greet only your own people, what are you doing more than others? Do not even pagans do that? Be perfect, therefore, as your heavenly Father is perfect.

God's character is reflected in the way a faith community administers justice. The people of God are to view human beings as majestic; they are created in God's own image. Dignity is not only given to the poor and landless, but even to villains. Justice is concerned with judging rightly and judging rightly includes seeing the human dignity in every person, even enemies and criminals.

2. Muzzling an Ox (25:4)

■ **4** When farmers thresh the grain, they would often muzzle oxen to keep them from stopping to eat the very grain they were treading. The alternative to muzzling an ox is to use a whip to prod the creature on in its work. The law is adamant that the creature is allowed a degree of contentment while working; the ox is not purely a machine for production. The question that haunts readers of this text is: Is Yahweh concerned for oxen? Before jumping to an allegorized interpretation, the reader of Deuteronomy must remember that there are decrees and regulations that convey concern for all life and nature itself.

There is no doubt that this prohibition against muzzling a working ox appears out of place if it is understood simply as a humanitarian concern for a domestic animal. The question the reader poses is: Why is this law here? Various interpreters understand this verse to be a metaphor. An example of this can be seen in 1 Cor 9:9, where Paul uses this text to imply that a worker deserves compensation for ministry. Nelson sees this as a law possibly inculcating a merciful stance toward the offender (2002b, 297). Perhaps this law is placed in this context to show the value of all of life. Even an ox deserves the dignity of being a living creature. This would imply a protection for the conception of life itself. If dignity is enlarged to include even oxen, then it must be extended to all people, even villains.

How would the ethos of a community that practices the dignity of life shape the character of individuals within the community? People, who even look upon an animal with nobility and majesty are shaped to see the world and all relationships within it as precious. This does not mean that oxen are not to thresh the grain and that villains are not to be punished, but they both, along with everything that lives, have a dignity given by the Giver of life.

3. Levirate Marriage (25:5-10)

■ **5-10** Levirate, which comes from the Latin *levir* (brother-in-law), associates with a polygamous communal situation. Brothers have an obligation to one another, according to this directive. If one of the brothers dies, the remaining brother is duty-bound to marry the wife of the deceased. The function of this marriage is not to comfort the grieving widow but to ensure that children will be born and carry on the name of the deceased brother. Because it is not until late in Israel's history that they believed in the resurrection of an individual life, the only way to preserve the life of the dead is through children and their children. These children and grandchildren carry on the family name. The other advantage of the Levirate law is that the widow will have the resources needed for survival. Married women are dependent on their husbands for economic support in ancient Israel. Women without husbands or sons, like Tamar or Ruth, are essentially without support. To protect the childless widow, the policy of levirate marriage is set in place.

The question that this law attempts to address is the refusal to carry out the Levirate law. What should be done? Possibly another question needs to be posed before answering this procedural question: Why would a brother refuse to carry out this Levirate law? The reader is not told why a brother may choose to not fulfill his obligations. In a contemporary setting one would give an answer that fits the values of the modern period, which would have to do with attraction or love. This most probably misses the point of the rejection. It is likely that the brother's own prospects in the family inheritance is affected by his marrying his dead brother's widow and producing children by her for his brother.

Whatever the reason, there is a procedure that is to be followed if the living brother refuses to marry the widow of his brother. Verses 7-10 stipulate a course of action by which the widow may come to the elders of the city to file a complaint and perform a ritual of public disgrace. The possibility that the living brother might not wish to carry out such a responsibility is plainly allowed for, and it is noteworthy that such a rejection is made through appeal to the elders. The elders of the town shall summon the living brother to speak to him. This interrogation by the elders subjects him to public humiliation.

Shame is the limit of the punishment by the elders for his refusal to fulfill the levirate obligation. But, if he continues in this refusal to marry the widow, then she can shame him further. This shame will continue beyond his lifetime into future generations. The widow shall, in the presence of the elders, pull off the brother's sandal, spit in his face, and declare, **This is what is done to the man who will not build up his brother's family line** (v 9). The widow of the diseased places a curse upon the living brother. She is given the authority to publicly attack her husband's brother through public ritual. The act of pulling off the sandal appears symbolic of a refusal to fulfill marital obligations or of a failure to take possession of property.

There are two very powerful narratives in the OT that describe the problems encased in this law. The first is the story of Tamar and Judah, which is found in Gen 38. The other is the story of Ruth. Both of these women lost their husbands to death and were vulnerable and in need of a redeemer, the next of kin. These narratives describe the dilemma that the law is attempting to resolve. They also narrate the justice that is described in the redeemer fulfilling the intention of the policy of levirate marriage.

4. Intervention in a Fight (25:11-12)

■ **11-12** A brawl among men is the context within which this statute is situated. The assumption is that the wife of one of the fighting men reaches out and intervenes inappropriately on behalf of her husband. She goes for the genitals of her husband's foe. Her contact with his genitals either humiliates him or causes him not to be able to be fruitful and multiply. The punishment for this humiliation or maiming is removing the woman's hand; she becomes maimed. She is to be given no pity by this policy. The lack of pity is usually reserved for the most extreme affronts. In ancient Israel this is evidently one of those most excessive offenses.

It should be obvious to the reader that this policy emerges from a world picture of male dominance. Male priority is unmistakable in this law. Social structures that give preference to any gender, race, or economic status are contrary to the Christian vision of God's purpose. "There is neither Jew nor Gentile, neither slave nor free, nor is there male and female" in the new people of God (Gal 3:28). The reader should regard the potential for fruitful life and honor as the intention of this law, but wooden readings of this policy should not allow for either violence to women or lowering the standard by which they are regarded.

5. Honest Weights and Measures (25:13-16)

■ **13-16** Equitable transactions, both buying and selling, are fundamental to the vision of a society committed to the common good. This requirement consists of two bans upon deceptive economic practices and two related affirmative declarations. These statements are concluded with a motivational clause. The bans are upon carrying two types of weights and measures. Fraudulent weights for business-related dealings are problematic in the ancient world. What is of interest is that there is no fixed punishment proposed for this crime. It must be extremely difficult to discover and take legal action against this kind of fraud in the ancient world. The positive assertions are that the business transactions are to have only full and honest weights and measures.

Because of the difficulty of discovering fraud, the law concludes with a strong reminder and warning: **For the LORD your God detests anyone who does these things, anyone who deals dishonestly** (v 16). Yahweh recognizes and is revolted by this type of abomination. The character and purpose of God is clearly witnessed to in this law. He is both honest and intends his people to be honest in all of their dealings. The purpose of this policy is discovered in the motive clause of the law. Sustainable life in the land is only possible if just and fair commercial practices are enacted. Christian readers of this text must realize that a follower of Jesus cannot compartmentalize life. All of life is under the care and conditions of God. Only neighborliness sustains a community committed to the common good. Deceptive economic practices destroy society as well as the members of that society.

6. Never Forget Amalek (25:17-19)

■ **17-19** Israel is encouraged to never forget Amalek. According to the canonical tradition, the animosity toward the Amalekites originated during the time close to the exodus itself, before Israel reached Mount Horeb (see Exod 17:8-16).

Amalekites, Israel's Perennial Enemy

Amalek was the leader of the first nation to attack Israel at Rephidim after the exodus. The problem with the perpetual enmity with the Amalekites is not addressed in the exodus story. It isn't until the text in Deut 25 that the narrative is given a warrant for the everlasting antagonism. The Amalekites launched their assault against the stragglers who were famished and weary (v 18). These were the weak, which were unable to keep up with the march through the wilderness. The failure to spare the weak and powerless is the act that provides the impetus for Israel's incessant loathing of the Amalekites. To take advantage of the weak is always to practice life in a way that reflects injustice and therefore the opposite of the politics of Yahweh.

The first chronicled attempt to eliminate the Amalekites appears in 1 Samuel. Samuel, speaking for Yahweh, says:

> This is what the LORD Almighty says: "I will punish the Amalekites for what they did to Israel when they waylaid them as they came up from Egypt. Now go, attack the Amalekites and totally destroy all that belongs to them. Do not spare them; put to death men and women, children and infants, cattle and sheep, camels and donkeys." (15:2-3)

King Saul ultimately lost the monarchy because of his disobedience to the command to destroy the Amalekites.

The Amalekites became the perennial enemy of Israel, but from a historical point of view they ceased to exist as a nation in the days of Hezekiah. Amalek functions, in due course, as a metaphor for the nemesis of Yahweh's people. Amalek is used conceptually as late as the book of Esther, where Haman is described as an Agagite; therefore, it relates him to Agag, the Amalekite enemy of King

Saul. This narrative brings to a close this warring with the Amalekites when the ten sons of Haman the Agagite are executed in the gallows their father erected for Mordecai.

Perhaps Deut 25:18 gives theological rationale into why this group is used as Yahweh's adversary: **they had no fear of God**. Most probably this phrase implies that they were both not astonished at the mystery of life and not anxious concerning their own judgment. They demonstrated their lack of fear of God by their total disregard for the **weary and worn out, they . . . attacked all who were lagging behind**. They are, in Israel's perception, a community of fools. Their foolishness will bring about their demise, because they pursue the way of death for others and for themselves.

Deuteronomy calls Israel to remember both what Yahweh did for her (ch 8) and what Amalek did to her (25:17). Remembering what Yahweh did for Israel involves her obedience to the will of Yahweh that is defined by Deuteronomy. Likely remembering Amalek is also tied to doing the will of Yahweh. This time it may point to the injustice brought about by the foolishness of Amalek. Israel must remember and never take advantage of the weak.

FROM THE TEXT

Is there a common theme or value that is expressed in these laws? The answer is yes; guard life particularly when it is vulnerable. When a person is being flogged, guard life. When an ox is used for production, guard its life. When a brother dies, guard his life and the life of his spouse. When there is a fight, never intervene in a way that harms or shames, but guard life. When one is engaged in business transactions, guard life through honest exchange. And never forget the eternal enemy of Yahweh, who took advantage of the weak and did not guard life. Guarding life, in a variety of practices, has a consequence on the culture of a community and the character of an individual. To practice the dignity of life in all of its manifestations is to become a people and a person that perceives rightly. Guarding the dignity of life is not a burden to be endured but a way of comprehending the meaning of all creation.

It should be remembered that Israel's existence emerges out of the disregard for life itself. People are understood as simply a means to an end. They become both a resource and a threat. The Egyptians did not regard Israel as if she had a story, but simply as an instrument to an economic objective. Because of her deliverance, she knows that life itself is a gift. To live within a community where the world is pictured as gift and blessing is to practice a political reality of guarding life. Therefore, she knows that even in the implementation of punishment, she is to guard the dignity of life. All life has a dignity to it, even the life of a criminal. Animals, used for sustaining life, must be acknowledged also as the living. Nothing is simply a means to an end! The dead and those who

25:1-19

depend on them are given the dignity of guarding their lives. Fighting is never understood as winning by any means possible, but there is a dignity that must be remembered even in the struggle. Commerce is not sectioned off to where one could say, "Well, this is business." In buying and selling, the people of God are to guard life. Sellers and buyers cannot place the other in a competitive win-at-all-costs position. Amalek is the chief exemplar of winning at all costs. The weak and vulnerable are disregarded for the sake of an advantage. Yahweh will have nothing to do with making life simply a category. It is the supreme gift. The people of God are called to practice a politic of guarding life.

L. Stewardship (26:1-15)

BEHIND THE TEXT

Most commentators regard these verses as a general conclusion to the whole of the Law section in chs 12—26. Some commentators interpret 26:16-19 as the genuine conclusion to the Law section (Olson 1994, 115). Deuteronomy 26:1-15 contains two declarative statements: the land is a gift of Yahweh's saving grace to Israel (vv 1-11), and Yahweh's gift of the land is intended to care for the disadvantaged people within the community (vv 12-15). These two types of offerings are placed one after the other and indicate a correlation linking gratitude and generosity.

Some scholars note the apparent inconsistency between vv 4 and 10, where the priest takes the basket of firstfruits and sets it before the altar, and where the worshipper places the basket before Yahweh. Many suggest that the passage has undergone editorial expansion. This seeming inconsistency may simply be that the two offerings take place in two very different settings: the place where Yahweh chooses and one's own town.

The first declaration is the firstfruits celebration, which is the earliest agricultural harvest of the year. It is possible that the tradition of Deuteronomy yearns for the community to experience again, on a yearly cycle, the gracious activity of Yahweh with the original generation of settlers. In this annual ritual subsequent generations remember the historical outcome of entering the land. Land is a result of fulfilled promise, and this promise has ongoing consequences in the form of economic well-being. It is the promise of land that flows with milk and honey. The form of life that the practice of firstfruits intends to generate is one where gift is recognized and celebrated in gratitude. All of Israel is to envision that they are part of the pioneer generation that enters into the land. When they bring their basket of produce to the priest, they are to respond by saying: "I declare today to the LORD your God that I have come to the land the LORD swore to our ancestors to give us" (v 3).

The second declaration is designed to care for the needy in the community. Israel remembers that her story transports her into solidarity with the needy. Her story narrates that she is an alien in the land of Egypt without authority or even the capability to provide for herself. She is not only an alien in Egypt, but she is also landless in Egypt just like the Levite, the orphan, and the widow. She finds herself, in her story, at the mercy of others. Yahweh's gracious gift of the land is designed to reinforce an everlasting concern for the most disadvantaged members of the community.

IN THE TEXT

■ **1-11** Salvation history is the framework within which the people are to interpret the provisions that sustain life. The focal point of vv 1-11 is the formal declaration of faith of vv 5-9. This affirmation is placed within the practice of firstfruits after the late summer harvest. Israel is reminded at least annually that Yahweh brought her up out of a land of bondage and gave her a land flowing with milk and honey. Possession of this land is portrayed as God's providence, which includes fertile soil. Firstfruits are a practice that tells Israel again that it is neither her strength nor the strength of the fertility gods that provide the fruitful land, but it is Yahweh's acts of promise, liberation, and land.

By the practice of firstfruits, each generation becomes present tense with the earliest generation of those who came to the fruitful land. A remarkable characteristic of this and other historical narrative summations is the consistent use of the first-person plural pronouns. Through the use of **we** and **us**, the confessors identify with the aforementioned salvation history of Yahweh's people.

The writer uses key words to convey the meaning of the practice of firstfruits. These words are: **to give/giving** and **land**. The key to understanding this section of the passage is the concept *nātan* ("to give"). The meaning of this pericope is especially shaped by the use of this word. It is used repeatedly in Deuteronomy to show the act and work of Yahweh in giving the land to Israel. (→ 2:1—3:22 for a detailed study of the way *nātan* is used in Deuteronomy.) Land as a gift brings the community to realize that everything produced upon the land is also a gift.

Verse 4 of ch 26 describes the placing of the basket before the altar of Yahweh. The contents of the basket become the possession of the priests, but the contribution functions as a gift to Yahweh. This contribution is not a gift to placate God or even to serve God, as if he needs food, but as an act of thanksgiving or gratitude. Gratitude is the instinctive response to the realization of receiving a gift. Perhaps Barth is right in his insistence that there is only one response to grace: gratitude.

Verses 5-9 are not a prayer or even an exhortation, but a confession of faith: a credo. These words sum up the most important events in Israel's saving history from the time of the patriarchs to the conquest. This may point to an early composition of the creedal confession. Von Rad believes that this credo is "probably the earliest and at the same time the most widely used . . . confessional formulae" of the saving history of Yahweh for Israel (1962, 121). He says that this credo "bears all the marks of great antiquity" (ibid., 122). What stands out in the confession is the absence of any reference to the events at Horeb/Sinai. The confession proceeds from the suffering in Egypt to the rescue out of anguish and bondage to entry into Canaan. This may imply that Horeb/Sinai did not belong to the salvation events narrated in this early summary of the tradition. If the credo is concerned with a land of promise, then it could make sense that the revelation of the Law is left out of the summary. Horeb/Sinai would function as a premise of both Deuteronomy and the form of life that the people are to take in the land, but not salvation history itself.

What the credo communicates is that from beginning to end communal identity and the land are woven together. Pre-Israel wandering Arameans are promised both identity and land. Simply moving out of Egypt, the house of bondage, does not complete the saving work of Yahweh. It will take moving into the land of promise, a land flowing with milk and honey. The credo makes it clear that the giving of the land of Canaan is the *telos* of the saving acts of Yahweh. It is Yahweh who **brought us to this place and gave us this land, a land flowing with milk and honey** (v 9). This confession is kept alive in the history of ancient Israel through singers and storytellers, and consists of both going from a place and going to a place.

26:12-15 The decree of firstfruits allows every generation to participate with the original gift of the land as the fulfillment of promise. This communal directive connects the gift of the land with the salvation story of the people. Through this annual ritual the identity of God's people is sustained through both narrative and practice. The preservation of Israel's character passes on communal convictions and values through the powerful flow of time. Israel's very identity calls for a response of gratitude.

■ **12-15** The second of the recitals emphasizes that God's gift of the land is designed to reinforce a concern for the most needy members of the community. The third-year tithe restates the themes of rich land and social concern from the previous eleven verses. The additional tithe offering scheduled for every third year could easily be discarded, but the theme of obedience to the Law is added (26:13). The reader should explore Deut 14:28-29, which also address the third-year tithe. Deuteronomy 26:12-15 specifies that every three years a tithe of the fruits of one's labor is offered to God and given to the needy. It is of note that vv 12 and 13 articulate twice who the needy members are: **the Levite, the foreigner, the fatherless and the widow.** These persons are all without land. This means that they do not have the possibility to reap the benefit of the gift of the land flowing with milk and honey. Therefore, if they are to benefit from the gift of Yahweh to Israel, they will need to receive

244

the bounty of the land in a different manner. They are to receive the fruit of the land that Yahweh gives to the people by an indirect route. A share of the bounty of the land is redirected to the poor and needy. Yahweh's blessed people are to practice generosity!

Distribution of the third-year tithe is a local activity, which takes place within one's own town. The earlier delivery of the tithe takes place where "the LORD your God will choose as a dwelling for his Name" (v 2). In the third year the people are told: **When you have finished setting aside a tenth of all your produce in the third year, the year of the tithe, you shall give it to the Levite, the foreigner, the fatherless and the widow, so that they may eat in your towns and be satisfied** (v 12). The emphasis is that the third-year tithes themselves remain at home.

The latter part of v 13 and all of v 14 describe the worshippers presenting their offering and declaring:

I have not turned aside from your commands nor have I forgotten any of them. I have not eaten any of the sacred portion while I was in mourning, nor have I removed any of it while I was unclean, nor have I offered any of it to the dead. I have obeyed the LORD my God; I have done everything you commanded me.

Even though this is an act of social righteousness and evenhandedness, it remains a theological practice. The recital of innocence articulates a contrast between the requirements of the politics of Yahweh and other alternatives that are available. The outcome of this practice of generosity is not only resourcing the needy within the community but also forming the character of individuals and the ethos of the group of people formed and disciplined by the integrity and purpose of Yahweh.

The final utterance of the worshipper is an entreaty to Yahweh to **look down from heaven, your holy dwelling place, and bless your people Israel and the land you have given us as you promised on oath to our ancestors, a land flowing with milk and honey** (v 15). **Look down** presupposes that Yahweh is both transcendent and attentive to the deeds and needs of creation. The second part of the final petition is that Yahweh will bless both Israel and the land. Again it should be noticed that communal identity and the land are tied together. The concept of blessing is narrated well in the priestly account of creation in Gen 1. God blesses living beings, humanity, and finally the Sabbath. The first two blessings are in order for all living beings to be fruitful and multiply. It follows that the Sabbath is designed for the same purpose, the ongoing abundance of life. Perhaps the land of promise is understood as an opportunity for creation to function within its original intent.

The plea for blessing is a desire for the people and the land to be fruitful and multiply. In other words, it is a prayer for life. This unmistakably brings

26:12-15

together a theology of salvation with a theology of creation. Deuteronomy's tradition is consistently proclaiming to Israel to "choose life" and not death. Life is the fulfillment of promise and life is what is extended to the least of these in the community.

FROM THE TEXT

Modern-day persons live in a culture that cultivates ravenous desire. Compilations of techniques of desire produce unjust yearnings and aspirations within individuals. These techniques are the practices and rituals of a culture. The question of contemporary readers is: How can present-day persons, whose desires are shaped by the techniques of capitalism, resist wrongful desiring?

For ancient Israel the practice of the stewardship of one's resources functions as a constructive custom that reforms the character of a person and the ethos of a community. Greed is transformed into generosity, and incessant striving is changed into gratitude. Israel's story is not a story of self-sufficiency but one of deliverance and gift. She confesses that her ancestors are wandering Arameans who went down into Egypt. They lived in Egypt as the landless, therefore the marginalized. Without power and authority, they found themselves relegated to hard labor without help or hope. All they can do is "cry" in their affliction. But Yahweh hears the cries of the afflicted and delivers the people. Yahweh himself leads them to a land flowing with all of the resources necessary for abundant life. He gives them the land!

Israel is a people formed out of the munificence of God. What are people who are formed out of bounteousness to do? They are to live their lives from gift as gift. This at least means that the virtues of gratitude and generosity are to become habituated within the ethos of the community and the character of individual persons. Habituation does not take place in a moment through a personal, heartfelt decision or even an earnest prayer, but through the persistent participation in practices and the perpetual storytelling that permeate a community's way of life. Identity is formed over time in both the community and the individual. The way people interpret the world and participate in that same world is formed by techniques of desire. These policies and practices are the community's framework or political reality.

Stewardship is a unique technique of desire. It shapes people to see the produce necessary for living as a gift. God provides for them through the gift of the land and the providence to work hard upon that same land. It is a land of milk and honey, and it is a gift. To bring a portion of the gift to God is not an act that appeases divinity but an act where the bearer of the portion realizes in ever-new ways that everything is a gift. If the world and all that is in it is interpreted as gift, then it generates the virtue of gratitude. Perhaps there is only one real response to grace—gratitude.

Stewardship also shapes a grateful people into a generous people. The landless and vulnerable are provided for. The Levite, the alien, the orphan, and the widow are generously resourced by the people of God as an extension of God's gifts. Generosity is not something that must be mustered within a person or a people but comes out of recognizing that everything is a gift to be extended to everyone. Providence is again a key theological concept at work in this world picture. God's providence provides the resources for not only oneself and one's family, but for all who are needy. One could say that generosity to the needy is almost a sacramental act. Those with the gifts of God are means of God's gifts to those in need. Milk and honey not only flow to those with property and wealth but flow through them to those who do not have the same resources.

The contemporary reader will want to explore the practice of stewardship, not as a way to pay the bills of the church or synagogue or even as a way of placating God, but as a way of participating in the blessings and gifts from God. How does the practice of stewardship shape the character of a person and the ethos of a community? Is gratitude and generosity habituating both individual and community? This passage, and perhaps the entire tradition of Deuteronomy, conveys the opportunity for the people of God to participate once more in the initial covenant of Yahweh with his people. The earliest covenant is declared once and for all, and yet it is reaffirmed in every new context to every generation. The practice of stewardship is an ongoing ritual whereby the people of God are persistently incorporated into the politics of Yahweh.

26:1-15

IV. BLESSINGS AND CURSES: 26:16—30:20

OVERVIEW

The closing sections of the book of Deuteronomy, 26:16—
34:12 address the present reality of how the people of Israel are to
prefer and personify the politics of their God. Deuteronomy's final
composition organizes 12:1—26:15 as the Deuteronomic Code,
enclosed by materials that narrate speeches given to the second
generation that did not know bondage in Egypt or life in the land of
promise. What are they and future generations to do with the policies and practices of the Deuteronomic Code, and how are they to
live in the land without Moses as their leader? These questions are
going to be answered in this final section of the book. Materials
that belong to the final section of the book contain blessings and
curses with the instruction to choose life (26:16—30:20), and a
narrative epilogue that reports the death of Moses and transition
of leadership to Joshua (31:1—34:12). The first part, Blessings and
Curses (26:16—30:20), has the following literary structure:

A. This Very Day . . . (26:16—27:10)
B. Keeping Boundary of Identity Safe and Secure
   (27:11-26)
C. Blessings and Curses (28:1-68)
D. Choose Life (29:1—30:20 [28:69—30:20 HB])

A. This Very Day . . . (26:16—27:10)

BEHIND THE TEXT

This segment functions as a transition from the decrees and laws in chs 12—26 to the epilogue that begins in 27:11. The literary suggestion is that Moses is finished explaining the laws and practices for Israel's new life in the land of promise. There is no scholarly consensus on how to structure the following passage. Many commentators place 26:16-19 with the earlier collection of laws in 12:1—26:15. If this is the case, then it is a concluding section for the law code and perhaps the entire section from ch 5 to 26:15. It is apparent that these verses are a closing exhortation to observe the earlier laws. However, 26:16-19 seems to both conclude the previous section and provide a transition to the following section. Most likely these verses are a later editorial postscript that leads to the concluding section of the book. The final section is concerned with future generations and their commitment to the policies and practices of Yahweh.

Some commentators also include 27:11-26 as part of the unit. The tone and character seem to shift in vv 11-26. Deuteronomy, in this latter section, is concerned with a series of curses on the people if they fail to embody Torah. Deuteronomy 26:16—27:10 has the following literary structure:

1. Making Promises "Today" (26:16-19)
2. Confirming and Writing Down the Torah (27:1-8)
3. Becoming the People of Yahweh "Today" (27:9-10)

Rhetorically, this passage underscores the current generation's responsibility for its own participation in the covenant. Multiple times the text exhorts the readers to recognize that the covenant is a matter of the present. It does this by using the phrase "this day." But this closing stage is not simply a literary end. The reader is again reminded of what ultimately matters when the policy of Torah is set forth: Israel's devotion today! Yahweh is Israel's God today. Israel is God's people today. The presentation of the commandments and ordinances, which will serve as a political guide for Israel in the land, must be renewed again and again.

IN THE TEXT

I. Making Promises "Today" (26:16-19)

■ **16-19** These verses differ from all the preceding units by what is absent: any new law. Even though these verses do not explicitly refer to covenant, their literary form presents the impression of a covenant/treaty in which the participants formulate their promises to Yahweh. This covenant is based upon the policies contained in the laws and practices of chs 12—26.

Moses verbalizes the declarations made by both covenant partners as though he is the covenant mediator. Both Israel and Yahweh make declarations regarding their relationship. Yahweh desires to be Israel's God, and Israel declares that it wishes to be Yahweh's people. The promise formula is bilateral, but the relationship is fundamentally one of nonequals. Yahweh instigates the relationship, and Israel can only respond. It is Yahweh who makes promises to the fathers, who liberates the people, and who is giving the land. The responsibilities of each party are interwoven with those of the other party. At the core of this covenant relationship are these reciprocal declarations between Yahweh and Israel.

Verse 16 announces the urgency of this passage with the phrase **this day**. The idiom is in the persuasive initial position of the clause; therefore, it functions by drawing the attention of each new generation to be present with Moses. Each generation must hear the words of Torah once again. Upon hearing God's word, they are given the opportunity to continue to live in covenant. **This day** is used again in vv 17 and 18. God is encountered today, in the present moment, as the community reads Torah.

The people are urged to obey the specific commands with **all** of their **heart** and with **all** of their **soul**. These words are reminiscent of ch 6. This phrase describes an all-encompassing reality of God upon Israel. The all-encompassing God requires an all-encompassing obedience, and this reminds the reader that divine instruction is not policy to be ignored but policy to be embodied in the life of the community and the lives of individuals as well.

Verses 17-18 demonstrate a connection to a segment of the covenant renewal ceremony, although the ceremony itself is not articulated explicitly. These words give the reader a hint as to the makeup of the covenant. They express a salient assertion of both Yahweh's and Israel's commitment to each other. This binary declaration is the confirmation of the covenant, and it should be noticed that Yahweh declares his faithfulness to Israel in response to Israel declaring her faithfulness to him. Israel's declaration of faithfulness is embodied through concrete acts of obedience as contained in the law code of 12:1—26:15.

The mutual commitment of Yahweh and Israel forms a rhetorical parallelism; each statement introduces a reciprocal commitment of Yahweh and Israel. Yahweh promises to be the God of his people. This means that he will watch over Israel, protecting her and providing for her. This is not a new conceptual picture of God for Israel. He has already been described through the actions of Israel's history as a protector, provider, and guide. The reader of these texts realizes that having Yahweh as God for Israel creates the possibility of the good life.

The text also seems to describe the reality that Yahweh is Israel's God whether or not the people like it. Yet, they are not forced into obedience. The gracious and liberating work of Yahweh led Israel into this covenant. The one who hears the cries of oppressed people, liberates them, and leads them, now requires of them a particular socially embodied way of life. They are to follow in his ways by keeping his commandments and obeying his voice. In other words, they are to practice the politics of Yahweh.

Verse 17 expresses three fundamental responses to Yahweh: that you will walk in obedience to him; that you will keep his decrees, commands, and laws; that you will listen to him. The way of the Lord is one of the most central metaphors to portray the ethical pilgrimage of a people or a person. To walk in a way is to comport oneself in a life direction. A reader of Scripture perceives examples of "walking in a way" from the call of Abraham to the calling of the disciples. The manner of the walking is described as keeping decrees, commands, and laws. The word translated **to keep** is literally **to watch**. It means significantly more than merely doing an act of obedience if one happens to remember the law, but it refers to a diligent focus that results in obedience. The final response of the people to Yahweh's covenant is to listen to Yahweh. The Hebrew word *šěmaʿ* is used in this verse. This concept means more than simply hearing a word or voice, but obedience is implied. Complete loyalty and obedience are required of a people who hear the voice of God. See Deut 6:4 ff. for an expression of this full habituation of Yahweh into the life of his people.

Deuteronomy 26:18-19 describes the status of the people in their covenant with God. Israel is Yahweh's special possession; she is set above all the nations, and she is a people holy to Yahweh. It should be noticed that God's grace and human responsibility appear to come together in these verses. The sentence structure points to obligations of the people who belong to Yahweh. Israel's faithfulness to Yahweh allows her to be distinguished among the nations; she is a people holy to Yahweh. This means that she is to witness before the nations to Yahweh's purpose and character for creation. Israel differentiates herself by reflecting the splendor and grandeur of Yahweh in her form of life. Israel's politics are to bear truthful witness to Yahweh's intention for creation.

2. Confirming and Writing Down the Torah (27:1-8)

■ **1-8** This section is most likely a text composed over time. The figure of Moses confers in essence the same directive twice, in vv 2-3 and vv 4 and 8. In the first instance the people are to set up some large stones and coat them with plaster as soon as they cross over the Jordan. They are then to **write on them all the words of this law** (v 3). Verses 4 and 8 point out Mount Ebal explicitly. This is "a site too far from the Jordan to reach on the day you cross. This suggests a later revision interested in pinpointing the locale of this action at Shechem" (Nelson 2002b, 316). Verses 5-7 point to the requirement for an altar and a sacrifice. This interrupts the command concerning stones. Nelson believes that the insertion of these verses reflects "a melding of separate traditions, one involving a stele and one an altar" (ibid., 317).

Verse 1 uses the phrase **keep all these commands**. This phrase is literally *commandment* (singular) in the Hebrew. Most translations translate *commandment* as plural, because it implies all of the commands given by God through Moses. This strange singular form means that the commandments are to be obeyed as a singular mandate by Yahweh. To keep the entire commandment is to be radically obedient to the politics of Yahweh. Deuteronomy, as a whole, is concerned with stories and practices that shape a political form of life for communal and personal well-being. This politic functions as a viewpoint to interpret experience, and therefore assigns to history a narrative shaped by God.

The reader should notice, in v 3, how the text describes **the land**: as a gift from Yahweh and as **a land flowing with milk and honey**. It is further described as a fulfillment of what Yahweh promised Israel's ancestors. A gift where the blessed life is possible is Deuteronomy's conception of the land. It should also be noted that the commandments or politics of Yahweh is a gift (v 2). Both land and commands allow for the abundant life to take place for the people of God. This gift is not given so that the people can know how to placate Yahweh, but to permit the people to inhabit the land of promise and blessing as they are being habituated by the will and purpose of Yahweh. They can choose life in abundance as they practice the political reality proclaimed in Deuteronomy.

In the context of this redacted passage, **when you have crossed the Jordan into the land** presents a problem. **Mount Ebal** (v 4) is thirty miles from Jericho and thousands of feet higher. Scholars have various ways of attempting to explain the location problem, but the function of this location is what is of greatest value. Mount Ebal is a very visible place where the covenant process is honored. It allows a person to see a vast section of the promised land, much like Moses is able to see from Mount Nebo. Because of this place Israel is habitually aware of the outlandish gift of the land and her unique responsibility to live as God's people in it. Israel's identity and Yahweh's political order are remembered and renewed at Mount Ebal.

Great stones, covered with plaster, are to have the politics of Yahweh written clearly. This visible public notice may function as a reminder of who Israel is or it may function as an alternative ideology, attempting to win over converts. Whether they are a reminder of who Israel is or what Israel is to be, these laws are at least the policies and practices of chs 12—26. They at least include the abbreviation of these laws, perhaps the Decalogue. "The purpose of all such billboards is to nurture and administer public opinion and public loyalty to persuade for this claim against all other claims" (Brueggemann 2001, 252).

A reader should also notice that the stones are not to have an iron tool wielded on them. These unhewn stones, as well as the stones used for the altar, are a reminder of the land that Yahweh created and gave to Israel as a possession.

Verses 6 and 7 describe the building of an altar and sacrifices that are to be made upon it: **Build the altar of the** L ORD **your God with fieldstones and offer burnt offerings on it to the** L ORD **your God** (v 6). This very likely implies that the stones are to keep their created condition and grandeur. Reshaping by human hands would distort their sacred form; they would become profane and unholy. The sacrifices are **burnt offerings** and *peace offerings*. In these offerings most of the meat is eaten by the worshippers and are proper for celebrations. These are not offerings to appease deity but to celebrate the gift of life in the land, to celebrate *shalom*.

3. Becoming the People of Yahweh "Today" (27:9-10)

■ **9-10** It is interesting to note the shift from the third-person reference of **Moses and the Levitical priests** in v 9 to first-person singular reference **that I give you today** in v 10. By joining the Levitical priests to Moses the text positions these leaders as those who will succeed Moses for the covenant renewal in Israel's future. The priests speak the singular **I** of Moses' voice to the people of Israel. Moses and the priests call on **all Israel** to be silent and listen to the voice of Yahweh in the present moment: **that I give you today**. In some way the reader comes to understand the voice of Moses is present in the voices of the priests in the coming generations.

The passage also points to the reality of God's grace enabling Israel to become a community of Yahweh's people. Once again the tradition of Deuteronomy insists upon a synergistic relationship between grace and responsibility. In order for Israel to sustain her communal identity she is obliged to **be silent . . . listen . . . obey** God's **commands and decrees**. Yahweh's promise to the fathers, deliverance from bondage, and gift of the land are acts of sheer grace, but communal identity is not prearranged, it must be habituated through practices and stories. Yahweh, in grace, gives the Torah to Israel, but Israel must embody that Torah. She is to live in the politics of Yahweh as the people of Yahweh. She is called to hear, but to hear is to obey, since without obedience the politics of Yahweh and its requirements would fail. Hearing and not obeying is like speaking without a form of life to make sense of that particular speech act. One might say that hearing without obedience is like language going on vacation. It doesn't work; it is meaningless.

FROM THE TEXT

What holds this section together is the prominence of the present moment. God's people are not satisfied to simply have a sacred text; the text is to become embodied "this day" by every generation. In other words, this text is a political reality to be practiced by God's people through history. It is not acceptable for a small group of teachers and scholars to read and understand the text; the people are called to perform the text as a form of life. The ancient people of God knew this and therefore, with great endeavor, Israel attempted to exemplify in her communal life the policies and practices of the politics of Yahweh.

Contemporary Christian congregations can learn a great deal from this passage: it is not simply enough to call the sacred texts God's Word or to memorize a few verses, but the people of God are called to be an alternative community. They are a community that traces its identity to the stories of promise and fulfillment. Promises are made to the patriarchs and through the prophets, and these promises are fulfilled in the gifts of land and messianic lordship. The genres of narrative and poem are woven together with strands of policies and practices. This forms a political identity that is more than a nation-state, but a peculiar people from every tribe, race, and period of time.

Only a sustained engagement with the Scripture allows for the habituation of a people across the expanse of time. Sacred texts must be read, interpreted, and embodied by the community. Markers, like the stones covered with plaster and law, must be placed as a sign of the form of life that the people are to participate within. This at least means that the Scriptures are given prominent and visible presence in worship and in the locations of worship. It is almost laughable that so many evangelicals insist that copies of the Decalogue be made visible in secular courthouses, but seldom if ever are these same expressions of Torah visible or even heard in the corporate worship of the same Christian congregations.

26:16—
27:10

A reader only has to read the laws of Deuteronomy to know that all of the laws should not become embodied within the congregations of Christian believers. There is no doubt that some of these laws are very specific to a worldview in a different time and place, but the depth grammar of these policies and practices should find place in the common life of the followers of Jesus Christ. Examples of this are implicit in the following questions: How do contemporary believers witness to the all-embracing reality of God? How are followers of Jesus to practice their lives in light of the needy and marginal in the community? What kinds of practices are necessary if the community is to remain an alternative people, a community of resident aliens? Hearing these words that are written on tablets and seeing their embodied way of life written into the lives of saints are necessary for contemporary believers to begin to practice the politics of the God revealed in the person of Jesus Christ. So when are Christians to get started? Today! The moment to commit to hearing and seeing is now, this day!

B. Keeping Boundary of Identity Safe and Secure (27:11-26)

BEHIND THE TEXT

In the final stage of the book of Deuteronomy, the Deuteronomic Code is framed by resources that direct the reader's attention toward the transition of Israel getting ready to enter into the land. The implicit audience of Moses' speeches is the second generation of Israelites, the age-group that was not familiar with bondage in Egypt and does not yet know life in the land of promise. This is the generation that will live through a changeover from the leadership of Moses to the leadership of Joshua. They will face the threat of the Canaanite form of life and its enticement in the direction of infidelity to Yahweh.

Verses 11-13 "are obviously not continuous with 27:14-26, but describe a distinct ceremonial of covenant solemnization" (Cairns 1992, 234). The implication is given that six of the tribes declare the blessings of covenant fidelity and six of the tribes announce curses on those who are unfaithful to the politics of the covenant. Verse 14 incorporates the Levites as the ones who proclaim to the tribes and the tribes are given the opportunity to respond to the message of the Levites with the word "Amen." It is interesting that in v 12 the tribe of Levi is recorded as one of the tribes among the six, while v 14 states that Levi is positioned as the preachers to all of Israel of the politics of Yahweh that include the results of curses and blessings.

Verses 15-26 embody a catalog of twelve curses representing the twelve tribes of Israel. This is a conventionalized list that functions in a way similar to the Decalogue. Whether or not this list is the sine qua non of outlawed practices is a matter of interpretation. They may very well constitute a way of life that will endanger the very core of what it means to be the people of Yahweh. Their stylized character allows the reader to distinguish them as a unit. What should be obvious is that this section has a history of development. This passage has the following structure:

1. Positioning the Twelve Tribes (27:11-14)
2. Twelve Curses Enumerated by the Levites (27:15-26)

IN THE TEXT

1. Positioning the Twelve Tribes (27:11-14)

■ **11-14** Moses gives orders to the people to divide the twelve tribes of Israel into halves upon entering the land of promise. Six of the tribes will stand on Mount Gerizim for the blessings and six of the tribes will stand on Mount Ebal for the curses. The demarcation of the two mountains frames the entire compilation of regulations and decrees found in chs 12—26. It is interesting that the mountain on which the practices and policies are written is on Mount Ebal, the mountain of curses. Transgressing the directives brings on curses that are articulated in greater detail in the ensuing chapters than are the blessings.

2. Twelve Curses Enumerated by the Levites (27:15-26)

■ **15-26** These verses comprise a stylized list of curses that have a liturgical form and function. Each curse is organized in a way that states a curse pronounced upon an unacceptable practice. After each warning the people respond, in a liturgical manner, with **Amen!** This word refers back to what has directly gone before and denotes concurrence with what is announced. The people, by saying **Amen**, are indicating that there is no excuse for their misconduct in the future. Breaking the mandate will result in catastrophe.

The twelve curses deal with behavior that Deuteronomy has already taken up eight times elsewhere in the book. The first two curses are represented in the Decalogue and the others have appeared elsewhere in the body of the book. Four prohibitions remain that have not been addressed in the laws of Deuteronomy up to this point: misleading the blind, having sex with any animal, striking a neighbor, and a generalized conclusion to not upholding the words of this Torah.

Verse 15 contains the first curse: **Cursed is anyone who makes an idol**. The NIV only makes reference to **idol**, but the Hebrew text denotes both an idol and a molten image. An idol is carved from wood and a molten image is cast in metal. Images in any form, whether made of wood or cast in metal, are resolutely forbidden by the second commandment (5:8-10). Many scholars believe that this curse is directed toward the undisclosed and sneaky nature of having small images venerated in a manner similar to contemporary good luck charms. These images are widespread in the ancient world, and legislation alone could not control them. It should be noted that many of the curses are possible actions that can be enacted in secrecy. Developing security, in secret, outside of trusting in Yahweh brings with it a total breakdown of the community.

Human beings venerate idols because they suppose that a god can be contained and therefore reduced to the finite. Once restricted to a location the god can be manipulated to some degree through its image and invocations. Yahweh is never "so ready to hand as the deity in the ritual forms of the ancient Near East, in which the image of the god was waited on, clothed, decorated, and fed, but also manipulated for mantic purposes" (Zimmerli 1978, 121). This unchanging, restricted, and convenient force could never be squared with the revelation of Yahweh. He is free *to be* what *he will be*. He is Yahweh: "I AM WHO I AM" (Exod 3:14). Yahweh will have none of this. Human beings cannot find in the world of God's creation any adequate representation of Yahweh. He will not become present for Israel by means of a static, earthly image. Yahweh is portrayed in language and story as actively involved in the life of his people.

His image can only be perceived in the tangible political authenticity of an obedient people within history.

The second curse is found in Deut 27:16: **Cursed is anyone who dishonors their father or mother**. Honoring parents is also found in the Decalogue. What is it that this directive wished most to safeguard? Scholars believe that the fifth commandment, like the other commandments in the Decalogue, has the adult members of the community notably in view. It is not intended primarily to champion the parents in their disciplining of disorderly children. It has in view the care of the aged, the treatment of old parents with dignity and thoughtfulness by their adult children (Harrelson 1997, 98). Therefore, the commandment would be misconstrued if it were thought of as designed to keep young children in line, to keep them obedient toward their elders.

The fifth commandment is the first with a promise attached to it. The promise of long life on the land God gives is a recurrent impetus in Deuteronomy. It is usually cited as a result of obedience to all the laws and statutes but may be joined to specific laws. The motivation clause in the fifth commandment points to a connection between a long and good life and keeping this commandment. This is in all probability to be understood as having to do with each generation learning how to care for its elderly so that each new generation can count on a long and good life as it is honored by the next generation. This commandment is not a promise as if enchantment is involved. There is no doubt that there are children who honor their aging parents but die prematurely, and others who dishonor their parents who live long lives. It should be obvious that this is once again a practice within the political reality of how the community is to function. When placed as a promised outcome of honoring father and mother, it suggests that each generation honoring and caring for its older members creates and maintains a societal ethos that increases the prospect of a good and long life for each person in the community and for the culture as a whole. To the extent that a lack of concern for and a disregard of the older generation becomes a societal pattern, the possibilities of a long and happy life are diminished for all.

Practicing proper respect of parents can instigate in the community a conversation about what kinds of associations warrant analogous attitudes of honoring other persons and what is the manifestation of such genuine respect. If there is real potency in the relationship of adult children to their elderly parents, there will be health in the other connections within the community.

For it is how one deals with the helpless, with those who can no longer fend for themselves, and with such helpless ones against whom one has a lifetime of grievances for wrongs done or imagined, that provides the test of one's moral and human commitments. Just as the treatment of orphans, widows, and the poor is the general test of justice within a society, so the treatment of the elderly parents by their children is the test of family relations as such. (Harrelson 1997, 103)

Verse 17 contains the third curse: **Cursed is anyone who moves their neighbor's boundary stone.** This curse relates to property rights. A similar law is found in 19:14 and deals with repositioning the boundary markers and thereby seizing someone else's land. To change the position of the boundary indicator is deliberately wicked, since embezzlement of the land deprives families of blessing and hope. It should not be forgotten that the land is Yahweh's gift to be disseminated among the tribes, clans, and families. Life and blessing are bestowed upon people by means of the land; therefore, to embezzle the land is a form of taking life. When boundary markers are moved, it could very well cause enormous controversy that would result in violence and hostility.

What makes this crime so complicated is that satisfactory proof is difficult to acquire. The nature of this crime is of such a kind that it is not normally attempted, except in circumstances that might lead the offender to think he could do it with impunity. Again, the reader of the curses notices the idea of secrecy. The curse highlights once again that this action is damned within the community, whether or not the offender is brought to the courts.

The fourth curse is aimed at the person **who leads the blind astray on the road** (27:18). This is a new prohibition for the book of Deuteronomy, but it is set up as a negative practice in Lev 19:14: "Do not curse the deaf or put a stumbling block in front of the blind, but fear your God. I am the Lord." Leading the blind astray can be understood literally, or it may have a metaphorical meaning. If these words are taken literally, then they point to some kind of behavior toward a blind person that would result in a personal advantage. A major problem with this type of treachery toward the blind is that they would not be able to adjudicate the case because they would not be able to identity the offender. Again the reader should notice the concealment of the offense and how it is noticed by Yahweh and would result in curse and destruction. A community cannot survive if it chronically abuses the vulnerable. The politics of Deuteronomy attempts to generate an ethos in the community where justice and human dignity permeate the society.

Deuteronomy 27:19 articulates the fifth curse: **Cursed is anyone who withholds justice from the foreigner, the fatherless or the widow.** This idiom designates the needy in Israel's culture and is found in numerous places in Deuteronomy (14:29; 16:11, 14; 24:19-21; 26:12-13). Aliens, orphans, and widows are landless and will perish without assistance from the community. Not only do these needy people rely upon the generosity of the community, but also the community must safeguard their protection against any misuse of justice. Israel is commanded to care for the most vulnerable in the community by both provision and protection against the powerful who, without being noticed, can withhold justice. One could say that the majority of Deuteronomy is a collection of justice decisions concerning the ways in which Israel is to apply the Decalogue to her life in the land that Yahweh is giving.

Justice usually means rendering a right judgment concerning a particular case. When justice is used in a general way it involves the entire social structure of policies and personnel. The prophets used this concept often to elucidate what is required of Israel as the covenant people. In most cases **justice** indicates a body of legal decisions resulting from the judgments of the courts. In the present context it is likely that denying justice to the needy is something that can be secretly pulled off. The implication is that the laws of Deuteronomy form a boundary to provide order for the community in the midst of the forces of chaos. The poor and needy are also included within the boundary lines that form the sacred community. The words of this curse remind the Christian reader of Jesus' words in Matt 25:45, "Truly I tell you, whatever you did not do for one of the least of these, you did not do for me."

Deuteronomy 27:20-23 contains four curses directed against sexual offenses of various types: with one's father's wife, any animal, one's sister, and one's mother-in-law. Only the prohibition against having sexual relations with one's father's wife is found elsewhere in the book of Deuteronomy (see 22:30). This reference is to marrying his father's wife. The nature of these sexual acts would more often than not be done surreptitiously; therefore, these acts would not come before the legal system. A man would be in a suspicious relationship if he was with another man's wife, but he would not be if seen in the company of his stepmother, sister, mother-in-law, or an animal. The reader of these prohibited practices should pay special attention to the secretive character of the curses. This likely means more than simply repulsive sex acts, but acts of abuse, especially of the vulnerable female members of a household. "Unmarried sisters, half-sisters, and widowed in-laws were all likely to have been part of a household and, therefore, susceptible to sexual abuse" (Clements 1998, 493).

Sexual union with an animal is a taboo that has at least two issues associated with it. This practice may have been a feature of certain ancient religious rituals. It clearly is a violation of the order of life in creation that is also at stake in this prohibition. Israel, as a community, understands itself as the holy people of Yahweh. This means that they are to remain pure and clean. Chaotic and anarchic sexual relations are looked upon as a unique hazard for a community that is to reflect the very character and purpose of God. The community is endangered by these reprehensible practices. It, along with those who participate in secret, is cursed!

The tenth curse is found in v 24: **Cursed is anyone who kills their neighbor secretly.** The word translated **kills** is literally *strike*. In this setting it means kill, because it is enacted in secrecy and there is no one to report the crime. Committing such a crime in secret assumes that, devoid of eyewitnesses, no indictment could be made in the legal system. The proviso of using **secretly** again refers to those violations that only God can know. Violence makes the entire community vulnerable to chaos. Israel is not to become a civilization that does not interpret the world through the lens of the covenantal politics of Yahweh.

Verse 25 contains the eleventh curse. This curse is in reference to **anyone who accepts a bribe to kill an innocent person.** Most likely **an innocent person** is an idiom that means a person with whom one has no dispute or fight. In other words, it is a person that one is neutral toward. In all probability this curse is in reference to a type of contract assassination. Again the reader should notice that it is difficult to discover the culprits in this hideous act of violence; therefore, the judicial structure is of no avail in bringing a person to justice. Some scholars believe that this curse refers to the perpetration of perjury in a capital court case that could lead to the death sentence being imposed upon the innocent party (Clements 1998, 493).

The concluding curse in this collection of twelve is located in v 26: **Cursed is anyone who does not uphold the words of this law by carrying them out.** For practical purposes, this is a summing up of all the previous curses and functions to underpin the clout that they have for Israel.

FROM THE TEXT

Every tradition authorizes core beliefs and values. These beliefs and values emerge from ideas or doctrines that make sense in light of the tradition itself. Certain beliefs and values shape and govern the center or core of the tradition. The center or core for Deuteronomy's tradition is revealed in the opening announcement of the Decalogue: "I am the LORD your God." This declaration is the keystone of all the commandments and undeniably of the full corpus of Deuteronomic law. These words are jointly a self-disclosure of divinity and an assertion about the community's highest good.

The questions that emerge in this declaration are: Who is Yahweh, and what does it mean for him to be Israel's God? Yahweh is the one who appeared at the sacred mountain to Moses and commanded him to go to Pharaoh and demand that the people be set free. He is the one who liberated a ragtag band of slaves from the oppressive hand of the Egyptian empire. He is the God who saves Israel! Israel remembers that it is out of the sheer free grace of God that he makes promises to the patriarchs, and it is out of that same grace that he both liberates the descendants of Abraham and reveals his purpose for them. The called, liberated people of God are to reveal his character and purpose in the world.

The one who saves Israel makes an exclusive claim on each descendant of Abraham: "You shall have no other gods before me" (Deut 5:7). This exclusive claim on Israel not only addresses the beliefs and values at the center of the tradition but also creates boundaries beyond which Israel would cease being Yahweh's truthful witness in the world. When they would cross the boundary line, they would bring on themselves curse and destruction. The twelve curses are declaring the limits in which Israel may practice its life together.

The recurring theme of Deuteronomy's tradition is that two ways are presented to the people of God: life/death, blessing/curse. This premise runs through the length of the entire belief system associated with Deuteronomy. Israel, in covenant, consents to what it means to be Yahweh's chosen and holy people. There is not only the awareness of significance for communal identity that goes with being Yahweh's people but also an adamant insistence of obedience from the people.

Obedience is not simply a matter of doing the righteous deed when people can see and know the endeavor, but it is to do the right thing even when no one will ever know. The people of God strictly forbid living a lie in the seclusion of secrecy. They are to live lives that reflect in the light of day and in the shadows of night the character and purpose of God. Only a people who in all the boundary activities of their lives together answer the question: Who is Yahweh, and what does it mean for him to be Israel's God?

27:11-26 For persons in the Western world, the regulating of a political order is necessary if trust and peace are to be realized. This regulation of order cannot simply be accomplished by the thrusting of unacceptable laws upon the populace. The people must be habituated into a way of life that is experienced in the ethos of the community as a whole and molds the character of individuals. How this ethos is developed takes place over time and includes certain boundary practices as a frontier never to cross. Only the cursed would cross such a horrific boundary. One does not need a rule book to know what is cursed and appalling; this knowledge is built into the communal psyche by means of the ongoing practices of the community. One might go so far as to say that people develop a tacit knowledge of the cursed life. It strikes one as horrendous and hideous. These are the boundary practices of a group of people that are built into the fabric of individuals through collective rituals.

Christians also have their own boundary practices. Many of these practices are the same as the ancient people of God; for example, both communities of faith are committed to loving God and neighbor. It is the definition of "neighbor" that the followers of Jesus are called to expand beyond their speaking of words to a form of life. Neighbors include those far and near. They include every class, race, and gender. They also include "the enemy." The question that Christian interpreters of the faith need to ask is not, How can one

DEUTERONOMY

love an enemy? but, How can loving one's enemy become a boundary practice? If Christians are to be transformed into the image of God, then a tacit awareness is necessary so that not loving one's enemy is experienced as horrendous and hideous. Followers of Christ must be habituated into a form of life that is experienced in the ethos of the community. The question is not, Who is my neighbor? or How can I love my enemy? but, What practices are necessary to shape a people into lovers of enemies?

C. Blessings and Curses (28:1-68)

BEHIND THE TEXT

Chapter 28 is extremely long and functions as a notification of the consequences of failing to practice the politics of Yahweh. A hasty reading of this chapter reveals several aspects worth noting. First, the ratio of blessing and curse is roughly one to four. The blessings go for only fourteen verses, but the curses run on for over fifty-four verses. Also, the tenor of several of the curses is particularly austere. Examples of this are: the people will be wholly eradicated, or reduced to cannibalism. Defiance of the covenant will devastate not only the community's life but also nature's balance. The consequences of disobedience will damage every element of Israel's life together. These wounds seem to be immutable.

Many scholars see a noticeable similarity to an ancient Near Eastern vassal treaty. These covenants would spell out terrifying peril for those who, having become partners to a treaty, break its requirements.

> From a literary perspective, therefore, it is undoubtedly conceivable that the authors of Deuteronomy were familiar with the employment of a series of threatening curses of warning and admonition to encourage the vassal to stick to the terms of the treaty. (Clements 1998, 500)

A vassal treaty genre would most likely make this chapter a relatively late stage of composition within the book of Deuteronomy.

Chapter 28 is divided into three major sections:
1. The Choice between Blessing and Curse (28:1-46)
2. The Certainty of Curse for the Disobedient (28:47-57)
3. The Purpose of the Law Book (28:58-68)

The first segment signifies the basis of the whole chapter; its purpose is focused on keeping the whole of the teaching rather than offering warnings concerning the hazards of failing to keep the Torah. The second section gives a markedly more ominous feel to the curses. It describes the misery of existence under the curse. It does this by narrating events that have come to pass among the people because of their disobedience. The final section presents even more specificity to the unbearable anguish of life under curse. Taken as a whole, these divisions form an arrangement that describes the responsibility of obedience to Yahweh's commands, the inescapability of catastrophe if the people fail to practice the politics of Yahweh, and the authority of the written Torah for the covenantal politics of Yahweh. Judgment, ecological disaster, national defeat, and disease are associated with the cursed life.

IN THE TEXT

Verses 1-46 have two subdivisions: "The Blessings" (vv 1-14) and "The Curses" (vv 15-46). In both parts, the concrete blessings and curses that are enunciated are declared in a few words. This section describes the outcome of both obedience and disobedience. The subject matter varies from personal domestic interests to nationwide consequences. The blessings are affirmed in vv 3-6 and the curses are confirmed in vv 16-19.

I. The Choice between Blessing and Curse (28:1-46)

■ **1-14** Verses 1-6 appear as a set pattern that includes the sixfold covenant blessing of vv 3-6. This formal pattern could very likely be an element of ancient worship. The opening two verses are dominated by the concept of obedience to the *voice* or will of Yahweh. The voice of Yahweh is not some subjective feeling that an individual might have, but it is understood to be the Torah proclaimed. The Hebrew word group *šāma'* dominates these two verses. The first verse opens with *šāma'* used twice (infinitive absolute and imperfect) as an emphatic expression. The NIV translates this phrase: **If you fully obey.** Literally it says: *If you hear hear* or *if you indeed listen;* this verb pair is followed by the customary prefixed noun *běqôl* ("to the voice of"). The phrase taken together (*šāma' běqôl*) conveys the idea of listening or hearing followed by the act of obedience. The second verse ends with the use of *šāma' běqôl.* Hearing the voice of Yahweh is not a matter of acknowledgment but enactment. For the people of God, to hear means to do. It should be obvious that mental assent and subjective feelings to and of God's will do not automatically result in the blessings of God. Blessing results in a people shaped by the political reality of Torah—concrete communal engagement in performing the will and purpose of God.

Verse 2 also makes an interesting claim: **All these blessings will come on you and accompany you.** This describes blessings as active and dynamic. The reader is not left with the impression that Yahweh doles out blessing to an individual as a result of each and every act of obedience, but as the consequence of an all-encompassing obedience or embodiment of the policies and practices of Yahweh's political order. Blessing *comes upon* and *overtakes* the people. Hearing and doing the politics of Yahweh is not magic, but the graced order of God allows for vitality and fruitfulness.

Blessing in the OT

Blessing is an interesting concept in the OT; it regularly refers to the fruitfulness of life. A wonderful example of this convention is found in the opening creation account in Genesis. The first use of the word follows the creation of life: "God blessed them and said, 'Be fruitful and increase in number'" (1:22). The next employment of the expression is found in 1:28, which follows the creation of humanity. The text declares, "God blessed them and said to them, 'Be fruitful and increase in number.'" It should be obvious that blessing and fruitfulness go hand in hand. Blessing is the gift of the flourishing of life. It makes perfect sense that the next use of blessing is in Gen 2:3, where God blesses the seventh day: "God blessed the seventh day and made it holy, because on it he rested from all the work of creating that he had done." The ongoing work of creation is in the hands of the hallowed, blessed rhythm of life. Keeping Sabbath and being obedient to the Torah of Deuteronomy demonstrate parallel ways of thinking; they allow for life to renew itself by functioning in its God-given manner. If this analysis is correct, then the gift of Torah, or the politics of Yahweh, is nothing other than a disclosure of how reality functions from the very beginning.

This brings the reader to the issue of divine agency. How does God work to bring about blessing or curse? Is there a fixed order in creation itself that corresponds between blessing and obedience, and curse and disobedience; or does Yahweh manage the course of blessing and curse? A case can be made for both understandings of divine agency in Deut 28:3-13. Verses 3-6 do not make an unequivocal declaration of God's supervising agency. Is it possible to believe that blessing and curse are placed into a fixed order of creation and that obedience is going with the flow of the universe? If so, the gift of Torah is then understood as a gift of revealing how reality functions.

On the other hand, vv 7-13 make Yahweh directly responsible for enacting blessings and curses upon the people. Yahweh is the agent of the blessing in these verses and his involvement is very personal. Phrases in vv 7-13, such as, "The LORD will grant . . . The LORD will send a blessing on your barns . . . The LORD your God will bless you . . . The LORD will establish you . . . The LORD will grant you abundant prosperity . . . The LORD will open the heavens . . . The LORD will make you the head . . ." demonstrate the direct intervention of Yahweh in enacting blessings for the obedient people.

Ancient Israel very likely had a twofold understanding of divine action in the world. Perhaps God sets the world up to operate in a specific way and when humanity goes against the order of creation, death ensues. This seems to articulate the wisdom tradition's web of belief. But clearly ancient Israel believed that God is always at work creatively in the world. He most of the time works with secondary causes by wooing creation toward his will and purpose. This is the understanding of the majority of the prophets. Yahweh used individuals and even entire nations to enact his will and purpose. It would make sense, in this understanding, that God uses all of creation in a similar fashion to the way he uses people, nations, and the course of history.

28:1-14

Six blessings are given in vv 3-6. These blessings reinforce the grace order that Yahweh placed in his creation. The word for "blessed" is a passive participle, and this asserts that the people will be acted upon. The vitality and fruitfulness of blessing is a gift or grace given to the people. What is interesting is that no cause is named as the immediate source of the blessing. Of course, Israel would believe that the ultimate source is Yahweh, but there is no specific mention of Yahweh in the text. Blessing as a result of obedience appears as a natural result in Israel's life together. The embodied politics of Yahweh produce "fruit" or "blessing" in all aspects of life: personal, communal, and in nature. This is not magic or an arbitrary action of Yahweh, but a grace-shaped result to a grace-formed people.

Beginning with the seventh verse, Yahweh becomes the operational means of blessing in a sequence of verbs. Six declarations are made, in which Yahweh personally and deliberately takes action to create blessing for Israel. This section most likely is a later addition that endeavors to portray how the blessings are enabled in the previous section. Yahweh will provide for the fortunes of his people. It is interesting to notice, side by side, how divine action is addressed in this book. Does God work directly or does God act through already established secondary causes? This is an interesting question to ponder, but in the end the people of God experience similar results, blessing and vitality.

The first blessing in this new subsection addresses the problem of enemies and the wreckage they bring to Israel. Any adversary who rises up against Israel will be overcome by the action of Yahweh. It is interesting to notice how the invaders are driven away in panic and confusion. The second blessing is a blessing of the land itself (v 8). It will be to produce such a harvest that the barns of the people will be full of produce.

The third blessing addresses the issue of the people's holiness (v 9). The blessing of holiness is conditioned by the clause that addresses the obedience of the people. In other words, holiness is a result of the action of God but is subject to the conformity of the people. This is not simply a singular act of commitment but an ongoing watchfulness (**keep**; *šāmar* means "to keep," "to observe," "to watch," "to guard") of the commandments of God and an ongoing ***walking in the ways*** of God. The word translated **if** may be translated ***as long as*** and implies that holiness is habituated in the character of persons and the ethos of a community. The communion of saints and individual saints are connected. Verse 10 makes it clear that the shape of the community, and persons within it, witness to **all the peoples on earth** that Israel is called by the name of Yahweh. Israel witnesses to Yahweh by the way she lives her life in obedience to Yahweh's will.

The final blessings of this subsection depict economic fulfillment (vv 11-14). The perspective of these blessings suggests that Israel will lead other nations economically. They **will lend to many nations but will borrow from none** and be **the head, not the tail** and be on **the top, never at the bottom**. This is not a promise to individual people in Israel but to Israel as a people. Blessing and economic prosperity go together in the convictions that shape the theology of this passage.

■ **15-46** The subject matter of these verses is opposite to the previous subsection. Words of curse draw a distinction from the preceding blessings that are pledged. The curse subsection is much longer and varied than the blessings expressed in the first fourteen verses. The structure of this subsection has some similarity to the subsection of blessings. Verse 15 has its counterpart in vv 1 and 2. A series of six passive participles, found in vv 16-19, corresponds to the passive participles of blessing found in vv 3-6. A reader should recognize that Israel's actions produce curse as an outcome of her waywardness. The second configuration, which has Yahweh as the cause of curses, is articulated in vv 20-29 and later in vv 35-37. This pattern directs the reader's attention once again to the direct involvement of Yahweh in Israel's story. Verses 36-37 and 38-44 seem to not require any direct agency of Yahweh for their fulfillment. The final part of this subsection, vv 45-46, focuses on Israel's culpability for its own calamity. Insolence and rebelliousness bring about wreckage and devastation.

A significant grammatical modification takes place in the enumeration of the curses in vv 45 ff. In the preceding inventory, the curses and blessings remain open possibilities and entirely dependent on the free decision to obey or to disobey: "If you fully obey the LORD your God . . ." (v 1); **if you do not obey the LORD your God** (v 15). But, beginning with v 45 the tone transitions from conditional to declarative: **All these curses will come on you.** "The curse shifts from a conditional possibility to a narrated future actuality" (Olson 1994, 123). Possibility changes to inescapability. Perhaps this is a redacted entry that is included during the exile. Deportation and banishment remove the provisional calculus of the riddle of blessing and curse, and resolve it with an unmovable conclusion of historical fact. Curses move from general to specific—general curse of the population and lack of fruitfulness (vv 15-19); death, sickness, and drought (vv 20-24); defeat in battle and shameful death (vv 25-26); diseases (vv 27-35); exile and humiliation (vv 36-46).

2. The Certainty of Curse for the Disobedient (28:47-57)

■ **47-57** There is a noteworthy modification that takes place in this section; explicit detail is given to the suffering of the people at the hands of their unspecified foe. Israel's undisclosed adversary is the instrument of God's curse upon his wayward people. Most likely this unnamed enemy is understood to be the experience of the people through the Assyrians and the Babylonians.

What is remarkable and terrifying is that there is no corresponding entry to the curses in this subsection. Curse looks as if it is irreversible and mortifying.

The first two verses of this subsection set up the conditions under which the irreversible curse will take place. Verse 47 gives the justification for the curse: **Because you did not serve the LORD your God joyfully and gladly in the time of prosperity.** A new addendum is added to the passage, that of gratitude and joy. The people of Israel experienced prosperity and peace, yet they did not serve Yahweh with gladness of heart.

There is a wordplay in vv 47-48. Because Israel did not **serve** Yahweh with a glad heart in times of blessing, she will **serve** her **enemies** as a curse in depravation. The NIV translates v 47: **Because you did not serve the LORD your God joyfully and gladly in the time of prosperity. Gladly** is literally *in a good heart*. Ancient Israel understood the "heart" not as the seat of emotion, like contemporary culture, but as the place where decisions are made. This is a clear reference to being aware, even at a tacit level, that Yahweh is the provider of blessing. The call is one of gratitude. Perhaps there is only one response to the grace of God, gratitude.

Verse 48 makes it clear that it is Yahweh who will bring curse through a secondary agent. The enemy is not the ultimate cause of the deprivation, but only a secondary cause as Yahweh's instrument of judgment. Yahweh's agent of judgment is described as bringing on complete removal of all resources: **hunger and thirst, in nakedness and dire poverty.** The picture painted for the reader is that the agent of Yahweh, the enemy, will bring about a protracted and dreadful siege that will produce horrific and unbearable deeds to the people and by the people.

Verses 49-52 describe the horrific acts of the enemy of Israel upon them; they will take the fruit of blessing away from the people. The strange people, who do not speak the same language of Israel, will show no

> **respect for the old or pity for the young. They will devour the young of your livestock and the crops of your land until you are destroyed. They will leave you no grain, new wine or olive oil, nor any calves of your herds or lambs of your flocks until you are ruined. They will lay siege to all the cities throughout your land until the high fortified walls in which you trust fall down. They will besiege all the cities throughout the land the LORD your God is giving you.** (Vv 50-52)

The fruitfulness of blessing will be turned into a barren fruitlessness of curse. Creation's purpose is reversed for the disobedient people of Israel.

What becomes so shocking is not simply the actions toward Israel by her enemy, but Israel's behavior in response to the curse executed upon her. She reacts to the persistent siege by horrific and grisly undertakings herself: she becomes a cannibal, even to her own children. A reader should notice that **fruit** is mentioned once again. The fruitfulness that is the blessing of God in creation, "Be fruitful and increase in number" (Gen 1:28), now becomes the fruit that is eaten to survive. Not only does the enemy devour the fruit, but also the fruit of Israel's seed is devoured by Israel herself. She eats her children. When personal survival takes priority over the survival of future generations, all is lost. The ultimate expression of curse is enacted. Despair and hopelessness overtake a people. The politics that keep chaos at bay collapse, and the people are infested with tragedy. Perhaps the contemporary world should contemplate what eating one's children might disclose for the future of humankind. When the creation is devoured in such a way that there is nothing for the future, perhaps the present generation is eating its own children.

3. The Purpose of the Law Book (28:58-68)

■ **58-68** The implication of a lingering period of exile is made in this subsection: **You will be uprooted from the land you are entering to possess. Then the LORD will scatter you among all nations, from one end of the earth to the other** (vv 63-64). For a people who received the land as gift, eviction from it takes on a foreboding tone; they are faced with the possibility that they may no longer be Yahweh's well-chosen people. There is no suggestion when or if this phase in Israel's story is to end, or even that she continues to have a story.

Curse returns Israel to the diseases and plagues of Egypt, even to the point of serving other gods and selling oneself and one's children into the service of slavery. This amounts to undoing the story of Yahweh's great deliverance from Egyptian bondage. What amounts to the promise to the patriarchs is reversed: **You who were as numerous as the stars in the sky will be left but few in number** (v 62). The exodus gave Israel an understanding that she has a unique identity as a people, but the totality of the curse is a loss not only of statehood but also of identity. There is a tragic reversal of Israel's destiny that moves Israel back into a complete loss of what it means to be the people of Yahweh.

The question that should engage both the ancient and modern readers' attention is: Can curse turn once again to blessing? An answer to this question may be found in what seems to be a hidden gospel. Good news is expressed in this final subsection by the conditional clause **if** of v 58. The conditional **if** is correlated with Torah: **If you do not carefully follow all the words of this law, which are written in this book, and do not revere this glorious and awesome name—the LORD your God.** Even though this conditional clause is expressed in a negative gist, the **if** of this section is still a note of hope and grace. Torah, or the politics of Yahweh, is what is to shape a people called by the name of Yahweh. These politics do not stipulate a land, but may be performed in a far-off land, even in slavery. To a people in exile, the only hope is to begin to allow the Torah to shape their life together. Is there a gospel in this horrific subsection of curse? Perhaps . . .

28:58-68

To many contemporary people the concept of blessing and curse is awkward and thorny. It implies to them that there might be powers that shape human destiny in supernatural ways. They imagine a god who keeps score and imposes on them the results of their actions in the world. In many ways this way of thinking leads to a legalism that brings paranoia and eventually despair. Often this manner of thinking conveys a judgmental view and a false sense of pride or shame. A question that contemporary Christian readers need to ask is: Is it possible to give full voice to this powerful passage of Deuteronomy without resorting to either magic or legalism? An answer to this question might be discovered in the use of law itself. Is law understood as a way of obtaining God's favor or is it God's gift to the community as a form of life? In other words, is Torah the politics of God?

Why should a people practice the politics of God? An answer to this question is given in this chapter: the way a community lives determines to a great degree whether life is experienced as blessed or cursed. A community that follows Torah, God's purpose for his people and creation, will be blessed and realize gladness and joy. On the other hand, communities who live contrary to God's purpose for creation will be subjected to curse and will undergo calamity and disaster. This is the conviction that presides over the whole Deuteronomic tradition.

A note of caution needs to be made; wretched lives do not necessarily mean that those persons, families, or even communities have violated the purposes of God. Theodicy is a thorny and challenging area of theological and philosophical inquiry, and simple answers should not be given in haste. Job is a prime example of simple answers given in haste by his friends. The conclusion of the book of Job makes it clear that the answers that the friends give are incorrect, and God vindicates Job of their charges.

Yet, there is a deep truth in the theological convictions of Deuteronomy. How communities organize their life together shapes a world that is experienced as blessing or curse. The ethos of a community and the character of a person are shaped by the political order, with its practices and values. This means that people will function in this political atmosphere in a way that either enhances life or diminishes it. This enhancement or diminishing of life is not necessarily person specific but shapes the whole people in such a way that individuals experience the outcome of the whole. It should be obvious to contemporary readers that the policies and culture of a people bring their own recompense. Examples in the culture of the USA can be demonstrated in the recreational use of sexuality and violence. One wonders why there is so much gun violence until one pays attention to the larger culture of guns and violence in America. Hosea articulates it well: "They sow the wind and reap the whirlwind" (8:7). How communities conduct their life together, their politics, shapes the reality of blessings or curses for the whole of the people.

The conclusion of this passage implies that the cursed life not only experiences the horrendous deeds of others but is shaped out of this desperation in such a way that the community participates in horrendous deeds: eating one's own children. This indicates that taboos are violated as a people become acculturated by the cursed life. What would the blessings of life look like if followers of Christ kept his Torah (Matt 5—7)? Would they not also be acculturated by the blessed life? "Blessed are the . . ." Perhaps they would be salt and light to the world in the way they live together and love even their enemies. Conceivably, their alien character (holiness) will be acknowledged and **all the peoples on earth will see that you are called by the name of the Lord** (Deut 28:10).

D. Choose Life (29:1—30:20 [28:69—30:20 HB])

BEHIND THE TEXT

Old Testament exegetes dispute whether Deut 29:1 [28:69 HB] represents the superscription to what follows or the conclusion of what began in 4:1 as the covenant at Horeb. Understood as a new superscription, Deut 29:1—30:20 [28:69—30:20 HB] is presented as the farewell address of Moses to the people. As the third of the great addresses of Moses, it frames the book of Deuteronomy. In its canonical form, this passage functions as a covenant-making ritual verbalized by Moses to the second generation of Israel on the edge of the promised land. It assumes the blessings and curses that are the focus of the previous passage in Deuteronomy.

Moses' speech is of substantial theological importance in Israel's history. It implicitly speaks to the community of Israel, who find themselves at a new crossroad in their story, having been driven out of the land promised to their ancestors. Enemies have laid waste the land. The land no longer continues under the influence of those whose sacred devotion is devoted to Yahweh. Israel is driven into exile. This new situation pictures the vulnerability of the people and their covenant way of life. In the eyes of the theologians of Deuteronomy it is a confirmation that Israel is defiant to the covenantal politics of Yahweh. The problem surfaces: How is Israel to maintain her identity without possession of the land?

Israel can only come into being by a new journey through the wilderness and a new act of taking possession of the land. Israel, in a sense, must be born again. Paul Hanson describes this new possibility, "The wilderness, as a return to the beginning, as a place for a new start, as an opportunity for covenant renewal, was the most promising place for the reformulation of the Yahwistic notion of the covenant community" (1986, 168). Only a return to the one true God can rescue Israel as a holy people who inhabit the politics of Yahweh. This political conviction is nothing less than the covenant of life.

This passage, in a compelling manner, allows the situation of exile to be seen through the lens of a people waiting in the plains of Moab to cross the Jordan and take possession of the land. In this farewell speech, Moses addresses a people who are landless, confused, and seeking a way forward. They need hope in the midst of what seems to be hopelessness. This speech of Moses can be understood as a fervent plea to accept the past catastrophe, to concede its own hopeless situation, and to come back to a rehabilitated loyalty to the covenant obedience within the politics of Yahweh. The passage can be divided into five sections:

1. Historical Assessment (29:1-9 [28:69—29:8 HB])
2. Endorse the Covenant (29:10-15 [9-14 HB])
3. Curses for Individuals and the Whole Community (29:16-29 [15-28 HB])
4. Returning to Yahweh (30:1-14)
5. Choose Life (30:15-20)

IN THE TEXT

I. Historical Assessment (29:1-9 [28:69—29:8 HB])

■ **1-9 [28:69—29:8 HB]** The first verse sets up the framework of Israel's prospects for newness when she found herself exiled from the land. She is once again in position to enter the land of promise. In some ways this is no different from her ancestors, when they were located across the Jordan in the plains of Moab. Just as Moses' address to her ancestors had amounted to a new covenant so also this new covenant is once again an untarnished opportunity. What is envisioned is not so much a completely new covenant but rather a fresh occasion to restart and revitalize the covenant. This covenant does not contain new or supplementary directives but is rather a restatement of the Horeb covenant. It is given again because Israel fails to measure up to its policies and practices. In other words, Israel failed to live within the political framework of the covenant.

Israel's narrative recounting (vv 2-8 [1-7 HB]) follows a somewhat stock line of recital that can be discerned to some extent in 26:5-6. This recital brings to mind a type of communal confession of identity. It begins with the miracles that take place in Egypt and continues through the provisions of the wilderness to the conquest of the land east of the Jordan. Israel has experienced the divine gifts of liberation, provision, and placement. The people are the result of grace.

A very interesting comment is made in vv 2b-4 [1b-3 HB]:

> Your eyes have seen all that the LORD did in Egypt to Pharaoh, to all his officials and to all his land. With your own eyes you saw those great trials, those signs and great wonders. But to this day the LORD has not given you a mind that understands or eyes that see or ears that hear.

Israel sees without seeing. What can this mean? The implication is that the people see all of the events but do not recognize them as the result of the agency of Yahweh. They are occurrences and incidents, but they are not the gift of God; they are not providence. Israel seems to consider herself fortunate, diligent, or even fated. She seems to consider the exodus to be a program, not a miracle. But she did not pool her military resources in order to defeat the Egyptians. Yahweh did all the fighting, and all she does is walk out of the land of bondage through a wilderness and into a land of promise. She exists from grace but does not understand herself as graced!

Verse 9 [8 HB] is the conclusion to this subsection, and it calls on the people to **carefully follow the terms of this covenant**. It is interesting that the people are not told to work on perceiving the hand of Yahweh in their lives, but that they are called to embody the policies and practices of God. Perhaps faith comes to a people as they tell stories and embody those stories through practices. It is socially construed narratives that allow for a people to have a **mind that understands** and **eyes that see** and **ears that hear** (v 4 [3 HB]). Israel perceives the world through a story-formed lens of Yahweh's amazing grace.

2. Endorse the Covenant (29:10-15 [9-14 HB])

■ **10-15 [9-14 HB]** The **you** of v 10 [9 HB] is "catholic" in character. All the people of God, from every social stratification and in every age, stand assembled together in their own moment in time to enter at that moment into covenant with God. This multigenerational inclusiveness brings with it accountability for each and for all to take up the covenant and become confirmed as Yahweh's own people. Covenant renewal appears to be indispensable in every **today** for communities and individuals to establish themselves as Yahweh's own people.

The obligation taken up in vv 10-11 [9-10 HB] does not simply address those responsible for the communal life of Israel: **your leaders and chief men, your elders and officials, and all the other men of Israel,** but also this duty attends to those who have a marginal role in the community: **together with your children and your wives, and the foreigners living in your camps who chop your wood and carry your water.** What does this imply about covenant commitment and requirement? Everyone in the community has a role to play in covenant faithfulness. The whole is dependent upon the parts to maintain integrity and consistency. This understanding not only places responsibility upon even the most unskilled persons within the community but also vali-

273

dates the value and importance of even the simple person for the community to function as Yahweh's people. The politics of Yahweh are not for a few to perform, but for the community in total to participate within. Israel is either living as God's people or they are not.

The scope of the covenant is extended to future generations. Verses 14-15 [13-14 HB] make it apparent that the **covenant** renewal ceremony is not only for those **who are standing here with us today in the presence of the LORD our God but also with those who are not here today.** This reference is to all future groups of people on whom the covenant conditions are also required. The Israelites, as they stand on the plains of Moab, undeniably renewed the covenant with God, but they are also prompted to grasp that they are but one part of a larger community. This community extends through time to include **those who are not here today.** This has at least two major implications. First, every generation is responsible before God to live within the covenantal politics of Yahweh. The present people of God cannot live on the past generations' faithfulness to God. Second, every present generation is responsible to pass on through its own faithful living the covenantal politics of Yahweh to the next generation. Proclaiming and practicing the political reality of covenant is the responsibility of one generation to the next.

3. Curses for Individuals and the Whole Community (29:16-29 [15-28 HB])

■ **16-29 [15-28 HB]** Israel experienced alien cultures with their systems of beliefs, values, and practices. These alien cultures are not to have an effect on the community's identity or an individual's character. Israel is a distinct people, holy to Yahweh. Only calamity and curse will encounter the people if she allows these strange and foreign practices a place in her social-political-religious milieu. This subsection articulates this hazardous warning for individuals (vv 16-20 [15-19 HB]) as well as the whole community (vv 21-28 [20-27 HB]).

The book of Deuteronomy makes it clear that the social, political, and religious are not separate spheres within which people live, but that all aspects of life are united under the rubric of the sacred. Yahweh's people are a chosen and therefore holy people. The whole of their life is to be shaped by this reality. What is held by a community, or dare it be said what holds a community, is what is considered ultimate. This is what people both give their lives for, as well as take the lives of others for. The demand to desist from alien cultures, with their beliefs and values, begins with a command to detest foreign gods and alien religious practices. The people of Yahweh recount what they have seen in their journey to the land: idols, the **detestable images** of **wood**, **stone**, **silver and gold**, dominated the cultures they passed through (v 17 [16 HB]).

274

This characteristic of alien modes of worship is abhorrent to the people of God. Why? What is so repugnant about an idol?

How is one to interpret the prohibition of idols? Is idolatry a separate commandment or is it an extension of the first commandment, elaborating and spelling it out. Is idolatry simply a prohibition concerning having other gods before Yahweh? If this is so, then this text is concerned with false beliefs that will eventually lead to false values. But the question that must be asked is, Did ancient Israel really believe that idols are gods? In fact, did people in the ancient world believe that idols are gods at all?

In order to understand this prohibition as something other than a demand to refrain from worshipping other gods, one must understand what an idol is in the ancient Near East and how it functions. The Scriptures do not articulate why the prohibition of idols is imposed on the people of Israel. The Bible simply demands the prohibition of idols and describes the results of idolatry. This directive expresses a conceptual view of reality that is very different from the worldview of other ancient Near Eastern people. The gods reveal themselves in an idol. They are at hand in the idol. Ancient pagan religions did not consider the deity as identical with the image. They knew that the gods are invisible and that they transcend all human comprehension. The crucial thing for the ancient Near East's conceptualization of idols is that the deity came near in the image. Idolatry is a practice that allowed the gods to be approached and influenced by means of the images (→ 27:15).

29:16-29

Verse 18 [17 HB] of ch 29 begins a very fascinating ban in opposition to the worship of foreign gods by individuals, families, or tribes in deceiving concealment. This prohibition is described as a **heart turns away from the LORD our God**. This **heart** belongs to either a man, woman, family, or tribe. A communal heart, as well as an individual heart, is implied. So what is a "heart"? It is nothing less than the beliefs, judgments, and purpose of a person or a people. The heart is the character of a person and the ethos of a people. It is the center where the premise for every question has its home and where assessment itself comes forth. A person or a people cannot choose their "heart"; they can only practice their lives in such a way that a fundamental core is formed.

A delusional center, whether of a person or a community, will result in a calamity that will lead to devastation. The metaphors of **root** and **bitter poison** signify an underground and hidden causative factor that controls the deadly outcome of the whole (v 18 [17 HB]). These metaphors are at the "heart" or core of persons and people groups. The way they believe, value, and even question is twisted and perverted by a poisonous bitter root. Curse and disaster will befall them as well as the whole populace. No person or group is an island unto themselves. When an individual or a group practices, even in private, an alternative belief and value system, it is like poison that spreads through the whole living organism. Far from being anonymous, each person bears a profound burden of liability for the whole social order. The totality of the society is influenced, for good or evil, by the dealings of its constituents. A people stands or falls together.

The grave deduction in vv 20-21 [19-20 HB] is that **all the curses of the covenant written in this Book of the Law** will be ratified until the people's very distinctiveness is utterly nullified. The next generation, resident aliens, as well as all the nations will ponder the devastation through a theological lens. They will ask, **Why has the LORD done this to this land? Why this fierce, burning anger?** (v 24 [23 HB]). The verification of judgment is instantly recognizable, because the ruin bears a resemblance to **Sodom and Gomorrah, Admah and Zeboyim** (v 23 [22 HB]). These are the result of Yahweh's **fierce anger.**

The answer to the question of "why" is found in vv 25-28 [24-27 HB]: **the people abandoned . . . they went off . . . they worshiped . . . and bowed down . . .** These people, and eventually all of Israel, refused to be Yahweh's people that the covenant renewal intended them to be. Disobedience to the politics of Yahweh brings a loss of land and identity. They are banished, exiled to a far-off land with alien beliefs, values, and purpose. The judgment of Yahweh is nothing less that exile. Yahweh, not the Babylonians, transports Israel to a far-off land.

This chapter concludes with an extraordinary theological statement: **The secret things belong to the LORD our God, but the things revealed belong to us and to our children forever, that we may follow all the words of this law** (v 29 [28 HB]). Beyond the wrath of Yahweh, which is experienced in exile, lie **secret things** that only Yahweh knows. The meaning of **secret things** is established by the context. Israel knows that disobedience to the policies and practices of Yahweh's covenant results in annihilation. She also knows that there are things that she does not know, but only Yahweh knows. These are dark things concerning her future; she cannot know these things. Only Yahweh knows his future plans for Israel or any people. Does the devastation brought about by disregard for the ways of God mean obliteration to the future of the people? Only God knows his plans, but people can hope. They hope in what they know, that God has **secret things.** Are these secret things tied to the character of Yahweh who is a promise and a blessing? Israel can only hope.

Israel knows that some things are secret only to God, but she does know other things. She knows that Torah is given to her to put into practice. The future belongs to God, but the purpose of God is given to his people. Israel may not be able to do anything about her future—it is dark and unknown— but she can be obedient to what is given to her: **but the things revealed belong to us and to our children forever, that we may follow all the words of this law** (v 29 [28 HB]). Israel understands that obedience leads to Yahweh's blessing

29:16-29

and that disobedience leads to Yahweh's curse. To go outside of this wisdom is to enter into the realm of the **secret things** understood only by God. Yahweh's people are not to comprehend what is incomprehensible—the future—but to inhabit God's will in the present.

4. Returning to Yahweh (30:1-14)

■ **1-10** Chapter 30 is a plea to a future generation to **return** to the politics of Yahweh (v 2). This chapter is held together by the repetition of **I set before you** (vv 1, 15, 19), *the blessing and the curse* (vv 1, 19), and *that I am commanding you today* (vv 2, 8, 11, 16). There is also a sevenfold repetition of the word **today** (vv 2, 8, 11, 15, 16, 18, 19). The chapter divides into three parts: an appeal for repentance (vv 1-10), a declaration that compliance is without a doubt achievable (vv 11-14), and a directive for the people to make a choice (vv 15-20).

Moses addresses a future generation and declares that beyond the wreckage of exile there is the hope of *return* for those who are *returning* to Yahweh. This homecoming begins in Israel's recognition that it is neither coincidence nor fate that created her exile, but the inescapable consequences of defiance to Yahweh's covenantal policies. *Returning* to the land begins with the people *returning* to Yahweh, which brings about Yahweh *returning* Israel's fortunes to them. Israel's repentance is not simply a turning away from evil but a wholehearted turning in responsibility to Yahweh's voice, which is Torah.

A wordplay with the Hebrew word *šûb* ("turn back," "return") occurs multiple times in this passage (vv 1, 2, 3). *Šûb* is the Hebrew word behind the translation "repent" in the English Bible, since *turning back* to God involves one's acknowledgment of *turning away* from God and the decision to return to him. The NIV **restore your fortunes** (v 3) can be translated as *turn your captivity*, but the phrase literally states: *to turn your turnings*. The *turning* of Israel caused a *turning* of her fate toward deportation. The wordplay is: Israel *turns* to her heart the blessings and curses that have befallen her (**take them to heart** [v 1]); then she *turns* in full obedience to Yahweh: **return to the LORD your God and obey him with all your heart and with all your soul** (v 2); so that Yahweh will *turn* her *turnings* toward life (**then the LORD your God will restore your fortunes** [v 3]). Israel's *turning* to Yahweh is matched by Yahweh's *turning* of Israel's fortunes.

The breathtaking implication of this text is found out of the bleak certainty of human insubordination and subsequently devastation. Into this horrific situation a new possibility rises. Beginning with v 6 the passage articulates hope beyond destruction to the very cause of humanity's defiance: **The LORD your God will circumcise your hearts and the hearts of your descendants, so that you may love him with all your heart and with all your soul, and live.** Israel's story makes it clear that people do not give full compliance to God's

30:1-10

purpose and ways. Only a gift from God, his grace, can transform the heart of a human being so that God's purpose becomes natural.

History makes it clear that such obedience cannot occur without a heart to know and obey God. Yahweh's proposal in this passage to triumph over human insubordination corresponds with the concept of the new covenant (see Jer 31:31-34). God's people are not simply exonerated and given another opportunity, but they are transformed and made new. The people of God are to become by grace what God is by nature (Athanasius, C. *Ar.* 1.39, 3.34). But how is this possible?

■ **11-14** What is of great interest to the reader is located in vv 11-14: that this possibility is **not too difficult for you or beyond your reach** (v 11). It **is very near you; it is in your mouth and in your heart so you may obey it** (v 14). In other words, it is in their language itself. It is in the way words are used and the form of life that these words correlate with. The transformation of human character is located in the language of the kingdom or the politics of God. A person must learn the language of Yahweh's political order by telling the story of God until one discovers one's owns story within it, and concurrently by practicing the politics of God until this political language becomes the presupposition for the interpretation of everything else. The people of God are called to sanctification, the transforming power to reflect truthfully God's character and purpose. Sanctification is a linguistic affair that is more than learning the meaning of words, but becoming baptized by the language so that perception, values, and even beliefs shape individuals and communities.

5. Choose Life (30:15-20)

■ **15-20** Emphatically the mandate bellows from the tradition of Deuteronomy: **choose** (v 19). Moses, as well as his successor Joshua, insists that Israel has an obligation to decide one way or another (v 19; Josh 24:14-15). Even though people are not independent and self-governing, they are responsible for the course their lives take. There is an interesting tension in the theology of Deuteronomy; Yahweh is singular and sovereign, yet the people are not puppets but co-creators of their own story. Israel does not have faith in luck or even fate, but that a person's as well as a people's destiny is shaped by choices within the providence of God. God is revealing and working for the good of his people.

So what is this **life** that is to be preferred, and how is it selected? Life is fruitfulness in the land that Yahweh is giving to his people: **See, I set before you today life and prosperity, death and destruction. . . . then you will live and increase, and the LORD your God will bless you in the land you are entering to possess** (vv 15-16). The original purpose of the creation of life is **be fruitful and increase in number and fill** (Gen 1:22; see v 28). Israel, in the land of promise, is to live and thus fulfill the purpose of creation. Is there any wonder as to why Deuteronomy constantly develops laws to protect life, especially vulnerable people? Justice, compassion, and generosity are the practices that maintain and sustain life. Life is the goal of creation.

So how are the people of God to select life? This passage makes it obvious: **to walk in obedience to him, and to keep his commands, decrees and laws; then you will live and increase** (Deut 30:16). The political order of Yahweh is to shape the people who are to bear witness to the character and purpose of God in the land of promise. The focal point of the politics of Yahweh is to **love the LORD your God, listen to his voice, and hold fast to him** (v 20; see also v 16). Loving God is expressed as obedience to his will and ways. To love God is to practice his political agenda; therefore, loving God comes out in loving one's neighbor.

A constant peril and danger for Israel is to allow something else to become the center of their affection and loyalty. These objects of devotion are **other gods** (v 17). The challenge of worshipping **other gods** is not that they may do something to the people; they do not exist. The challenge is that they bring with their veneration a bundle of convictions, values, and the very goal of existence itself. To worship other gods is to enter into a different story and to practice a different set of policies. This social performance is linguistically enacted; it is political. These foreign gods shape perception of the people and their understanding of life's purpose. They subsist by conforming people to an alien story, opposite from the story of Yahweh and his people. The conclusion of this alien narrative is not blessing and life but curse and death. The *telos* of these strange and outlandish stories is violence and the demise of life. Israel is summoned to **love the LORD your God, listen to his voice, and hold fast to him. For the LORD is your life, and he will give you many years in the land he swore to give to your fathers, Abraham, Isaac and Jacob** (v 20). Yahweh is Israel's life; all other gods are her demise, downfall and death!

FROM THE TEXT

The vital concern throughout chs 29 and 30 is Yahweh's absolute claim upon his people. The present-day reader should realize that God is not in want of the unconditional allegiance of his people, as if he is insecure or needy, but that the very existence of people is dependent upon their faithful obedience to Yahweh's will and purpose. Without Israel's fidelity she will fall into corruption and decay, and so it is for the church in the twenty-first century. Curse and death are at hand. The church, like Israel, must choose life, the purpose and way of God. This choice is not once and for all, but every generation is responsible for choosing to renew the covenant, the politics of God.

Like Israel, the church is always under the threat to forget the story of grace and to enter into a counterfeit narrative: stories of other gods and values,

279

with other purposes and practices. These gods will forge God's people into something foreign and unfamiliar. Alien gods will attempt to write the narrative of the church as a detestable story full of poison and death. This toxin will have its way with the people, and it will contaminate and destroy. Curse and death will be the end of such a story, not blessing and life.

The wonderful news of this passage and its contemporary application is that the policies and practices that produce blessing and life are "not too difficult for you or beyond your reach" (30:11). The decrees that give life to the communities that practice them are "very near you; it is in your mouth and in your heart so you may obey it" (v 14). The language of the gospel, God's kingdom, is to convert persons into a socially construed narrative of grace. This transformation of human character is located in the language of the faith itself: the politics of Jesus.

Contemporary Christians, like their ancient forbearers of the faith, learn the language of God's political order by telling the story of God in Christ, and simultaneously practice the politics of Jesus until one's own self emerges within that narrative. The goal is for the language of the kingdom, the gospel, to become the assumption that elucidates the world. One could call this making gospel sense. This is an act of moral transformation, which not only attempts to act differently but also is a conversion that brings about a new identity and a new lens within which to perceive everything else. The transformed people of God not only envision the world differently but also are a picture that reflects the character and purpose of God. The church confesses that this is only possible by the *life-giving breath* of the Holy Spirit, which linguistically forms individuals into saints and communities into the *sanctorum communio*. "The Son of God became man that we might become god" (Athanasius, C. *Ar.* 1.39, 3.34).

V. THE DEATH OF MOSES AND THE TRANSITION OF YAHWEH'S GUIDANCE: 31:1—34:12

BEHIND THE TEXT

Deuteronomy 31:1—34:12 forms what can be described as the epilogue to the book of Deuteronomy. With the death of Moses drawing near, the question that Israel asks is: How is the heritage of Moses preserved? This final section forms the answer to this question. A number of events and genres are included in this final section: the appointment of Joshua as Moses' successor, provision for the reading of the Torah, a poetic song of Moses, a poetic blessing of Moses, and an account of the death of Moses. Each of these subsections has particular theological significance, but the entire section ought to be understood theologically as well.

The structure of this last large section can be divided into five main sections: Moses' Successor (31:1-29); Moses' Song (31:30—32:47); Moses' Death Foretold (32:48-52); Moses' Final Blessing on Israel (33:1-29); and Moses' Death (34:1-12). The reader should notice that all of these sections involve Moses releasing the vision of Yahweh's covenant order over to the next generation. Most of these sections have clear subdivisions. The extended structure of the passage is:

A. Moses' Successor (31:1-29)
    1. Joshua to Succeed Moses (31:1-8)
    2. Communal Reading of Torah (31:9-13)
    3. Commission and Collapse (31:14-23)
    4. Israel's Defiance Predicted (31:24-29)
B. Moses' Song (31:30—32:47)
    1. Presenting Moses' Song (31:30)
    2. Ascribe the Greatness of Yahweh (32:1-6)
    3. Reflect on the Past (32:7-18)
    4. Yahweh Proposes to Destroy Israel (32:19-25)
    5. Yahweh Vindicates Israel (32:26-43)
    6. Take to Heart These Words (32:44-47)
C. Moses' Death Foretold (32:48-52)
D. Moses' Final Blessing on Israel (33:1-29)
    1. Yahweh Came from Sinai (33:1-5)
    2. Blessing the Twelve Tribes (33:6-25)
    3. Blessed Are You, Israel! (33:26-29)
E. Moses' Death (34:1-12)

IN THE TEXT

A. Moses' Successor (31:1-29)

At the end of his life Moses is described as letting go of his exclusive leadership, his purpose, and his life. Moses' mission is completed, and now the question comes into view: How will Israel move forward? Who will lead the people into the land of promise? How can the people go on in Yahweh's guidance? This chapter is Deuteronomy's answer to these crucial questions. Joshua receives confirmation to lead the people on their journey into the land of promise. His leadership of the nation does not take the place of Yahweh's continued guidance of his people. Israel, through her interpretive performance of Torah, remains under the guidance of Yahweh.

1. Joshua to Succeed Moses (31:1-8)

■ 1-8 The background for this subsection is portrayed in Deut 3:23-29. Moses knows that he is not going to enter the land of promise and must provide transition for the guidance of the people. The literary-historical circumstance places Israel on the boundary between the fulfillment of promise and the disorientation of marching in circles. These landless people long to be home; a homeland they never occupied, and yet they persistently longed for it. Moses, the leader that summoned the courage of the people to set out from a place of bondage, is now about to die. Deuteronomy has described Israel's arduous journey under Moses' leadership to the edge of the land, which she will call home.

Israel, as well as the reader, knows that all leaders eventually die and the task of their lives is left incomplete. The fact of history is that great leaders, even of the stature of Moses, leave their work unfinished. Moving forward beyond Moses is a key theme of Deuteronomy. In 1:38 and 3:28 this change is already implied. Other people will have to complete what is started, but who can even imagine taking Moses' place and leading this ragtag band into the place of promise under the politics of Yahweh? Joshua is to take over the leadership of Israel. Moses' responsibility is to make this transition transparent in the presence of all Israel (31:7).

Fulfilling the mission of occupying the land is not up to Joshua but belongs to Yahweh: **The LORD your God himself will cross over ahead of you. He will destroy these nations before you, and you will take possession of their land** (v 3). It is Yahweh who calls Moses and goes with him into Egypt. It is also Yahweh who calls Joshua and will go with him into the land of promise. The mission to enter into the land continues to be the mission of God. He not only promises the land but also ultimately gives it to Israel. But Joshua is needed in the mission of God. Joshua is the commissioned human representative of Yahweh's leadership.

There is no conjunction in v 3: **Joshua also will cross over ahead of you, as the LORD said.** The implication is that in Joshua's crossing over ahead of the people, Yahweh is crossing over ahead of the people. The assignment that God gives may be larger than any one person is able to complete, but if the task is ultimately the mission of God, then he will accomplish this task through other people. Hope is not based upon the talents and strengths of any individual but upon the faithfulness of Yahweh. God's mission belongs to God, but he partners with human beings to synergistically accomplish his mission. Joshua will lead the people over into the land of promise.

Moses' task is now to encourage Joshua to **be strong and courageous, for you must go with this people into the land that the LORD swore to their ancestors to give them** (v 7). The reason Joshua is to **be strong and courageous** is because the people are to **be strong and courageous. Do not be afraid or terrified because of them, for the LORD your God goes with you; he will never leave you nor forsake you** (v 6). Human leadership is called to courage in order to allow the people of God to have courage in the promise of God's abiding presence and strength. The people will experience the land of promise as home because God will give it to them.

2. Communal Reading of Torah (31:9-13)

■ **9-13** Israel cannot simply exchange Joshua for Moses. Moses is more than a leader, he also is the one who approaches Yahweh and proclaims his will and purpose to the people. Torah is the inheritance and witness of Moses to Israel. Moses hands over Torah to Israel! Can a new leader receive Torah in the way that Moses takes delivery of Torah? How will Israel preserve the way of life that Moses hands over to them? Torah occupies a central place in the communal life of Israel, and it must be preserved if the people are to inhabit the politics of Yahweh. Through the interpretative performance of Torah, Moses' unique ministry survives. His guidance is permanently continued in the politics of Yahweh. God's people are built up through formative instruction. Torah, with its policies and practices, forms the culture of a people. For Israel, Torah is the law that Moses hands over to God's people.

This subsection of Deuteronomy provides detailed directives that are intended to demonstrate how the content of Torah is to be preserved, protected, and processed. The mandate to write down the Torah and the directive to read it every seven years is frequently interpreted in the setting of an obligation for the regular public recital of an inscribed treaty document. This ancient custom may have its setting in life with Israel's neighbors: "The ancient Near Eastern treaty texts prescribed that the treaty be read periodically to the vassal's subjects" (Cairns 1992, 273). There are other scholars who think it is likely that this practice originated with ancient Israel (Mayes 1979, 374).

Whatever the setting of this public reading may have been, it seems that the public reading of the law every seven years is astonishingly occasional, in light of how necessary the law is for Israel's well-being. Life and death are at stake in the internalization of Torah. Why only read this law publicly every seven years? The contemporary reader should presume that this refers to a unique public recognition of the supremacy of Torah as a political standard for the life of the people who belong to Yahweh. It should be noticed that it is during **the year for canceling debts** (v 10) that the Torah is read. The year of remission is profoundly political; therefore, this public reading is a reminder of the political nature of Israel's covenant with Yahweh.

3. Commission and Collapse (31:14-23)

■ **14-23** Verses 14-15 form a beginning for Joshua's commission. Yahweh himself, in v 23, gives the conclusion to this charge to Joshua. He reinstates the promise of the people entering into the land, but this time the promise is made to Joshua: **Be strong and courageous, for you will bring the Israelites into the land I promised them on oath, and I myself will be with you.** Biblical leadership is characterized in the commission of Joshua as not simply ruling over people, but going before them in the presence of God. It also reveals that the place of leadership's origin emerges in the midst of the people.

Sandwiched between these verses of commission is an ominous forecast concerning the people's infidelity to the politics of Yahweh: **These people will soon prostitute themselves to the foreign gods of the land they are entering. They will forsake me and break the covenant I made with them** (v 16). Brueggemann says it well when he writes, "What a sorry future it is! It is marked by 'prostitution,' that is, Israel will 'shack up' with other gods, when its proper partner is YHWH only" (Brueggemann 2001, 273). Israel's infidelity is not a matter of causally changing gods, but by changing gods she changes her story and identity. Her beliefs, values, and even practices will all eventually change in the worshipping of other gods. She will be a different people, with a different way of seeing the world and narrating her own history. Hosea, who is a part of the tradition that includes Deuteronomy, articulates this concept well when he names his third child Lo-Ammi. "Then the LORD said, 'Call him Lo-Ammi (which means "not my people"), for you are not my people, and I am not your God'" (Hos 1:9). New gods mean a new story, which means a new identity . . . "not my people."

4. Israel's Defiance Predicted (31:24-29)

■ **24-29** Moses writes down the words of this Torah and entrusts it to the Levites. The scroll is then placed near the ark of the covenant. The ark of the covenant is an extremely sacred article in ancient Israel. It is adorned with cherubim and this symbolizes the enthronement of Yahweh. The ark contains the stone tablets of the Decalogue, and it is carried into battle ahead of Israel's army. The presence and power of Yahweh is associated with the ark in both positive and negative ways. A great story that illustrates both the positive and negative power associated with the ark is found in 1 Sam 4—6. By means of the ark, Yahweh delivers and destroys. It is holy: a magnificent and treacherous object. "According to ancient Near Eastern custom, the original copy of the vassal treaty was stored in the central shrine of the kingdom, indicating that the god of the shrine was guardian of the treaty" (Cairns 1992, 277).

The physical existence of the Torah scroll alongside the ark bears witness that Israel agrees to the policies and practices contained within it. This is wonderful and risky, especially knowing the subject matter of the song that is about to be introduced and sung and the content of the future of Yahweh's people. Torah is the abiding standard of covenantal obligations. For this reason, Torah is consigned to the Levites. They are the custodians of the ark and the Torah; covenantal policies, practices, and purpose are in their care. Israel must live within the presence and politics of Yahweh.

Is there any wonder that the Levites would migrate south, after the horrifying fall of the northern tribes to the Assyrians, and bring with them their guardian responsibilities of covenant obligations to Judah? What has transpired in the north must not be allowed to take place in the south. Yahweh has a standard politic for his people. Blessing and life is the result of practicing this political reality. Curse and death is the result of abandoning the way of life prescribed by the Torah. Second Kings 22:8 narrates the discovery in the temple of the scroll of the Torah. What power the Torah has; a political reform would ensue under young King Josiah. Did these guardians of covenant policies and practices place it there in the temple to be discovered?

The function of the Torah placed beside the ark of the covenant is to serve as **a witness against** Israel when she rebels against Yahweh (v 26). Words of the Torah are spoken in the hearing of the elders and officials of the tribes of Israel; moreover, **the heavens and the earth** are witness of the words of the Torah. They will be called upon to **testify against** Israel when she rebels against the words of the Torah (v 28).

B. Moses' Song (31:30—32:47)

The song of Moses is designed for singing or chanting along the journey of Israel's history. It allows the people of God to recall their past when Yahweh elected them and faithfully led them and provided for them. The song also clearly indicates that Israel, God's people, is historically "corrupt . . . warped and crooked" (32:5-6). Israel's response to Yahweh's faithfulness is that they "abandoned the God who made them and rejected the Rock their Savior" (v 15). As this poem becomes a part of communal consciousness, Israel becomes skilled at interpreting the present in light of her past. She assumes that she is not left to her own contriving and devastation, for Yahweh will once again bring order out of chaos, even if that chaos is a result of her own rebellion.

Israel's experience of tragedy and devastation is given theological significance by Moses' song. It affirms not only Israel's culpability for the disaster of deportation, but it also announces the possibility of renewal and reinstatement. Israel's devastation is not an accident of history by the power of another nation or even their gods, but the righteous judgment of Yahweh upon his people. Moses' song is therefore a type of theodicy that confesses Yahweh as the one and only God who remains both upright in his judgments and yet steadfast to Israel. But, because Israel's devastation is an act of Yahweh, she has hope. The God who judges them is the God who saves them, **The LORD will vindicate his people and relent concerning his servants when he sees their strength is gone and no one is left, slave or free** (v 36). As such, this song seeks not only to warn Israel but also to give assurance and hope in Yahweh. The function of this poem moves toward the praise of God who creates, judges, and renews!

The song's pattern of argument is similar to the genre of a prophetic lawsuit. However, a comparison to the book of Psalms suggests that the genre classification of hymn is more appropriate (Nelson 2002a, 369). There are a few themes that are persistent in the Song of Moses. Some of these themes are: the powerlessness of other gods, Israel's familial bond to Yahweh, and Yahweh will fight for his people. The organizing principle of the song is Israel's history with Yahweh: the election of Israel that leads to settlement in the land (vv 6-14), Israel's infidelity (vv 15-18), Yahweh's initial proposal of ruin and annihilation (vv 19-25), and finally Yahweh's change of heart and vengeance on Israel's enemies (vv 26-43). Scholarly attempts to date the song of Moses have been inconclusive. It likely "came into existence quite independently of Deuteronomy" (von Rad 1975, 195).

1. Presenting Moses' Song (31:30)

■ **30** This verse functions as an introduction to Moses' song, which follows in its entirety in ch 32. This song recounts the greatness of God, the failure of Israel, and Yahweh's compassionate vindication of his people. The reader assumes that it is the leadership of Israel that needs to hear this truthful yet hopeful song of Moses, but this introduction makes it clear that all of Israel is to sing the song. Political responsibility for the course of Israel's history is dependent upon not only the leadership class but also the populace as a whole. This prologue makes it obvious that the song includes a message for the totality of Israel.

2. Ascribe the Greatness of Yahweh (32:1-6)

■ **1-6** The first verse summons all of creation, the heavens and the earth, as a witness to the song of Moses. The implication is that the song functions as a lawsuit in the legal arrangement of ancient Israel's social order. Scholars call this type of literature a *rib*. In the literary context of this passage, Yahweh is both the plaintiff and the judge. What is of special interest is that the setting of the song is referring to a future state of affairs for the people of God. This lawsuit is what will happen and the verdict is already enacted upon the people in the future. Israel is both indicted and rescued by Yahweh in this future state of affairs. All of creation witnesses silently to this future lawsuit by the plaintiff-judge: Yahweh. This song is most likely sung at the covenant renewal ceremony.

Verse 2 addresses the desired outcome of the song, the soothing quickening of the life of the people. Metaphors are used to describe the way the words would touch the life of the community: **fall like rain . . . descend like dew, like showers on new grass, like abundant rain on tender plants**. These images imply that the song would permeate the covenant community and mold the character of persons within the culture itself.

The reason why the song can permeate the community and individuals is discovered in v 3: **I will proclaim the name of the LORD**. Yahweh is the premise of the song. The future belongs to Yahweh in the same way that the past belongs to Yahweh.

> To name Yahweh is not simply to pronounce the "sacred letters" but to focus on Yahweh's character . . . on the generous favors which flow from that character . . . and on the obligation to grateful obedience which the disclosure of that character entails. (Cairns 1992, 281)

Israel can count on the character of their God in both judgment and restoration. No wonder the song erupts with: **Oh, praise the greatness of our God!**

Verses 4-6 depict a disproportionate disparity between the fidelity of Yahweh and the infidelity of his people. Modifiers such as **the Rock, perfect . . . works, just,** and **faithful** are used to portray God. Expressions such as **corrupt, not his children, shame, warped, crooked generation, foolish and unwise people** are used to expose Israel. These metaphors are used to show the utter contrast between the character of Israel and her God. Being faithful to the covenant politics is the premise upon which both God and Israel are being judged in these verses. Yahweh practices covenant faithfulness and his people do not; therefore, they do not correspond to their Father and Creator who made them and formed them (v 6).

Your Creator in v 6 is not a noun, but a Hebrew verb (*qāneka* from *qānâ*, which means "to get" or "to acquire," "to buy"); the phrase literally means, *he bought you* or *he acquired you*. However, it is possible that this phrase is similar in meaning to the following phrase: *he made you and formed you*. Thus the phrase could be translated as *he brought you into being* or *he gave you life*. The second half of v 6 describes the electing grace of God in making the people Israel. Its meaning would involve the narrative world of promise to the Fathers, exodus from bondage, guidance in the wilderness, the gift of Torah, and the gift of the land.

3. Reflect on the Past (32:7-18)

■ **7-18** Yahweh is given the title **Most High** in v 8. This title calls attention to the sovereignty and authority that Yahweh employs over all nations and people. Not the gods, but Yahweh gives to all nations their inheritance and boundary. The boundaries are fixed **according to the number of the sons of Israel.** This is a very difficult phrase, and there are various translations. The NIV is a literal rendering of the Hebrew text. The NRSV rendering "gods" is based on the Dead Sea Scrolls and the Septuagint reading. The NRSV reading conveys the idea that in accordance with the number of gods, Yahweh divided humankind into separate peoples. Verse 9 asserts that Yahweh has chosen Israel to be **his** own **people.** This reading also seems to imply that Yahweh "determined where each nation should live, each with its own god, which he chose" (Bratcher and Hatton 2001, 538). Whatever the origin intent of the phrase is, it communicates that Yahweh, and not another god or power, is sovereign over all reality.

In a desert land he found him, in a barren and howling waste. He shielded him and cared for him (v 10) is not a reference to the forty years that Israel spent wandering in the wilderness after their escape from Egypt. This is a reference to the nomadic beginnings of Israel when they followed the promise of Yahweh to the place he would show them. Israel begins with a promise and leaves the settled life to practice the way of the nomad.

Analogies are extracted from the natural world to describe the providential care of Yahweh for his people in their wilderness journey (vv 10-11). The most prevailing image is that of **an eagle** (v 11). It could be incited by the nomadic memory of the desert itself. The word picture intends to show the protective care of God for his people. During their nomadic journeys it is Yahweh who led them; no foreign god was with them to help them. All too often communities and individuals believe that it is something else that provides for them: a god, hard work, capitalism, society, talent, luck, or even fate. The people of God understand that God leads and provides; yet he does this without force and coercion. The sovereignty of God is hidden yet in plain sight, like all characteristics of the mystery of God.

Yahweh and his ways are not the only mystery in this passage; the other great mystery is narrated beginning in v 15: **Jeshurun . . . abandoned the God who made them and rejected the Rock their Savior.** Jeshurun is a seldom used but affectionate name for the people of Israel. This term emerges again in Deuteronomy two more times in 33:5, 26. This name means the "upright" and is used that way in ch 33. In this passage it is used in a satirical way. Yahweh is *upright* but the people are anything but upright. This indictment is set up by covenant expectations: Israel is to be *upright*; she is to be faithful to Yahweh.

The exploits of unfaithful Israel are described in vv 16 and 17: **They made him jealous with their foreign gods and angered him with their detestable idols. They sacrificed to false gods, which are not God—gods they had not known, gods that recently appeared, gods your ancestors did not fear.** By abandoning Yahweh to go after unfamiliar and alien gods, the people shatter the covenantal politics of Yahweh by violating the first commandment. When Israel breaches the first commandment, the entire political premise is destroyed. It is impossible to be the people of Yahweh, living within a culture of policies and practices that reflect him, when the people worship other gods. To worship other gods is to take on their character and their ways.

The reader is confronted by a vexing question: How is it possible to abandon the source of the community's creation and treat with contempt the very cause of her salvation? This is a mystery almost as great as the mystery of God himself. The answer that this passage gives to this mystery of infidelity is found at the beginning of v 15: the people have grown **fat and kicked; filled with food, they became heavy and sleek. Kicked** means to rebel against the policies of Yahweh, therefore to rebel against God. This sorry condition of the people is not because they are in want but because they have gorged and have become satiated and obese. The irony is that Israel was more faithful in their dependent journey in the wilderness than in the settled comfort and security of the land. When

32:7-18

they were on the move, they were dependent upon Yahweh for guidance and provision. In the settled land they forget the nomadic God and his provisions. They suppose that something else provides for their well-being.

4. Yahweh Proposes to Destroy Israel (32:19-25)

■ **19-25** These verses make a sudden variation in tone. They depict the eruption of Yahweh's passionate judgment. Israel will receive the payment for her infidelity. Cairns makes an interesting observation concerning these verses. He sees here a tit for tat (1992, 285). Yahweh spurns Israel (v 19), Israel spurned Yahweh (31:16); Yahweh provokes Israel (32:21), Israel provoked Yahweh (vv 19, 21); Yahweh hides his face (31:17-18; 32:20), Israel turns their face away (31:18); and finally Yahweh stirs Israel to jealousy (32:21), Israel stirs Yahweh to jealousy (v 21). What this may imply is that Yahweh is predictable psychologically and will return evil for evil.

What does it mean for God to be jealous and angry? Does God have emotions like a human being? These expressions seem anthropomorphic and may only be a way of depicting the mystery of human failure and the tragedies that proceed from this downfall. Perhaps wrath and judgment are built into the very fabric of creation itself. If this is so, then the Torah is not a test for people to live up to, but a gift that discloses the nature of the way the universe operates. One thing is for sure; the consequence coming to Israel is best understood in light of the curses from ch 28. When humanity goes against the grain of God's universe, they acquire toxic splinters in their lives. Paul is correct, "the wages of sin is death" (Rom 6:23).

5. Yahweh Vindicates Israel (32:26-43)

■ **26-43** With v 26 there is a noteworthy advancement in the song; judgment has a limit. Even though judgment is warranted, the complete annihilation of the people is restrained. Yahweh's wrath and fury has limits. Israel's God did not intend the watching nations to presume that they themselves defeated Israel and her God. Without eyes shaped by the Torah, the nations do not understand the course of history. They do not discern that the event of Israel's demise is an act of Yahweh's judgment upon his own people. Therefore, Yahweh does not allow the wide-ranging annihilation of his people. The nations do not understand that the **Rock** of Israel's salvation sold them and that it is Yahweh who gives them up (v 30).

The dilemma that the text addresses is that these nations see the world and the events taking place in the world through the spectacles that are shaped by the practices, values, and beliefs connected with their gods. Verses 28-29 make it clear that they are a people who have no discernment: **They are a nation without sense, there is no discernment in them. If only they were wise and would understand this and discern what their end will be!** The nations perceive the universe differently from Israel, because they have a different narrative picture of the world. The text implies that it is because of this lack of discernment on the part of the nations that Yahweh backs away from the complete destruction of his people. The nations see but don't see, and they hear but don't hear. They have become habituated by the beliefs, practices, and values of gods that are not divinity. It is interesting that the very people groups that God uses to judge his people conduct their way of life in a manner that Israel is being judged for. Yet, Yahweh uses these nations for judgment against Israel.

Verses 32-35 articulate a picture of not only the vindication of Yahweh's people but at the same time the judgment of the nations. High-quality vines engender superior fruit, but the nations' **vine comes from the vine of Sodom and from the fields of Gomorrah.** Therefore: **Their grapes are filled with poison, and their clusters with bitterness. Their wine is the venom of serpents, the deadly poison of cobras** (vv 32-33). The nations' beliefs, values, and practices produce a harvest of death and destruction. Yahweh will judge the nations as well as Israel. The reader must remember, to go against the way of the universe is to inhabit the *telos* of death. The politics of Yahweh pointed Israel to the ways of life, but she chose the way of death. She chose the form of life of her neighbors, with their gods and practices. Now these neighbor nations will also experience the judgment of God. Death is the end of their form of life.

In judging the nations, Yahweh also delivers his people. Verse 36 points out an interesting aspect of Yahweh's judgment upon the nations; in this act he has compassion on his servants. The way forward begins where there is no path for the nomadic people of God. Yahweh's people will prosper and flourish when they recognize their weakness. Exile, both in reality and metaphorically, is a time to come to grips with powerlessness, disorientation, and displacement. Second Corinthians 12:9 express this assertion well: "My grace is sufficient for you, for my power is made perfect in weakness." In frailty Israel welcomes the amazing grace of God. Perhaps the grace of God is not perceived until people have exhausted all other sources for their own survival. In judgment as well as vindication God is at work.

Life and death remain in the hands of Yahweh since, as v 39 makes plain: **There is no god besides me.** This is one of the clearest and most forceful declarations of the radical monotheism in the OT. This affirmation signifies that everything is dependent in the singularity of Yahweh. Both the way of creation and course of history depend upon Yahweh. God is the source of reality, the foundation of redemption, and the meaning and goal of the universe. Even though God uses secondary causes in both creation and history, it is God who is ultimately the source. Life and death, health and sickness, victory and

32:26-43

defeat are all in the hands of the living God. Nothing is outside of the care and control of the God of Israel who raised Jesus from the dead!

Is there any wonder that the song ends with a doxology, a call to the **nations** to **rejoice** with Yahweh's **people** (v 43)? Doxology is appropriate for those who experience the devastation brought about by their own sin, for it is God who acts, not some other god, nation, or situation. Doxology is also appropriate for those who experience redemption, for it is God who sets free. God judges and God delivers; praise God. When a contemporary reader considers the song of Moses as a whole, it is obvious that grace and mercy prevail over judgment. Christian readers confess that God is the first and last word, and he has spoken most clearly in the person of Jesus Christ. Praise God from whom all blessings flow!

6. Take to Heart These Words (32:44-47)

■ **44-47** The framing conclusion of the ode reiterates once again the urgency of its message. Life is at stake; this is no inconsequential affair. These words are not simply to be a public ritual, but they are to **take to heart**. How do people *place on* their **heart** anything? This is the question that the attentive reader should ponder over and over. Perhaps the remainder of this section gives a hint as to how this internalization takes place: adults are to command their children to *watch and do all the words of this Torah.* In other words, the Torah-song of Moses is to be an influence in the political reality of the community. Tacit knowledge comes by participating in a way of life, a politic. Children are shaped by the way of life that the adults in the community live out.

These words are to be habituated in the life of the community. This exclusive love and loyalty toward God is to be upon the **heart**. The heart, in this context, points to the forming of a person's character or disposition. John Wesley called this disposition "affections." (See Wesley's sermon on "The Circumcision of the Heart," January 1, 1733.) Affections are formed through the habituation of a person's life. The question is: How are the words to become a part of the living fabric of a person? This can happen only if the words become a part of the living fabric of the community. The Torah is passed on to the next generation, not by a coercive enforcement, but by making it the framework of everyday life.

Habituation is not something an individual is capable of doing alone. Individuals are persons in social networks; therefore, to have Torah embodied in one's own life takes the political embodiment of Torah in the life of the whole community. Enacting Torah is social and political in nature. The exclusive loyalty to Yahweh and his covenant policies is to comprise the whole of Israel's life; it is to become a political reality. Israel is to have a way of life that demonstrates undivided loyalty to Yahweh and his purpose.

C. Moses' Death Foretold (32:48-52)

■ **48-52** This subsection provides a new rationale for Moses' sanction from the land by the assessment narrated in Num 20:10-13 and 27:12-14. Earlier in Deuteronomy (1:37; 3:23-29; 4:21), Moses is given an explanation for his death outside the promised land; it is because of the people's sin. In this passage (32:51) the reader is given another reason for Moses' exclusion, because he **broke faith** with Yahweh and **did not uphold my holiness among the Israelites**. This extreme change has many scholars wondering if 32:48-52 is a later addition by the editor from the priestly tradition.

What does the breaking of faith and not upholding holiness in the midst of the people of Israel suggest? **You broke faith with me** presumably refers to Moses' lack of self-control by striking the rock rather than by speaking to it as Yahweh instructed him in Num 20:8. In his irritation at the people he raised his staff and struck the rock twice (Num 20:11). Yahweh, in this priestly text of Num 20:12 says, "Because you did not trust in me enough to honor me as holy in the sight of the Israelites, you will not bring this community into the land I give them." Perhaps these two expressions are only one expression. If this is the case, then breaking faith is failing to act in a holy manner and failing to act in a holy manner is breaking faith. In both of these expressions, obedience to the voice of God is the issue. Moses, Israel, and the whole of the people of God are called to obedience. The end never justifies the means. The means, obedience, is the end of the politics of Yahweh.

32:48-52

D. Moses' Final Blessing on Israel (33:1-29)

Moses has accomplished all that he will personally do; he must now trust Yahweh to bring to completion what he started. It seems natural that the final act of "the man of God" (v 1) is to bless the children of Israel. Perhaps this kind of blessing is what Israel understands as the final act of a leader/patriarch. An obvious example of this type of blessing is Jacob (Gen 49). In this Genesis passage Jacob gives a similar farewell blessing to his family, Israel. The setting in life, for this particular genre, is near the moment of the death of a patriarch. A special blessing is imparted upon the children. In Deuteronomy, the whole people of Israel are metaphorically the children of Moses.

Moses is recognized as "the man of God." This is a title that is usually applied to prophets. This means that Moses is speaking the word of God. Such a blessing is more than simply a barren wish or even predicting the future, but a word that creates the very reality that is spoken. One could say this type of speech is not fortune-telling but forthtelling. The stories of Balaam in Num 22 and Jonah are great examples of how a prophetic word is believed to create the reality that is spoken. Balaam is hindered from speaking, and Jonah is upset because what he speaks does not come to pass. This passage in Deuteronomy pictures Moses as a prophet who is capable of uttering Yahweh's creative word.

Israel is addressed one tribe at a time in this passage. Each tribe obtains its exclusive blessing from the creative words of Moses. These blessings are to communicate Yahweh's grace and authority for the sake of each tribe. Each blessing is a type of prayer-pronouncement, which as a speech-act appeal to and from God for assistance in accomplishing what human beings cannot do. This type of prayer presupposes human limitation and a need for outside assistance.

The blessing of Moses is written in poetic form. This may indicate that it is sung or recounted in a particular ritual, perhaps in the covenant renewal ceremony. This poetic blessing is divided into two major sections. The framework (vv 1-5 and 26-29) encompass the blessings upon the tribes. The blessing itself is located in vv 6-25.

I. Yahweh Came from Sinai (33:1-5)

■ **1-5** Blessing (*bĕrākâ*) is one of the most interesting concepts in the Bible. The Hebrew word is used twice in the first verse of this chapter. The Hebrew text literally reads: **This is the blessing *with which* Moses the man of God blessed the sons of Israel before his death**. The typical way of referring to the act of speaking a blessing in English is to pronounce a blessing; therefore, the translation **pronounced** in the NIV.

A blessing is a gift from God to increase the fruitfulness of life. Deuteronomy 1:11 expresses this blessing this way: "May the LORD, the God of your ancestors, increase you a thousand times and bless you as he has promised!" Blessing is used in the Genesis creation story for the fertility of both animal and human life (see 1:22, 28). Genesis 12:1-3 also discloses the meaning of blessing, this time to Abram:

> The LORD had said to Abram, "Go from your country, your people and your father's household to the land I will show you. I will make you into a great nation, and I will bless you; I will make your name great, and you will be a blessing. I will bless those who bless you, and whoever curses you I will curse; and all peoples on earth will be blessed through you."

Again, the emphasis is upon the fertility and abundance of life itself.

The blessing uttered by Moses is introduced with a brief narration of God's deeds on behalf the people. This narration depicts Yahweh striding from the holy mountain with his sacred army: **myriads of holy ones** (v 2). This phrase is literally *from the ten thousands of holy ones*. It is likely that the **holy ones** are understood as heavenly attendants; therefore, a heavenly army surrounds him. The picture of a heavenly army is implied in Josh 5:13-15:

> Now when Joshua was near Jericho, he looked up and saw a man standing in front of him with a drawn sword in his hand. Joshua went up to him and asked, "Are you for us or for our enemies?"

"Neither," he replied, "but as commander of the army of the LORD I have now come." Then Joshua fell facedown to the ground in reverence, and asked him, "What message does my Lord have for his servant?" The commander of the LORD's army replied, "Take off your sandals, for the place where you are standing is holy."

The metaphor of **myriads of holy ones** implies that Yahweh is coming with the power and might to enact his will in the world. Blessing, when seen in this context, is understood as a sure reality for Israel.

Three names are used in this passage for the mountainous terrain that is regarded as Yahweh's home: **Sinai, Seir,** and **Paran**. What is curious is the use of Sinai rather than Horeb. This is the only occasion in Deuteronomy where the word **Sinai** is used rather than Horeb. According to the source theory of the Pentateuch, the documentary hypothesis, Sinai is only used by the Yahwist (J) and Priestly (P) sources. The Elohist (E) and Deuteronomist (D) use Horeb. Therefore, the use of Sinai in this final portion of Deuteronomy almost certainly points to a late editorial insertion into the text from the southern tribe.

The reference to **king over Jeshurun** in v 5 is interesting. Jeshurun here depicts Israel (see 32:15). It is a seldom used but loving title for the people of Israel. This name is a play on words for the *upright*. The people of Israel are to be upright or righteous in their living out the politics of Yahweh's covenant.

Does the king refer to Saul or David, or is it a reference to Yahweh sitting on his throne? In the tradition that Deuteronomy belongs to, a human king is culpable for the downfall of the people and their judgment in exile. If this is a reference to an earthly king, then it is either a warning or satire. If the reference is to Yahweh, it points directly to his political rule of Israel. Under the kingship of Yahweh the people would live out **the law that Moses gave** them (v 4). They would reside in the political reality of King Yahweh.

2. Blessing the Twelve Tribes (33:6-25)

■ **6-25** The blessings themselves point the reader to the shared interests of the united tribes of Israel and to the conditions the individual tribes face in their future. These blessings are amazingly concise, with the exception of the tribes of Levi and Joseph. On the whole, they communicate a tribe's achievement in a particular situation.

The pronouncement of blessings begins with **Reuben** (v 6), the firstborn of the sons of Jacob; as the firstborn, he receives the first place in the list of tribes. This blessing suggests that Reuben is in decline in power and influence because of its declining numbers. Moses speaks a creative word of blessing for the continued life, not necessarily for Reuben's success.

The blessing in v 7 is for the tribe of **Judah**, and it is more of an intercessory prayer. Judah put down roots in the south and found itself separated from the other tribes. It is for this reason that Moses appeals to Yahweh to bring

33:6-25

Judah into unity with the whole people of Israel. This prayer for the unity of Judah with the rest of the nation may have its context early in Israel's history. This is very likely a northern viewpoint on Judah's standing in the era following the splitting up of the nation into northern and southern kingdoms.

In vv 8-11 **Levi** is the object of blessing. Genesis 34:25-29 depicts the tribe of Levi in a forceful and militaristic way as a tribe that participated in the killing and looting of the unsuspecting citizens of the city of Shechem. The Levites slaughtered the people who worshipped the golden calf at Mount Sinai at the command of Moses (Exod 32:25-29). The blessing portrays the Levites as those who have demonstrated utter devotion to Yahweh; devotion to Yahweh was more important to them than devotion to their parents, brothers, or even their own children. The text does not make clear the role of the Levites **at Massah** and **at the waters of Meribah** (Deut 33:8). These are mentioned only in this text and are most probably a story in Levi's oral legends. What all of this points to is Levi's unique role based upon the tribe's surrender of everything for the sake of Yahweh. Because of this devotedness, they observe Yahweh's word, teach the nation God's ordinances and Torah, and lead Israel in worship.

Benjamin (v 12) is the youngest of the sons of Jacob. He is considered, along with Joseph, the favorite. In this blessing, Benjamin is called **the beloved of Yahweh**, and this refers to his status in the story of Jacob. He is given the

creative word of blessing so that he is able to **rest secure in him, for he shields him all day long**. The strife implied in this blessing could be in light of the contention between Saul, a Benjamite, and David, a Judahite.

Joseph's blessing (vv 13-17) is disproportionate to the other tribes. It depicts a lush fertile land, abundant descendants, strength, and riches. The central hill country is by far the most fertile, as it is watered by the dew and the springs beneath the soil. This blessing presupposes that the Joseph tribes, **Ephraim** and **Manasseh**, are the most favored in Israel. This may point to the northern beginnings of the tradition of Deuteronomy and the move toward the south when the Assyrians desolated Israel. With the horns of a wild ox Joseph's descendants will drive out all of their enemies and drive them to the ends of the earth.

Zebulun and **Issachar** regularly appear together in tribal lists and this can be seen this way not only in the blessing of Moses (vv 18-19) but in the blessing of Jacob (Gen 49:13-15). The blessings of these two tribes signal the type of commerce they are engaged in. Zebulun is to rejoice **in your going out, . . . they will feast on the abundance of the seas**; this suggests her seafaring ways. Issachar is told that in their **tents . . . they will feast . . . on the treasures hidden in the sand**. These two northern tribes settled in the vicinity of the seaports of Tyre and Sidon; their neighbors would be the seafaring Phoenicians. They profited from the sea trade that developed there and feasted on the economic resources associated with this location.

Gad's blessing signals a point in time when he carried out a leadership role amongst the tribes (vv 20-21). This tribe settled east of the Jordan and developed a reputation for being aggressive. Genesis 49:19 articulates this aggressive nature well: "Gad will be attacked by a band of raiders, but he will attack them at their heels." There is no apparent clarification given for Gad's praiseworthy activity of carrying **out the** LORD's **righteous will, and his judgments concerning Israel.** The key covenantal concepts of "righteousness" and "justice" are again used by Deuteronomy to reinforce the political agenda of the book.

The tribe of **Dan** is blessed in Deut 33:22. This tribe journeyed from its original territory between Judah and Ephraim to capture Laish at the foot of Mount Hermon in the north. The blessing of Moses correlates this migration with a possible wordplay on Laish, meaning lion: **Dan is a lion's cub, springing out of Bashan.**

Naphtali is blessed in v 23. In the beginning, Naphtali owned only a small territory south of Hermon. Moses states that the tribe's extension toward the sea to the south is evidence of Yahweh's favor. The blessing of **Asher** is toward the tribe that lived in the fertile region of central Galilee (vv 24-25). This area is known for its olive production. The suggestion is that the fruitfulness of the tribe indicates that they enjoy an existence of comparative comfort.

3. Blessed Are You, Israel! (33:26-29)

■ **26-29** Moses' blessing opens (vv 1-5) and closes (vv 26-29) with an inspired word that creates fortification and fruitfulness for the people of God. **Jeshurun** is referenced once again (v 26; see v 5); in vv 2-5, Yahweh reassures the people of his love for Israel and the giving of his instructions and stipulations for their way of life. In v 26, the focus is on the incomparable **God of Jeshurun,** the one **who rides across the heavens** to help Israel. This metaphor indicates the awe-inspiring capacity of God for the well-being of his people.

God's people find their dwelling place and their security in the presence of the Almighty. Verse 27 makes this point in a poetic fashion when it states: **The eternal God is your refuge, and underneath are the everlasting arms. He will drive out your enemies before you, saying, "Destroy them!"** These metaphors portray not only Yahweh's victory over the forces that would destroy his people but also that this victory is brought about by the ongoing, never-ending strength of God. The **eternal God** has **everlasting arms** to protect and cover his people. Verse 28 joins together the themes of safety and the fertile land that produces **grain and new wine** because of the dew that drops from heaven. These verses celebrate the grace of God, which enables the people to achieve victory and fruitfulness because God, the Divine Warrior, is the one who comes to their rescue, fights for them, and blesses them with the resources from heaven.

Israel's history illustrates the certainty that life is not passive seclusion from the forces that are hostile toward God's people. Israel suffers much by the forces that would destroy her. But, the good news is that Israel is repeatedly saved, in the midst of the most terrifying circumstances of history, by the creative strength of God. No nation on earth has experienced Yahweh's salvation like Israel (v 29). **Shield**, **helper**, and **sword** are metaphors that suggest Yahweh's strength in times of hardship. In triumph, the blessings end with the declaration that the enemies of the people of God **will cower before** Yahweh, because he is their strength and provision.

E. Moses' Death (34:1-12)

■ **1-5** After bestowing his blessing, Moses departs the plains of Moab and scales **Mount Nebo**. **Pisgah**, the other mountain mentioned, is most likely the summit and means "ridge" in Hebrew. From the summit of the mountain, Moses can catch a glimpse of the immense vista of the land that Yahweh promised to the patriarchs.

The author envisages Moses standing with Yahweh on Pisgah, and having his gaze directed north along the east side of Jordan right to Hermon, then back down west Jordan through Naphtali, and on through Ephraim-Manasseh to Judah to the south and the Negeb to the deep south. Then the gaze is shifted to Jericho at the north end of the Dead Sea and due west of Pisgah, and from there runs right down the east shore of the Dead Sea to the southernmost extreme. Thus the whole land is sighted. (Cairns 1992, 304)

Yahweh keeps his promise; he is faithful!

Subsequent to this far-off glimpse of Yahweh's fulfilled promise, Moses dies. So what is the meaning of Moses' death in the last chapter of Deuteronomy? It at least indicates that a single lifetime is too short to complete the mission of God. Episodes in the ongoing narrative of promise and fulfillment last only over the course of a generation or two. God's story is ongoing and unfolds through multiple generations. Moses, the man of God, is no exception. His life, as important as it is, is but an episode in the story of God.

So who is this Moses? Verse 5 gives one of the most compelling answers to this question: he is **the servant of the LORD**. If Moses were to have an epitaph it would read: "Moses the servant of Yahweh." This title makes a profound statement about leadership among the people of God; they are his servants. The Hebrew word for **servant** (*'ebed*) is often translated *slave*. The Decalogue in Deuteronomy uses this word to describe Israel's status in Egyptian bondage. In 5:6, the Decalogue begins, "I am the LORD your God, who brought you out of Egypt, out of the land of *slavery.*" The Sabbath commandment also uses the same Hebrew word in a verbal form as well as a noun. In 5:13 it reads, "Six days you shall *labor* and do all your work." Also, the motivational clause in 5:15 uses this word, "Remember that you were *slaves* in Egypt." To be a servant of Yahweh is to do the work of Yahweh, because Yahweh possesses his servant. This may be the most notable description for people who participate in the purpose of God for his creation!

■ **6-9** These verses describe Moses at the time of his death and the transition of leadership to Joshua. Unlike some of the patriarchs before him, Moses does not die feebly in his old age, but with vitality: **his eyes were not weak nor his strength gone** (v 7). He dies only because he reaches the end of his responsibility in Yahweh's mission for Israel. The removal of Moses makes it possible for the people of God to move on under the guidance of a new leader. The next phase of Israel's story is connected to the past by the successful transition of leadership to Joshua from Moses: **Now Joshua son of Nun was filled with the spirit of wisdom because Moses had laid his hands on him. So the Israelites listened to him and did what the LORD had commanded Moses** (v 9).

Moses is truly the greatest leader in Israel's history, but he is not indispensable because it is Yahweh who ultimately leads his people. He leads them from the calling of Abraham through the doldrums and deception of the patriarchs to the despair of bondage and finally to the assistance of Moses. It is Yahweh who protects baby Moses, who trains him in Pharaoh's house, who calls him in his melancholy in the wilderness, who delivers and guides Israel through him. Yahweh and Yahweh alone is Israel's leader. He will guide his people through Joshua and then through the judges and kings. He will lead them into and out of Babylonian captivity. Israel does not belong to Moses or any leader; they belong to Yahweh!

No one knows the location of Moses' burial site (v 6). The implication is that his burial is supernatural, much like the unnatural events that envelop his infancy, calling, exodus leadership, and Torah revelation. There will be no pilgrimage to his tomb. Moses is not to become a dead icon for the people but is a voice that continues to exist as Israel embodies the Torah. The tradition that Moses participates in will continue to have a home in the lives of future generations as they practice the vision of the politics of Yahweh revealed to Moses. The only shrine needed for the continual memory of Moses is an embodied Torah in people called Israel.

■ **10-12** These verses function as a eulogy for the greatest leader in the history of Israel. It is remarkable that this concluding tribute to Moses does not categorize him as a king or even a judge, but a prophet: **No prophet has risen in Israel like Moses, whom the LORD knew face to face.** Yahweh knowing Moses **face to face** is figurative for a deep intimacy that exists between Yahweh and Moses. This understanding is similar to the relationship that exists between a husband and wife. This is a knowledge that no other person in Israel's history will experience, until the Messiah. Therefore, the words of Moses that emerge from this intimacy are held in highest regard.

Prophets will appear in the unfolding of Israel's story, but none will be like Moses. For this reason, Deuteronomy functions like a collection of sermons from Israel's greatest prophet; a man who knows and is known by God face-to-face. Future generations of prophets and sages will have to weigh their words against the words of Moses. Torah is the definitive standard for the politics of Yahweh. The people of God are to hear, watch, and do the will of God revealed in the Torah. Only the incarnation of Yahweh could be held as a norm that supersedes the words of Moses. No wonder the identity of Jesus the Messiah was so challenging to recognize: "You have heard that it was said to the people long ago . . . but I tell you . . ." (Matt 5:21-22).

FROM THE TEXT

The final section of Deuteronomy is a way of bringing theological closure to the book. Deuteronomy is not the story of Moses that concludes with his demise, but the story of God that continues beyond the life span of any individual or even people group. This does not mean that Moses is unimportant, for clearly Moses is the most significant character in Israel's storied world. But, Moses is simply a character in the ongoing drama of God. The question the book of Deuteronomy and this final section puts before the reader is: How is Israel to go on without Moses?

The answer to this question is that they will not go on without him because Moses continues to play an important role in Israel, even after his death. Israelites will never make pilgrimages to his grave; no one knows where he is buried and it is unimportant anyway. Israel will also not reinvent itself, because who she is continues to form her identity in the future. The ministry of Moses will continue because he is the servant of Yahweh and his mission.

How Moses' servanthood persists is recognized in two decisive ways: the mentoring and appointing of Joshua, and the embodiment of Torah in the politics of the people of Israel. The servant ministry of Moses continues in the personification of the people of Israel as they live out the politics of Yahweh. The goals, leadership, policies, and practices are established in a particular context of time and space. Yet if the people are to have a continuity of identity, they will need to embody a form of life that moves toward a historically established purpose. Change the form of life, the politics, and you change the identity of the people. Change the historical purpose of the tradition, and you change the identity of the people. Yet, history itself brings changes to be confronted by a people group. The question is: How can a community of memory remain who they are in light of new circumstances and challenges? The ability to not simply repeat a past action but to "go on" becomes the true test of understanding the meaning and purpose of a tradition.

In a contemporary context, readers should be aware of two important principles that emerge from reflecting on this text: no single life or generation is irreplaceable, and an embodied faith must be handed on to the next generation if the community is going to be faithful to its role in the mission of God. When leadership or even a generation clutches at its role of leadership, it fails to respect the transitions necessary for meaningful engagement in the mission of God.

Moses guides Israel to the edge of realizing the fulfillment of promise, but a transition of leadership is required to take the people into the land of promise. The reader is told that Moses' eyes are not weak nor his strength gone, but that it is time for him to let go of the responsibility of leading the people. When a generation of leaders linger until they no longer are able to see or have the strength to accomplish the mission of God for the community, they have stayed too long. It is reassuring to realize that God makes it known to both the leader and the people when the time is right for transition. There is a time and season for leading, and there is a time and season for removing oneself from leadership.

Moses' transition is not made in resentment or weakness, but by finishing his service for the mission of Yahweh: he passes the faith and leadership on to the next generation. He passes the torch of leadership to Joshua by a process of recognizing the call of God upon Joshua's life, mentoring Joshua, and finally publicly handing over leadership to Joshua. The transition of leadership is not an impulsive decision, but a long process of discernment, engagement, and relinquishment.

31:1—
34:12

Moses also passes the faith along to future generations. The insights of revelation may have been given to Moses, but the ability to pass this vision, with its policies and practices, on to the next generations is a task that takes a community to accomplish. It is interesting to notice the recurring aphorism of not only hearing the words of Torah but enacting the Torah. In other words, faith is passed on to the next generation through a form of life within which words find their meaning. Ludwig Wittgenstein says it well when he is asked the meaning of a word; he states, "The meaning of a word is its use in the language" (1953, 43). How anyone uses a word, doctrine, or idea is connected to a form of life. Torah's meaning is discovered in an embodied community.

Each generation must grasp what is at stake in its embodied faith, life itself. God's people are constantly reevangelizing the community through the story of grace. Stories, whether sung or narrated, help shape the identity, beliefs, and values of a community of memory. They remind, warn, and energize present and future generations. This is true concerning the song of Moses, and it is also spot on today.

The ministerial task is not complete until the present generation realizes the need to bless future generations. Passing on the faith does not come from compulsion or even duty, but from the wellsprings of love that take pleasure in the future generations of God's people. Blessing is an act of compassionate imagination. It sees, like Moses, from afar and anticipates a future full of opportunity as well as challenge. Moses does this in a remarkable way; he sees the challenges and opportunities of specific situations and speaks a creative word of God into the lives of future generations; he blesses the tribes. Whether or not this is a later addition from redactors, it implies the need to recognize challenge and opportunity and speak grace into future situations.

What an amazing confidence that allows a generation to release a lifelong zeal of ministry and entrust it to future servants of God. Each generation has a responsibility to pass the faith along. As the writer of Hebrews states in 11:39-40: "These were all commended for their faith, yet none of them received what had been promised, since God had planned something better for us so that only together with us would they be made perfect." The completion of faith takes place across time and not in a single person or generation. The completion of Moses' service and faith required Joshua, Joshua requires judges, and judges require kings and prophets, and so forth. A community of faith does not finish anything, as if one could put a period at the end of a story. The community of faith is in a story that is larger than a lifetime. It is a story that stretches from creation to consummation. It is God's story of grace and love. Each generation is called upon to live faithfully within this story and to pass this faithfulness along to the next generation. Rather than a period, one could say that one places an ellipsis at the closing stages of a generation's episode within the story, with a blessing: "to be continued . . ."